# AS YOU LIKE IT

## William Shakespeare

Heather Dubrow, Editor
Fordham University

J. J. M. Tobin, General Editor
University of Massachusetts–Boston

WADSWORTH
CENGAGE Learning™

Australia • Brazil • Japan • Korea • Mexico • Singapore • Spain • United Kingdom • United States

WADSWORTH
CENGAGE Learning

**Dedication for *As You Like It***
To the memory of the late Gwynne Blakemore Evans and to Maynard Mack, Jr.— astute Shakespeareans, dedicated teachers, and generous colleagues

**Evans Shakespeare Series:
As You Like It
Heather Dubrow, Editor
J. J. M. Tobin, General Editor**

Senior Publisher: Lyn Uhl

Publisher/Exectutive Editor: Michael Rosenberg

Development Editor: Michell Phifer

Assistant Editor: Erin Bosco

Editorial Assistant: Rebecca Donahue

Media Editor: Janine Tangney

Senior Marketing Manager: Melissa Holt

Marketing Communications Manager: Glenn McGibbon

Content Project Manager: Aimee Chevrette Bear

Art Director: Marissa Falco

Print Buyer: Betsy Donaghey

Rights Acquisition Specialist, Text: Katie Huha

Rights Acquisition Specialist, Images: Jennifer Meyer Dare

Production Service: MPS Limited, a Macmillan Company

Cover Designer: Walter Kopec

Text Designer: Maxine Ressler

Cover Image: Melinda Parrett (left) as Rosalind and Quinn Mattfeld as Orlando in the Utah Shakespeare Festival's 2009 production of *As You Like It.* (Photo by Karl Hugh. Copyright Utah Shakespeare Festival 2009.)

Compositor: MPS Limited, a Macmillan Company

For product information and technology assistance, contact us at **Cengage Learning Customer & Sales Support, 1-800-354-9706**

For permission to use material from this text or product, submit all requests online at **www.cengage.com/permissions**
Further permissions questions can be emailed to **permissionrequest@cengage.com**

Library of Congress Control Number: 2010942859

ISBN-13: 978-0-495-91117-3

ISBN-10: 0-495-91117-8

**Wadsworth**
20 Channel Center Street
Boston, MA 02210
USA

Cengage Learning is a leading provider of customized learning solutions with office locations around the globe, including Singapore, the United Kingdom, Australia, Mexico, Brazil, and Japan. Locate your local office at: **international.cengage.com/region**

Cengage Learning products are represented in Canada by Nelson Education, Ltd.

For your course and learning solutions, visit **www.cengage.com**

Purchase any of our products at your local college store or at our preferred online store **www.cengagebrain.com**

Printed in the United States of America
1 2 3 4 5 6 7 14 13 12 11

Other titles in the *Evans Shakespeare Editions*
from Cengage Learning

**Hamlet**
J. J. M. Tobin, Volume Editor

**King Lear**
Vincent F. Petronella, Volume Editor

**Macbeth**
Katherine Rowe, Volume Editor

**Measure for Measure**
John Klause, Volume Editor

**A Midsummer Night's Dream**
Douglas Bruster, Volume Editor

**Richard III**
Nina Levine, Volume Editor

**The Tempest**
Grace Tiffany, Volume Editor

**The Winter's Tale**
Lawrence F. Rhu, Volume Editor

# Table of Contents

Modern Essays

# ACKNOWLEDGMENTS

For assistance throughout my work on this volume, I thank Richard Knowles, Donald Rowe, and especially Jeffrey Theis and John Tobin, as well as a series of excellent research assistants, Amanda Auer, Anna Beskin, Sarah Iovan, Jason Siegel, and Aaron Spooner. For incisive observations about the play, I am indebted to many Fordham University and University of Wisconsin students—in particular, Jon Baarsch, Andrea Benton, Daniel Gibbons, Will Rogers, and Patrick Murphy. The staff of the Harvard Theater Collection and the Fogg Museum rendered valuable assistance, as did Liviu Ciulei, Joan Holcomb of the Guthrie Theater, and Paul Bentzen and Evelyn Matten of the American Players Theater. Like all the editors, I am indebted to the astute and generous counsel of Mark McNeil, Susannah Tobin, and Grant Ujifusa. The funding and released time associated with the John D. Boyd, SJ Chair in the Poetic Imagination at Fordham helped me to complete the project.

# LIST OF ILLUSTRATIONS

## Color Plates

## Illustrations in the Text

# ABOUT THIS SERIES

## J. J. M. Tobin

T HE EVANS Shakespeare Editions are individual editions of essential plays by William Shakespeare, edited by leading scholars to provide college and university students, advanced high school students, and interested independent readers with a comprehensive guide to the plays and their historical and modern contexts.

The volume editor of each play has written an introduction to the play and a history of the play in performance on both stage and screen. Central sources and contexts for the play are included, and each editor also has surveyed the critical commentary on the play and selected representative influential essays to illuminate the text further. A guide to additional reading, viewing, and listening concludes the volume and will continue the reader's relationship with the play.

Each volume includes an overview of Shakespeare's life and the world of London theater that he inhabited. Our goal for these editions is that they provide the reader a window into Shakespeare and his work that reminds us all of his enduring global influence.

The text for these plays comes from *The Riverside Shakespeare*, edited with notes and textual commentary by the late Gywnne Blakemore Evans. Evans was known for his unrivaled scholarly precision, and his *Riverside* text is an essential and much-admired modern edition of Shakespeare. The Evans Shakespeare Editions preserve the *Riverside* line numbering, which is the numbering used in the invaluable *Harvard Concordance to Shakespeare* by Marvin Spevack.

Beyond his scholarly work, Evans was a generous mentor to many of the editors in this series and a tremendous influence on all of us. His kind-hearted nature made it impossible for him truly to dislike anyone. However, despite an identification with the most traditional and canonical of cultural texts, he reserved a raised eyebrow and stern words for those whose politics lacked empathy and understanding for the full diversity of human experience. In this attitude too, as in all his writing and teaching, it was evident that he was a scholar who understood Shakespeare. This series is dedicated to his memory.

# SHAKESPEARE'S LIFE

*J. J. M. Tobin*

S HAKESPEARE WAS a genius, but he was no unreachable ivory-tower poet. Instead, Shakespeare was a young man from the provinces who made good in the big city of London. Just when and how he came from the provinces remains a mystery. He was born in 1564, the eldest son of an initially quite successful father whose position as alderman and then bailiff (mayor) of the town of Stratford allowed his son to attend the local Latin Grammar School. There, Shakespeare received an education that, contrary to some critics' belief, provided him with the historical perspective and verbal flexibility that helped define his writing.

The schoolboy grew into a young man who married an older woman, Anne Hathaway, and became the father of a daughter and a set of twins, a boy and a girl, by the age of twenty-one. The boy, Hamnet, would die before his twelfth birthday. When the playwright's father, John Shakespeare, only recently recovered from two decades of legal and financial difficulties, died in 1601, having earlier secured the coat of arms of a gentleman (Duncan-Jones 90–102), Shakespeare was left in Stratford with a family of four women: his wife, his two daughters, and his mother, Mary, *née* Arden. Shakespeare's own familial experiences, from the fluctuations of his father's fortunes, to the strong influence of several female relatives, to the tragic loss of a beloved son, doubtless added heart and depth to the incisive portrayals of characters that he created in his plays and poems.

Accordingly, given the fact that all description is necessarily selective, Shakespeare often had in mind his own experiences when he chose narrative and dramatic sources for the foundation of his comedies, histories, and tragedies. The few facts of his life that survive are open to all sorts of interpretations, some of which reveal more about the interpreter than about the facts themselves, while others carry with them a greater degree of likelihood. A few critics have noted that Shakespeare was the eldest boy in a patriarchal world, the first surviving child born in a time of plague after the infant deaths of two siblings. As a child, he doubtless saw and remembered his father dressed in the furred scarlet gown of a bailiff in 1568, going about his appointed supervisory tasks, a figure both familiar as a person and strangely exalted as an official, and as Stephen Greenblatt has noted, all by means of a costume (Greenblatt 30–31). He was likely to have been the indisputable favorite of his mother, acquiring a self-confidence that often leads young men with even a modicum of talent on to success.

Richard Wheeler has pointed out that Shakespeare's choice of source material in which a female is disguised as a boy, best illustrated in *Twelfth Night*, has psychological roots in the playwright's wish to have repaired the loss of his son, Hamnet, whose twin sister, Judith, remained a constant reminder of the absent boy (Wheeler 147–53). Finally, although his marriage and fatherhood indicate some clear grounds for heterosexuality, Shakespeare also wrote beautiful poems about a young man, and his plays often feature male bonding and pathetic male isolation when the bond is broken by marriage, as in the instances of Antonio and Bassanio in *The Merchant of Venice* and a second Antonio and Sebastian in *Twelfth Night*. These scenarios offer putative evidence of at least homosociability.

Of course, over-reliance on causal links between the playwright and the experiences of his creations would logically have Shakespeare a conscience-stricken killer like Claudius or Macbeth, a disoriented octogenarian like Lear, and a suicidal queen like Cleopatra—interpretative leaps that even the most imaginative critic is unwilling to make.

Between the birth of the twins in February 1585 and the writer Robert Greene's allusion to Shakespeare as an actor-turned-playwright in September 1592, there is no hard evidence of his whereabouts, although many theories abound. Perhaps he was a schoolmaster in the country; perhaps he was attached to the household of a Catholic landowner in Lancashire. Certainly one of the most plausible theories is that Shakespeare joined the traveling theatrical troupe called the Queen's Men in 1587 as it passed through Stratford and then came to London as a member of their company. If so, he joined an exciting theatrical world with competition for the entertainment dollar among several companies with plays written by both authors who were university graduates and a minority who were not. It was a world that on its stages carefully reflected the political issues and events of the moment, but did so indirectly because of restrictions created by governmental censorship and by the potential dangers posed by a personal response to criticism by the powerful men of the time.

These dramas were composed for a public audience of mixed class and gender, from work-cutting apprentices to lords of the realm and every possible class gradation in between. They were also performed occasionally for a private audience of higher status in smaller indoor venues.

The London of these plays was a fast-growing city, even in a time of plague, full of energy, color, commerce, varieties of goods, animals, and people of all social degrees. The population numbered perhaps 200,000 by the end of the sixteenth century. It was governed by a Lord Mayor and a municipal council quite concerned about issues of crowd control, the spread of disease, crime, and the fallout of all three in neighborhoods either just at the edge of their partial jurisdiction, Shoreditch in the north and Southwark, Bankside, in the south, or fully within it, like the Blackfriars. Playhouses, three-tiered amphitheaters, and the earlier open-plan inn-yards with galleries above, brought together all three of these problems and more, and they were threatened constantly with restriction by the authorities, who also had the subtle financial desire of taxing players whose performances were not protected by aristocratic patronage.

By the time he joined the newly formed Lord Chamberlain's Men in 1594, Shakespeare had already written his first four history plays (*1, 2, & 3 Henry VI* and *Richard III*), the farcical comedies *The Taming of the Shrew* and *The Comedy of Errors*, and the grotesquely interesting tragedy *Titus Andronicus*. Many, but certainly not all, of his 154 sonnets were also written in the mid-1590s. When the Lord Chamberlain's Men moved into the newly constructed Globe Theater in late 1599, having had five good years at the Theater and the nearby Curtain in Shoreditch, Shakespeare had scripted four more history plays, *King John, Richard II*, and *1 & 2 Henry IV* (and part of a fifth play, *Edward III*), six comedies, including *The Two Gentlemen of Verona, Love's Labour's Lost*, three of the five so-called "golden comedies" (*A Midsummer Night's Dream, The Merchant of Venice,* and *Much Ado About Nothing*), and *Romeo and Juliet,* the tragic companion to *A Midsummer Night's Dream.*

The opening season at the Globe doubtless included the last of the English history plays written solely by Shakespeare, *Henry V*, the pastoral comedy both debunking and idealistic, *As You Like It,* and the most frequently taught of the plays focused on Roman history, *Julius Caesar*. Before the death of Queen Elizabeth in late March of 1603, Shakespeare had certainly written his most famous play, *Hamlet*, his most intensely claustrophobic tragedy, *Othello*, the bourgeois domestic comedy *The Merry Wives of Windsor*, the last of the "golden comedies," which we find alloyed with both satire and melancholy, *Twelfth Night*, and the uniquely powerful satirical comedy *Troilus and Cressida*, as well as the enigmatic poem about martyrdom, *The Phoenix and Turtle*.

Outbreaks of the plague affected Shakespeare both as a dramatist and as a poet, for the virulence of the disease, when deaths reached more than fifty a week in London, forced the authorities to close the theaters in order to restrict contagion. Shakespeare was thus left with added time free from the incessant pressure to produce dramatic scripts, and he then composed his two Ovidian narrative poems, *Venus and Adonis* (1593) and *The Rape of Lucrece* (1594). The most extended theater closings were from June 1592 to May 1594 and from March 1603 to April 1604, but there were other, briefer closings. The plague was an abiding and overpowering presence in the lives and imaginations of the poet and his audiences.

After the accession in 1603 of James VI of Scotland as James I of England, when the Lord Chamberlain's Men became the King's Men and before the company activated for themselves the lease in 1608 of the Blackfriars, a smaller, indoor theater that was to draw a higher and more homogeneous class of spectator, Shakespeare created his other great tragedies, *King Lear, Macbeth, Antony and Cleopatra,* and *Coriolanus,* as well as the bitter *Timon of Athens* (although there is no record of its ever having been performed), and the two "bed-trick" plays, *All's Well That Ends Well* and *Measure for Measure,* comedies in which a lecherous man is fooled by the substitution of one woman for another in the darkness of the night. For that indoor spectacle-friendly Blackfriars theater, Shakespeare wrote the romances *Pericles, Cymbeline, The Winter's Tale,* and *The Tempest,* with their wondrous atmospheres and radiant daughters. By 1611, Shakespeare was moving into partial retirement, co-authoring with John Fletcher, his younger colleague and successor as principal playwright of the King's Men, *Henry VIII, The Two Noble Kinsmen,* and, probably, the lost *Cardenio.*

The division of his plays into these categories—comedies, histories, tragedies, and romances—reminds us that the first step taken by the playwright (indeed any playwright) was to determine the basic genre or kind of play that he wished to write, however much he might expand its boundaries. Genre creates expectations in the mind of the audience, expectations that no dramatist of the time was willing to frustrate. Regarding kind, Polonius tells us with unconscious humor of the versatility of the players who come to Elsinore: "The best actors in the world, either for tragedy, comedy, history, pastoral, pastoral-comical, historical-pastoral, tragical-historical, tragical-comical-historical-pastoral" (2.2.396–399). In that boundary-blurring, increasingly capacious definition of genre, he also informs us of Shakespeare's own gift in all kinds of writing and the fact of his often combining many of these genres in a single work. When, at the end of Plato's *Symposium,* Socrates argues that logically, the greatest tragic writer should also be the greatest comic writer, he was prophetic of Shakespeare, even if he doesn't go on to argue that these principles of tragedy and comedy could and should be connected in the same play. And Shakespeare indirectly repays Socrates for his prophecy by alluding to the philosopher's death in Mistress Quickly's description of the dying Falstaff in *Henry V,* 2.3.

Shakespeare is Shakespeare because of a combination of philosophical tolerance, psychological profundity, and metaphoric genius; that is, he is generous-minded, aware of what makes people tick, and is able to express himself more vividly and memorably than anyone else in the language. And it is his language that truly sets him apart, while simultaneously creating some occasional static in the mind of the modern reader.

There are six areas of this problematic language worth special attention: word choice, false friends, allusions, puns, iambic rhythm, and personification. Shakespeare's vocabulary has words that are no longer part of today's language, chiefly because they refer to things and concepts no longer in use, such as "three-farthings," coins of small value, in the Bastard's metaphoric "Look where three-farthings goes" (*King John*, 1.1.143). Such terms are easily understood by looking at the footnotes, or by checking *The Oxford English Dictionary* or a Shakespearean lexicon, like that of Schmidt; C. T. Onions's *A Shakespeare Glossary;* or *Shakespeare's Words,* by David and Ben Crystal. More difficult are false friends, words spelled the same as words we use today but that have different meanings. One example of this issue is "brave," which as an adjective in the sixteenth and early seventeenth centuries meant primarily "splendid" or "glorious," as in Miranda's expression of awe and excitement in *The Tempest*: "O *brave* new world/That has such people in't" (5.1.183–84), or "virtue," which in Shakespeare's language usually means "strength or power," as in Iago's argument for personal responsibility to Roderigo and the latter's lament that "it is not in my *virtue* to amend it [being in love with Desdemona]": "*Virtue*? A fig! 'tis in ourselves that we are thus or thus" (*Othello*, 1.3.318–20).

Equally problematic, but just as easily understood by reference to footnotes, are instances of classical and biblical allusion, where Shakespeare assumes a recognition by all or some of the audience of glancing references to Greek and Roman deities, frequently to elements in that most abiding narrative in Western literature, the Trojan War, as well as historical and legendary figures, as in Hamlet's "My father's brother, but no more like my father/Than I to *Hercules*" (1.2.152–53) or his subconscious reminder in the graveyard of the fact that his father was the victim of fratricide, "How the knave jowls it to the ground, as if 'twere *Cain*'s jaw-bone" (5.1.76–77).

More difficult at times are Shakespeare's puns—plays on words, sometimes comedic and sometimes intentionally non-comedic, but in each case designed to bring more than one meaning in a single word to the attention of the audience and the reader. Shakespeare's puns are almost always thematically significant, revelatory of character, or both, and attention to the possibilities of the presence of punning can only increase our understanding and pleasure in the lines. There are such simple etymological puns as "lieutenant," the military title of Cassio in *Othello*, where the word is defined as one who holds the place of the captain in the latter's absence—exactly the fear Othello has about the relationship that he imagines exists between his wife, Desdemona, and Lieutenant Cassio. There are also puns that fuse the physical and the moral, as in Falstaff's comment that his highway robbery is condoned by the goddess of the moon, "under whose *countenance* we steal" (*1 Henry IV*, 1.2.29) where the word "countenance" means both "face" and "approval." Falstaff's pun is in prose, a good example of how Shakespeare, commonly regarded as the greatest of English poets and dramatists, wrote often in prose, which itself is full of the linguistic devices of poetry.

When Shakespeare was writing in verse, he used iambic pentameter lines, ten syllable lines with five feet, or units, of two syllables each, in the sequence of short-long or unstressed-stressed. Consider, for example, Romeo's "But soft,/what light/through yond/er win/

Fig. 1. Joseph Fiennes as William Shakespeare fighting through writer's block in the film *Shakespeare in Love*: a handsome dramatist without the receding hairline of contemporary portraits and busts.

8

dow breaks" (*Romeo and Juliet*, 2.2.1), or Antony's "If you/have tears/ prepare/to shed/them now" (*Julius Caesar*, 3.2.169).

Scanning the rhythm of these lines is made easier by our knowledge that Shakespeare and the English language are both naturally iambic and that proof of the correct rhythm begins with marking the stress on the final syllable of the line and moving right to left. The rhythm with the emphasized syllables will lead the actor delivering the lines to stress certain words more than others, as we imagine Shakespeare to have intended, even as we know that stage delivery of lines with an unexpected stress can create fruitful tension in the ear of the audience. For example, Barnardo's "It was about to speak when the cock crew" (*Hamlet*, 1.1.147) is a pentameter line, but the expected iambic rhythm is broken in the last two feet, especially in the sequentially stressed final two syllables, which by their alliteration and double stress combine in form to underscore the moment of interruption in the play's narrative. Such playing off the expected is part of Shakespeare's arsenal of verse techniques.

In addition to these issues of unknown terms, false friends, allusions chiefly classical and biblical, meaningful puns, and verse rhythm itself, there is the metaphoric language that is the glory of Shakespeare, but each instance of this feature demands careful unpacking. Consider the early example of Romeo's personifying Death as an erotic figure keeping Juliet as his mistress, linking the commonly joined notions of love and death: "Shall I believe/That unsubstantial Death is amorous,/ And that the lean abhorred monster keeps/Thee here in dark to be his paramour?" (5.3.102–05). This link already had been anticipated by the Chorus in the prologue to the play, which speaks of "The fearful passage of their death-marked love" (1.6).

More compactly, later in his career, Shakespeare will have Hamlet, in prose, combine Renaissance and medieval views in similes and metaphors, comparisons with and without "like" or "as," in order to describe the multifaceted nature of man: "...how like an angel in apprehension, how like a god! The beauty of the world; the paragon of animals; and yet to me what is this quintessence of dust?" (*Hamlet*, 2.2.306–08). Macbeth in his play will argue against his wife's view that a little water will cleanse his guilty hands, "No; this my hand will rather/The multitudinous seas incarnadine,/Making the green one red" (2.2.58–60). Here Shakespeare has been careful to combine the mouth-filling hyperbole and its Latinate terms "multitudinous" and "incarnadine" (an illustration of the technique that he had learned from Christopher Marlowe) with a crystal-clear synonymous expression, "Making the green one red" for the benefit of all in the theater, even as everyone hears the hypnotically mellifluous line that came before it.

Sometimes Shakespeare scorned the opportunity to use high-flown language, even when one might expect it most, as in the Roman play *Antony and Cleopatra*, when the queen uses a noun as a verb in her bitter image of herself live on the Roman stage played by a child actor, "And I shall see/Some squeaking Cleopatra *boy* my greatness/I'th' posture of a whore" (*Antony and Cleopatra*, 5.2.219–221). Shakespeare gives to Cleopatra's handmaiden Charmian the least hyperbolic expression in a context linking the erotic and funereal (analogous to that situation described by Romeo), "Now boast thee, death, in thy possession lies/A *lass* unparallel'd" (5.2.315–16), where the simple pastoral monosyllable charms the audience, which all along had sensed the antithesis of the playful girl within the cunningly imperious and imperial queen.

While nothing can fully explain the development of this language, its raw material comes largely from Shakespeare's reading, as do the basic elements of plot and character. The same man who was to save and increase his money and property in London and Stratford was, as a craftsman, equally economical, preferring to alter and expand upon material given to him in the literary sources that lie behind all his compositions rather than to create from experience alone. He is the chief counter-example to Polonius's admonition "Neither a borrower nor a lender be" (*Hamlet* 1.3.75)—Shakespeare is a world-class borrower, but one who reshapes and transforms the borrowed materials.

Certainly he had a most retentive memory and could and did recall, at times subconsciously, both single expressions and rather lengthy passages from his reading. "It is often as if, at some deep level of his mind, Shakespeare thought and felt in quotation," as Emrys Jones has noted (Jones 21). Dryden's comment that Shakespeare "needed not the spectacles of books to read Nature; he looked inwards and found her there" ignores Shakespeare's conscious manipulations of his reading as a chief source for his achievement. Nevertheless, Dryden gives us the basic image useful for picturing Shakespeare's genius. The playwright's metaphorical spectacles had two lenses, one of which was focused on life as he knew it and one on the writings of his predecessors and contemporaries: historians both classical and English, proto-novelists, poets, pamphleteers, and essayists, and playwrights who had in their own ways dealt with themes that interested him.

It is by looking at what Shakespeare himself perused that we see his manipulative genius at work, omitting, adding, preserving, and qualifying those plots, motifs, and images viewed through one lens of his binoculars. An important question is just how much of the original theme and significance is brought over in the creative borrowing, a question made more difficult to answer by the fact that in the composition of his plays, Shakespeare often modified and sometimes even inverted the gender and number of the persons in the original material. See, for example, the model in the story of Cupid and Psyche from Apuleius' *The Golden Asse* (1566), where Psyche almost murders Cupid, for the description of the deaths of the little princes in *Richard III*, as well as for the presentation of the murder of Desdemona in *Othello*. The closer one looks at this source and the affected passage, the more one sees that the young man from Stratford, despite being accused by his London-educated colleague and rival Ben Jonson of having "small Latin and less Greek," was a sufficiently good Latinist to check the translation of Apuleius that he was using against the original, even as he would later check Golding's translation of the *Metamorphoses* against Ovid's Latin for use in *The Tempest*.

We don't know the workplace of Shakespeare, the desk or table where he kept his books, nor do we know for certain who provided him with these volumes, some of which were quite expensive, such as *Holinshed's Chronicles*, North's *Plutarch*, and bibles, both Bishops' and Geneva. But, if we imagine a bookshelf above his desk and envision the titles that he might have ordered there chronologically, we would first see the classics, most importantly Ovid and Virgil; then the Bible, especially Genesis, the Gospel of St. Matthew, and the Book of Revelation; medieval and Renaissance writers, including Chaucer and Erasmus; and then his own immediate predecessors and colleagues, especially Thomas Kyd, Christopher Marlowe, Robert Greene, and Thomas Nashe. Sometimes the most unlikely source can provide a motif or a character, but for more important ideas, we may note what he would have learned from four exemplary volumes on this imagined shelf.

From Seneca, the Roman philosopher, tutor to the emperor Nero and playwright of closet tragedies (that is, of plays meant to be read in the study rather than performed on stage), Shakespeare learned to balance a sensational theme—fratricide and incest—with a plot structured with care and characters subtly developed with an attitude quite fatalistic. From Plutarch, the Greek historian who wrote parallel lives of Greek and Roman leaders, he learned the importance of the nature of the private man when serving in public office and how that nature is revealed in small gestures with large significance—what James Joyce, the "spiritual son" of Shakespeare, would later refer to as "epiphanies." From Machiavelli, the notorious early-sixteenth-century political theorist, or from the image of Machiavelli, he saw what he had already known about the role of deception and amorality in political life. From Michel de Montaigne, the sixteenth-century father of the essay, he added to his already operative skepticism, a capacity to question received notions about the consistency of the "self" and the hierarchical place of human beings in creation.

Mr. WILLIAM

# SHAKESPEARES

COMEDIES,
HISTORIES, &
TRAGEDIES.

Published according to the True Originall Copies.

*Martin Droeshout sculpsit London.*

*LONDON*
Printed by Isaac Iaggard, and Ed. Blount. 1623.

Fig. 2. Later, on other writers' bookshelves, would be Shakespeare's own First Folio (1623), containing thirty-six plays, half of them appearing in print for the first time. It does not, however, include any of the longer poems or sonnets.

To enjoy Shakespeare, it is not at all necessary to understand the sources that he mined, but to study Shakespeare, the better to appreciate the depth and complexity of the work, it is extremely useful to examine the foundations upon which he has built his characters and plots. We can trace, for example, the many constituent elements that have gone into the creation of Falstaff, who, together with Hamlet, is the most discussed of Shakespeare's creations. The elements include, among still others, the Vice of the morality plays; the rogue from Nashe's *The Unfortunate Traveller;* the *miles gloriosus* or cowardly braggart warrior from the Roman comic playwright (and school text) Plautus; the cheerful toper from the Bacchus of Nashe's *Summer's Last Will and Testament;* parodically, the Protestant martyr Sir John Oldcastle from Foxe's *Book of Martyrs;* and even the dying Socrates of Plato's *Phaedo.* Not that Falstaff is at all times all these figures, but in the course of his career in four plays, alive in *1 & 2 Henry IV,* dying offstage in *Henry V,* and radically transformed in *The Merry Wives of Windsor,* he is each of them by turn and counterturn, and still so much more than the mere sum of all these literary, dramatic, and historical parts.

In terms of giving voice to multiple perspectives, to characters of different ages, genders, colors, ethnicities, religions, and social ranks, Shakespeare is unrivaled. No other playwright, then or since, makes other selves live while simultaneously concealing his own self or selves, a talent described by Keats as "negative capability." Shakespeare was also an actor; that is, a person interested in imitating imaginary persons. He was thus doubly a quite creative mimic. Some of the selves mimicked are versions of the "Other," those foreigners or aliens from around the world, including Africans (Aaron, Morocco, Othello), Jews (Shylock, Tubal, Jessica), Frenchmen and Frenchwomen (the Dauphin, Joan of Arc, Margaret of Anjou), non-English Britons (Irish: Macmorris; Scots: Jamy; Welsh: Fluellen), as well as such other continental Europeans as Spaniards (Don Armado) and Italians (including several Antonios), to say nothing of the indefinable Caliban.

Some of his topics, his subjects for dramatic treatment, came often from already set pieces at school, as Emrys Jones, among others, has shown. For example, a set question to be answered, pro and con, was, should Brutus have joined the conspiracy to assassinate Caesar, the answer to which helps create the tensions in *Julius Caesar* (Jones 16). Such an on-the-one-hand and on-the-other school exercise became part of Shakespeare's dramatic strategy, where plays provide the tension created by opposites and the consequent rich ground for multiple interpretations by readers and audiences. There were also sources in earlier stage productions, including plays about Romeo and Juliet, King John, King Lear, and Hamlet. Marlowe especially provided structures to imitate and diverge from in his plays of a weak king (*Edward II*) and of several extraordinary ambitious characters, among whom are a villainous Jew (*The Jew of Malta*), and a rhetorical conqueror (*Tamburlaine*), brilliant efforts which become in Shakespeare's hands the still more dramatic *Richard II*, *The Merchant of Venice*, and *Henry V*.

Shakespeare's borrowing was frequent and pervasive, but his creative adaptations of those raw materials have made him ultimately not just a borrower but in fact the world's greatest lender, giving us four hundred years of pleasure and providing countless artists, whether painters, novelists, film directors, or even comic book writers, with allusive material. Of course, we would happily surrender our knowledge of a number of these borrowings if only we could have some sense of the quality of the voice of the leading man Richard Burbage, of the facial expressions of the comic actor Will Kemp, the sounds of the groundlings' responses to both the jokes and the set soliloquies, and the reactions of both Queen Elizabeth, who allegedly after watching *1 & 2 Henry IV* wanted to see Falstaff in love, and King James, who doubtless loved the image of his ancestor Banquo in *Macbeth*.

Shakespeare's last years before his death in April 1616 were spent back in Stratford. Although little is known of that time, we are left with the enigmatic coda to his life: his will, in which he famously left to his wife, Anne Hathaway Shakespeare, "the second-best bed"—it is unclear whether it was a cruel slight or a fondly personal bequest. Care of his estate went to his elder daughter, Susannah, while a lesser inheritance went to his wayward younger daughter, Judith, and any children she might have. He died a landowner, a family man, and a once well-known playwright. His will did not cite what has become his greatest legacy—the plays and poems that we read today—but the clues that these works leave about his life, and certainly the testament to his talent that they represent, are more valuable than even the most detailed autobiography. To be sure, however, the local boy who made good, worked hard, had flaws, and lived a complicated family life has more in common with many of his readers, then and now, than does the iconic Shakespeare, who has been mistakenly portrayed as a distant genius paring his fingernails while creating many of the greatest works in world literature.

# ELIZABETHAN THEATER

*J. J. M. Tobin*

MASS ENTERTAINMENT today has become ever more fractured as technology provides myriad ways to take in a film (and myriad ways for Hollywood to try to make money). Movie theaters now have to compete with home theaters and couches in a way they never had to before in order to put people in the seats. The attractions of high-definition screens and stereo surround-sound are not the draw they once were now that individuals can access such technology in their own homes, and stadium seating and chair-side concessions don't make up the difference. The appeal of first-run films is fading too, now that movies go to DVD in a matter of weeks and are also available for immediate streaming through a Netflix subscription. All of these technologies, however, whether enjoyed in the cinema or at home, contribute to the moviegoer's sensation of being transported to another time and place (a journey, moreover, that lasts not much longer than an hour and a half). Hard to imagine, then, that a little over four hundred years ago, when the battle for the entertainment dollar took place on the stage rather than the screen, most members of the Elizabethan audience gladly stood for more than two hours without benefit of a padded seat, buttered popcorn, or Junior Mints (although they did have dried fruit and nuts), or the pause button in order to watch the plays of Shakespeare and his fellow dramatists performed. The legendary plays we read today on these pages were once the sixteenth- and early-seventeenth-century equivalents of the *Harry Potter* series or *Avatar*—artistic creations to be sure, but first and foremost moneymakers for their producers.

Theatrical performances in Elizabethan England took place all over the country in a wide variety of venues. As we know from the work of A. Gurr and others, if we put aside the sites used by touring companies like the Queen's Men of the 1580s (to which Shakespeare himself may have been attached), the guildhalls and marketplaces in cities and towns like Norwich, Bristol, and Stratford, or the halls of the universities of Oxford and Cambridge, and instead concentrate on London itself, we see that there were five basic performance locales (Gurr, esp. 115 ff.). There were, of course, the inns and inn-yards, in large part roofed against the weather and useful especially during the winter months.

The most celebrated of these inns in the history of London theater were the Bel Savage, the Bull, and the Cross Keys, these latter two on the same London street. These were the locations most frequently of concern to the mayor and other municipal authorities anxious about unruly crowds and increased chances of plague contagion, until 1594, when it was declared by the Lord Chamberlain of the Queen's court that there would be only two adult companies—his own, the Lord Chamberlain's Men (Shakespeare's group) and his father-in-law's, the Lord Admiral's Men, troupes that would upon the succession of King James be called the King's Men and Prince Henry's Men—and they would not perform anymore in city inns.

Second, there were two indoor halls, one in a building abutting St. Paul's Cathedral, not too far from the Bel Savage Inn, and the other in the refectory of the old Blackfriars monastery, each used by the children's companies of boys who put on plays with adult political and moral themes. Shakespeare and his company in 1596 had hoped to use the Blackfriars because Blackfriars was a liberty—that is, a district that, for reasons of its religious history, was independent of the secular control of the sheriff—but were refused by a powerful NIMBY (not in my backyard) movement of influential residents. They then leased the building to a second generation of a children's company and had to wait until 1608 to take possession of what would turn out to be both a "tonier" and quite lucrative theatrical space.

Third were the dining halls of the Inns of Court, the London law schools or, perhaps, more accurately, legal societies, where noteworthy performances of *The Comedy of Errors* (Gray's Inn) and *Twelfth Night* (the Middle Temple) took place. There, special audiences with their appetite for contemporary satire allowed for the lampooning of particular individuals whose traits and foibles would be represented by grimace, gesture, voice imitation, and even clothing, as in the case of Dr. Pinch in *The Comedy of Errors*, Malvolio in *Twelfth Night*, and Ajax in *Troilus and Cressida*. When these plays were moved to the larger public stage, the personalized elements could be withdrawn and the characters could continue as general, non-specifically humorous figures.

Fourth was the Queen's court itself (after the death of Elizabeth in 1603, it became the King's court), where at Christmastide, the major companies would be invited to perform for the pleasure of the monarch. Indeed, throughout the long period of tension between the city authorities and the court, the justification for allowing the players to perform their craft in public was that they needed to practice in order to be ready at year's end to entertain the monarch. This argument assumed a quite disproportionate ratio of practice to performance, but it was a convenient semi-fiction that seemed to satisfy all concerned. These court performances were rewarded financially by the Master of the Revels and were less expensive than other kinds of royal entertainment, including masques with elaborate scenery and complicated production devices, the high costs of which later contributed to the downfall of Charles I, James's son and successor. Legend has it that Queen Elizabeth so enjoyed some of the performances featuring the character of Falstaff that she wished to see him in love, a comment which was allegedly the stimulus for *The Merry Wives of Windsor*, which was said to have been written in two weeks, the better to satisfy the queen's request. A close look at the multiple sources used in the creation of this middle-class comedy suggests that the legend may be well founded.

Last, there are the purpose-built amphitheaters, beginning with James Burbage's the Theater (1576) in Shoreditch, just to the north of the city limits; and the Curtain (1578) nearby. To the south, across the Thames, were the Rose (1587), the site of the Lord Admiral's company and most notably the performances of Christopher Marlowe's plays; the Swan (1596); the Globe (1599), built with the very timbers of the Theater transported across the river in the winter of 1598 after the twenty-one-year lease on the old property had expired and several subsequent months of renting; and, back to Shoreditch in the north, the Fortune (1600), explicitly built in imitation of the triple-tiered Globe.

There was competition for the same audience in the form of bull-baiting, bear-baiting and cockfighting, and also simple competition for attention from such activities as royal processions, municipal pageants, outdoor sermons, and public executions with hangings, eviscerations, castrations, and quarterings, not to mention the nearby temptation of the houses ("nunneries") of prostitution. Nonetheless, these theatrical structures proved that, if you build it, they will come.

And come they did, with hundreds of performances each year of thirty or more plays in repertory for each company, plays of chronicle history, romance, tragedy (especially revenge tragedy), satire, and comedy (slapstick, farcical, situational, verbal, and, from 1597, "humorous"; that is, comedy dependent upon characters moved by one dominant personality trait into behavior mechanical and predictable, almost monomaniacally focused). The two major companies could and did perform familiar plays for a week or more before adding a new play to the repertory. A successful new play would be performed at least eight times, according to Knutson, within four months to half a year (Knutson 33–34). New plays were house-fillers, and entrance fees could be doubled for openings. When sequels created a two-part play, performances were only sometimes staged in proper sequence, even as moviegoers will still watch on cable *Godfather II* or *The Empire Strikes Back* without worrying that they had not just seen *The Godfather* or *Star Wars*.

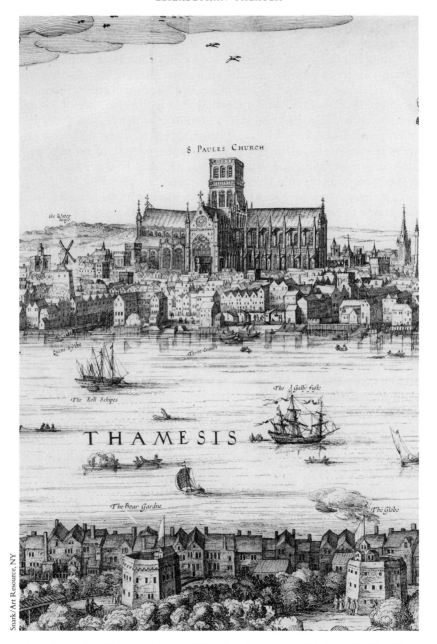

Fig. 3. Part of J. C. Visscher's view of London (c. 1616 or slightly earlier) looking north from the Bankside and showing the Beargarden theater and, to the right, the Globe theater (or possibly the Swan).

The players seemed willing to play throughout the week and throughout the year, but municipal officials repeatedly insisted that there be no performances on Sundays and holy days and holidays, nor during Lent. These demands had some effect, although their repetition by the authorities clearly suggests that there were violations, with performances on occasional Sundays, even at court, on some holidays, and on some days in Lent.

Of course, even though almost half of Shakespeare's plays had already been performed at the Theater and elsewhere, we think of the Globe, open for business probably in the late summer of 1599, as the principal venue for Shakespeare's work, perhaps with *As You Like It* the first production. The current New Globe on the Bankside in Southwark, erected in careful imitation of what we know to have been the methods and materials of the sixteenth century, allows for a twenty-first-century experience analogous to that of the Elizabethan theatergoer. It may be that the diameter of the current theater, of one hundred feet, is a bit too wide, and that seventy-two feet is rather closer to the exact diameter of not only the Globe but several of these late-sixteenth-century London theaters. If so, the judgment that such Elizabethan theaters could hold between 2,000 and 3,000 people suggests that spectators, particularly the groundlings—those who had paid a penny to stand throughout the two-to-three hour performance—were packed in cheek by jowl.

The geometry of the Globe itself is that of a polygon, but it appears circular. From a distance, one would know that a play was to be performed that day by the presence of a flag flying high above the tiring house, the dressing area for the actors. Once inside the building, the theatergoer would note the covered stage projecting from an arc of the circle almost to the center of the uncovered audience space, such that the groundlings would be on three sides of the stage, with those in the front almost able to rest their chins on the platform which was raised about five feet from the floor. This stage was not raked—that is, inclined or tilted towards the audience—as it often is in modern theaters today. Raking both creates better sightlines and potentially affects stage business, as in the case of a fallen Shylock in productions of *The Merchant of Venice*, who at one point struggles in vain to stand on a pile of slippery ducats (gold coins). This move is made even more difficult by the slight incline. However, instead of raking the stage, the Rose, and perhaps the Globe and the Fortune, had the ground on which the audience stood slightly raked (Thomson 78–79), to the great advantage of those in the back of the theater.

Behind the stage, protected by a backdrop on the first level, was the tiring house where the actors dressed and from which they came and went through two openings to the left and right. There were few surprise entrances in the Elizabethan theater, as the audience could always see before them the places of entry. Covering the upper stage and a large part of the outer stage would be the "heavens," supported by two columns or pillars behind which characters could hide in order to eavesdrop and which could serve metaphorically as trees or bushes. The underside of the "heavens" was adorned with signs of the zodiac, the better to remind the audience that all the world is a stage. At the back of the stage in the center, between the two openings of exit and entrance, was a discovery space within which, when a curtain was drawn, an additional mini-set of a study, a bed, or a cave could be revealed.

From below the stage, figures, especially ghosts, could ascend through a trapdoor, and mythological deities could be lowered from above. From the second tier of the galleries, still part of the tiring house, characters could appear as on battlements or a balcony. Music was a very great part of Elizabethan theater, and musicians would be positioned sometimes on that second level of the tiring house. Less musical but still necessary sound effects, say one indicating a storm and thunder, were achieved by such actions as the offstage rolling of a cannonball down a metal trestle or repeated drumming.

Although the groundlings were the closest to the talented actors, for those members of the audience who wished to sit in the galleries (Stern, esp. 212–13) and were willing to pay more money for the privilege, there would have been the comfort of the familiar, as V. F. Petronella has pointed out, inasmuch as these galleries included rooms not unlike those in the domestic buildings near the Globe. However, the familiar was balanced with the rare via the figures on the stage who represented kings, nymphs, fairies, and ghosts, personages not usually found in the Southwark area (Petronella, esp. 111–25). These audiences themselves came from a great range of Elizabethan society, male and female, from aristocrats to lowly apprentices, with all gradations of the social spectrum in between. The late Elizabethan and early Jacobean period is so special in theatrical history in part because of the work of a number of gifted playwrights, Shakespeare preeminent among them, but also in part because of the inclusive nature of the audiences, which were representative of the society as a whole.

When the King's Men in 1609 began to perform in the smaller, indoor Blackfriars Theater while still continuing at the Globe in the summer months, they were able to charge at Blackfriars five or six times the entry fee at the Globe for productions that pleased a grander and wealthier group, but at the cost of having a more socially homogeneous audience. Although the Blackfriars was a more lucrative venue,

Shakespeare's company still profited from productions at the Globe, to the degree that when the Globe burned down during a performance of *Henry VIII* on June 29 1613, the company immediately set about rebuilding the structure so that it could reopen the very next year. One wonders whether Shakespeare came down from semi-retirement in Stratford for the new opening or was already in London working yet again in collaboration with John Fletcher, his successor as principal playwright of the King's Men.

In the more heterogeneous atmosphere at the Globe, whether the first or second version, audiences watched action taking place on a platform of about twelve hundred square feet, a stage which could be the Roman forum at one moment, the senate house at another, and a battlefield at still another. Yet the audience was never at a loss in recognizing what was what, for the dramatist provided place references in the dialogue between and among characters (and some plays may also have featured signs indicating place). The action was sometimes interrupted by informative soliloquies, speeches directed to the audience as if the character speaking on the stage were totally alone, whether or not he or she actually was. By convention, what was said in a soliloquy was understood to be the truthful indication of the character's thoughts and feelings. These soliloquies must have been in their day somewhat analogous to operatic arias—plot-useful devices, but also stand-alone bravura exercises in rhetorical display. Othello's "flaming minister" speech (5.2.1–22) is a good example of the show-stopping effect of the soliloquy, and Edmund's defense of bastardy in *King Lear* (1605; 1.2.1–22), in a passage of identical length seldom fails to elicit applause at the last line even from today's audiences, who otherwise are accustomed not to interrupt the flow of a performance.

The actors and the audience were proximate and visible to each other during these daylight performances, putting them on more intimate terms than is the case in theaters today. Performers were dressed onstage in contemporary Elizabethan clothing, with the kings and dukes wearing specially purchased, costly garments whose fate as they grew worn and tattered was to outfit the clowns with social pretensions. There were also attempts to provide historical atmosphere when needed with helmets, shields, greaves and togas appropriate to the ancient world. Perhaps as few as ten men and four boys, who would play the women's roles in this all-male theatrical world, could perform all sixteenth-century plays. The boys would remain with the company until their voices cracked, and some then became adult members of the company when places became available. They were apprentices in a profession where the turnover was not great—a bonus to the dramatist who could visualize the actor who would be playing the character he was creating but not so advantageous for a young actor looking for a permanent place within a stable group. Because plays were very seldom performed in an uninterrupted run, actors needed powerful memories. It was a time when the aural rather than the visual understanding was much greater than in our own time, but even so, the capacity of actors to hold in their heads a large number of roles from many different plays was extraordinary, and new plays were constantly being added to the repertory.

Even as one man in his time plays many parts, so did Shakespeare's company of actors. The skills and particular strengths of these actors must have given Shakespeare a great deal of confidence about the complexity of the roles that he could ask them to create. Such an element of the familiar increased the pleasure of the audience when it could recognize the same actor behind two different characters whose similarity might now be perceived. Celebrated instances of doubling include, in *A Midsummer Night's Dream*, Theseus/Oberon and Hippolyta/Titania; and, in *Hamlet*, Polonius/First Gravedigger and, most strikingly, the Ghost/Claudius. The audience would likewise be affected by their experience with an actor in a current play having performed in a previous play that they had also seen. One example of this link between roles that allows the audience to anticipate the plot comes in *Hamlet,* when Polonius tells us of his having played Caesar. Caesar, of course, was killed by Brutus in Shakespeare's *Julius Caesar.* The actor now playing Polonius had played Caesar previously in *Julius Caesar,* and in that production, he was killed by Brutus, played by Richard Burbage (son of James). In this performance of *Hamlet*, Burbage was playing Hamlet, and he would shortly kill Polonius, in a repeat of history.

The theater is the most collaborative of enterprises. We should think of Shakespeare as a script-writer under considerable pressure to provide material for his colleagues, all of whom viewed the play to come as a fundamentally money-making project. Shakespeare had multiple advantages beyond his inherent verbal and intuitive gifts. Not only did he write for a group of actors whose individual talents he could anticipate in the composition of his characters, but the script that he was creating was often a response to recent successes by rival companies with their own revengers, weak and strong English kings, and disguised lovers.

The performances themselves relied greatly on the power of the audience's imagination to fill in what was missing because of the limitations of the Elizabethan stage, as the self-conscious Prologue in *Henry V* (1599) makes clear by appealing to the audience to imagine whole armies being transported across the sea. Other Elizabethan dramatists did attempt to be "realistic" in ways that are laughable even beyond the well-intended efforts of Quince, Bottom, and the other Mechanicals in *A Midsummer Night's Dream* (1596). Consider, as noted by G. B. Evans, Yarrington's *Two Tragedies in One* (1594–c. 1598), 2.1: "When the boy goeth in to the shop, Merry striketh six blows on his head and, with the seventh, leaves the hammer sticking in his head; the boy groaning must be heard by a maid, who must cry to her master." Three scenes later, a character "Brings him forth in a chair with a hammer sticking in his head" (Evans 71). Such grossly imperfect efforts increasingly gave way to conventional signals expressive of the limitations of the stage. Four or five men with spears and a flag could represent an army, and a single coffin could represent a whole graveyard. While the Globe stage lacked scenery as we know it, it was not lacking in props. Not only were there a trapdoor grave and a bank of flowers, but also a good number of handheld props like swords, torches, chalices, crowns, and skulls, each a real object and potentially a symbol.

Sometimes convention and symbolism gave way to nature in the case of live animals. Men in animal skins are safer, of course, but some animals, like dogs and bears, are trainable. It is certain that Crab, the dog in the *Two Gentlemen of Verona* (1595–96), was "played" by a true canine, and it is quite likely that the bear that pursues Antigonus in *The Winter's Tale* was only sometimes a disguised human being; but at other times, it was a bear, managed but real, possibly even a polar bear reared from the time of its capture as a cub. Further reflection on the known dangers associated with working with bears and our knowledge of the props listed in *Henslowe's Diary* of 'j beares skyne' (Henslowe 319) suggest that Elizabethan actors were more comfortable with artificial bears, thereby avoiding any sudden ursine aggression, revenge for all the suffering their colleagues had endured at the bear-baiting stake.

The authorities whose powers of censorship were real and forceful did not worry much about whether animals were live onstage or not, but they did care about theological issues being discussed explicitly and about urban insurrection, as we know from the strictures applied to *The Book of Sir Thomas More*, a manuscript play in which Shakespeare most probably had a hand. For all their apparent sensitivity to political issues, the government seems not to have interfered with plays that show the removal—or even the murder—of kings, although the scene of the deposing of Richard in *Richard II* (1596) was thought too delicate to be printed during the lifetime of Queen Elizabeth, who recognized Richard as a parallel figure and pointedly said: "Know ye not I am Richard the Second." Scholars debate whether some of these potent themes regarding right versus might, illegitimate succession, and successful usurpation were recognized imperfectly by the government and so escaped into performance if not always into print. Another theory is that the authorities allowed the audiences to be excited and then pacified by these entertaining productions, a release of energies that returned the audience at the play's end to an unchanged social and political reality.

While it is now customary to refer to this reality as part of the Early Modern Period, it is still important to remember that the two main cultural forces of the time, the Renaissance and the Reformation, came together in a perfect storm of new ideas about values. The Renaissance brought us the rebirth of classical culture and an emphasis on the dignity of human beings, and the Reformation stripped levels of interpretative authority in favor of the individual's more direct reliance on Scripture. These new ideas, sometimes in concert and sometimes in tension, have led increasingly over four hundred years to our current distant but clearly related theories of skepticism and pragmatism.

It is just as important to remember that when James Burbage built his theater in 1576, he was not so much interested in the idea of the dignity of human beings or in the proper interpretation of Scripture as in the making of money. When his son, Richard, and his son's friend and partner, William Shakespeare, and their fellow shareholders were creating and performing their scripts, they were counting the house above all else. Theater was an essential part of the entertainment industry, and for some, it was especially lucrative. If a man was an actor, he made a little bit of money; if a playwright, a little more; if a shareholder in the company that put on the play, a very great deal more; and if a householder in the building in which the plays were performed, even more still. Shakespeare was all four, and as we read his scripts, we should remember that the artist was also a businessman, interested in the box office as much as or more than any hard-to-imagine immortality. The Elizabethan theater was the forerunner of the multiplex, a collaborative, secular church in which the congregation/audience focused on the service before them, and Shakespeare and his fellows focused on both the service and the collection plate.

And yet with all the primary focus on material gain, Shakespeare and his competitors and collaborators were aware of the cultural importance and historical traditions of drama itself. Their own work continued myths and rituals that had begun in Athens and elsewhere more than two thousand years ago. It may well be true, as Dr. Samuel Johnson famously said, that no man but a blockhead ever wrote for anything but money, and Mozart might have been partially correct when he said that good health and money were the two most important elements in life. Yet we also know that just because a work has been commissioned doesn't rule out the presence of beauty and truth, as indeed Mozart's own works reveal. Michelangelo was paid by Pope Julius II to paint the Sistine Chapel, but nobody thinks of the fee the artist earned when she or he looks at the creation of Adam or the expulsion of Adam and Eve from the Garden of Eden. Shakespeare's career in the Elizabethan theatrical world turned out to be quite lucrative, but given the many profound reasons for which we read and study *A Midsummer Night's Dream, King Lear,* and *The Tempest* today (among so many other plays and poems), we see that the dramatist who created these works and gained so much material success was nevertheless grossly underpaid.

## WORKS CITED

Crystal, David and Ben Crystal. *Shakespeare's Words.* London: Penguin, 2002. Print.

Duncan-Jones, Katherine. *Ungentle Shakespeare: Scenes from His Life.* London: Arden Shakespeare-Thomson, 2001. Print.

Evans, G. Blakemore. *Elizabethan-Jacobean Drama.* London: A&C Black, 1988. Print.

Foakes, R. A., ed. *Henslowe's Diary.* 2nd ed. Cambridge: Cambridge UP, 2002. Print.

Greenblatt, Stephen. *Will in the World: How Shakespeare Became Shakespeare.* New York: Norton, 2004. Print.

Gurr, Andrew. *The Shakespearean Stage 1574–1642.* 3rd ed. Cambridge and New York: Cambridge UP, 1992. Print.

Jones, Emrys. *The Origins of Shakespeare.* Oxford: Clarendon, 1977. Print.

Knutson, Rosalyn. *The Repertory of Shakespeare's Company, 1594–1603.* Fayetteville: U of Arkansas P, 1991. Print.

Onions, C. T. *A Shakespeare Glossary.* Oxford: Clarendon, 1911. Print.

Petronella, Vincent F. "Shakespeare's Dramatic Chambers." *In the Company of Shakespeare: Essays on English Renaissance Literature in Honor of G. Blakemore Evans.* Eds. Thomas Moisan and Douglas Bruster. Madison and London: Fairleigh Dickinson and Associated UPs, 2002. 111–38. Print.

Schmidt, Alexander. *Shakespeare Lexicon.* Berlin: Georg Reimer, 1902. Print.

Stern, Tiffany. "'You that walk i' in the Galleries': Standing and Walking in the Galleries of the Globe Theater." *Shakespeare Quarterly* 51 (2000): 211–16. Print.

Thomson, Peter. *Shakespeare's Professional Career.* Cambridge: Cambridge UP, 1992. Print.

Wheeler, Richard P. "Deaths in the Family: The Loss of a Son and the Rise of Shakespearean Comedy." *Shakespeare Quarterly* 51 (2000): 127–54. Print.

# The Critical Introduction

## "speak'st thou in sober meanings?" (5.2.69): reading *As You Like It*

The title of *As You Like It* suggests accord and harmony, but in fact, conflicting interpretations of the play abound. Whereas most readers would agree on certain fundamental points—this is a pastoral comedy whose central concerns involve love and marriage, gender, nature and the natural world, and theater itself—intense disagreements about other issues are expressed in critical commentary on the play and enacted in the telling differences among productions.

Many debates involve how Rosalind is represented and the consequent implications about gender, arguably the predominant issue in the play. A figure for the playwright, among her many other roles, does she skillfully direct the action in ways that demonstrate and celebrate female power and agency, is her apparent independence illusory throughout the text, or does the conclusion of the play reactively wrest from her the very potency earlier permitted her?[1] These and related questions engender more abstract ones: Does the play insistently distinguish male and female, disrupt those categories without offering an alternative, or celebrate the admixture of male and female characteristics, androgyny? This query in turn invites an even broader one: In its treatment of not only gendered divides but also other distinctions and rankings (notably social status), is *As You Like It* deeply conservative, or does it challenge widely accepted hierarchies, boldly going where few plays had gone before? Delighting like its heroine in paradoxes, equivocations, and unanswered riddles (Young), *As You Like It* resists easy answers to such questions; its multivalent title arguably invited its original audience to formulate interpretations that pleased them. Similarly, the complexities of *As You Like It* invite contemporary readers, whether students or scholars, to assess evidence carefully and craft their own interpretations of the issues discussed below.

---

**1.** The critical commentary on this issue is extensive. For the argument that female power is emphasized in the play, see, e.g., Latham, esp. lxxii, and Nevo, while Shakespeareans focusing primarily on its limitations include, among many others, Erickson and Green. A number of critics negotiate compromises between those positions; see in particular Carlson, who suggests that female freedom is asserted but later undercut, and Howard, who maintains that the gender system is threatened yet preserved.

In any event, the structure of the plot is clear. Written in or around 1599, *As You Like It* interweaves its narrative about love with stories involving inheritance and political power. Its action opens on the conflict between two brothers, with the evil and elder Oliver denying the virtuous and younger Orlando what his father's will had stipulated and even plotting for him to be killed, first by a wrestler and then through arson. Exploring reflections and refractions of many sorts, the play also includes another set of brothers: his kingdom usurped by his unscrupulous sibling Duke Frederick, Duke Senior lives in exile in the Forest of Arden, surrounded by a group of courtiers that includes the melancholy Jaques. Rosalind, daughter of Duke Senior and niece of Duke Frederick, falls in love with Orlando, and when her uncle banishes her, she and her friend Celia, Duke Frederick's daughter, run away to the forest of Arden. Disguised as the male character Ganymede (who was cupbearer to and, in many versions of the myth, the lover of the king of the gods, Jove), Rosalind encounters Orlando there; she tells him she ("he") will pretend to be Rosalind to cure him of love. This process, enacted through several interchanges between them, mirrors other love plots, notably the Fool Touchstone's courtship of Audrey and Silvius's wooing of the disdainful Phebe. Eventually, Oliver, repenting of his previous unbrotherly cruelty and rescued from death by its victim, Orlando, falls in love with Celia; Duke Frederick also repents and restores the kingdom to Duke Senior. The play concludes with the marriage of four sets of couples.

## "I COULD MATCH THIS BEGINNING WITH AN OLD TALE" (1.2.120): CULTURAL AND LITERARY ROOTS

We cannot be certain whether Shakespeare knew a medieval text with a similar plot, *The Tale of Gamelyn,* and neither do scholars agree on whether he drew on the anonymous sixteenth-century play *Sir Clyomon and Sir Clamydes.* But certainly his principal source is the sixteenth-century writer Thomas Lodge's prose romance entitled *Rosalynde* (1590), itself based on *The Tale of Gamelyn.* As the excerpts included in this edition demonstrate, many similarities link the plot of *Rosalynde* to *As You Like It*: An evil ruler, the current king of France, seizes power by banishing the beneficent former king, an elder brother mistreats his younger brother, the character corresponding to Orlando is aided by a faithful servant, and so on.

But what isn't copied from a source—the dog that didn't bark in the night, as Sherlock Holmes put it in his own sleuthing—or what is copied with salient differences is as telling in literary investigations as in Holmes's detection. *As You Like It* demonstrates that comparing a play and its literary sources can effectively reveal the aims and anxieties that drive it. Shakespeare's usual preoccupations with pairings and with familial tensions emerge when his text makes Duke Frederick and Duke Senior, the characters corresponding to Lodge's deposed king and deposer, brothers. Behind the interest in pairing throughout Shakespearean drama lies a concern, even an obsession, with one of its sources and consequences, competition in its many forms—between suitors for the same woman, between brothers, and even between genres.

In Lodge's *Rosalynde,* the elder brother resents the younger for inheriting more land, whereas in Shakespeare's rendering, the elder brother inherits the estate and fails to take care of his younger sibling, reminding us that the play is about material needs as well as erotic drives (Montrose; Phillips, 212–13). Shakespeare's version accords with and comments on contemporary laws and customs connected to bequests: Although the practices informing inheritance differed from one part of the country to the next, bestowing the entire estate on the eldest male heir, a practice known as primogeniture, was common in many regions of England, rendering younger children dependent on the largesse of potentially selfish older siblings. In addition, the death of a parent could leave all the offspring, not just the younger ones, vulnerable to unscrupulous relatives and stepparents trying to gain their inheritances. Many members of Shakespeare's original audience would have been all too familiar with such threats: For example, nearly half the women in London had experienced the demise of their fathers by the time they were twenty (Dubrow [1999], 161–62). Yet, like other historically specific concerns in the play, the frequency of early parental loss has resonances for our own culture, although today, comparable conflicts with siblings and stepparents are more likely to result from divorce than death.

The most noticeable differences between *Rosalynde* and *As You Like It*, however, revolve around a diminution and deflection of violence. In Shakespeare, we are briefly told that the wrestler causes the death of his previous opponents, and his fate after being overthrown by Orlando is described ambiguously; in Lodge, his destruction of his victims is recounted in much more detail, and he is himself indubitably killed by the hero corresponding to Orlando. Similarly, Torismond, the counterpart to Duke Frederick, dies in battle rather than retreating to a life of religion. The most obvious explanation for these and many cognate changes is generic, since comedy is generally less bloodthirsty than many other genres, including prose romance. But they also introduce a larger pattern central to the play: Shakespeare's text typically at once incorporates and delimits threats of many types.

Another related difference between *Rosalynde* and *As You Like It* is in the treatment of that cultural violence against women, misogyny.

Overt and relentless in Lodge, emphasized by his repeated references to those temptresses from Greek mythology known as the sirens misogyny is far from absent in *As You Like It*. Indeed, Rosalind herself expresses stereotyped critiques of her sex ("Do you not know I am a woman? when I think, I must speak" [3.2.249–50]). But such sentiments are certainly less prominent in Shakespeare's play; on this issue, it both controls and conceals aggression.

As we have just seen, the relationship between *Rosalynde* and *As You Like It,* like the relationship between that play and such cultural problems as inheritance, is too dynamic to accord to the simple, one-way impact implicit in terms like "source" and "background." Rather, the play rethinks, reconsiders, and reshapes the literary texts and cultural events that in turn shape it. Nowhere is this pattern more apparent than in its relationship to another type of "source," contemporary documents on and debates about forests. In creating the forest of Arden, Shakespeare alludes both to the area in France known as the Ardennes and to the English forest of Arden (Arden was also the last name of his mother); at the same time, he creates a space that is in some ways an idealized imaginary world and in others the arena for problems that were occurring in literal forests.

In so doing, Shakespeare draws not only on more than one geographical locale but also on the several meanings of the very term *forest* (Daley). First, in his era, as now, that word certainly could be used to refer to dense woodlands. Contemporary documents sometimes describe them as what we today would call "high-crime areas," the locale for thievery in particular, one of the most feared felonies in Shakespeare's period. The hostilities between the native Irish and Englishmen attempting to colonize Ireland—particularly heated in 1599—activated cognate anxieties: Lawless Irish rebels were often represented as living in the woods. At the same time, events closer to home seemed to substantiate the association of the forest with transgression: the late sixteenth and seventeenth centuries witnessed substantial migrations to wooded areas, and contemporary documents often condemned squatters and other woodland inhabitants as dangerous outlaws.

In informing the cultural matrix of forests, interpretations of historical events like those in Ireland and England interacted with a series of legends and folk tales, notably stories about the so-called green man, a figure representing fertility and agency but also wildness. But the best known legendary inhabitant of woodlands is introduced in an early scene of *As You Like It:* "They say he is already in the forest of Arden, and a many merry men with him; and there they live like the old Robin Hood of England" (1.1.114–16). Other, more latent connections, such as the way Amiens's song in Act 2 echoes Robin Hood ballads (Knowles, 487), recur.

The legend thus evoked was well known to Shakespeare's audience: many contemporary ballads and plays detailed Robin Hood's résumé, including two dramas performed in London in 1598 (Bullough, 143), while he also featured in festivities, notably May games and those ritualized performances known as morris dances. Although they vary in other respects, tales about Robin Hood typically involve many issues central to *As You Like It:* Their plots often pivot on challenges to authority much as the play is fundamentally concerned with norms and their violation; both share an interest in at once displaying and delimiting violence; and, above all, Robin Hood's penchant for inversions of power and social leveling recall the ways that *As You Like It* overturns and turns inside out the disposition of social rank and gender. Indeed, more specifically, the practice of a man representing Maid Marian in Robin Hood folk games not coincidentally anticipates Rosalind's cross-dressing (Wilson, 73), and some Robin Hood plays contemporaneous with *As You Like It* draw attention to the ambiguous gendering of this figure (Shapiro, 82–87). An intriguing ballad reproduced in this edition narrates a fight between a cross-dressed Maid Marian and Robin Hood, who, like Orlando, does not recognize his beloved. The Robin Hood story, then, is one of many reasons Shakespeare's sixteenth-century audience would have connected woodlands both with freedom and with dangerous wildness, meanings on which the text repeatedly plays.

Also germane to *As You Like It*, however, is the second denotation of *forest*, a royal preserve where the monarch or those he designated had the right to hunt. Associated with both authority and challenges to it, such areas occupied a paradoxical status very relevant to this play. A royal forest was often not entirely or even mainly woodlands; it could, for example, include pastures like those to which *As You Like It* refers. As stressed in the excerpt in this volume from John Manwood's *Treatise and Discourse of the Lawes of the Forrest* (1598), the principal sixteenth-century tract on these royal forests, they were exempt from common law and had their own regulations and courts. Those distinctive laws were invoked on numerous occasions, since poachers regularly violated the king's exclusive and exclusionary privileges; according to legend, Shakespeare himself had been a poacher. Moreover, although Manwood emphasizes the rights of the lower classes living within forest territory, in fact royal forests were often the site of disputes about the conflict between the king's asserted prerogatives over the land and other types of land use by less privileged members of the culture. These struggles could intensify when a monarch defined as royal forest land that had not previously been classified that way, as in the royal proclamation also included in this edition. Thus, debates about hunting and poaching often coded broader, coded arguments about social rank and the control of space (Theis [2001]; [2009], esp. 125–52).

The legal status of forests was further complicated by the regions on the edge of the forest, the so-called purlieux, which function as both setting and metaphor for this play; previously part of the forest, these areas enjoyed a peculiarly ambiguous status, marginal not only in the literal and spatial senses but legally as well, as the excerpt from Manwood incorporated into this edition testifies. Hunting rights were extended more widely, with such areas being regulated differently from both the royal forests *per se* and from land totally unconnected to those forests.

Critics of the play generally simply assert that Rosalind inhabits the forest, but in fact, it is crucial that she lives in the purlieux (Dubrow [2006]). *As You Like It* concerns itself with boundaries and borders of many types, and it is no accident that its heroine, who locates herself on the borders of gendered categories, is twice described in the play as dwelling in a territory that is edgy in more senses than one. Nor is it an accident that the character who variously asserts autonomy and apparently surrenders herself to patriarchal authority ("To you I give myself, for I am yours" [5.4.116–117]) dwells in an area associated both with a monarch's prerogatives and their extension to others. In short, the character and the play that delight in the conditional "if" involve a spatial construct described by Manwood as "but conditionally in some sort *Forrest*" (Manwood, 153).

## "ARE YOU NATIVE OF THIS PLACE?" (3.2.338): GENERIC DEBTS AND EXPERIMENTS

By locating most of the action of the play in the forest, Shakespeare signals its affiliations with pastoral; but just as the royal forest consists of several types of terrain, the landscape of this text juxtaposes many different genres, some peacefully coexisting in neighboring patches and others, like the king and the less obedient denizens of his forests in early modern England, struggling for power.[2]

To begin with, the play's engagement with form in its many senses is manifest in its preoccupation not only with literary types like comedy but also with so-called speech genres, a category that includes invitations, commands, and promises. *As You Like It* invites us to see threats, whose centrality to this play I have emphasized, as a genre of language, and

---

**2.** I am indebted to Jon Baarsch and Jeffrey Theis for many useful observations about the interplay of genres in this text.

the interest in them is one component of a larger engagement with the distinctive workings of other forms of speech, such as promises, vows (Scott), and the conditionals (Athanasiadou and Dirven, Kuhn, Traugott et al.) and riddles (Young) discussed later in this introduction.

*As You Like It* is clearly a comedy, providing a textbook example of many characteristics widely seen as distinguishing that mode from tragedy. Thus, like comedies ranging from Shakespeare's own *A Midsummer Night's Dream* to such classic movies as *The Philadelphia Story*, it ends with a celebration of marriage, in contrast to the predilection of tragedies for ending in death. This is not to say that death is wholly absent from the world of this or other comedies (Barton, 163–67); indeed, like many of Shakespeare's other sorties into this genre, it opens on the consequences of losing a parent. But the prevalence of death is diminished and its most destructive effects played down in comedy, recalling how other threats that we have already identified are also checked. Unlike his counterpart in *Rosalynde,* Duke Ferdinand gets religion rather than getting killed; Orlando eventually acquires his inheritance.

Comedy is also often associated with certain structural movements much in evidence in *As You Like It.* It may involve a shift from a rigid world to a freer one, with the action often ending in a milieu that compromises between rigidity and license. We find a latter-day version of this pattern in movies designed for a teenage audience that show rebellions against a rule-bound school principal, while in *As You Like It,* freedom is signaled by the intriguing observation that "there's no clock in the forest" (3.2.300–301). And comedies often chart a movement from emotional bonds centered on what sociologists today call the "family of origin" and on friendships with members of the same sex to marriage.

Variously developing and differing from theories like these, the critic C. L. Barber influentially maintains that Shakespeare's later comedies constitute a distinctive form that he terms "festive comedy." He links *As You Like It* and other plays in this category to Elizabethan holidays and festivals, asserting that they include a period of release, exemplified by the freedom that disguise offers Rosalind, and a clarification of our relationship to nature in its many senses.

Arguably the most reflexive of all Shakespeare's comedies, *As You Like It* repeatedly examines—and sometimes undermines—comedic norms. For instance, another contrast often posited between comedy and tragedy is that the former includes only folly and the latter vice, but surely the behavior of both Oliver, who twice plots to murder his brother, and Duke Frederick is indeed vicious. Elsewhere, the play questions comedy by reminding us of the perils just beneath its surface: The sport of wrestling can turn into manslaughter, especially when Oliver, in some senses a rival playwright to Rosalind, attempts to rewrite the script. And even more tellingly, as we will see, this comedy parodies the traditional comic ending by marrying off not one or two but four couples, while also repeatedly reminding us that this form of closure is to a degree anticlosural, for, as Jaques emphasizes, they are not all likely to live happily ever after.

Pastoral often interacts with comedy, and in many respects *As You Like It* offers a textbook instance of that dynamic, as well as exemplifying the workings of pastoral in numerous other respects (Woodbridge). Rather than simply describing the countryside, this genre typically contrasts it with the worlds of court and city, thus exploring, among many other questions, the relationship between the natural and artificial. As the performance history in this volume indicates, directors have interpreted that contrast in a range of ways, including rendering it merely illusory. The dialogic interactions, such as disagreements between two parties and songs for two voices, that characterize pastoral are apparent in the many two-person debates in *As You Like It*. The signature concerns of this genre—love, death, and community—are also evident throughout the play.

The introduction of social rank and status into classical pastoral introduces the topic of alienation as well, as Rosalie L. Colie points out (253). In the instance of Christian pastoral, implicit or explicit reminders of the loss of the Garden of Eden may intensify that threat of alienation the Biblical narrative is activated here by the name "Arden," so close in sound to "Eden"). Subterranean but significant, the preoccupation with alienation in pastoral often emerges as a longing for home and inability to fit into a pastoral landscape. Throughout *As You Like It,* as in so many other pastorals, loss and alienation recur: Belongings and belonging are repeatedly imperiled, Aliena's name, though borrowed from Lodge, signals the significance of exile, a preoccupation throughout the play (Dusinberre, 70–71), as does Rosalind's telling choice of words when she faints, "I would I were at home" (4.3.161). And at the conclusion of the play, Jaques stresses his alienation and in effect exiles himself from the characters who are ending their exile, as though he has become their lightning rod. Finally, Paul Alpers trenchantly associates pastoral with the suspension, as opposed to reconciliation, of tensions and oppositions (Alpers, 68–69), and nowhere is that process more intriguingly realized than in a pattern that we have already noted: the control of threats throughout *As You Like It*.

Although these and many characteristics typically recur in pastoral, the mode itself assumes a range of forms, many of which are exemplified by this text. Formulating the concept of "sylvan pastoral," Jeffrey Theis has trenchantly argued that the forest setting creates a significantly distinctive form of the genre; sylvan landscapes, he demonstrates, are associated with borders and boundaries (Theis [2009], esp. 130–32, 249–53). Others distinguish the many versions in which nature is welcoming and beneficent from so-called "hard pastoral," in which the physical world is associated with discomforts and even threats, and, as my essay on performance indicates, many directors have developed the text's potential connections with that harsher mode.

In the context of genre, "romance" suggests not simply a story about love but rather a literary form with a whole range of specified characteristics (that mass-market literary form known as the "Harlequin romance" shares the name but lacks most of those salient characteristics and should not be confused with the genre itself). Even when one delimits the term *romance* in these ways, it encompasses many different forms, stretching chronologically and tonally from medieval poems such as "Sir Gawain and the Green Knight" to Nathaniel Hawthorne's *The Scarlet Letter* and *The House of the Seven Gables* in the nineteenth century and A. S. Byatt's novel *Possession* and the films in the *Shrek* series in the twentieth and twenty-first centuries. Romance typically treats both love and heroic adventure, recounted through several interlocking plots rather than the single plot characteristic of epic. Characters, often presented in black-and-white terms, may include magicians and witches, one of the many ways that romance is connected to the supernatural. The quest that motivates romance generally terminates in finding something or someone who had been lost. In this and many other ways, romance is about return and returning: Nostalgic at its core, the genre itself enacts a retreat to an older and simpler world.

Even this brief summary demonstrates that *As You Like It,* like a number of other Shakespearean comedies, is affiliated with romance. The wrestling match, for example, exemplifies the trials that a romance hero must undergo, and a daughter is returned to her father, another common motif. Variously represented as a relative of a magician and as a sorcerer herself, Rosalind thus figures further connections to the genre that so often includes magicians. Like that hybrid pastoral romance, the play delights in an abundance of songs. And, as I will emphasize, the entrance of Hymen arguably effects the introduction of the supernatural (Fig. 7).

Although comedy, pastoral, and romance are the main generic coordinates of the play, it alludes to many other literary types, flirting with a range of generic norms, much as it flirts with erotic possibilities. In its hints of tragic consequences, it gestures towards another hybrid form, tragicomedy (Hattaway, 1–2). Jaques and Touchstone introduce a world of satire, often seen as the opposite of pastoral. And, as we will also see shortly, *As You Like It* incorporates that curious dramatic form, the masque.

## "TELL THIS YOUTH WHAT 'TIS TO LOVE" (5.2.83): PRINCIPAL ISSUES AND IDEAS

Like other pastorals, *As You Like It* engages with the relationship between a natural world and civilized realms; in so doing, it draws attention as well to the relationship between nature and fortune, discussed overtly in a dialogue between Rosalind and Celia. But in this play, again like many other pastorals, the contrasts between the values of the natural and the civilized world are not necessarily clear-cut. Shakespeare, who characteristically delights in first establishing and then blurring various binary distinctions (tavern versus court and battlefield in *1 Henry IV*, Claudius versus Hamlet, Sr. in *Hamlet,* and so on), does so here as well. If the court is the world where Duke Frederick has usurped his brother's throne, that brother proceeds, Jaques asserts, to treat the deer the same way: "swearing that we/Are mere usurpers, tyrants" (2.1.60–61).

Equally apparent and equally significant is the play's preoccupation with the workings of love and marriage. *As You Like It* suggests the suddenness and intensity of desire through not only Rosalind's response to Orlando but also the even more rapid attraction between Oliver and Celia. The dialogues between Celia and Rosalind repeatedly draw attention to how irrational love is; when, for example, Rosalind is distressed that Orlando is late, she shifts in seconds from dismissing his hair color as "dissembling" (3.4.7) to lavishly praising it.

Love and much else is explored here through a recurrent issue that enfolds many of the other concerns of the text: This is a play about conventions, norms, games, and rules (Marshall [1993]).[3] Romeo, Juliet observes wryly, "kiss[es] by th'book" (1.5.110), and Orlando loves by the book in that he follows the conventions of Petrarchism, the style of writing and desiring associated with the work of the Italian poet and thinker Francesco Petrarch (1304–74)and his many imitators in England and on the continent. Petrarchan poems typically involve a poet lavishing idealized and conventionalized praise on a beautiful but distant woman who does not return the lover's affection.

---

**3.** Carlson's feminist analysis traces the structure of the play in terms of the sequential presence, inversion, and reestablishment of norms, though our interpretations of their workings differ significantly.

Although Orlando does not compose sonnets, he, unlike his more poetically competent counterpart in *Rosalynde,* establishes a branch library of truly dreadful verse; thus the play mocks Petrarchism, much as *A Midsummer Night's Dream* and *Hamlet* mock the pedestrian plays that coexisted with the splendid achievements of their age. The praise of women lacking the characteristics generally considered beautiful, the so-called ugly beauty tradition, was at once a version and a critique of Petrarchism, and, through transforming Phebe from her indubitably attractive counterpart in *Rosalynde* to one that Rosalind describes as very unattractive, Shakespeare participates in this subdivision of Petrarchism as well.

But Petrarchan love is just one of the codes and conventions that the play calls into question. It does so with comedy and with the social and legal practice of primogeniture, as we have already seen. Above all, in its investigation of conventions and norms, the play asks what happens if a game, that most conventional and rule-bound activity, becomes serious, or if we are forced to confront serious, even fatal consequences that it has contained all along. The wrestling match is potentially deadly (Marshall [1993], 278); Jaques emphasizes that the ritualized sport of hunting is much less fun for the deer; Rosalind's suggestion that she and Celia play at falling in love is succeeded by the painful complications of love itself.

The most intriguing instances of games turning serious and conventions being questioned involve marriage, and in particular the mock marriage in the woods. Rosalind, pretending to be Ganymede (who is in turn pretending to be Rosalind), encourages Orlando to pretend to marry her:

ROSALIND  Come, sister, you shall be the priest, and marry us. Give
    me your hand, Orlando. What do you say, sister?
ORLANDO  Pray thee marry us.
CELIA  I cannot say the words.
ROSALIND  You must begin, "Will you, Orlando"—
CELIA  Go to! Will you, Orlando, have to wife this Rosalind?
ORLANDO  I will.
ROSALIND  Ay, but when?
ORLANDO  Why, now, as fast as she can marry us.

(4.1.124–134)

Why does Celia, who actually proposes the mock marriage in Lodge, so nervously resist it here? And why does Rosalind insist on specifying its time? The customs and regulations surrounding marriage were fraught and fluid at the time the play was written, far more so than pat generalizations about the position of women in the culture sometimes

Fig. 4. Rosalind (Vanessa Redgrave) and Orlando (Ian Bannen) stage a marriage ceremony in the woods, with Celia (Rosalind Knight) looking on, in Michael Elliott's 1961 production.

acknowledge; its members disagreed, for example, about what role, if any, the church should play in what some saw as a secular event. But according to widespread theories, a valid marriage could be effected if two people declared they wanted to wed and exchanged appropriately worded vows—and it became valid immediately if they specified in those vows that they wanted it to be. Thus, arguably Rosalind is engineering an actual marriage, ensuring its immediate validity by forcing her groom to specify the time. No wonder Celia can barely say the words.

This mock marriage on this stage thus enlarges the play's concern for norms by insisting that we think about what series of norms in fact create a legal marriage off the stage, a problem posed as well by that dubious minister Sir Oliver Martext. The episode also has consequences for the fraught question of female agency, for in setting it up, Rosalind surely asserts her power, no matter how much it may be qualified later on.

In addition, the mock marriage serves to draw attention to both the power and limitations of that serious game drama itself, reminding us that theater and theatricality also rank high among the concerns of this text. Within the mock marriage that Rosalind engineers, the splendidly multivalent phrase "have to wife *this* Rosalind"(4.1.130–131; italics inserted), like the query slightly earlier in the scene, "Am I not *your* Rosalind?" (4.1.88; italics inserted), wittily develops these issues about theatricality. On one level, both statements stress that the speaker is giving herself to the man before her, and in so doing celebrating presence and immediacy. But on another, contradictory level, "this" and "your" remind us how many Rosalinds appear in the play (the character created by a boy actor, the Rosalind posing as Ganymede, and the Rosalind who, while posing as Ganymede, also poses as Rosalind), while "your" also suggests that Rosalind is the creation and creature of Orlando's imagination and thus implies that women are not autonomous agents but rather male fantasies (Green). Similarly, "am I not your Rosalind?" asks if there is something serious, real beyond acting— and also raises the troubling possibility that Orlando's Rosalind, like the beloved of some members of the theatrical audience, may be playing a role. If pastoral is, as David Young observes, a world of "if's" (Young, 46–50), so too is theater, and, as the performance histories in this volume indicate, numerous productions have drawn attention to such questions about theatricality.

The questions about theatricality thus raised signal another of the play's concerns, whether the stability and sameness implicit in the very concept of identity are illusory. Central to the question of what constitutes the self is the influence of gender categories, a problem to which this introduction necessarily returns repeatedly. But for now, we can note that the very text that emphasizes Rosalind's cross-dressing at several junctures suggests, though not without some qualifications and complications, that she maintains some inner, quintessentially feminine qualities unaffected by her outer appearance. The complexities of the passages in question insistently demonstrate that reading the play well involves reading it closely and slowly, focusing intensely on the nuances of particular words. For example, in Act I, scene 3, when Rosalind first proposes to dress as a man, she observes, "and— in my heart/Lie there what hidden woman's fear there will" (118–19). This formulation surely suggests an inner female characteristic; notice, however, that its presence is delimited by the indeterminacy of "what . . . there will" (119), a version of the delight in "if's" we encounter throughout the play; and notice too that only two lines later, she refers to "mannish cowards" (121), with the adjective "mannish" representing masculinity not as something essential and immutable but rather as contingent. Later passages, however, suggest a stable inner femininity without such qualifications. In the second scene of the third act, for example, Rosalind asks Celia, "dost thou think, though I am caparison'd [dressed] like a man, I have a doublet and hose in my disposition?" (194–96). Above all, at the moment in Act 4, scene 3 when, seeing Orlando's blood, this master of feints is mastered by a faint, she and Oliver treat that response as a sign of essential femininity.

The issues about the self raised by gender are also related to the problem of to what extent that self is constructed by the culture rather than by the individual and hence to the subject of social rankings, another preoccupation of the play. In particular, Shakespeare plays on and with the changing valences of the terms *clown* and *villain*, which could either be general indications of opprobrium or refer very specifically to a place in the pecking order (Crane). Critics debate whether Shakespeare's plays typically favor the socially elite or show sympathy for the commoners [Marshall (2004), 4]. In the instance of this text, the most persuasive argument is the mediation between those positions negotiated by Mary Thomas Crane, who argues that the play at once excludes, at times mockingly, the lower social orders and draws attention to the dubious strategies used to do so, especially the use of labels like *clown* and *villain*.

As the frequency of those terms in the play reminds us, word usage can be a helpful index to a writer's concerns, especially those not overtly highlighted. *Father* and its cognates *fathers* and *father's* appear no fewer than thirty-eight times in the first act alone, and sporadically thereafter. As in so many of Shakespeare's plays, mothers are

Fig. 5. *Haec-Vir,* like its companion text *Hic-Mulier,* both published in London in 1620, illustrate their culture's preoccupation with cross-dressing.

tellingly absent, although the images of the lioness and doe gesture toward them (Rose); but paternity in several senses is an important though sometimes neglected issue. In particular, old Sir Rowland, although he is never onstage, is a ghost persistent and pertinent enough to anticipate old Hamlet.

Why the concern flagged by this pattern of word usage? Louis Montrose's influential emphasis on the material consequences of parental loss is a crucial answer, but also a partial one.[4] More broadly, as we have seen, many members of the culture had lost their fathers, and in its references to both the death of paternal figures and their recovery in various forms—for example, Duke Senior finds in Orlando's face many characteristics of Sir Rowland's, a visual analog realized linguistically in the similarity of their names and materially when he regains his father's estate—the drama participates in the process of mourning that was so frequent in its culture and in the fantasy of recovery that mourning so often engenders. And the references to fathers thematize Shakespeare's interaction with his own literary paternity in the form of Lodge's *Rosalynde*.[5]

Other explanations for the frequency with which *father* and its cognates appear lie in that comedic pattern of moving from the world of parents to that of the younger lovers (Dolan, xxxv), apparently enacted linguistically in the diminution of references to fathers after the first act. Whereas this text incorporates in its concluding scene that romance motif of returning the child to her father, it devotes much less attention to the moment of restoration than most romances do. The comedic emphasis on moving forward to the world of wedded love overrides romance's nostalgic delight in restoration.

Overrides, not obliterates. Critics have sometimes exaggerated and oversimplified the putative shift from fathers to spouses, for *As You Like It,* which stages so many other debates, is also the arena for one between the comedic drive to move away from fathers and the impulse, common in romance and pastoral, to move backward toward what paternity can represent: a golden world of the past, authority, protection. Notice that whereas Orlando's counterpart in Lodge is called "Rosader," thus linking him to his beloved as names often do in prose romances, Shakespeare substitutes a name that anagrammatically links the character both to his father and his beloved. Observe too how the

---

4. Montrose's influential study, one of the few extensive discussions of fathers in the play, focuses primarily on inheritance and the redefinition of filial bonds, in contrast to my compatible but different emphasis on nostalgia for an idealized and hypostasized world.

5. For a related but different argument, see Nevo's suggestion that Rosalind's off-hand dismissal of fathers tropes Shakespeare's own independence from the paternalistic New Comedy (180–81).

text signals the connection between pastoral and the absent character who embodies many of its values through another verbal echo: the play on Sir Rowland's name, "du Boys," and the French term for woodlands, *bois*. We find the same conservative nostalgia in the celebration of Adam as a representative of an older ideal of service.[6] The very transgressiveness of the play's questions about gender may breed a reactive attraction to the safety, or apparent safety, of an older world and older, paternalistic values; similarly, the political chaos in *Richard II* motivates the idealized view, expressed in particular by the Duchess of Gloucester, of another ghost who never actually appears on stage, King Edward III.

My enumeration of some of the principal concerns of *As You Like It*—nature, love, conventions, the construction of the self, social rankings, theatricality, and fathers—also draws attention to its connections, some of which we have already examined, with cognate plays by its author. Among the links with *King Lear*, noted by many readers, are the presence of brothers who disagree over an inheritance and a political leader who is exiled, the attraction to a lost world of loving and dutiful service, the focus on pastoral and on its cynical brother anti-pastoral. The similarities and differences between the ways that Jaques and Kent resist invitations to join a community at the end of their respective plays also lend themselves to intriguing analysis. Less frequently noted but arguably no less revealing are the connections with *Hamlet*. Subterranean in *As You Like It*, nostalgia for a lost father and the idealized world that he represents surface overtly in *Hamlet;* rather than hovering at the edges as in the earlier comedy, these ghostly desires actually appear onstage. In the relationship between Laertes and Hamlet, we find another instance of brotherly rivalry, while Hamlet himself embodies in intensified form the alienation experienced by several characters in *As You Like It*.

## "FOR HERE COMES MORE COMPANY" (4.3.74): CAST OF CHARACTERS

If the changes in the plot of *Rosalynde* crystallize many of Shakespeare's driving interests, so do additions to its personages draw attention to his central concerns. In particular, neither Touchstone nor Jaques has his counterpart in the prose romance. In creating Touchstone, however, Shakespeare is drawing on extensive traditions of fools and clowns

---

**6.** The nostalgia of the play is discussed, though from angles different from my own, by Peter Milward, who connects it to the movement away from Catholicism; by Robert Watson (esp. 77–80), who links it to the anxiety that we can know things only through imperfect likenesses of them; and by Joshua Phillips (226–29), who relates it to a desire for communal identity.

in Elizabethan life and literature (Billington, Welsford, Wiles). In general, Fools were typically characters whose utterances were irrational or opaque (although often incisive, despite or because of that), who challenged social conventions and truisms, and who had an unconventional or grotesque appearance. The so-called natural fool, whose behavior and appearance were congenital, was often distinguished from the artificial fool, who played a part—thus reminding us that the Fool in the play, like so much else, is connected to theatricality.

Fools were often members of large households, especially courts. These household fools had many similarities with stock theatrical characters, notably the Vice figure, a type of devil developed in medieval plays and appearing in different forms in Renaissance drama, and the clown or buffoon. Another version of the Fool was a character in village festivities, fairs, and morris dances. The Fool's habit of breaking away from the other dancers in the morris group has been analyzed as a type of improvisation (Wiles, 5), but no less significant for our purposes is the way this action, like pastoral, creates an alternative world, and also actually stages a kind of exile.

Touchstone himself serves several functions in the play. His witty comments explicate many of its concerns; in Act 1, scene 2, for example, he demonstrates how to protect honor—"if you swear by that that is not, you are not forsworn" (76–77)—thus introducing the exploration of equivocation that is to culminate in his observation at the end of the play: "much virtue in If" (5.4.103). Above all, his courtship of Audrey, a cynical attempt to satisfy his sexual desires, parodies the more idealistic wooing by others in the play and reminds us that even, or especially, Orlando's admiration of Rosalind is driven in part by erotic urges.

For all the bawdiness of his courtship, Touchstone is not a buffoon but rather an intellectually alert and wry observer. It is possible, though not certain, that Shakespeare created this type of Fool partly in response to changes in the cast of characters in his own acting company.[7] Will Kemp had played the more raucous, buffoon-like Fools in the earlier plays, as well as performing the dance known as a jig on which Elizabethan plays often terminated. Leaving Shakespeare's theatrical company at around the time *As You Like It* was written, Kemp was replaced by Robert Armin, apparently more ratiocinative and less rambunctious in manner and endowed with a singing voice.

---

7. Such speculations are tempting, especially since a Fool is named "Tutch" in one of Armin's writings; but they need to be approached with care since we cannot be sure exactly when Armin replaced Kemp. Dusinberre, for example, argues that Kemp may have initially played Touchstone (4, 111–12). For a valuable summary of these and other debates, see Knowles, 5–6 and 374–77.

Shakespeare's delight in pairings often involves juxtaposing characters who are both compared and contrasted (Hamlet and Fortinbras, Falstaff and the Chief Justice, and so on), and here Jaques is both the twin and opposite number to Touchstone. Jaques represents the melancholic temperament, a concept of character based on a classical theory of physiology that declares that bodies contain four principal fluids known as the humors: black bile or melancholy, choler, phlegm, and blood. According to this model, disease results from disproportions of the humors. And even in the healthy individual, temperaments are determined by the proportion of the humors—someone with too much choler would be prone to anger, someone with too much melancholy to what we today would call depression.

Jaques also exemplifies another stereotype, that of the so-called Malcontent. This figure, represented by the speakers in the satire that flourished in the 1590s as well as by a host of stage characters, was traditionally an outsider, complaining of the follies of his culture as Jaques does in his attack on hunting. Thus, the Malcontent may also serve the role of a type of character common in comedy, the so-called blocking figure, who attempts to prevent or forestall the happy denouement. By creating a Jaques who not only does not marry but also refuses the role of beneficent onlooker assumed by Duke Senior, Shakespeare embodies the discordant responses to love and its genre comedy that cannot be, as it were, swept under the green carpet of the forest. In contrast, Jaques's equivalent in Charles Johnson's adaptation, *Love in a Forest* (1723), falls in love with and marries Celia.

Often read out of context, Jaques's description of the seven ages of man might appear to establish him as a sage. But that speech works very like the couplets of many of Shakespeare's sonnets: If at first glance it seems to edify, it instead proves to simplify. Here the entrance of Adam, apparent exemplar of the old age being described, calls Jaques's neat generalizations into question.

The shepherds of the play differ among themselves a great deal, thus representing the range of ways that the pastoral world and genre are presented here. Whereas Lodge's shepherds are typically dignified, Shakespeare's desire to undermine pastoral values no less than to celebrate them is evident in his adding a figure like William, who, rather than Touchstone, becomes the buffoon of the play. An even more telling change in the treatment of the shepherds in Shakespeare's source is the redefinition of Phebe from the striking beauty in Lodge to a woman whose appearance Rosalind mocks. To understand further why Shakespeare makes this change, however, we need to turn to Rosalind.

Most critics have been charmed by Rosalind, many actresses have been eager to play her, and Shakespeare's own interest in the character is reflected in the fact that Celia becomes less central than her counter-part in *Rosalynde*, ceding center stage, as it were, to Rosalind. She joins a line of vivacious, energetic heroines, like Portia, Helena, and Beatrice, who use their wits and their wit to get their man and to help oth-ers. Whether Shakespeare thus celebrates powerful women, as the first generation of feminist Shakespeare critics asserted, or demonstrates the temporary or even illusory quality of such women's attempts to assert power in a patriarchal culture is one of the central questions for students of the play, whether they be undergraduates confronting it for the first time or actors and directors fashioning an interpretation.

A more specific question is why Rosalind interacts with Orlando as she does in the forest, pretending to be Ganymede acting the part of Rosalind. After all, she could have abandoned her doublet and identi-fied herself to Orlando when she discovered his presence in Arden. Not the least way the play is affiliated with romance is its incorpora-tion of the testing of the hero, and not only Orlando's responses to the female lion threatening his brother but also his replies to that lionized female Rosalind exemplify the process of trial. Some claim that in this way, Rosalind exorcises her own fear of marriage (Bono, 204). Most readers have also assumed that Rosalind's interchanges with her lover serve to instruct him about love—and in the process, some assert, instructing herself as well.

But the influence of romance and the theory of exorcising fears are only partial explanations for Rosalind's behavior in the woods, and the text at best sporadically substantiates the argument about education. Comments like her observations on adultery might serve her pretense of curing the lovesick, but they do not provide the type of schooling that would advance her relationship with Orlando, and in any event, most of the dialogue between Rosalind and Orlando is unrelated to any form of pedagogy. Instead, the principal episode in question, Act 4, scene 1, explores a process that intrigued Shakespeare, as the dialogues between Beatrice and Benedict in *Much Ado About Nothing* demon-strate as well: that is, how lovers use wit to express desire while also holding it at bay. And indeed, surely the primary explanation for this wordplay, which is also a type of foreplay, is that Rosalind wants to encourage Orlando to court her—after all, much of the scene in ques-tion is devoted to the mock marriage that she instigates—while also in some senses controlling that courting. To label her "a domineering woman," as one critic regrettably does (Berry, 183), is far too harsh, but he is quite right that this play, like so much of its author's canon and culture, is very concerned with power struggles. In short, a drive to engineer events rather than a drive to educate Orlando impels her behavior in the forest.

Recurrent linguistic mannerisms often reveal character—witness, for example, Prospero's and Othello's propensities for storytelling. In this instance, Rosalind's drive to take charge of events customarily run by men is manifest in her predilection for actual riddles and for riddle-like statements (Jenkins, 50), for riddles typically locate power in the person posing them unless and until they are successfully answered. And riddles, like the disguised Rosalind, involve frustrated desire, whether to possess a solution or a body. They involve the mysterious and occluded, too, characteristics that at once link them to representations of the female body and to wooded areas (forests are in fact often mentioned in certain riddles)[8].

Riddles are a form of disguise, and Rosalind poses them while dressed in male clothing, although the exact meaning of her cross-dressing is itself one of the principal riddles of the play. Other English playwrights had presented women dressed as men and vice versa (for example, the plot of Ben Jonson's *Epicoene* turns on a woman eventually proving to be a man), but none does so as frequently or intriguingly as Shakespeare (Howard, Rackin). Behind his interest in cross-dressing lies its resemblance to and implicit commentary on theater itself, most obviously on the practice of boy actors taking female roles, a custom often condemned by those who attacked the theaters as immoral in the late sixteenth and seventeenth centuries. But drama was not the sole transgressor in this regard; other modes, such as prose romances like Sir Philip Sidney's *Arcadia,* also represented cross-dressing. And literary versions of that practice, like the references to inheritance and to forests that we examined earlier, also interact with quotidian experiences. On the streets of London were a number of women dressed as men, a practice that generated both positive and negative commentaries in a series of pamphlets in the early seventeenth century (Fig. 5), while James I, the king who succeeded Elizabeth in 1603, also expressed his opposition to it.

Students of theatrical cross-dressing debate whether it is an expedient to foster heterosexual love, an avenue to same-sex romantic relationships, or both. And does it serve to celebrate an androgynous ideal, reaffirm traditional concepts of gender, or muddy them without offering a clear-cut alternative? Addressing these questions in *As You Like It* demands detailed attention to the special form that it takes: a male actor representing Rosalind assumes the name of Ganymede and then agrees with Orlando that she/he will pretend to be Rosalind. Why Ganymede? The use of that name in Lodge's *Rosalynde* is a partial but by no means complete explanation. The legend in question was

---

**8.** I am indebted to Patrick Murphy for this information.

well known in the period, appearing in some two hundred Renaissance and baroque art works (Saslow, 1); in addition, two Latin texts widely read in the Elizabethan era, Virgil's *Aeneid* and Ovid's *Metamorphoses,* include the tale of Ganymede. Versions of it vary in some details, but essentially Ganymede is a youth who is seized while hunting by the king of the gods, Jupiter (Zeus in Greek mythology), and carried off to heaven. Appointed cupbearer to the gods, Ganymede displaces Hebe, the daughter of Jupiter's wife Juno, from that post, incurring Juno's wrath for that and other reasons.

The other reasons for Juno's anger relate to one of the many interpretations of the myth: Ganymede is often represented as Jupiter's sexual partner. A number of English texts focus on this meaning of the legend, and the term *ganymede* was sometimes used during this period for a boy participating in a sexual relationship with an older man, so many members of Shakespeare's original audience would surely have been aware of this interpretation. Hence, its presence here certainly mirrors a substratum of hints of homoerotic relationships at several points in the play: Might Orlando be attracted not to the female character that Ganymede plays but to the young man himself? Should we read Phebe's interest in Rosalind in a similar way? And what do we do with the hints that Rosalind encourages Phebe's desire for her, as Valerie Traub has rightly argued (126)? One can develop Traub's observations by focusing on Rosalind's interjection of "If you will know my house, /'Tis at the tuft of olives here hard by" (3.5.74–75) into a speech that is ostensibly aimed at discouraging Phebe's affections. So troubling is this invitation that it is often cut by directors; some editors attempt to finesse the problem by claiming, without much evidence, that Rosalind is addressing Sylvius, not Phebe.

Such passages indubitably direct our attention to homoerotic possibilities, and the name "Ganymede" emphasizes that reading (Orgel, 57–58; Traub, 124–25). At the same time, however, the text deflects and downplays—but never demolishes—these readings. In this, as in so many other arenas, we encounter the partially successful attempts to defuse threats, attempts that are, this introduction suggests, central to the play. First of all, the word "Ganymede," sprinkled liberally throughout Lodge's text, appears only seven times in the play; two are in the scene when Rosalind faints and three others appear in Phebe's formulaic speeches in Act 5, scene 1. Both of these contexts insistently remind us that the name was assumed by a woman as a disguise. Similarly, by revising his source to make Phebe physically unappealing, Shakespeare plays down the likelihood that Rosalind is attracted to her. Moreover, whereas the legend of Ganymede itself indubitably introduces homoerotic readings, it also permits alternative

Fig. 6. In this drawing by Michelangelo, an eagle that represents the god Jove is carrying away Ganymede.

explanations for why Shakespeare preserves Lodge's use of that name. Ganymede's status as a hunter, signaled by Rosalind's reference to carrying a boar-spear only six lines before she assumes the name in question (1.3.118), is surely germane to a play concerned with hunting. Juno's jealousy about her daughter's being displaced as cupbearer recalls the emphasis on rivalry, and more broadly on displacement, throughout *As You Like It*. Ganymede was associated with intelligence, so the reference to him is another compliment to Rosalind. And the legend is also sometimes interpreted as the soul's desire for the divine, so one might even speculate that it hints at Christian theology and at the desire to move from the everyday world of comedy to the more numinous realms of romance.

We should not merely dismiss these alternative interpretations of the myth in question as decoys for the introduction of its homoerotic meanings: As we have already seen, the text is indeed interested in Rosalind's intelligence and in hunting. At the same time, arguably one reason Shakespeare is attracted to the Ganymede legend is that it allows him at once to flirt with and to rein in homoerotic meanings through the presence of alternative interpretations of the myth, much as Rosalind arguably flirts with the possibility of flirting with Phebe.

## "TRUE DELIGHTS" (5.4.198):
## CONCLUSIONS AND EPILOGUES

Closure is one of the many literary concepts with analogs in everyday life: Debates about to what extent texts may resolve issues reassuringly ("and they lived happily ever after") mirror commonplace issues ranging from why it is rude to hang up a phone on someone to how to terminate a visit to relatives. Interpreting the ending of this play at once demonstrates the workings of closure outside this drama and in so doing, also crystallizes the central questions about gendering and other, related forms of potential transgression that arise within and throughout *As You Like It.*

Central to analyses of the play is whether its conclusion resolves volatile issues about gender. Are the forms of rebellion that the play has earlier represented curtailed—is an independent woman reinserted into patriarchal structures (Cohen, 35–36; Erickson, 21–25, 33–34; Montrose, 51–52)? Certain critics claim that a reassertion of conservatism is typical of Shakespearean comedies, including this one. Are homoerotic possibilities thus transformed to heterosexual actualities here (Barber, 230–31; Bono, 203–04; Dolan, xxxvii–xxxviii)? Or, alternatively, is the disruption of gender categories maintained and even intensified at the conclusion of *As You Like It* (Belsey, 180–84; Masten, 153–63)?

My own response assumes that we cannot simply generalize about the ending of the play because each of its component parts— the masque, the final scene as a whole, and the Epilogue—works in distinctive ways. When we acknowledge that, we find two patterns. First, the control of transgressive possibilities posited by Barber, Bono, Dolan, and others does indeed mark the final act of the play, including the masque; but this pattern differs in degree rather than kind from the agenda of controlling threats that occurs throughout. In the conclusion as in many earlier instances, such control is partly but not entirely successful. Second, the free play of gendered and other disruptions that other critics find in the play's conclusion is in fact characteristic of the Epilogue, although not of much of what precedes it. To put it another way, the final scene of the play repeatedly enacts and emphasizes reassuring, even complacent, values, yet another instance of containing threats. In particular, female power and agency are indeed curtailed. But at the same time, an undertow of doubt and disagreement about this and many other questions remains throughout the final scene— and it becomes not an undertow but the powerful current in which we swim, or flail, or delightedly float in the Epilogue.

Masques were a form of court entertainment that flourished in the sixteenth and seventeenth centuries, typically involving elaborate and courtly spectacle, allegorical plots, and mythological characters. One persuasive explanation for Hymen's appearance and the masque-like spectacle that ensues, then, is that Shakespeare, who in his role as "sharer" benefited financially as well as in less tangible ways from the success of its plays, was drawing on the popularity of masques. Further interpretations of the significance of the masque depend on determining whether Hymen, who presides over marriage in many classical texts, should be read as a numinous visitor from another realm—the introduction of the supernatural element associated with romance, as we have already observed—or simply as the final device in Rosalind's capacious bag of tricks. Does he take over the responsibility for marrying the couples and assuring closure, thus contributing to her demotion, or does he demonstrate her continuing power? In other words, is he her master or her minion? As the analyses of productions elsewhere in this volume demonstrate, directors, like critics, continue to disagree on this issue.

Given the text's delight in mixing genres and the unease with Rosalind's power registered in its occasional misogynistic comments, it is best to read Hymen as a presence from a more magical world who challenges Rosalind for power, an analog and reference to the *deus ex machina* (god from the machine) figure in classical drama. Notice a telling sequence of speeches:

ROSALIND  I'll have no father, if you be not he;
  I'll have no husband, if you be not he;
  Nor ne'er wed woman, if you be not she
HYMEN  Peace ho! I bar confusion,
  'Tis I must make conclusion
    Of these most strange events.
  Here's eight that must take hands
  To join in Hymen's bands,
    If truth holds true contents.

(5.4.122–130)

While Rosalind seems to be making straightforward promises when one reads each of her three lines separately, read in conjunction, the second and third in effect form one of the riddles in which she delights. Surely Hymen's pronouncement should be interpreted in part as a rebuttal to all these linguistic games, an assertion that he will substitute firm conclusions for the strange events of the play and the confusing riddles of its heroine. Twice in the lines quoted above and once a few lines later in the same speech, he uses "must," a telling contrast with all the "if's" in preceding speeches by other characters. Similarly, the one "if" clause that he does use ("If truth holds true contents" [130]), essentially disarms the ambiguities latent in that formulation, since, as many editors uneasily agree, the line can probably best be glossed through the tautology "if truth is true."

But in so doing, *As You Like It* does not definitively erase female power, as many critics have claimed. Rather, throughout the conclusion, several characters—Jaques, Hymen, Duke Senior, and Rosalind herself—seem bent on having the final word, thus producing what we might call "contestatory closure," a phenomenon that is also seen in, for example, the distinctive and differing closural gestures of Horatio and Fortinbras in *Hamlet*. In other words, Hymen threatens Rosalind's power as stage manager and playwright but does not definitely—closurally as it were—take it from her.

A similar type of cycle between closure and anticlosure may be found at several points in the dialogue of the scene. For instance, "If there be truth in sight, you are my daughter" (118), Duke Senior declares, and Orlando echoes the sentiment immediately afterwards by saying, "If there be truth in sight, you are my Rosalind" (119). But the reliability of the visual realm has been challenged throughout the play (Ronk), and in this instance, the audience's impression that they are indeed seeing Rosalind is complicated by recurrent questions about who or what Rosalind is and by Orlando's pronoun "my."

Fig. 7. Hymen (Michael Follis) descends from heaven in Trevor Nunn's Royal Shakespeare Company production in 1977, exemplifying the possibility of interpreting this figure as supernatural rather than earthly, as other directors have done.

Yet nowhere is this tension between the predominant emphasis on returning to traditional values and a persistent critique of them more evident than in the tantalizing line, "To you I give yourself, for I am yours" (116–17), which Rosalind delivers first to Duke Senior, then repeats to Orlando. Recalling that each member of the couple promised him- or herself as part of the prenuptial contract, we can with justice find in the lines at least a hint of that contract and a reference to the mock marriage earlier; from this perspective, Rosalind is not surrendering power when she speaks to Orlando, who would deliver similar words in such a contract himself, but rather buttressing a wedding she had stage-managed earlier. But of course, she delivers the same line, more problematically, to her father, and some readers have found in these words further evidence that she is indeed surrendering power, even while maintaining a pretense of at least controlling the surrender (Erickson, 24–25). These acknowledgments of the paradoxical, divided agenda of the line are extended in one acute reading that finds in it evidence of a divided self; on the one hand, Rosalind is asserting power, but on the other hand, her very claim to be a creator able to do so depends on being the creature of two men ("for I am yours"). At the same time, the fact that, here and elsewhere in the text, her claims to power occur onstage allows the audience to dismiss their validity (Wofford, 163–69).

But we need to expand and qualify these and similar interpretations by acknowledging that Rosalind is yet again delivering a riddle. That is, if she belongs to Orlando and Duke Senior, she has neither the need nor the right to give herself to them. Thus, she in effect builds in the hedging "if" without deploying it specifically. Hence, she is indeed giving up power; but at the same time, she is doing so in a linguistic form that offers not a pretense of the continuation of power but the thing itself.

If the dialogue in the concluding scene is divided in these ways, the Epilogue is more unsettling. Certain things about it are clear: Again located on the purlieux—in this instance, the borders between the stage and the "real world"—the Epilogue draws attention to the illusions of theater and theatricality. On many other points, however, critics and readers demonstrate the disagreements that this play so often provokes. Do the transgressive ideals apparently dismissed in the final scene reassert themselves (according to some readers, Rosalind regains power, an ideal of androgyny emerges again, and so on), or do the reminders that it is all make-believe further diminish the agency of that master and slave of make-believe, Rosalind?

The most persuasive answer, as I have already suggested, is that Rosalind is disrupting the forces that have attempted, with at best partial success, to achieve some measure of closure in the earlier scene. In a number of other plays, the jigs by Will Kemp had challenged the playwright's power to have the last word. Here, Rosalind is in effect doing the same thing, replacing those stately and communal "dancing measures" (5.4.193) to which Jaques refers with her own idiosyncratic, verbal jig, a dance whose syncopated rhythms unsettle the categories and hierarchies of male and female. Thus, for example, when she opens by saying, "It is not the fashion to see the lady the epilogue"(1), she calls into question both theatrical and social practices: Rosalind is clearly taking the role of Epilogue, and the character she represents is a lady in both gender and social position, while the actor playing the role is a lady in neither of those senses. Her subsequent statements are also loaded with the equivocations that have characterized the play in general and her language in particular throughout—"If it be true," "to like as much of the play as please you," "If I were a woman." Whereas in the final scene various forms of closure are both presented and undermined, thus exemplifying the pattern of partly containing forms of transgression I have traced throughout the play, the Epilogue devotes its energies instead largely to the unsettling of meanings and categories. Tellingly, Rosalind herself glosses the speech with "My way is to conjure you" (11), choosing the verb associated with magic in its many forms, not least trickery.

In short, then, the Epilogue summarizes and intensifies the questions that the text has explored all along—notably the dynamic interplay between conventional modes of speaking, writing, loving, and marrying on the one hand and challenges to them on the other.

# PERFORMANCE HISTORY

*A*s *you like it* is intrigued with—arguably obsessed with—the workings of theater and theatricality; and their workings in productions of the play are intriguing as well. This essay is designed to supplement, not merely replicate, the many other analyses of performance represented in this edition, notably in the critical essays; hence, I draw attention to certain productions too recent to be discussed in most previous performance histories, and, rather than attempting the sort of comprehensive survey that Cynthia Marshall, as well as many other critics, so ably provide, I offer a brief chronological overview, then focus on five of the principal decisions a director and his or her company must make.

## "THE OLD NEWS" (1.1.98–99): AN OVERVIEW OF PRODUCTIONS

Although most of Shakespeare's plays are hard to date precisely, considerable evidence suggests that *As You Like It* was first performed in 1599. Previous critics and editors have assumed that this initial production occurred in the Globe, the public theater where many of Shakespeare's other plays were put on, but Juliet Dusinberre (37–46) has recently offered evidence that his company, the Lord Chamberlain's Men, first staged this drama in a royal palace called Richmond Palace on Shrove Tuesday, February 20, 1599. If she is right—the evidence, though plausible, is as inconclusive as so much else about this and other early Shakespeare productions—the date has many implications for issues discussed elsewhere in this volume. It increases the likelihood, for example, that Touchstone was initially played by Will Kemp rather than the actor who replaced him, Robert Armin; and it suggests that *As You Like It* was first produced in a rural setting closer to its forest than the milieu of the Globe would have been.

All hypotheses about performances between 1599 and 1740 are highly speculative. In particular, the possibility that the play was put on before King James at Wilton House in December 1603 has interested theater historians but cannot be substantiated. We do know, however, that on January 9, 1723, Charles Johnson's *Love in a Forest,* the drama loosely based on *As You Like It* that was discussed briefly in the Introduction, was first performed. Contemporary debates about hunting rights may have intensified interest in it.

In 1740, *As You Like It* itself was revived at Drury Lane. Apparently well received in that instance, the play soon became a favorite of the London season. Eighteenth- and nineteenth-century productions initiated the tradition, still alive and well today, of well-known actresses eagerly welcoming the opportunity to interpret the part of Rosalind; reviews and other records suggest that viewers also often focused on how and by whom that role was played. One distinguished Shakespeare editor observes that "The stage history of *AYL* since 1740 is in large part a history of famous Rosalinds" (Knowles, 635); yes, that is indeed true, but, as I will suggest below, the treatment of other characters, notably Hymen, and of the setting itself merit more attention from students of stage history than they sometimes receive.

In the second half of the nineteenth century, interest in the play further intensified in both England and the United States. Often these productions were graced, or disgraced, by very elaborate illusionistic settings, including one with cascading water and stage grass constructed from feathers. The nineteenth-century stage history of *As You Like It,* however, should be expanded to include not only versions like these but also the mirror image of its own plot: That is, during that period, life imitated art inasmuch as numerous actresses, including no less a figure than Sarah Bernhardt, regularly played male Shakespearean characters, notably Hamlet, assuming what were known as "breeches parts" (Wadsworth). This type of cross-dressing elsewhere in the theater surely alerted Victorian audiences to the theatricality—in more senses than one—of Rosalind's own behavior and arguably also diminished its potential threats.

Twentieth-century stage productions have differed in telling ways that variously demonstrate and even enlarge the wide range of interpretive possibilities discussed in my introduction. The periods in which these versions are set or to which they allude have ranged from the medievalism suggested by costumes and sets in Nigel Playfair's 1919 Stratford version, to a U.S. Civil War setting used by Edward Payson Call's 1966 production in Minneapolis's Guthrie Theater, to many modern-dress versions, including one in which Sir Oliver Martext rides a bicycle. Both Anglo-American and continental productions have sometimes taken place outdoors; for example, Jacques Copeau put on the play in Florence's Boboli Gardens in 1938. Representations of the principal characters have also varied tellingly, of course. To winnow just two examples, in the 1961 production at Stratford directed by Michael Elliott, Vanessa Redgrave's Rosalind charmed critics with the "energy, commitment and sheer rapture" of her performance (Smallwood, 108); issues of gender were cleverly represented by her wearing a cap from which her long hair could on occasion be released, and in a tribute and allusion to that production, many subsequent Rosalinds sport caps as well (Figs. 4, 9). When, however, Sophie Thompson assumed the same part in the version that John Caird directed in the same theater twenty-eight years later, her childlike demeanor, intensified by clothes that were too big, pleased some reviewers and antagonized others.

The twentieth century witnessed not only television productions but also a number of significant films of *As You Like It*. Paul Czinner's 1936 version is of particular interest in part because it was the first Shakespeare movie with speaking parts and in part because a young Laurence Olivier plays Orlando, reminding us of his early career as a romantic lead. If Olivier is handsome, as Figure 8 suggests, the version itself can justly be described as pretty in both the positive senses of

© 20th Century Fox/Everett Collection, Inc.

Fig. 8. Orlando (Laurence Olivier) kneels before Rosalind (Elisabeth Bergner) in the film version that Paul Czinner directed in 1936. Should we interpret the stick Rosalind holds as a weapon? A phallic symbol? An instance of the magical branches associated with forests?

Fig. 9. In Christine Edzard's cinematic version (1992), in contrast to the films of Paul Czinner and Kenneth Branagh and many theatrical renditions, Arden is a harsh world, with the poems hung on trees transformed into graffiti.

charm and the more dubious senses of fluffiness. In contrast, Christine Edzard's 1992 film (Fig. 9) transforms Arden into the sordid world of the London docks. Kenneth Branagh's Shakespeare movies cleverly reimagine settings; his *Hamlet* includes a palace with a hall of mirrors that conceal passages behind them, and his *Much Ado About Nothing* borrows the charm of a nineteenth-century Italian town for its locale. Far bolder in its conception and far more controversial in its workings was his decision to locate his *As You Like It* (2006) in a violent Japan (Color Plates 1, 2, and 4).

The best way to analyze this radical decision by Branagh and many other issues about productions in both cinematic and theatrical versions is to turn to topical comparisons. I have winnowed from the many and motley areas that distinguish such productions five intersecting and overlapping touchstones, as it were—the treatment of the woods, of theatricality, of violence, of gender, and of Hymen and the concluding masque—because they are intriguing in themselves and also variously source and symptom of many other decisions, potentialities, and problems.

## "TONGUES IN TREES" (2.1.16): DECISIONS ABOUT THE SYLVAN SETTING

Directorial interpretations of both the forest and the court offer perspectives on not only literary cruxes directly connected with those settings but also the broader questions about theatricality and representation that are so central to the play. One central issue, how different the woods are from the court, draws attention to a problem central to pastoral: Can one escape the values and problems to which it purports to offer an alternative, or is fallen man doomed vainly to attempt—in both senses of the adverb *vainly*—to reenter lost Edens? A number of productions have used their sets to evoke a dramatic contrast between the rule-bound court and the green world of the woods, thus responding positively to the possibility of discovering, or recovering, a better world. The lush vegetation in Color Plate 3 demonstrates this approach. Similarly, in the 2000 Royal Shakespeare Company version directed by Gregory Doran, the set for the court was black and white, its elaborate designs suggesting embroidery and hence art, artifice, and stasis; in contrast, the forest was festooned with giant flowers that shifted color in the course of the play, thus associating nature with freshness and change (Color Plate 4).

Other productions have emphasized the distinction between two worlds but reinterpreted each of them, often in the interests of exploring broader political issues. As noted above, Christine Edzard's 1992 film transports sylvan pastoral to the London docks, thus establishing a pointed social contrast between the elegant court and the world of the socially and economically dispossessed. Rather than hang poems on trees, Orlando scrawls graffiti on walls; and this Rosalind wears a cap that is less jaunty and stylish and more utilitarian than Vanessa Redgrave's famous headgear (Figs. 4, 9). Critics also interpreted the chilled yet communal world that provides an alternative to the elegance of the court in this film as an alternative to and critique of the capitalist values of Margaret Thatcher's Britain (Marshall, 86). Produced in 2002 by the Worth Street Theater Company in New York and directed by Jeff Cohen, a cognate version represented the court as urban corporate America (the wrestling match took place in the Duke Frederick Sports Arena, and Amiens was a fashionably dressed personal assistant to that duke), while the pastoral realm was represented as the world of urban poverty, with the deer not animals but a rival gang. Tim Ocel's 2010 production at the American Players Theater in Wisconsin connects court and woods by using the same set, but it distinguishes them innovatively when a limping Charles the wrestler is welcomed into the woods, implicitly contrasting Duke Frederick's apparent rejection of him with the sylvan commitment to community.

Many productions, however, stress not distinctions but similarities between the two worlds, sometimes signaled theatrically by how one travels from one to the other (or, indeed, does not need to travel) and by the characterological analog to the absence of travel, the version of doubling in which the same actor represents both dukes. Three productions illustrate the range of theatrical techniques through which the similarities between court and woods can be expressed. In the 1961 Royal Shakespeare Company production directed by Michael Elliott, a single set was used, but different actors represented the two dukes. Twenty-four years later, when Adrian Noble directed the play for the same company, the actor playing both parts becomes Duke Senior by casting a cloth over himself and entering Arden through a mirror that aptly functions as a visual emblem for the doubling of one actor as both dukes. Similarly, in the 2010 Brooklyn Academy of Music (BAM) Bridge production, Duke Frederick turns himself into Duke Senior—and his courtiers simultaneously transform themselves into their counterparts in the world of the banished duke—by ceremoniously putting on country clothes. Such versions clearly imply that the distinctions between the two worlds are neither clear-cut nor immutable, thus gesturing towards Jaques's claim that Duke Senior, like his brother, is a usurper and also emphasizing the topic to which I will turn shortly, the role of theater and theatricality.

In that BAM production, snow falls as those characters don their country attire, reminding us again of how often productions of this play interrogate not only the reality but also the attractiveness of pastoral. Much as many literary texts evoke worlds variously described as "hard" pastoral and anti-pastoral, so numerous productions of *As You Like It* have developed the references to harsh weather in Duke Senior's first speech. In a 1996 version, Adam actually dies onstage of the cold. In other versions, however, living in the woods is, as it were, a walk in the park, and a park in springtime at that.

## "IF THERE BE TRUTH IN SIGHT" (5.4.117,119): APPROACHES TO THEATRICALITY

As we just saw, representations of the forest often introduce the questions about theatricality, conventionality, and game-playing that are so central to the play. Moving from illusionistic sets and props that straightforwardly represent a forest (a production in 1907 is reported to have used 2,000 pots of ferns) to ones that draw attention to the act of representation encourages the audience to reflect on how, both within a theater and outside it, pastoral is not discovered but created by craft in its disparate senses. Comparing the 1936 film directed by Czinner and starring Olivier and many subsequent productions demonstrates the range of ways that the pastoral realm of the forest can be represented. The film's rendition relies on recognizable, realistic trees (Fig. 8), while in contrast, the 1967 stage version that Clifford Williams directed with an all-male cast represents the woodlands through tubular projections, an insistently theatrical allusion to trees. And when the Eastern European director Liviu Ciulei put on the play in the Guthrie Theater in Minneapolis in 1982, he used cognate techniques to defamiliarize the pastoral landscape and thus make his audience more familiar with issues about theatrical game-playing: The trees of the forest were represented by dancers, and by putting down a blue ribbon to represent water, his actors literally construct a pastoral realm. (Dancers also were associated with the forest in the version that the same director staged in Bucharest in 1961; in this earlier production, he underscored questions about theatricality by displaying near the actual, live spectators murals that represented an Elizabethan audience.) Similarly, other productions have linked Arden to the realms of the imagined and performed by creating sets that allude to "real" objects while determinedly differing from them, such as a red tree or an exceptionally large one. Returning to the BAM production in 2010, the floor was covered with strawlike projections whose color was changed by lighting, including a brief—but only brief—period in which they turned green and hence resembled grass (though only slightly). Perhaps the allusion to straw also suggested that pastoral performances turn what was once live into something dried and preserved and artificial.

Although the pastoral setting is one of the most effective ways of asking what is "real," and who decides, and to what ends, those questions have been staged in other ways as well. For example, in the Royal Shakespeare Company version that John Caird directed in 1989, as the audience walked in, actors, some dressed like theater staff, were dancing with each other on a set that replicated the dress-circle bar in the theater itself, thus, among many other implications, blurring the distinction between the staged and the "real."

But arguably no production has explored such issues more thoroughly or imaginatively than Branagh's film, represented by three color plates at the beginning of this volume. The very decision to set it in Japan, a culture so deeply if stereotypically associated with convention, introduces questions about theatricality, and these questions are pushed to the forefront when the wrestling match is preceded by a series of ritualized moves and gestures. Branagh has many aims in supplementing Shakespeare's text with its backstory— that is, at the beginning of the movie, characters are watching a play, which is violently interrupted by events that we come to realize are the overthrow of Duke Senior—but not the least is to create the Chinese-box effect of a play within a play and thus introduce the issues about cinema and drama that are to recur throughout. Adapting and alluding to techniques that he also explored in his *Henry V,* the director proceeds repeatedly to draw attention to the fact that we are indeed viewing a film. Symmetrically, the movie that opens on that representation of characters viewing a play ends on a film set, and "cut" is the final word we hear.

"IT IS THE FIRST TIME THAT EVER I HEARD BREAKING OF RIBS WAS SPORT FOR LADIES" (1.2.138—139): VIOLENCE AND/OR
*AS YOU LIKE IT*

As my introduction emphasized, the diminution of violence indisputably distinguishes Shakespeare's play from its principal source, Lodge's prose romance—but the extent of violence in the drama remains a complex interpretive conundrum with implications for gender in particular. First, how threatening is Duke Frederick's court? At one extreme, the Ciulei production of 1982 in the Guthrie Theater in Minneapolis cleverly played up the comedic and played down the suffering associated with other genres when Duke Frederick delivered his attack on his niece while he was taking a shower behind a screen. The potentiality for brute force comes out in the wash. In other productions, that duke is far more ominous; he variously wears clothing that recalls the scales of a beast (Color Plate 1), oversees the torture of Oliver (on occasion portrayed as waterboarding), and strides into Rosalind's chamber to banish her when she is in her nightclothes, making her seem more vulnerable to his power.

Comparing various treatments of the hunt also demonstrates a range of responses to the potentialities for violence. Cynthia Marshall persuasively demonstrated that productions in the 1960s and 1970s tended to intensify the pain and violence elsewhere in the play as well (76–79), and among her examples are one production in which hunting involves a gun rather than a bow and arrow and another in which the stag is actually gutted. But in Branagh's film, bloody in so many other respects, the erstwhile hunters enjoy a vegetarian repast.

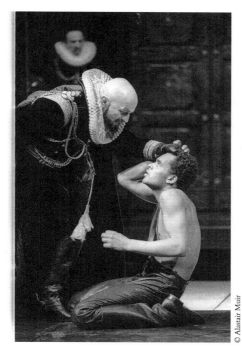

Fig. 10. Duke Frederick (Andrew Jarvis) reacts angrily to the news of Orlando's (Peter de Jersey) parentage in David Thacker's 1992 Royal Shakespeare Company production.

© Alastair Muir

## "NAY, YOU MUST CALL ME ROSALIND" (3.2.434): CHARACTERS AND GENDERS

Among the most important characterological decisions a director and his company must make is the extent to which normative gendering is disrupted, whether by specific characters or by the interplay between them. Several overlapping and intersecting choices can contribute to either containing or intensifying such disruptions. For example, what type of costume and body language should Rosalind sport? Possibilities range from clothes and gestures that play up her femininity by making her attempts to look like a boy risible to ones that render her quite masculine. Should the homoerotic possibilities in the relationships between Rosalind and Celia, Rosalind and Phebe, and Orlando and Ganymede be virtually erased, exposed but not stressed, or emphasized? And to what extent, if at all, does Orlando or any of the other characters sense that Rosalind is not in fact male?

Especially germane to such questions is the issue of how unsettling, even threatening, the cross-dressing is made to seem. It may, of course, merely be reduced to a lark. But the potential transgressiveness behind this and many other episodes involving gender in the play is neatly captured in Branagh's film when Rosalind suggests both fear and excitement by dropping her voice to a whisper in the final three words of "Were it not better . . . that I did suit me all points like a man" (1.3.114, 116).

That cross-dressing is of course both troped and troubled in all-male productions, notably the version directed in 1967 by Clifford Williams for the National Theater and Declan Donnellan's production for the experimental theater company Cheek by Jowl in 1991. Many critics have observed that the impact of this sort of casting on an audience unaccustomed to it is likely to be different from its effects on the original Elizabethan playgoers—but that observation merely introduces, rather than resolves, analyses of those effects and their relationship to broader questions about cross-dressing. Both James C. Bulman's essay, included in this volume, and the study by Cary M. Mazer cited in the suggestions for further reading comment trenchantly on the extraordinary moment when Jaques reacts to touching the chest of the male actor playing Rosalind as though he has encountered a female breast; as their analyses suggest, this episode

Fig. 11. Rosalind (Adrian Lester) dances with Celia (Simon Coates) in the 1994–95 all-male production by Cheek by Jowl (a revival of the 1991 version by the same company).

© John Haynes/Lebrecht Music & Art

aptly provides a microcosm for the workings of gender-bending, not only in all-male castings of this play but also in other productions and in the text itself.

## "HYMEN FROM HEAVEN BROUGHT HER" (5.4.112): MYTHOLOGY AS TRANSFORMATIVE OR MYTHOLOGY AS TRANSFORMED

The treatment of Hymen, as my introduction argues, deserves far more attention than it often receives from critics since it encapsulates several other issues crucial to the play. How, and by whom—and how successfully—is closure realized? In particular, is a diminution in Rosalind's power signaled by her yielding sovereignty over the action to Hymen, much as she yields, or apparently yields, control over her body and being to husband and father? Is a shift from the comedic to romance or proto-romance effected by the appearance of Hymen, much as the masque of Jupiter shifts tone in *Cymbeline?* Does the celebration of marriage supersede and suppress the hints that that institution is being rendered ironically?

In negotiating such questions, directors must decide whether they want any suggestion of the supernatural and numinous, an interpretation for which this edition and some other critical analyses have argued (Hunt, 44). In an interview, the director Steven Pimlott establishes a firm position: "I think one has to take the Folio at its word and see this as a theophany [the appearance of a god]: the god comes to earth . . . Hymen is the final manifestation of Arden's magic" (Smallwood, 190). Not only Pimlott's own 1996 version but many others have indeed approached Hymen in this way. In Trevor Nunn's Stratford production in 1977, Hymen and his attendants appear in a cloud, recalling the concept in classical drama of the *deus ex machina,* the god who appears in a magical vehicle (Fig. 7). Other productions, however, play down Hymen's agency, often with the aim of restoring power to Rosalind. In Czinner's movie, Hymen is a child led in with Rosalind and Celia each holding one of his hands. Although visually this scene associates Hymen with Cupid, the main effect is to reduce the figure to an ineffective though lovable toddler.

In those instances when doubling is used to suggest subterranean links between characters, that can shape how Hymen is viewed. Directors have experimented with a range of possibilities, including even recycling the wrestler Charles as Hymen (Hunt). The productions that cast Hymen and Corin as the same actor associate him with the earthly realm of pastoral rather than the supernatural; in one version, he even arrives in a rustic cart. This connection also aptly links the pastoral and georgic world to the wedding, that celebration of potential fertility.

In an engaging American Players Theater production directed by Jonathan Smoots in 2001, Adam dies onstage but reappears as Hymen, repeating Adam's characteristic gesture, cupping his hand around Orlando's face, to signal that this is not merely the doubling of a role but a kind of rebirth. That form of reincarnation introduces the magic associated with romance, even as it simultaneously links Hymen with the everyday rather than the luminous and numinous.

## WORKS CITED IN INTRODUCTION AND PERFORMANCE HISTORY

Alpers, Paul. *What Is Pastoral?* Chicago: U of Chicago P, 1996.

Athanasiadou, Angeliki, and René Dirven, eds. *On Conditionals Again. Current Issues in Linguistic Theory, 143.* Amsterdam: John Benjamins Publishing Company, 1997.

Barber, C. L. *Shakespeare's Festive Comedy: A Study of Dramatic Form and Its Relation to Social Custom.* Princeton: Princeton UP, 1959.

Barton, Anne. "*As You Like It* and *Twelfth Night*: Shakespeare's Sense of an Ending." In *Shakespearian Comedy,* Stratford-upon-Avon Studies. Ed. Malcolm Bradbury and David Palmer. London: Edward Arnold, 1972. 160–80.

Belsey, Catherine. "Disrupting Sexual Difference: Meaning and Gender in the Comedies." In *Alternative Shakespeares.* Ed. John Drakakis. London: Methuen, 1985. 166–90.

Berry, Ralph. *Shakespeare's Comedies: Explorations in Form.* Princeton: Princeton UP, 1972.

Billington, Sandra. *A Social History of the Fool.* Sussex and New York: The Harvester Press and St. Martin's Press, 1984.

Bono, Barbara J. "Mixed Gender, Mixed Genre in Shakespeare's *As You Like It.*" In *Renaissance Genres: Essays on Theory, History, and Interpretation.* Ed. Barbara Kiefer Lewalski. Cambridge, MA: Harvard UP, 1986. 189–212.

Bullough, Geoffrey. *Narrative and Dramatic Sources of Shakespeare.* Vol. II: The Comedies, 1597–1603. London and New York: Routledge and Kegan Paul and Columbia UP, 1958.

Carlson, Susan. "Women in *As You Like It*: Community, Change, and Choice." *Essays in Literature* 14 (1987): 151–69.

Cohen, Stephen. "(Post)modern Elizabeth: Gender, Politics, and the Emergence of Modern Subjectivity." In *Shakespeare and Modernity: Early Modern to Millennium.* Ed. Hugh Grady. London: Routledge, 2000. 20–39.

Colie, Rosalie L. *Shakespeare's Living Art.* Princeton: Princeton UP, 1974.

Crane, Mary Thomas. *Shakespeare's Brain: Reading with Cognitive Theory.* Princeton: Princeton UP, 2001.

Daley, A. Stuart. "Where Are the Woods in *As You Like It?*" *Shakespeare Quarterly* 34 (1983): 172–80.

Dolan, Frances E. Introduction. *As You Like It,* by William Shakespeare. *The Pelican Shakespeare.* New York: Penguin, 2000. xxxi–xliv.

Dubrow, Heather. *Shakespeare and Domestic Loss: Forms of Deprivation, Mourning, and Recuperation.* Cambridge, UK.: Cambridge UP, 1999.

———— "Fringe Benefits: Rosalind and the Purlieux of the Forest." *Notes and Queries* 53 (2006): 67–69.

Dusinberre, Juliet. Introduction. *As You Like It,* by William Shakespeare. *The Arden Shakespeare.* London: Thomson Learning, 2006. 1–142.

Erickson, Peter. *Patriarchal Structures in Shakespeare's Drama.* Berkeley: U of California P, 1985.

Green, Douglas E. "The 'Unexpressive She': Is There Really a Rosalind?" *Journal of Dramatic Theory and Criticism* 2 (1988): 41–52.

Hattaway, Michael. Introduction. *As You Like It,* by William Shakespeare. *The New Cambridge Shakespeare.* Cambridge, UK: Cambridge UP, 2000. 1–66.

Howard, Jean E. "Crossdressing, the Theater, and Gender Struggle in Early Modern England." *Shakespeare Quarterly* 39 (1988): 418–40.

Hunt, Maurice A. *Shakespeare's "As You Like It": Late Elizabethan Culture and Literary Representation.* New York: Palgrave, 2008.

Jenkins, Harold. "*As You Like It.*" *Shakespeare Survey* 8 (1955): 40–51.

Knowles, Richard, ed. *As You Like It.* A New Variorum Edition of Shakespeare. New York: Modern Language Association, 1977.

Kuhn, Maura Slattery. "Much Virtue in *If.*" *Shakespeare Quarterly* 28 (1977): 40–50.

Latham, Agnes. Introduction. *As You Like It,* by William Shakespeare. *The Arden Shakespeare.* 1975; rpt. Waltham-on-Thames: Thomas Nelson & Sons, 1997. lxiii–lxxv.

Lodge, Thomas. *Rosalynde. Euphues golden legacie.* In Geoffrey Bullough, *Narrative and Dramatic Sources of Shakespeare.* 158–256.

Manwood, John. *A Treatise and Discourse of the Lawes of the Forrest.* London, 1598.

Marshall, Cynthia. "Wrestling as Play and Game in *As You Like It.*" *Studies in English Literature* 33 (1993): 265–87.

———— Introduction. *As You Like It,* by William Shakespeare. *Shakespeare in Production.* Cambridge, UK: Cambridge UP, 2004. 1–95.

Masten, Jeffrey. "Textual Deviance: Ganymede's Hand in *As You Like It.*" In *Field Work: Sites in Literary and Cultural Studies.* Ed. Marjorie Garber, Paul B. Franklin, Rebecca L. Walkowitz. New York: Routledge, 1996. 153–63.

Mazer, Cary M. "Rosalind's Breast." In *Shakespeare Re-Dressed: Cross-Gender Casting in Contemporary Performance.* Ed. James C. Bulman. Madison, NJ: Fairleigh Dickinson UP, 2008. 96–115.

Milward, Peter. "Religion in Arden." *Shakespeare Survey* 54 (2001): 115–21.

Montrose, Louis Adrian. "'The Place of a Brother' in *As You Like It:* Social Process and Comic Form." *Shakespeare Quarterly* 32 (1981): 28–54.

Nevo, Ruth. *Comic Transformations in Shakespeare.* London: Methuen, 1980.

Orgel, Stephen. *Impersonations: The Performance of Gender in Shakespeare's England.* Cambridge, UK: Cambridge UP, 1996.

Phillips, Joshua S. *English Fictions of Communal Identity, 1485–1603.* Aldershot: Ashgate Publishing, 2010.

Rackin, Phyllis. "Androgyny, Mimesis, and the Marriage of the Boy Heroine on the Renaissance English Stage." *PMLA* 102 (1987): 29–41.

Ronk, Martha. "Locating the Visual in *As You Like It.*" *Shakespeare Quarterly* 52 (2001): 255–76.

Rose, Mary Beth. "Where Are the Mothers in Shakespeare? Options for Gender Representation in the English Renaissance." *Shakespeare Quarterly* 42 (1991): 291–314.

Saslow, James M. *Ganymede in the Renaissance: Homosexuality in Art and Society.* New Haven: Yale UP, 1986.

Scott, William O. "'A woman's thought runs before her actions': Vows as Speech Acts in *As You Like It.*" *Philosophy and Literature* 30 (2006): 528–39.

Shapiro, Michael. "Cross-dressing in Elizabethan Robin Hood Plays." In *Playing Robin Hood: The Legend as Performance in Five Centuries.* Ed. Lois Potter. Newark and London: U of Delaware P and Associated University Presses, 1998. 77–90.

Smallwood, Robert. *As You Like It. Shakespeare at Stratford.* London: Thomson Learning, 2003.

Theis, Jeffrey S. *Writing the Forest in Early Modern England: A Sylvan Pastoral Nation.* Pittsburgh: Duquesne UP, 2009.

—— "The 'ill kill'd Deer': Poaching and Social Order in *The Merry Wives of Windsor.*" *Texas Studies in Literature and Language* 43 (2001): 46–73.

Traub, Valerie. *Desire and Anxiety: Circulations of Sexuality in Shakespearean Drama.* London: Routledge, 1992.

Traugott, Elizabeth Closs, Alice ter Meulen, Judy Snitzer Reilly, Charles A. Ferguson, eds. *On Conditionals.* Cambridge, UK: Cambridge UP, 1986.

Wadsworth, Frank W. "Hamlet and Iago: Nineteenth-Century Breeches Parts." *Shakespeare Quarterly* 17 (1966): 130–39.

Watson, Robert. *Back to Nature: The Green and the Real in the Late Renaissance.* Philadelphia: U of Pennsylvania P, 2006. Esp. Chapter 3, 77–107.

Welsford, Enid. *The Fool: His Social and Literary History.* London: Faber and Faber, 1935.

Wiles, David. *Shakespeare's Clown: Actor and Text in the Elizabethan Playhouse.* Cambridge, UK: Cambridge UP, 1987.

Wilson, Richard. *Will Power: Essays on Shakespearean Authority.* New York: Harvester/Wheatsheaf, 1993.

Woodbridge, Linda. "Country Matters: *As You Like It* and the Pastoral-Bashing Impulse." In *Re-Visions of Shakespeare: Essays in Honor of Robert Ornstein.* Ed. Evelyn Gajowski. Newark: U of Delaware P, 2004. 189–214.

Wofford, Susanne L. "'To You I Give Myself, For I Am Yours': Erotic Performance and Theatrical Performatives in *As You Like It.*" In *Shakespeare Reread: The Texts in New Contexts.* Ed. Russ Mcdonald. Ithaca: Cornell UP, 1994. 147–69.

Young, David. *The Heart's Forest: A Study of Shakespeare's Pastoral Plays.* New Haven: Yale UP, 1972.

# Abbreviations

★=additional material added by the volume editor
F1, F2, etc. First Folio, Second Folio, etc.
conj. conjecture
ed. editor; edition
l(l). line(s)
om. omit(s), omitted
o.s.d. opening stage direction
s.d(d). stage direction(s)
s.p(p). speech-prefix(es)
subs. substantially

# KEY TO WORKS CITED IN EXPLANATORY AND TEXTUAL NOTES

Reference in explanatory and textual notes is in general by last name of editor or author. Not included in the following list of works so cited are editions of individual plays or special studies referred to in the selected bibliographies appended to the "Note on the Text" following each of the plays and poems.

CAMBRIDGE, *Works,* ed. W. G. Clark and W. A. Wright, 1863–66 (9 vols.); ed. W. A. Wright, 1891–93 (9 vols.)

CAPELL, Edward, ed., *Works,* [1768] (10 vols.)

COLLIER, John P., ed., *Works,* 1842–44 (8 vols.); 1853; 1858 (6 vols.)

CRAIG, William J., ed., *Works,* 1891

DOUAI MS (*Twelfth Night, As You Like It, Comedy of Errors, Romeo and Juliet, Julius Caesar, Macbeth*), Douai MS. 7.87, in the Douai Public Library (see G. B. Evans, *PQ,* XLI [1962], 158–72)

DYCE, Alexander, ed., *Works,* 1857 (6 vols.); 1864–67 (9 vols.); 1875–76 (9 vols.) *Works of Beaumont and Fletcher,* 1843–46 (11 vols.)

FURNESS, H. H., ed., *New Variorum Edition,* 1871–1928 (vols. 1–15; vols. 16–21 by H. H. Furness, Jr.)

HANMER, Thomas, ed., *Works,* 1743–44 (6 vols.); 1745; 1770–71 (6 vols.)

HINMAN, Charlton, *The Printing and Proof-Reading of the First Folio of Shakespeare,* 1963 (2 vols.)

JOHNSON, Samuel, ed., *Works,* 1765 (2 eds., 8 vols.); 1768 (8 vols.)

KITTREDGE, George L., ed., *Works,* 1936

KNIGHT, Charles, ed., *Works,* 1838–43 (8 vols.); 1842–44 (12 vols.)

MALONE, Edmond, ed., *Works,* 1790 (10 vols.)

MUNRO, John, ed., *Works* (The London Shakespeare), 1958 (6 vols.)

POPE, Alexander, ed., *Works,* 1723–25 (6 vols.); 1728 (8 vols.)

ROWE, Nicholas, ed., *Works,* 1709 (2 eds., 6 vol.); 1714 (8 vols.)

SINGER, S. W., ed., *Works,* 1826 (10 vols.); 1855–56 (10 vols.)

STEEVENS, George, ed., *Works,* 1773 (with Samuel Johnson, 10 vols.); 1778 (10 vols.); 1793 (15 vols.)

THEOBALD, Lewis, ed., *Works,* 1733 (7 vols.); 1740 (8 vols.); 1757 (8 vols.) (with Thomas Seward and J. Sympson), *Works of Beaumont and Fletcher,* 1750 (vol. X: *The Two Noble Kinsmen*)

UPTON, John, *Critical Observations on Shakespeare,* 1747

WARBURTON, William, ed., *Works,* 1747 (8 vols.)

WELLS, Stanley and Gary Taylor, et al., eds., *William Shakespeare: The Complete Works, Original Spelling Edition* (1986) *William Shakespeare: A Textual Companion* (1987)

WHITE, Richard Grant, ed. *Works,* 1857–66 (12 vols.); 1883 (6 vols.)

WILSON, John Dover (with A. Quiller-Couch et al.), ed., *Works* (New Shakespeare), 1921–66 (39 vols.)

# AS
# YOU LIKE
# IT

# DRAMATIS PERSONAE

DUKE SENIOR, *living in banishment*
DUKE FREDERICK, *his brother, and usurper
of his dominions*
AMIENS ⎫
JAQUES ⎭ *lords attending on the banished Duke*
LE BEAU, *a courtier attending upon Duke Frederick*
CHARLES, *wrestler to Duke Frederick*
OLIVER ⎫
JAQUES ⎬ *sons of Sir Rowland de Boys*
ORLANDO ⎭
ADAM ⎫
DENNIS ⎭ *servants to Oliver*
TOUCHSTONE, *a clown*
SIR OLIVER MARTEXT, *a vicar*
CORIN ⎫
SILVIUS ⎭ *shepherds*
WILLIAM, *a country fellow, in love with Audrey*
*A person representing* HYMEN
ROSALIND, *daughter to the banished Duke*
CELIA, *daughter to Duke Frederick*
PHEBE, *a shepherdess*
AUDREY, *a country wench*
LORDS, PAGES, FORESTERS, *and* ATTENDANTS

SCENE: *Oliver's house; Duke Frederick's court; and the
forest of Arden*

# Act I

SCENE I

*Enter* ORLANDO *and* ADAM.

ORLANDO As I remember, Adam, it was upon this
fashion bequeath'd me by will but poor a thousand
crowns, and, as thou say'st, charg'd my brother,
on his blessing, to breed me well; and there begins
my sadness. My brother Jaques he keeps at                        5
school, and report speaks goldenly of his profit.
For my part, he keeps me rustically at home, or (to
speak more properly) stays me here at home unkept; for
call you that keeping for a gentleman of
my birth, that differs not from the stalling of an              10
ox? His horses are bred better, for besides that
they are fair with their feeding, they are taught
their manage, and to that end riders dearly hir'd;
but I (his brother) gain nothing under him but growth,
for the which his animals on his dunghills are                  15
as much bound to him as I. Besides this nothing
that he so plentifully gives me, the something that
nature gave me his countenance seems to take from
me. He lets me feed with his hinds, bars me the

*Words and passages enclosed in square brackets in the text above are either emendations of
the copy-text or additions to it. The Textual Notes immediately following the play cite the
earliest authority for every such change or insertion and supply the reading of the copy-text
wherever it is emended in this edition.*

1.1. Location. The garden of Oliver's house. **2,3. bequeath'd, charg'd.** The
understood subject is *he,* i.e. Orlando's father. **2. poor a:** a poor. **4. on his blessing:**
i.e. on pain of losing his blessing. **breed me:** bring me up. **5–6. keeps at school:**
maintains at the university. **6. goldenly:** in glowing terms. **profit:** progress.
**7. rustically:** like a peasant; cut off from civilized society. **8. stays:** detains.
**8–9. unkept:** without proper maintenance. **12. fair:** in fine physical condition. **13. manage:** manege, paces and movements of a trained horse. **dearly:** at
great expense. **16. bound:** indebted. **18. countenance:** behavior, or (ironically)
favor, patronage. **19. hinds:** farm laborers. **bars me:** excludes me from.

place of a brother, and as much as in him lies,                    20
mines my gentility with my education. This is it,
Adam, that grieves me, and the spirit of my father,
which I think is within me, begins to mutiny against
this servitude. I will no longer endure it, though
yet I know no wise remedy how to avoid it.                         25

*Enter* OLIVER.

ADAM Yonder comes my master, your brother.
ORLANDO Go apart, Adam, and thou shalt hear how
   he will shake me up.
OLIVER Now, sir, what make you here?
ORLANDO Nothing. I am not taught to make any thing.              30
OLIVER What mar you then, sir?
ORLANDO Marry, sir, I am helping you to mar that
   which God made, a poor unworthy brother of yours,
   with idleness.
OLIVER Marry, sir, be better employ'd, and be naught            35
   a while.
ORLANDO Shall I keep your hogs and eat husks with
   them? What prodigal portion have I spent, that
   I should come to such penury?
OLIVER Know you where you are, sir?                              40
ORLANDO O, sir, very well; here in your orchard.
OLIVER Know you before whom, sir?
ORLANDO Ay, better than him I am before knows me.
   I know you are my eldest brother, and in the gentle
   condition of blood you should so know me.                      45
   The courtesy of nations allows you my better, in
   that you are the first born, but the same tradition
   takes not away my blood, were there twenty brothers
   betwixt us. I have as much of my father in me

21. **mines:** undermines. **with my education:** by the way I am brought up.
28. **shake me up:** berate me (cf. *blow me up*). 29. **make you:** are you doing (but
Orlando quibbles on the more usual sense of *make*). 31. **mar.** Commonly used
in antithesis to *make,* as in *Othello,* I.v.4: "It makes us, or it mars us." 32. **Marry:**
why, indeed (originally the name of the Virgin Mary used as an oath). 35. **be**
**naught:** a mild curse, equivalent to "Go to the devil." 37–39. **Shall . . . penury.**
An allusion to the parable of the prodigal son (Luke 15:11–32), who, having wasted
his portion of his father's possessions, was forced to become a swineherd and
envied the hogs their husks. 40. **where:** i.e. in whose presence (but Orlando
again quibbles). 41. **orchard:** garden. 44–45. **gentle . . . blood:** feeling proper
to gentle birth. 46. **courtesy of nations:** generally accepted convention; here, the
custom of primogeniture. **allows:** acknowledges.

as you, albeit I confess your coming before me is            50
nearer to his reverence.
OLIVER  What, boy! [*Strikes him.*]
ORLANDO  Come, come, elder brother, you are too
young in this. [*Collaring him.*]
OLIVER  Wilt thou lay hands on me, villain?                  55
ORLANDO  I am no villain; I am the youngest son of
Sir Rowland de Boys. He was my father, and he
is thrice a villain that says such a father begot
villains. Wert thou not my brother, I would not
take this hand from thy throat till this other had          60
pull'd out thy tongue for saying so. Thou hast
rail'd on thyself.
ADAM  Sweet masters, be patient, for your
father's remembrance, be at accord.
OLIVER  Let me go, I say.                                     65
ORLANDO  I will not till I please. You shall hear me.
My father charg'd you in his will to give me good
education. You have train'd me like a peasant,
obscuring and hiding from me all gentleman-like
qualities. The spirit of my father grows strong             70
in me, and I will no longer endure it; therefore
allow me such exercises as may become a gentleman,
or give me the poor allottery my father left me
by testament, with that I will go buy my fortunes.
OLIVER  And what wilt thou do? beg, when that is             75
spent? Well, sir, get you in. I will not long be
troubled with you; you shall have some part of
your will. I pray you leave me.
ORLANDO  I will no further offend you than becomes
me for my good.                                              80
OLIVER  Get you with him, you old dog.
ADAM  Is "old dog" my reward? Most true, I
have lost my teeth in your service. God be with my
old master, he would not have spoke such a word.
                                *Exeunt Orlando, Adam.*

---

**50–51. your . . . reverence:** i.e. your being my senior gives you a better claim
to the respect which was due him.  **54. young in this:** i.e. inexperienced in
fighting.  **56. villain:** the quarrel involves alternative meanings: someone evil
or someone of low birth.★  **63. be patient:** control yourselves.  **70. qualities:**
accomplishments.  **72. exercises:** occupations, training.  **73. allottery:** portion.
**78. your will:** what you want.

OLIVER  Is it even so? Begin you to grow upon me?                    85
I will physic your rankness, and yet give no thousand crowns
neither. Holla, Dennis!

*Enter* DENNIS.

DENNIS  Calls your worship?
OLIVER  Was not Charles, the Duke's wrastler, here
to speak with me?                                                    90
DENNIS  So please you, he is here at the door, and
importunes access to you.
OLIVER  Call him in.
'Twill be a good                                        [*Exit Dennis.*]
way; and to-morrow the wrastling is.

*Enter* CHARLES.

CHARLES  Good morrow to your worship.                               95
OLIVER  Good Monsieur Charles, what's the new
news at the new court?
CHARLES  There's no news at the court, sir, but the
old news: that is, the old Duke is banish'd by his
younger brother the new Duke, and three or                         100
four loving lords have put themselves into voluntary exile
with him, whose lands and revenues enrich the new
Duke; therefore he gives them good
leave to wander.
OLIVER  Can you tell if Rosalind, the Duke's daughter,             105
be banish'd with her father?
CHARLES  O no; for the Duke's daughter, her cousin,
so loves her, being ever from their cradles bred together,
that [she] would have follow'd her exile, or
have died to stay behind her. She is at the court,                 110
and no less belov'd of her uncle than his own daughter,
and never two ladies lov'd as they do.
OLIVER  Where will the old Duke live?
CHARLES  They say he is already in the forest of Arden,
and a many merry men with him; and there                           115

---

**85. grow upon me:** i.e. get so big that you crowd me.  **86. physic your rankness:**
administer a dose that will cure your overgrowth.  **89. wrastler:** wrestler.
**95. morrow:** morning.  **104. leave:** permission.  **110. to stay:** at being forced
to stay.  **114. forest of Arden.** The setting of much of the action of Lodge's
*Rosalynde,* where it signifies the forest of Ardennes in present-day Belgium, Lux-
embourg, and France; but Shakespeare (and his audience) would doubtless have
in mind as well the forest of Arden in Warwickshire.

they live like the old Robin Hood of England. They
say many young gentlemen flock to him every day,
and fleet the time carelessly, as they did in the golden
world.

OLIVER What, you wrastle to-morrow before the                    120
new Duke?

CHARLES Marry, do I, sir; and I came to acquaint
you with a matter. I am given, sir, secretly to
understand that your younger brother, Orlando,
hath a disposition to come in disguis'd against me     125
to try a fall. To-morrow, sir, I wrestle for my
credit, and he that escapes me without some broken
limb shall acquit him well. Your brother is but
young and tender, and for your love I would
be loath to foil him, as I must for my own honor     130
if he come in; therefore out of my love to you,
I came hither to acquaint you withal, that either
you might stay him from his intendment, or brook
such disgrace well as he shall run into, in that it
is a thing of his own search, and altogether against     135
my will.

OLIVER Charles, I thank thee for thy love to me,
which thou shalt find I will most kindly requite.
I had myself notice of my brother's purpose
herein, and have by underhand means labor'd to     140
dissuade him from it; but he is resolute. I'll tell
thee, Charles, it is the stubbornest young fellow of
France, full of ambition, an envious emulator of
every man's good parts, a secret and villainous
contriver against me his natural brother; therefore     145
use thy discretion—I had as lief thou didst break
his neck as his finger. And thou wert best look
to 't; for if thou dost him any slight disgrace, or if
he do not mightily grace himself on thee, he
will practice against thee by poison, entrap thee by     150
some treacherous device, and never leave thee till

**118. fleet:** pass. **carelessly:** free from care. **118–19. the golden world:** the Golden
Age, i.e. the primal age of innocence and ease. **126. fall:** bout. **127. credit:**
professional reputation. **128. shall:** must. **130. foil:** defeat. **132. withal:**
therewith. **133. brook:** endure. **135. search:** seeking. **140. underhand:** indirect. **143. emulator:** rival. **144. parts:** qualities. **145. contriver:** schemer. **natural:** own. **146. lief:** willingly. **147. thou . . . look:** you had better give serious
attention. **149. grace . . . thee:** gain honor at your expense. **150. practice:** plot,
act treacherously.

he hath ta'en thy life by some indirect means or
other; for I assure thee (and almost with tears I
speak it) there is not one so young and so villainous
this day living. I speak but brotherly of 155
him, but should I anatomize him to thee as he is, I
must blush and weep, and thou must look pale and
wonder.

CHARLES  I am heartily glad I came hither to you.
If he come to-morrow, I'll give him his payment. 160
If ever he go alone again, I'll never wrastle for prize
more. And so God keep your worship! *Exit.*

[OLIVER]  Farewell, good Charles. Now will I
stir this gamester. I hope I shall see an end
of him; for my soul (yet I know not why) hates 165
nothing more than he. Yet he's gentle, never school'd
and yet learned, full of noble device, of all sorts
enchantingly belov'd, and indeed so much in the
heart of the world, and especially of my own
people, who best know him, that I am altogether 170
mispris'd. But it shall not be so long, this wrastler
shall clear all. Nothing remains but that I kindle
the boy thither, which now I'll go about. *Exit.*

## SCENE 2

*Enter* ROSALIND *and* CELIA.

CELIA  I pray thee, Rosalind, sweet my coz, be
merry.

ROSALIND  Dear Celia—I show more mirth than I am
mistress of, and would you yet [I] were merrier?
Unless you could teach me to forget a banish'd 5
father, you must not learn me how to remember
any extraordinary pleasure.

CELIA  Herein I see thou lov'st me not with the full
weight that I love thee. If my uncle, thy banish'd

---

**155. brotherly:** i.e. with brotherly reticence about his vices.  **156. anatomize:**
dissect, lay open.  **161. go alone:** walk without help.  **164. stir:** stir up (to compete in
the wrestling). **gamester:** sportive fellow.  **166. gentle:** of gentlemanly character.
**167. device:** devising, purposes. **of all sorts:** by people of every rank.
**168. enchantingly:** as if by enchantment.  **171. mispris'd:** despised.  **172. clear:**
settle. **kindle:** incite.  **173. thither:** i.e. to court, for the wrestling.  **1.2.** Location:
Lawn before the Duke's palace.  **1. sweet my coz:** my dear cousin.  **3–4. am
mistress of:** have at my command, i.e. actually feel.  **6. learn:** instruct.

father, had banish'd thy uncle, the Duke my 10
father, so thou hadst been still with me, I could
have taught my love to take thy father for mine;
so wouldst thou, if the truth of thy love to me were
so righteously temper'd as mine is to thee.

ROSALIND Well, I will forget the condition of my estate, 15
to rejoice in yours.

CELIA You know my father hath no child but I,
nor none is like to have; and truly when he dies,
thou shalt be his heir; for what he hath taken
away from thy father perforce, I will render thee 20
again in affection. By mine honor, I will, and when
I break that oath, let me turn monster. Therefore,
my sweet Rose, my dear Rose, be merry.

ROSALIND From henceforth I will, coz, and devise
sports. Let me see—what think you of falling in love? 25

CELIA Marry, I prithee do, to make sport withal.
But love no man in good earnest, nor no further
in sport neither, than with safety of a pure blush
thou mayst in honor come off again.

ROSALIND What shall be our sport then? 30

CELIA Let us sit and mock the good huswife
Fortune from her wheel, that her gifts may henceforth
be bestow'd equally.

ROSALIND I would we could do so; for her benefits
are mightily misplac'd, and the bountiful blind 35
woman doth most mistake in her gifts to women.

CELIA 'Tis true, for those that she makes fair she
scarce makes honest, and those that she makes honest
she makes very ill-favoredly.

ROSALIND Nay, now thou goest from Fortune's office 40
to Nature's. Fortune reigns in gifts of the world,
not in the lineaments of Nature.

---

**11. so:** provided that. **14. righteously temper'd:** rightly compounded.
**15. estate:** state, circumstances. **20. perforce:** by force. **25. sports:** amusements.
**28. safety:** safeguard. **pure:** innocent. **29. come off:** escape. **31. huswife:**
housewife, manager of household affairs. The conventional image of Fortune with
her wheel is playfully altered (by the adjective *good*) to a domestic picture of an
industrious matron at her spinning wheel. Cf. *the false huswife Fortune* in *Antony and
Cleopatra,* IV.xv.44, where *huswife* = hussy. **38. honest:** chaste. **39. ill-favoredly:**
ugly. **40. office:** function. **41. gifts . . . world:** i.e. well, power, and the like, as
contrasted with beauty and intelligence, the gifts of Nature. This distinction was
an Elizabethan commonplace. **42. s.d. Touchstone.** The audience does not learn
the Clown's name until II.iv.19.

*Enter Clown* [TOUCHSTONE].

CELIA  No; when Nature hath made a fair creature,
　　may she not by Fortune fall into the fire?
　　Though Nature hath given us wit to flout at　　　　　45
　　Fortune, hath not Fortune sent in this fool to cut off
　　the argument?
ROSALIND  Indeed there is Fortune too hard for Nature,
　　when Fortune makes Nature's natural the cutter-off
　　of Nature's wit.　　　　　　　　　　　　　　　50
CELIA  Peradventure this is not Fortune's work
　　neither, but Nature's, who perceiveth our natural
　　wits too dull to reason of such goddesses, [and] hath
　　sent this natural for our whetstone; for always the
　　dullness of the fool is the whetstone of the wits.　　55
　　How now, wit, whither wander you?
TOUCHSTONE  Mistress, you must come away to your
　　father.
CELIA  Were you made the messenger?
TOUCHSTONE  No, by mine honor, but I was bid to　　60
　　come for you.
ROSALIND  Where learn'd you that oath, fool?
TOUCHSTONE  Of a certain knight, that swore by his
　　honor they were good pancakes, and swore by his
　　honor the mustard was naught. Now I'll stand to it,　　65
　　the pancakes were naught, and the mustard was good,
　　and yet was not the knight forsworn.
CELIA  How prove you that, in the great heap of
　　your knowledge?
ROSALIND  Ay, marry, now unmuzzle your wisdom.　　70
TOUCHSTONE  Stand you both forth now. Stroke your
　　chins, and swear by your beards that I am a
　　knave.
CELIA  By our beards (if we had them) thou art.
TOUCHSTONE  By my knavery (if I had it) then I were.　　75
　　But if you swear by that that is not, you are not
　　forsworn. No more was this knight, swearing by

---

**45. flout:** mock, jeer.　**47. argument:** discussion, witty exchange.　**49. natural:**
idiot, simpleton.　**56. wit . . . you.** Celia turns to her purpose an expression
ordinarily addressed to one who was talking too much or not to the point, or
giving other such evidence that his wits were deserting him. For another example
see IV.i.166, "Wit, whither wilt?" (i.e. whither wilt thou go?).　**65. naught:** bad.
**67. forsworn:** perjured.

his honor, for he never had any; or if he had, he
had sworn it away before ever he saw those pancakes
or that mustard.                                                      80
CELIA  Prithee, who is't that thou mean'st?
TOUCHSTONE  One that old Frederick, your father, loves.
[CELIA]  My father's love is enough to honor him
    enough. Speak no more of him, you'll be whipt for
    taxation one of these days.                                       85
TOUCHSTONE  The more pity that fools may not speak
    wisely what wise men do foolishly.
CELIA  By my troth, thou sayest true; for since the
    little wit that fools have was silenc'd, the little
    foolery that wise men have makes a great show.                    90
    Here comes Monsieur [Le] Beau.

*Enter* LE BEAU.

ROSALIND  With his mouth full of news.
CELIA  Which he will put on us, as pigeons feed
    their young.
ROSALIND  Then shall we be news-cramm'd.                              95
CELIA  All the better; we shall be the more marketable.
    *Bon jour,* Monsieur Le Beau. What's the
    news?
LE BEAU  Fair princess, you have lost much good
    sport.                                                            100
CELIA  Sport! of what color?
LE BEAU  What color, madam? How shall I answer
    you?
ROSALIND  As wit and fortune will.
TOUCHSTONE  Or as the Destinies decrees.                              105
CELIA  Well said—that was laid on with a trowel.
TOUCHSTONE  Nay, if I keep not my rank—
ROSALIND  Thou losest thy old smell.
LE BEAU  You amaze me, ladies. I would have
    told you of good wrestling, which you have lost                   110
    the sight of.
ROSALIND  Yet tell us the manner of the wrestling.

---

**85. taxation:** censure, slander.  **88. troth:** faith.  **93. put:** force.  **96–97. more
marketable.** As a fowl fattened by forced feeding would be.  **101. color:**
sort.  **106. with a trowel.** Deliberately ambiguous: (1) with telling force; (2)
unsubtly. Touchstone blandly ignores the second possibility.  **107. rank:** i.e. status as
a witty jester. Rosalind puns on the sense "bad-smelling."  **109. amaze:** bewilder.

LE BEAU  I will tell you the beginning; and if it
    please your ladyships, you may see the end, for
    the best is yet to do, and here where you are, they        115
    are coming to perform it.
CELIA  Well, the beginning, that is dead and buried.
LE BEAU  There comes an old man and his three
    sons—
CELIA  I could match this beginning with an old tale.        120
LE BEAU  Three proper young men, of excellent
    growth and presence.
ROSALIND  With bills on their necks, "Be it known unto
    all men by these presents."
LE BEAU  The eldest of the three wrastled with        125
    Charles, the Duke's wrastler, which Charles in a
    moment threw him, and broke three of his ribs,
    that there is little hope of life in him. So he serv'd
    the second, and so the third. Yonder they lie, the
    poor old man, their father, making such pitiful dole        130
    over them that all the beholders take his part with
    weeping.
ROSALIND  Alas!
TOUCHSTONE  But what is the sport, monsieur, that the
    ladies have lost?        135
LE BEAU  Why, this that I speak of.
TOUCHSTONE  Thus men may grow wiser every day.
    It is the first time that ever I heard breaking of ribs
    was sport for ladies.
CELIA  Or I, I promise thee.        140
ROSALIND  But is there any else longs to see this broken
    music in his sides? Is there yet another dotes upon
    rib-breaking? Shall we see this wrastling, cousin?
LE BEAU  You must if you stay here, for here is
    the place appointed for the wrastling, and they are        145
    ready to perform it.
CELIA  Yonder sure they are coming. Let us now
    stay and see it.

---

**115. to do:** to be done.    **120. I . . . tale:** i.e. that isn't a very original beginning. The motif of the father with three sons is common in folktales.    **121. proper:** handsome.    **123. bills:** placards.    **124. these presents:** this present document (with obvious pun on *presence*).    **128. that:** so that.    **130. dole:** lamentation.    **141–42. broken music:** i.e. noisy breaking of ribs. Rosalind twists to her own purposes a term used of music arranged for instruments of more than one kind.    **148. s.d. Flourish:** trumpet fanfare (announcing an important personage).

*Flourish. Enter* DUKE [FREDERICK], LORDS, ORLANDO,
CHARLES, *and* ATTENDANTS.

DUKE FREDERICK  Come on. Since the youth will not be
  entreated, his own peril on his forwardness.                    150
ROSALIND  Is yonder the man?
LE BEAU  Even he, madam.
CELIA  Alas, he is too young! yet he looks
  successfully.
DUKE FREDERICK  How now, daughter and cousin? are you            155
  crept hither to see the wrastling?
ROSALIND  Ay, my liege, so please you give us leave.
DUKE FREDERICK  You will take little delight in it, I can
  tell you, there is such odds in the man. In pity of
  the challenger's youth I would fain dissuade                    160
  him, but he will not be entreated. Speak to him,
  ladies, see if you can move him.
CELIA  Call him hither, good Monsieur Le Beau.
DUKE FREDERICK  Do so; I'll not be by.
LE BEAU  Monsieur the challenger, the princess                   165
  calls for you.
ORLANDO  I attend them with all respect and duty.
ROSALIND  Young man, have you challeng'd Charles
  the wrastler?
ORLANDO  No, fair princess; he is the general challenger.        170
  I come but in, as others do, to try with him
  the strength of my youth.
CELIA  Young gentleman, your spirits are too bold
  for your years. You have seen cruel proof of this
  man's strength. If you saw yourself with your eyes,            175
  or knew yourself with your judgment, the
  fear of your adventure would counsel you to a more
  equal enterprise. We pray you for your own sake
  to embrace your own safety, and give over this attempt.
ROSALIND  Do, young sir, your reputation shall                   180
  not therefore be mispris'd. We will make it our suit
  to the Duke that the wrastling might not go forward.

---

**150. entreated:** persuaded (to desist). **his own . . . forwardness:** i.e. let him
assume the risk for his own rashness.    **151. yonder.** A demonstrative pronoun,
not an adverb.    **153–54. successfully:** like a winner.    **157. liege:** sovereign.
**159. odds:** disparity, i.e. superiority. **the man:** i.e. Charles.    **160. fain:** gladly.
**175–76. If . . . judgment:** i.e. if you used your powers of observation and your
judgment on yourself.    **177. fear:** danger. **your adventure:** your venture, the risk
you are taking.    **178. equal:** commensurate with your powers.    **181. therefore:**
on that account. **mispris'd:** despised.

ORLANDO  I beseech you, punish me not with your hard
thoughts, wherein I confess me much guilty to deny
so fair and excellent ladies any thing. But let your                185
fair eyes and gentle wishes go with me to my
trial; wherein if I be foil'd, there is but one sham'd
that was never gracious; if kill'd, but one dead that
is willing to be so. I shall do my friends no wrong,
for I have none to lament me; the world no injury,                 190
for in it I have nothing. Only in the world I fill up a
place, which may be better supplied when I have
made it empty.

ROSALIND  The little strength that I have, I would it
were with you.                                                     195

CELIA  And mine, to eke out hers.

ROSALIND  Fare you well; pray heaven I be deceiv'd
in you!

CELIA  Your heart's desires be with you!

CHARLES  Come, where is this young gallant that is so           200
desirous to lie with his mother earth?

ORLANDO  Ready, sir, but his will hath in it a more
modest working.

DUKE FREDERICK  You shall try but one fall.

CHARLES  No, I warrant your Grace, you shall not               205
entreat him to a second, that have so mightily persuaded
him from a first.

ORLANDO  You mean to mock me after; you should not
have mock'd me before. But come your ways.

ROSALIND  Now Hercules be thy speed, young man!              210

CELIA  I would I were invisible, to catch the strong
fellow by the leg.          *Wrastle.*

ROSALIND  O excellent young man!

CELIA  If I had a thunderbolt in mine eye, I can tell
who should down.          [*Charles is thrown.*] *Shout.* 215

DUKE FREDERICK  No more, no more.

ORLANDO  Yes, I beseech your Grace, I am not yet
well breath'd.

---

**183–84. punish . . . thoughts:** don't think ill of me if I refuse to withdraw.
**184. wherein:** with reference to which.   **188. gracious:** in favor, esteemed.
**196. eke out:** supplement.   **197–98. deceiv'd in you:** i.e. mistaken about your
chances.   **203. modest working:** decorous operation (Orlando is playing on
the sexual implications of line 201).   **209. come your ways:** come along and
begin.   **210. be thy speed:** aid you, give you success.   **218. well breath'd:** i.e.
warmed up.

DUKE FREDERICK  How dost thou, Charles?

LE BEAU  He cannot speak, my lord.                            220

DUKE FREDERICK  Bear him away. What is thy name, young man?

ORLANDO  Orlando, my liege, the youngest son of Sir
  Rowland de Boys.

DUKE FREDERICK  I would thou hadst been son to some man else:
  The world esteem'd thy father honorable,                   225
  But I did find him still mine enemy.
  Thou shouldst have better pleas'd me with this deed
  Hadst thou descended from another house.
  But fare thee well, thou art a gallant youth.
  I would thou hadst told me of another father.              230
                    *Exit Duke [with Train and Le Beau].*

CELIA  Were I my father, coz, would I do this?

ORLANDO  I am more proud to be Sir Rowland's son,
  His youngest son, and would not change that calling
  To be adopted heir to Frederick.

ROSALIND  My father lov'd Sir Rowland as his soul,           235
  And all the world was of my father's mind.
  Had I before known this young man his son,
  I should have given him tears unto entreaties,
  Ere he should thus have ventur'd.

CELIA                           Gentle cousin,
  Let us go thank him, and encourage him.                    240
  My father's rough and envious disposition
  Sticks me at heart. Sir, you have well deserv'd.
  If you do keep your promises in love
  But justly as you have exceeded all promise,
  Your mistress shall be happy.

ROSALIND                        Gentleman,                   245
                    *[Giving him a chain from her neck.]*
  Wear this for me: one out of suits with Fortune,
  That could give more, but that her hand lacks means.
  Shall we go, coz?

CELIA                 Ay. Fare you well, fair gentleman.

ORLANDO  Can I not say, I thank you? My better parts

---

**226. still:** ever, always.  **231. do this:** behave thus.  **233. calling:** name.  **238. unto:** in addition to.  **241. envious:** malicious.  **242. Sticks:** stabs.  **244. But justly as:** to the same degree in which. **promise:** expectation (of success in the wrestling match).  **246. one . . . Fortune:** one whose petitions to Fortune are rejected (?) or one who no longer wears the livery of Fortune, i.e. one cast out of Fortune's favor (?).  **247. could:** would wish to.

Are all thrown down, and that which here stands up          250
　Is but a quintain, a mere liveless block.
ROSALIND  He calls us back. My pride fell with my fortunes,
　I'll ask him what he would. Did you call, sir?
　Sir, you have wrastled well, and overthrown
　More than your enemies.
CELIA                                Will you go, coz?          255
ROSALIND  Have with you.—Fare you well.

                                    *Exit [with Celia].*
ORLANDO  What passion hangs these weights upon my tongue?
　I cannot speak to her, yet she urg'd conference.

                    *Enter* LE BEAU.

O poor Orlando! thou art overthrown,
　Or Charles, or something weaker, masters thee.          260
LE BEAU  Good sir, I do in friendship counsel you
　To leave this place. Albeit you have deserv'd
　High commendation, true applause, and love,
　Yet such is now the Duke's condition
　That he misconsters all that you have done.          265
　The Duke is humorous—what he is indeed
　More suits you to conceive than I to speak of.
ORLANDO  I thank you, sir; and pray you tell me this:
　Which of the two was daughter of the Duke,
　That here was at the wrastling?          270
LE BEAU  Neither his daughter, if we judge by manners,
　But yet indeed the [smaller] is his daughter.
　The other is daughter to the banish'd Duke,
　And here detain'd by her usurping uncle
　To keep his daughter company, whose loves          275
　Are dearer than the natural bond of sisters.
　But I can tell you that of late this Duke
　Hath ta'en displeasure 'gainst his gentle niece,
　Grounded upon no other argument
　But that the people praise her for her virtues,          280
　And pity her for her good father's sake;
　And on my life his malice 'gainst the lady

---

**251. quintain:** wooden figure used as a target in tilting. **liveless:** lifeless.
**256. Have with you:** let us go together. **257. passion:** violent emotion.
**258. urg'd conference:** invited conversation. **260. Or:** either. **264. condition:**
state of mind. **265. misconsters:** misconstrues. **266. humorous:** temperamental, given to shifting moods or notions. **279. argument:** reason, grounds.

Pl. 1. Clad in dark armor that makes them seem only half human, Duke
Frederick's attendants form a menacing tableau in Kenneth Branagh's 2006 film.
Duke Frederick himself (Brian Blessed) is also a threatening figure, and Celia
(Romola Garai) to his left and Rosalind (Bryce Dallas Howard) to his right
appear potentially vulnerable in comparison.

Pl. 2. The marriage of Rosalind (Bryce Dallas Howard) and Orlando (Adrian
Lester), with Touchstone (Alfred Molina) in the background. Branagh's 2006
film version of the play exemplifies recent experiments with colorblind casting
that have engaged both cinematic and theatrical directors.

Pl. 3. Branagh's cinematic interpretation (2006) evokes an lushly idyllic Forest of Arden. Her bouquet links Celia (Romola Garai) to the beauty and peace of the natural world.

Pl. 4. The huge flowers in Gregory Doran's Royal Shakespeare Company production (2000) create an Arden as idyllic as but far more stylized than Branagh's (Color Plate 3) These flowers contrast with the suggestions of winter in Arden earlier in the play and with the monochromatic court. Anthony Howell plays Orlando and Alexandra Gilbreath Rosalind.

Will suddenly break forth. Sir, fare you well.
Hereafter, in a better world than this,
I shall desire more love and knowledge of you.                    285
ORLANDO  I rest much bounden to you; fare you well.

*[Exit Le Beau.]*

Thus must I from the smoke into the smother,
From tyrant Duke into a tyrant brother.
But heavenly Rosalind!                                           *Exit.*


## SCENE 3

*Enter* CELIA *and* ROSALIND.

CELIA  Why, cousin, why, Rosalind! Cupid have
    mercy, not a word?
ROSALIND  Not one to throw at a dog.
CELIA  No, thy words are too precious to be cast
    away upon curs, throw some of them at me. Come            5
    lame me with reasons.
ROSALIND  Then there were two cousins laid up, when
    the one should be lam'd with reasons, and the other
    mad without any.
CELIA  But is all this for your father?                          10
ROSALIND  No, some of it is for my child's father. O
    how full of briers is this working-day world!
CELIA  They are but burs, cousin, thrown upon
    thee in holiday foolery; if we walk in the trodden
    paths, our very petticoats will catch them.                 15
ROSALIND  I could shake them off my coat; these
    burs are in my heart.
CELIA  Hem them away.
ROSALIND  I would try, if I could cry "hem" and have
    him.                                                        20
CELIA  Come, come, wrastle with thy affections.

---

**284. in . . . world:** i.e. when circumstances are more favorable.  **286. bounden:** indebted.  **287. from . . . smother:** i.e. out of the frying pan into the fire. 1.3. Location: The Duke's palace.  **6. reasons:** explanations (of your silence). **9. mad:** crazed.★  **11. my child's father:** i.e. Orlando. In her love melancholy Rosalind is dreaming of the future.  **14. holiday foolery.** In retort to *working-day world,* line 12 (Wilson).  **18. Hem them away:** i.e. cough them away, like any other choking obstruction in the throat or chest.  **19–20. cry . . . him:** win him merely by clearing my throat (with a play on *hem* and *him*).

ROSALIND  O, they take the part of a better wrastler
than myself!

CELIA  O, a good wish upon you! you will try in
time, in despite of a fall. But turning these                    25
jests out of service, let us talk in good earnest. Is
it possible, on such a sudden, you should fall into so
strong a liking with old Sir Rowland's youngest son?

ROSALIND  The Duke my father lov'd his father
dearly.                                                          30

CELIA  Doth it therefore ensue that you should
love his son dearly? By this kind of chase, I should
hate him, for my father hated his father dearly;
yet I hate not Orlando.

ROSALIND  No, faith, hate him not, for my sake.                  35

CELIA  Why should I not? Doth he not deserve
well?

*Enter* DUKE [FREDERICK] *with* LORDS.

ROSALIND  Let me love him for that, and do you love
him because I do. Look, here comes the Duke.

CELIA  With his eyes full of anger.                              40

DUKE FREDERICK  Mistress, dispatch you with your safest
haste,
And get you from our court.

ROSALIND                         Me, uncle?

DUKE FREDERICK                                    You, cousin.
Within these ten days if that thou beest found
So near our public court as twenty miles,
Thou diest for it.

ROSALIND              I do beseech your Grace                    45
Let me the knowledge of my fault bear with me:
If with myself I hold intelligence,
Or have acquaintance with mine own desires;
If that I do not dream, or be not frantic
(As I do trust I am not), then, dear uncle,                      50

---

**22. take . . . of:** (1) side with; (2) require the agency of.   **25. in despite of:** notwithstanding the danger of.   **25–26. turning . . . service:** dismissing this levity.
**31. therefore ensue:** follow as a consequence.   **32. By . . . chase:** by pursuing this
course of argument.   **33. dearly:** intensely.   **36–37. deserve well:** i.e. well deserve
to be hated (but Rosalind pretends to misunderstand).   **41. your safest haste:** i.e.
utmost speed, since in speed lies your safety.   **42. cousin.** Used of aunts, uncles,
nieces, and nephews, as well as cousins in the modern sense.   **47. hold intelligence:** am in communication.   **49. If that:** if. **frantic:** raving mad.

Never so much as in a thought unborn
Did I offend your Highness.

DUKE FREDERICK                    Thus do all traitors:
If their purgation did consist in words,
They are as innocent as grace itself.
Let it suffice thee that I trust thee not.                              55

ROSALIND Yet your mistrust cannot make me a traitor.
Tell me whereon the [likelihood] depends.

DUKE FREDERICK Thou art thy father's daughter, there's enough.

ROSALIND So was I when your Highness took his dukedom,
So was I when your Highness banish'd him.                        60
Treason is not inherited, my lord,
Or if we did derive it from our friends,
What's that to me? my father was no traitor.
Then, good my liege, mistake me not so much
To think my poverty is treacherous.                                   65

CELIA Dear sovereign, hear me speak.

DUKE FREDERICK Ay, Celia, we stay'd her for your sake,
Else had she with her father rang'd along.

CELIA I did not then entreat to have her stay,
It was your pleasure and your own remorse.                       70
I was too young that time to value her,
But now I know her. If she be a traitor,
Why, so am I. We still have slept together,
Rose at an instant, learn'd, play'd, eat together,
and whereso'er we went, like Juno's swans,                        75
Still we went coupled and inseparable.

DUKE FREDERICK She is too subtile for thee, and her smoothness,
Her very silence, and her patience
Speak to the people, and they pity her.
Thou art a fool; she robs thee of thy name,                        80
And thou wilt show more bright and seem more virtuous
When she is gone. Then open not thy lips:
Firm and irrevocable is my doom

---

**53. purgation:** exoneration.    **54. grace:** virtue.    **57. likelihood:** supposition that it is
likely.    **62. friends:** relatives.    **64. good my liege:** my good lord duke (*liege* = sovereign).
**65. To:** as to.    **67. stay'd her:** kept her here.    **68. rang'd:** roamed.    **70. remorse:**
pity, compassion (prompted by conscience).    **71. that time:** at that time. The line
suggests that some considerable time has passed since Duke Senior was banished.
This is not the impression conveyed by I.i, but cf. II.i.2.    **73. still:** always.    **74. at an
instant:** at the same moment.    **75. Juno's swans.** Swans were associated with Venus,
not Juno.    **77. subtile:** subtle, cunning.    **80. name:** i.e. due praise.    **81. show:**
appear. **virtuous:** filled with admirable qualities.    **83. doom:** judgment, sentence.

Which I have pass'd upon her; she is banish'd.

CELIA Pronounce that sentence then on me, my liege,   85
   I cannot live out of her company.

DUKE FREDERICK You are a fool. You, niece, provide yourself;
   If you outstay the time, upon mine honor,
   And in the greatness of my word, you die.

                     *Exit Duke [with Lords].*

CELIA O my poor Rosalind, whither wilt thou go?   90
   Wilt thou change fathers? I will give thee mine.
   I charge thee be not thou more griev'd than I am.

ROSALIND I have more cause.

CELIA              Thou hast not, cousin,
   Prithee be cheerful. Know'st thou not the Duke
   Hath banish'd me, his daughter?

ROSALIND               That he hath not.   95

CELIA No, hath not? Rosalind lacks then the love
   Which teacheth thee that thou and I am one.
   Shall we be sund'red? shall we part, sweet girl?
   No, let my father seek another heir.
   Therefore devise with me how we may fly,   100
   Whither to go, and what to bear with us,
   And do not seek to take your change upon you,
   To bear your griefs yourself, and leave me out;
   For by this heaven, now at our sorrows pale,
   Say what thou canst, I'll go along with thee.   105

ROSALIND Why, whither shall we go?

CELIA To seek my uncle in the forest of Arden.

ROSALIND Alas, what danger will it be to us,
   Maids as we are, to travel forth so far!
   Beauty provoketh thieves sooner than gold.   110

CELIA I'll put myself in poor and mean attire,
   And with a kind of umber smirch my face;
   The like do you. So shall we pass along
   And never stir assailants.

ROSALIND              Were it not better,
   Because that I am more than common tall,   115
   That I did suit me all points like a man?

---

**87. provide yourself:** make your preparations.   **89. in . . . word:** upon my word as duke.   **91. change:** exchange.   **102. change:** i.e. of fortune.   **110. provoketh:** arouses.   **111. mean:** lowly.   **112. umber:** brown pigment.   **116. suit:** dress. **all points:** in every respect.

A gallant curtle-axe upon my thigh,
A boar-spear in my hand, and—in my heart
Lie there what hidden woman's fear there will—
We'll have a swashing and a martial outside,     120
As many other mannish cowards have
That do outface it with their semblances.

CELIA What shall I call thee when thou art a man?

ROSALIND I'll have no worse a name than Jove's own page,
And therefore look you call me Ganymed.     125
But what will you [be] call'd?

CELIA Something that hath a reference to my state:
No longer Celia, but Aliena.

ROSALIND But, cousin, what if we assay'd to steal
The clownish fool out of your father's court?     130
Would he not be a comfort to our travel?

CELIA He'll go along o'er the wide world with me;
Leave me alone to woo him. Let's away,
And get our jewels and our wealth together,
Devise the fittest time and safest way     135
To hide us from pursuit that will be made
After my flight. Now go [we in] content
To liberty, and not to banishment.     *Exeunt.*

117. **curtle-axe:** short sword. 120. **swashing:** blustering, swashbuckling. 121. **mannish:** man-like (often used contemptuously for a woman or someone effeminate).★ 122. **outface it:** boldly carry off a situation. **semblances:** (mere) appearances. 125. **Ganymed:** Ganymede, kidnapped by the king of the gods (Jove or Jupiter) and became his cupbearer and, in some versions, lover.★ 128. **Aliena:** the estranged one (Latin). 129. **assay'd:** attempted. 133. **woo:** coax, persuade. 137. **content:** contentment.

# Act 2

## SCENE I

*Enter* DUKE SENIOR, AMIENS, *and two or three* LORDS, *like foresters.*

DUKE SENIOR  Now, my co-mates and brothers in exile,
    Hath not old custom made this life more sweet
    Than that of painted pomp? Are not these woods
    More free from peril than the envious court?
    Here feel we not the penalty of Adam,               5
    The seasons' difference, as the icy fang
    And churlish chiding of the winter's wind,
    Which when it bites and blows upon my body
    Even till I shrink with cold, I smile and say,
    "This is no flattery: these are counsellors        10
    That feelingly persuade me what I am."
    Sweet are the uses of adversity,
    Which like the toad, ugly and venomous,
    Wears yet a precious jewel in his head;
    And this our life, exempt from public haunt,     15
    Finds tongues in trees, books in the running brooks,
    Sermons in stones, and good in every thing.
AMIENS  I would not change it. Happy is your Grace,
    That can translate the stubbornness of fortune
    Into so quiet and so sweet a style.             20
DUKE SENIOR  Come, shall we go and kill us venison?
    And yet it irks me the poor dappled fools,

---

2.1. Location: The forest of Arden.   o.s.d. **like:** in the guise of.   **2. old:** long-continued.   **3. painted:** artificial, specious.   **4. envious:** malicious, spiteful. **5. feel we not:** i.e. we do not suffer seriously from. Many editors emend *not* to *but* (after Theobald).   **5–6. penalty . . . difference:** banishment from Eden, where it was perpetual spring.★   **6. as:** such as.   **7. churlish:** rough, rude.   **11. feelingly:** through my senses.   **12. uses:** benefits.   **13–14. toad . . . head.** A widespread belief. The jewel was supposed to have great curative power against disease. **14. his:** its.   **15. exempt:** cut off. **public haunt:** the society of men.   **19. translate:** transform.   **22. irks:** distresses. **fools:** innocents (expressive of affectionate pity).

Being native burghers of this desert city,
Should in their own confines with forked heads
Have their round haunches gor'd.
1. LORD                  Indeed, my lord,      25
The melancholy Jaques grieves at that,
And in that kind swears you do more usurp
Than doth your brother that hath banish'd you.
To-day my Lord of Amiens and myself
Did steal behind him as he lay along      30
Under an oak, whose antique root peeps out
Upon the brook that brawls along this wood,
To the which place a poor sequest'red stag,
That from the hunter's aim had ta'en a hurt,
Did come to languish; and indeed, my lord,      35
The wretched animal heav'd forth such groans
That their discharge did stretch his leathern coat
Almost to bursting, and the big round tears
Cours'd one another down his innocent nose
In piteous chase; and thus the hairy fool,      40
Much marked of the melancholy Jaques,
Stood on th' extremest verge of the swift brook,
Augmenting it with tears.
DUKE SENIOR            But what said Jaques?
Did he not moralize this spectacle?
1. LORD   O yes, into a thousand similes.      45
First, for his weeping into the needless stream:
"Poor deer," quoth he, "thou mak'st a testament
As worldlings do, giving thy sum of more
To that which had too [much]." Then being there alone,
Left and abandoned of his velvet [friends]:      50
"'Tis right," quoth he, "thus misery doth part

---

**23. desert:** uninhabited by men, "unpeopled" (3.2.126). **24. confines:** territories. **forked heads:** two-pronged hunting arrows; antlers, which often symbolized cuckoldry.★ **26. Jaques.** Pronounced as a dissyllable throughout. **30. along:** stretched out. **31. antique:** ancient. **32. brawls:** noisily courses. **33. sequest'red:** separated from the herd. **39. Cours'd:** pursued (a hunting metaphor, picked up by *chase,* line 40). **41. marked of:** observed by. **42. extremest verge:** very edge of the bank. **44. moralize:** interpret morally or symbolically. **46. needless:** having no need (of additional water). **48. worldlings:** mortals; worldly men. **sum of more:** additional amount. **50. of:** by. **velvet:** i.e. in flourishing condition. There is perhaps an allusion to the so-called "velvet" on the antlers of deer during the stage of rapid growth, as well as to the rich clothing of "worldlings." **51. 'Tis right:** just so. **part:** depart from.

The flux of company." Anon a careless herd,
Full of the pasture, jumps along by him
And never stays to greet him. "Ay," quoth Jaques,
"Sweep on, you fat and greasy citizens,                          55
'Tis just the fashion. Wherefore do you look
Upon that poor and broken bankrupt there?"
Thus most invectively he pierceth through
The body of [the] country, city, court,
Yea, and of this our life, swearing that we                      60
Are mere usurpers, tyrants, and what's worse,
To fright the animals and to kill them up
In their assign'd and native dwelling-place.

DUKE SENIOR  And did you leave him in this contemplation?
2. LORD  We did, my lord, weeping and commenting              65
Upon the sobbing deer.

DUKE SENIOR                    Show me the place.
I love to cope him in these sullen fits,
For then he's full of matter.

1. LORD  I'll bring you to him straight.              *Exeunt.*


SCENE 2

*Enter* DUKE [FREDERICK] *with* LORDS.

DUKE FREDERICK  Can it be possible that no man saw them?
It cannot be. Some villains of my court
Are of consent and sufferance in this.

1. LORD  I cannot hear of any that did see her.
The ladies, her attendants of her chamber,                        5
Saw her a-bed, and in the morning early
They found the bed untreasur'd of their mistress.

2. LORD  My lord, the roynish clown, at whom so oft
Your Grace was wont to laugh, is also missing.
Hisperia, the princess' gentlewoman,                             10
Confesses that she secretly o'erheard
Your daughter and her cousin much commend

---

**52. flux:** continuous stream. **Anon:** just then, presently. **careless:** carefree.   **56. just:** exactly.   **57. broken:** ruined.   **58. invectively:** in abusive language.   **61. mere:** out-and-out. **what's worse:** whatever may be worse.   **62. up:** off (intensive).   **67. cope:** deal with, converse with. **sullen:** melancholy.   **68. matter:** substance, good sense.   **69. straight:** straightway. 2.2. Location: The Duke's palace.   **3. Are . . . in:** i.e. have connived at.   **8. roynish:** scurvy, paltry.

The parts and graces of the wrastler
That did but lately foil the sinowy Charles,
And she believes, where ever they are gone,                    15
That youth is surely in their company.
DUKE FREDERICK  Send to his brother; fetch that gallant hither.
If he be absent, bring his brother to me;
I'll make him find him. Do this suddenly;
And let not search and inquisition quail                       20
To bring again these foolish runaways.            *Exeunt.*


## SCENE 3

*Enter* ORLANDO *and* ADAM, *[meeting].*

ORLANDO  Who's there?
ADAM  What, my young master? O my gentle master,
O my sweet master, O you memory
Of old Sir Rowland! Why, what make you here?
Why are you virtuous? Why do people love you?                  5
And wherefore are you gentle, strong, and valiant?
Why would you be so fond to overcome
The bonny priser of the humorous Duke?
Your praise is come too swiftly home before you.
Know you not, master, to [some] kind of men                    10
Their graces serve them but as enemies?
No more do yours. Your virtues, gentle master,
Are sanctified and holy traitors to you.
O, what a world is this, when what is comely
Envenoms him that bears it!                                    15
[ORLANDO]  Why, what's the matter?
ADAM                                O unhappy youth,
Come not within these doors! Within this roof
The enemy of all your graces lives.
Your brother—no, no brother, yet the son
(Yet not the son, I will not call him son)                     20
Of him I was about to call his father—
Hath heard your praises, and this night he means

13. **parts and graces:** talents and accomplishments.  14. **sinowy:** sinewy.
19. **suddenly:** quickly.  20. **inquisition:** inquiry. **quail:** slacken.  21. **again:** back.
2.3. Location: Before Oliver's house.  3. **memory:** reminder.  4. **make you:**
are you doing.  5. **virtuous:** full of good qualities.  7. **fond:** foolish. **to:** as to.
8. **bonny priser:** strapping prize-fighter. **humorous:** capricious.  11. **graces:**
virtues.  12. **more:** i.e. better.

To burn the lodging where you use to lie,
And you within it. If he fail of that,
He will have other means to cut you off;                25
I overheard him, and his practices.
This is no place, this house is but a butchery;
Abhor it, fear it, do not enter it.
[ORLANDO] Why, whither, Adam, wouldst thou have me go?
ADAM No matter whither, so you come not here.                30
ORLANDO What, wouldst thou have me go and beg my food?
    Or with a base and boist'rous sword enforce
    A thievish living on the common road?
    This I must do, or know not what to do;
    Yet this I will not do, do how I can.                35
    I rather will subject me to the malice
    Of a diverted blood and bloody brother.
ADAM But do not so. I have five hundred crowns,
    The thrifty hire I sav'd under your father,
    Which I did store to be my foster-nurse,                40
    When service should in my old limbs lie lame,
    And unregarded age in corners thrown.
    Take that, and He that doth the ravens feed,
    Yea, providently caters for the sparrow,
    Be comfort to my age! Here is the gold,                45
    All this I give you, let me be your servant.
    Though I look old, yet I am strong and lusty;
    For in my youth I never did apply
    Hot and rebellious liquors in my blood,
    Nor did not with unbashful forehead woo                50
    The means of weakness and debility;
    Therefore my age is as a lusty winter,
    Frosty, but kindly. Let me go with you,
    I'll do the service of a younger man
    In all your business and necessities.                55
ORLANDO O good old man, how well in thee appears
    The constant service of the antique world,

---

**23. use:** are accustomed.   **26. practices:** treacherous plots.   **27. place:** dwelling place. **butchery:** slaughterhouse.   **32. boist'rous:** violent.   **35. do . . . can:** whatever happens to me.   **37. diverted blood:** disaffected kinship.   **39. thrifty . . . sav'd:** money I thriftily saved from my wages.   **41. When . . . lame:** when my duties as a servant would be performed haltingly because of my aged limbs.   **42. thrown:** be thrown.   **43–44. He . . . sparrow.** Alluding to such Biblical passages as Job 38:41, Luke 12:6, 24.   **47. lusty:** vigorous.   **49. rebellious:** injurious to health.   **53. kindly:** (1) natural; (2) pleasant.   **57. constant:** faithful.

When service sweat for duty, not for meed!
Thou art not for the fashion of these times,
Where none will sweat but for promotion,          60
And having that do choke their service up
Even with the having. It is not so with thee.
But, poor old man, thou prun'st a rotten tree,
That cannot so much as a blossom yield
In lieu of all thy pains and husbandry.          65
But come thy ways, we'll go along together,
And ere we have thy youthful wages spent,
We'll light upon some settled low content.
ADAM  Master, go on, and I will follow thee
To the last gasp, with truth and loyalty.          70
From [seventeen] years till now almost fourscore
Here lived I, but now live here no more.
At seventeen years many their fortunes seek,
But at fourscore it is too late a week;
Yet fortune cannot recompense me better          75
Than to die well, and not my master's debtor.

*Exeunt.*

## SCENE 4

*Enter* ROSALIND *for Ganymed,* CELIA *for Aliena,*
*and Clown, alias* TOUCHSTONE.

ROSALIND  O Jupiter, how [weary] are my spirits!
TOUCHSTONE  I care not for my spirits, if my legs were
not weary.
ROSALIND  I could find in my heart to disgrace my
man's apparel and to cry like a woman; but I          5
must comfort the weaker vessel, as doublet and hose
ought to show itself courageous to petticoat; therefore
courage, good Aliena.
CELIA  I pray you bear with me, I cannot go no
further.          10
TOUCHSTONE  For my part, I had rather bear with you
than bear you. Yet I should bear no cross if I did

**58. sweat:** sweated. **meed:** reward. **65. lieu of:** return for. **68. low content:**
lowly contented state. **74. a week:** i.e. a time. 2.4. Location: The forest of
Arden. **6. weaker vessel:** i.e. woman (see 1 Peter 3:7). **doublet and hose:** jacket
and breeches. **9. cannot go no.** Elizabethan double negative. **12. cross:** (1)
burden; (2) the device stamped on a penny.

bear you, for I think you have no money in your
purse.

ROSALIND  Well, this is the forest of Arden.                         15

TOUCHSTONE  Ay, now am I in Arden, the more fool I.
When I was at home, I was in a better place, but
travellers must be content.

*Enter* CORIN *and* SILVIUS.

ROSALIND  Ay, be so, good Touchstone. Look you,
who comes here, a young man and an old in solemn      20
talk.

CORIN  That is the way to make her scorn you still.

SILVIUS  O Corin, that thou knew'st how I do love her!

CORIN  I partly guess; for I have lov'd ere now.

SILVIUS  No, Corin, being old, thou canst not guess,        25
Though in thy youth thou wast as true a lover
As ever sigh'd upon a midnight pillow.
But if thy love were ever like to mine—
As sure I think did never man love so—
How many actions most ridiculous                               30
Has thou been drawn to by thy fantasy?

CORIN  Into a thousand that I have forgotten.

SILVIUS  O, thou didst then never love so heartily!
If thou rememb'rest not the slightest folly
That ever love did make thee run into,                        35
Thou hast not lov'd;
Or if thou hast not sat as I do now,
Wearing thy hearer in thy mistress' praise,
Thou hast not lov'd;
Or if thou hast not broke from company               40
Abruptly, as my passion now makes me,
Thou hast not lov'd.
O Phebe, Phebe, Phebe!                                      *Exit.*

ROSALIND  Alas, poor shepherd, searching of [thy wound],
I have by hard adventure found mine own.                     45

TOUCHSTONE  And I mine. I remember when I was
in love, I broke my sword upon a stone, and bid him
take that for coming a-night to Jane Smile; and I

---

20. **solemn:** serious.  **31. fantasy:** fanciful love-thoughts.  **38. Wearing:**
wearying.  **44. searching of:** probing.  **45. hard adventure:** ill chance.
**48. a-night:** at night.

remember the kissing of her batler and the cow's
dugs that her pretty chopp'd hands had milk'd;                                    50
and I remember the wooing of a peascod instead of
her, from whom I took two cods, and giving her
them again, said with weeping tears, "Wear these
for my sake." We that are true lovers run into
strange capers; but as all is mortal in nature,                                 55
so is all nature in love mortal in folly.

ROSALIND  Thou speak'st wiser than thou art ware of.

TOUCHSTONE  Nay, I shall ne'er be ware of mine own
wit till I break my shins against it.

ROSALIND  Jove, Jove! this shepherd's passion                                   60
Is much upon my fashion.

TOUCHSTONE  And mine, but it grows something stale
with me.

CELIA  I pray you, one of you question yond man,
If he for gold will give us any food;                                           65
I faint almost to death.

TOUCHSTONE                Holla! you clown!

ROSALIND  Peace, fool, he's not thy kinsman.

CORIN                              Who calls?

TOUCHSTONE  Your betters, sir.

CORIN                    Else are they very wretched.

ROSALIND  Peace, I say. Good even to [you], friend.

CORIN  And to you, gentle sir, and to you all.                                  70

ROSALIND  I prithee, shepherd, if that love or gold
Can in this desert place buy entertainment,
Bring us where we may rest ourselves and feed.
Here's a young maid with travel much oppressed,
And faints for succor.

CORIN                Fair sir, I pity her,                                       75
And wish, for her sake more than for mine own,
My fortunes were more able to relieve her;
But I am shepherd to another man,

49. **batler:** a club for beating clothes while washing them.  50. **chopp'd:**
chapped.  51. **peascod:** pea pod; but here apparently the whole plant. Country
swains thought that peascods presented to and worn by their mistresses brought
good luck in their wooing. There is, Wilson suggests, a bawdy undertone in
the lines as a whole, turning on *peascod* and *codpiece.*  52. **whom, her.** Both
words refer to the pea plant.  55. **mortal:** subject to death.  56. **mortal:** i.e.
humanly faulty.  57. **ware:** aware. Touchstone then quibbles on the sense "wary."
61. **upon:** after.  62. **something:** somewhat.  66. **clown:** country fellow. Rosalind
quibbles on the sense "jester."  68. **wretched:** low in rank and means.  72. **enter-**
**tainment:** accommodation.  75. **faints for succor:** is faint for lack of aid (i.e. food).

And do not shear the fleeces that I graze.
My master is of churlish disposition,                                                80
And little reaks to find the way to heaven
By doing deeds of hospitality.
Besides, his cote, his flocks, and bounds of feed
Are now on sale, and at our sheep-cote now
By reason of his absence there is nothing                                        85
That you will feed on; but what is, come see,
And in my voice most welcome shall you be.
ROSALIND What is he that shall buy his flock and pasture?
CORIN That young swain that you saw here but erewhile,
    That little cares for buying any thing.                                             90
ROSALIND I pray thee, if it stand with honesty,
    Buy thou the cottage, pasture, and the flock,
    And thou shalt have to pay for it of us.
CELIA And we will mend thy wages. I like this place,
    And willingly could waste my time in it.                                        95
CORIN Assuredly the thing is to be sold.
    Go with me; if you like upon report
    The soil, the profit, and this kind of life,
    I will your very faithful feeder be,
    And buy it with your gold right suddenly.                    *Exeunt.* 100


SCENE 5

*Enter* AMIENS, JAQUES, *and others.*

SONG

[AMIENS]        Under the greenwood tree
                Who loves to lie with me,
                And turn his merry note
                Unto the sweet bird's throat,
            Come hither, come hither, come hither!                    5
                    Here shall he see
                    No enemy
                But winter and rough weather.

**79. do . . . graze:** i.e. am not the owner who profits from the shearing of the sheep
I graze.  **80. churlish:** miserly.  **81. reaks:** recks, cares.  **83. cote:** cottage. **bounds
of feed:** areas in which he has grazing rights.  **87. in my voice:** as far as my word
carries weight.  **88. What:** who.  **89. erewhile:** a short time ago.  **91. stand:** be
consonant.  **93. to pay:** i.e. the money to pay.  **94. mend:** increase.  **95. waste:**
spend.  **99. feeder:** servant.  **100. suddenly:** speedily.  2.5. Location: The forest.
**3. turn:** adapt, i.e. attune.

JAQUES  More, more, I prithee more.

AMIENS  It will make you melancholy, Monsieur                    10
Jaques.

JAQUES  I thank it. More, I prithee more. I can
suck melancholy out of a song, as a weasel sucks eggs.
More, I prithee more.

AMIENS  My voice is ragged, I know I cannot                      15
please you.

JAQUES  I do not desire you to please me, I do desire
you to sing. Come, more, another stanzo. Call you
'em stanzos?

AMIENS What you will, Monsieur Jaques.                           20

JAQUES  Nay, I care not for their names, they owe
me nothing. Will you sing?

AMIENS  More at your request than to please myself.

JAQUES  Well then, if ever I thank any man, I'll                 25
thank you; but that they call compliment is like th'
encounter of two dog-apes; and when a man thanks
me heartily, methinks I have given him a penny, and
he renders me the beggarly thanks. Come, sing;
and you that will not, hold your tongues.                        30

AMIENS  Well, I'll end the song. Sirs, cover the
while; the Duke will drink under this tree. He hath
been all this day to look you.

JAQUES  And I have been all this day to avoid him.
He is too disputable for my company. I think               35
of as many matters as he, but I give heaven thanks,
and make no boast of them. Come, warble, come.

SONG                    *All together here.*

Who doth ambition shun,
And loves to live i' th' sun,
Seeking the food he eats,                                        40
And pleas'd with what he gets,
Come hither, come hither, come hither!
Here shall he see
[No enemy
But winter and rough weather].                                  45

**15. ragged:** raspy.  **18. stanzo:** stanza.  **21–22. they . . . nothing.** Debtors signed
their names in the lender's record book.  **26. compliment:** formal courtesy.
**27. dog-apes:** baboons.  **29. beggarly:** i.e. excessive, like those of an effu-
sively grateful beggar.  **31. cover:** set the table.  **31–32. the while:** meanwhile.
**33. look:** look for.  **35. disputable:** fond of argument.  **39. live . . . sun:** i.e. live
a free open-air life.

JAQUES I'll give you a verse to this note, that I made
    yesterday in despite of my invention.
AMIENS And I'll sing it.
[JAQUES] Thus it goes:

> If it do come to pass              50
> That any man turn ass,
> Leaving his wealth and ease
> A stubborn will to please,
> Ducdame, ducdame, ducdame!
>    Here shall he see            55
>    Gross fools as he,
> And if he will come to me.

AMIENS What's that "ducdame"?
JAQUES 'Tis a Greek invocation, to call fools into a
    circle. I'll go sleep, if I can; if I cannot, I'll rail      60
    against all the first-born of Egypt.
AMIENS And I'll go seek the Duke, his banket is prepar'd.     *Exeunt.*

## SCENE 6

*Enter* ORLANDO *and* ADAM.

ADAM Dear master, I can go no further. O, I die
    for food! Here lie I down, and measure out my grave.
    Farewell, kind master.
ORLANDO Why, how now, Adam? no greater heart in
    thee? Live a little, comfort a little, cheer thyself      5

**46. note:** tune.   **47. in . . . invention:** notwithstanding my lack of imagination.
**50–57. If . . . me.** Jaques' stanza serves as a realistic, if cynical, antidote to the out-right romanticism of Amiens' song. Such undercutting of the romantic attitude is an important function of Jaques' role throughout.   **54. Ducdame.** Trisyllabic. Not satisfactorily explained, despite numerous ingenious suggestions, e.g. that it is related to Latin *duc ad me*, "lead (him) to me"; to Welsh *dewch da mi*, "come to me"; or to Gipsy *dukrā mē*, a fortuneteller's cry to attract customers. The last of these is tempt-ingly appropriate for an invitation to a gipsy existence in the forest and would clarify the reference in line 61 to "all the first-born of Egypt," i.e. all highborn persons who have adopted a gipsy life; but there is no evidence that an audience could have recognized any such derivation. *Ducdame* may well be a meaningless invented word; when Jaques tells Amiens that it serves "to call fools into a circle" (lines 59–60), probably part of his meaning is that only fools will draw round to ask what it means.
**57. And if:** if only.   **59. Greek.** This word could be used of any unintelligible utter-ance, or, more specifically, of sharpers' cant.   **61. first-born of Egypt.** See note to line 54. *First-born* would suggest in particular the elder of the two dukes. The phrase itself is a Biblical echo, from the account of the death of all the first-born of Egypt in Exodus 11–12.   **62. banket:** banquet, i.e. light repast of fruit, sweetmeats, and wine.
2.6. Location: The forest.   **5. comfort:** take heart. (So also *be comfortable* in line 9.)

a little. If this uncouth forest yield any thing
savage, I will either be food for it, or bring it for
food to thee. Thy conceit is nearer death than
thy powers. For my sake be comfortable, hold
death a while at the arm's end. I will here be with          10
thee presently, and if I bring thee not something to
eat, I will give thee leave to die; but if thou diest
before I come, thou art a mocker of my labor. Well
said, thou look'st cheerly, and I'll be with thee
quickly. Yet thou liest in the bleak air. Come,             15
I will bear thee to some shelter, and thou shalt not
die for lack of a dinner if there live any thing in this
desert. Cheerly, good Adam!                     *Exeunt.*


### SCENE 7

*[A table set out.] Enter* DUKE SENIOR, [AMIENS,]
*and* LORD[S], *like outlaws.*

DUKE SENIOR  I think he be transform'd into a beast,
  For I can no where find him like a man.
1. LORD  My lord, he is but even now gone hence;
  Here was he merry, hearing of a song.
DUKE SENIOR  If he, compact of jars, grow musical,          5
  We shall have shortly discord in the spheres.
  Go seek him, tell him I would speak with him.

*Enter* JAQUES.

1. LORD  He saves my labor by his own approach.
DUKE SENIOR  Why, how now, monsieur, what a life is
  this,
  That your poor friends must woo your company?      10
  What, you look merrily!
JAQUES  A fool, a fool! I met a fool i' th' forest,
  A motley fool. A miserable world!

---

**6. uncouth:** strange, wild.  **8. conceit:** imagination.  **11. presently:** immediately.  **13–14. Well said:** well done.  **14. cheerly:** cheerful.  2.7. Location: The
forest.  **2. like:** in the form of.  **5. compact of jars:** composed entirely of discords.
**6. discord . . . spheres.** It was thought that a ravishingly beautiful harmony was produced by the movement of the crystal spheres in which, according to the Ptolemaic
system, the planets and stars revolved round the earth. It was inaudible to human ears.
**13. motley:** wearing motley, the parti-colored costume of professional jesters.

As I do live by food, I met a fool,
Who laid him down, and bask'd him in the sun,                    15
And rail'd on Lady Fortune in good terms,
In good set terms, and yet a motley fool.
"Good morrow, fool," quoth I. "No, sir," quoth he,
"Call me not fool till heaven hath sent me fortune."
And then he drew a dial from his poke,                           20
And looking on it, with lack-lustre eye,
Says very wisely, "It is ten a' clock.
Thus we may see," quoth he, "how the world wags.
'Tis but an hour ago since it was nine,
And after one hour more 'twill be eleven,                        25
And so from hour to hour, we ripe and ripe,
And then from hour to hour, we rot and rot;
And thereby hangs a tale." When I did hear
The motley fool thus moral on the time,
My lungs began to crow like chanticleer,                         30
That fools should be so deep contemplative;
And I did laugh sans intermission
An hour by his dial. O noble fool!
A worthy fool! Motley's the only wear.
DUKE SENIOR What fool is this?                                   35
JAQUES O worthy fool! One that hath been a courtier,
And says, if ladies be but young and fair,
They have the gift to know it; and in his brain,
Which is as dry as the remainder biscuit
After a voyage, he hath strange places cramm'd                  40
With observation, the which he vents
In mangled forms. O that I were a fool!
I am ambitious for a motley coat.
DUKE SENIOR Thou shalt have one.
JAQUES                                It is my only suit—
Provided that you weed your better judgments                     45
Of all opinion that grows rank in them
That I am wise. I must have liberty
Withal, as large a charter as the wind,

17. set: forthright, outspoken.    19. Call . . . fortune. An allusion to the proverb
"Fortune favors fools."    20. dial: portable sundial. poke: pocket, pouch.    23. wags:
goes on its way.    29. moral: moralize.    30. crow: i.e. with laughter. chanticleer:
a cock.    31. deep: profoundly.    32. sans: without.    34. wear: costume.    39. dry.
Dryness of the brain was supposedly connected with good memory. remainder
biscuit: stale hardtack.    41. vents: utters.    44. suit: (1) petition; (2) clothing
(cf. line 34).    46. rank: wild.    48. Withal: also. charter: privilege, license.

To blow on whom I please, for so fools have;
And they that are most galled with my folly,                    50
They most must laugh. And why, sir, must they so?
The why is plain as way to parish church:
He that a fool doth very wisely hit
Doth very foolishly, although he smart,
[Not to] seem senseless of the bob; if not,                    55
The wise man's folly is anatomiz'd
Even by the squand'ring glances of the fool.
Invest me in my motley; give me leave
To speak my mind, and I will through and through
Cleanse the foul body of th' infected world,                   60
If they will patiently receive my medicine.
DUKE SENIOR  Fie on thee! I can tell what thou wouldst do.
JAQUES What, for a counter, would I do but good?
DUKE SENIOR  Most mischievous foul sin, in chiding sin:
For thou thyself hast been a libertine,                         65
As sensual as the brutish sting itself,
And all th' embossed sores, and headed evils,
That thou with license of free foot hast caught,
Wouldst thou disgorge into the general world.
JAQUES Why, who cries out on pride                             70
That can therein tax any private party?
Doth it not flow as hugely as the sea,
Till that the weary very means do ebb?
What woman in the city do I name,
When that I say the city-woman bears                           75
The cost of princes on unworthy shoulders?
Who can come in and say that I mean her,
When such a one as she, such is her neighbor?
Or what is he of basest function,

---

**50. galled:** rubbed on a sensitive spot.   **53. He . . . hit:** he that is wittily attacked by a fool.   **54. Doth:** acts, behaves.   **55. senseless of:** insensible to. **bob:** jibe, taunt.   **56. anatomiz'd:** dissected, laid bare.   **57. squand'ring glances:** random hits. **63. counter:** a disk or coin of no value, used in computation. Jaques humorously adapts a betting formula: "I'll wager a counter you can't tell me . . ." **66. sting:** lust.   **67. embossed:** swollen. **headed evils:** sores that have come to a head.   **68. license . . . foot:** i.e. the privilege of living like a libertine (uncontrolled).   **69. general:** whole.   **70. pride:** ostentation and extravagance. **71. tax:** take to task, censure. **private party:** particular individual.   **73. the weary very means:** i.e. the source itself, becoming exhausted (?). Various emendations have been proposed, e.g. *wearer's* for *weary.*   **75. city-woman .. shoulders:** citizen's wife who dresses extravagantly.★   **79. basest function:** lowest office or rank.

That says his bravery is not on my cost,                    80
Thinking that I mean him, but therein suits
His folly to the mettle of my speech?
There then! how then? what then? Let me see wherein
My tongue hath wrong'd him; if it do him right,
Then he hath wrong'd himself. If he be free,              85
Why then my taxing like a wild goose flies,
Unclaim'd of any man. But who [comes] here?

*Enter* ORLANDO [*with his sword drawn*].

ORLANDO  Forbear, and eat no more.
JAQUES                      Why, I have eat none yet.
ORLANDO  Nor shalt not, till necessity be serv'd.
JAQUES  Of what kind should this cock come of?           90
DUKE SENIOR  Art thou thus bolden'd, man, by thy distress?
   Or else a rude despiser of good manners,
   That in civility thou seem'st so empty?
ORLANDO  You touch'd my vein at first. The thorny point
   Of bare distress hath ta'en from me the show         95
   Of smooth civility; yet am I inland bred,
   And know some nurture. But forbear, I say,
   He dies that touches any of this fruit
   Till I and my affairs are answered.
JAQUES  And you will not be answer'd with reason,         100
   I must die.
DUKE SENIOR  What would you have? Your gentleness shall force,
   More than your force move us to gentleness.
ORLANDO  I almost die for food, and let me have it.
DUKE SENIOR  Sit down and feed, and welcome to our table.   105
ORLANDO  Speak you so gently? Pardon me, I pray you.
   I thought that all things had been savage here,
   And therefore put I on the countenance
   Of stern command'ment. But what e'er you are
   That in this desert inaccessible,                     110
   Under the shade of melancholy boughs,

---

**80. bravery:** splendid dress. **on my cost:** at my expense. **81. suits:** (1) dresses;
(2) makes conformable. **82. mettle:** substance, tenor **84. right:** justice.
**85. free:** innocent. **94. vein:** condition, state of mind. **at first:** i.e. in the first
explanation you suggested. **96. smooth:** mild. **inland bred:** i.e. reared in a
centre of civilized behavior, not on the wild or rustic outskirts. **97. nurture:**
education, good training. **99. answered:** satisfied. **100. And:** if. **reason.** With
a pun on *raisin* (then closer in pronunciation to *reason* than now). The fruits on
the table may well have included grapes. **102. force:** press home, urge. **104. for
food:** i.e. for lack of food. **109. command'ment:** command, authority.

Lose and neglect the creeping hours of time;
If ever you have look'd on better days,
If ever been where bells have knoll'd to church,
If ever sate at any good man's feast,      115
If ever from your eyelids wip'd a tear,
And know what 'tis to pity, and be pitied,
Let gentleness my strong enforcement be,
In the which hope I blush, and hide my sword.
DUKE SENIOR True is it that we have seen better days,      120
And have with holy bell been knoll'd to church,
And sat at good men's feasts, and wip'd our eyes
Of drops that sacred pity hath engend'red;
And therefore sit you down in gentleness,
And take upon command what help we have      125
That to your wanting may be minist'red.
ORLANDO Then but forbear your food a little while,
Whiles, like a doe, I go to find my fawn,
And give it food. There is an old poor man,
Who after me hath many a weary step      130
Limp'd in pure love; till he be first suffic'd,
Oppress'd with two weak evils, age and hunger,
I will not touch a bit.
DUKE SENIOR          Go find him out,
And we will nothing waste till you return.
ORLANDO I thank ye, and be blest for your good comfort! [*Exit.*] 135
DUKE SENIOR Thou seest we are not all alone unhappy:
This wide and universal theater
Presents more woeful pageants than the scene
Wherein we play in.
JAQUES          All the world's a stage,
And all the men and women merely players;      140
They have their exits and their entrances,
And one man in his time plays many parts,
His acts being seven ages. At first the infant,
Mewling and puking in the nurse's arms.
Then the whining schoolboy, with his satchel      145
And shining morning face, creeping like snail
Unwillingly to school. And then the lover,

---

**114. knoll'd:** rung. **115. sate:** sat. **118. enforcement:** compulsion. **125. upon command:** at your will. **126. wanting:** need. **132. weak:** enfeebling. **134. waste:** consume. **137. This . . . theater.** Thought to be a reference to the Globe theater, built in 1599, and its motto, *Tòtus mundus agit histrionem* (The whole world plays the actor). **144. Mewling:** crying. **puking:** vomiting.

Sighing like furnace, with a woeful ballad
Made to his mistress' eyebrow. Then a soldier,
Full of strange oaths, and bearded like the pard,                    150
Jealous in honor, sudden, and quick in quarrel,
Seeking the bubble reputation
Even in the cannon's mouth. And then the justice,
In fair round belly with good capon lin'd,
With eyes severe and beard of formal cut,                            155
Full of wise saws and modern instances;
And so he plays his part. The sixt age shifts
Into the lean and slipper'd pantaloon,
With spectacles on nose, and pouch on side,
His youthful hose, well sav'd, a world too wide                     160
For his shrunk shank, and his big manly voice,
Turning again toward childish treble, pipes
And whistles in his sound. Last scene of all,
That ends this strange eventful history,
Is second childishness, and mere oblivion,                          165
Sans teeth, sans eyes, sans taste, sans every thing.

*Enter* ORLANDO *with* ADAM.

DUKE SENIOR  Welcome. Set down your venerable burthen,
  And let him feed.
ORLANDO  I thank you most for him.
ADAM                                So had you need,
  I scarce can speak to thank you for myself.                  170
DUKE SENIOR  Welcome, fall to. I will not trouble you
  As yet to question you about your fortunes.
  Give us some music, and, good cousin, sing.

SONG

[AMIENS]         Blow, blow, thou winter wind,
          Thou art not so unkind                175
            As man's ingratitude;
          Thy tooth is not so keen,
          Because thou art not seen,
            Although thy breath be rude.

**148. Sighing like furnace:** i.e. emitting sighs as a furnace emits smoke.
**150. bearded . . . pard:** with long mustaches like the feelers of the leopard or
panther.   **151. Jealous in honor:** jealously protective of his honor. **sudden:**
rash.   **154. with . . . lin'd.** Perhaps with satiric reference to the bribing of judges
with capons.   **156. saws:** maxims. **modern instances:** trite illustrations.   **157. sixt:**
sixth.   **158. pantaloon:** foolish old man (from the name of a stock character in
Italian comedy).   **163. his:** its.   **165. mere:** utter.   **167. burthen:** burden.

Heigh-ho, sing heigh-ho! unto the green holly,          180
Most friendship is feigning, most loving mere folly.
　　　　　　[Then] heigh-ho, the holly!
　　　　　　This life is most jolly.


　　　　　Freeze, freeze, thou bitter sky,
　　　　　That dost not bite so nigh          185
　　　　　　As benefits forgot;
　　　　　Though thou the waters warp,
　　　　　Thy sting is not so sharp
　　　　　　As friend rememb'red not.
Heigh-ho, sing, etc.          190
DUKE SENIOR  If that you were the good Sir Rowland's son,
As you have whisper'd faithfully you were,
And as mine eye doth his effigies witness
Most truly limn'd and living in your face,
Be truly welcome hither. I am the Duke          195
That lov'd your father. The residue of your fortune,
Go to my cave and tell me. Good old man,
Thou art right welcome as thy [master] is.
Support him by the arm. Give me your hand,
And let me all your fortunes understand.          *Exeunt.* 200

**180. holly.** An emblem of mirth.  **187. warp:** freeze (?) or contort by freez-
ing (?).  **192. faithfully:** with assurances of good faith.  **193. effigies:** likeness,
image.  **194. limn'd:** portrayed.

# Act 3

*Enter* DUKE [FREDERICK], LORDS, *and* OLIVER.

DUKE FREDERICK  Not see him since? Sir, sir, that cannot be.
    But were I not the better part made mercy,
    I should not seek an absent argument
    Of my revenge, thou present. But look to it:
    Find out thy brother, wheresoe'er he is;          5
    Seek him with candle; bring him dead or living
    Within this twelvemonth, or turn thou no more
    To seek a living in our territory.
    Thy lands and all things that thou dost call thine
    Worth seizure do we seize into our hands,       10
    Till thou canst quit thee by thy brother's mouth
    Of what we think against thee.
OLIVER  O that your Highness knew my heart in this!
    I never lov'd my brother in my life.
DUKE FREDERICK  More villain thou. Well, push him out of doors,   15
    And let my officers of such a nature
    Make an extent upon his house and lands.
    Do this expediently, and turn him going.        *Exeunt.*

## SCENE 2

*Enter* ORLANDO *[with a paper].*

ORLANDO  Hang there, my verse, in witness of my love,
    And thou, thrice-crowned queen of night, survey

---

3.1. Location: The Duke's palace. **2. better:** i.e. greater. **made:** made of. **3. argument:** subject. **6. with candle.** An allusion to the parable in Luke 15:8 which describes how a woman who has lost a coin lights a candle and diligently searches the house until she has found it. **7. turn:** return. **11. quit:** acquit. **mouth:** testimony. **15. More villain thou.** The irony of this charge nicely points up the parallel between Oliver and Duke Frederick. **16. of . . . nature:** whose duty it is to see to such matters. **17. extent:** seizure by writ. **18. expediently:** quickly. **turn him going:** get him on his way. 3.2. Location: The forest.

With thy chaste eye, from thy pale sphere above,
Thy huntress' name that my full life doth sway.
O Rosalind, these trees shall be my books,                                5
And in their barks my thoughts I'll character,
That every eye which in this forest looks
Shall see thy virtue witness'd every where.
Run, run, Orlando, carve on every tree
The fair, the chaste, and unexpressive she.                   *Exit.* 10

*Enter* CORIN *and* CLOWN [TOUCHSTONE]

CORIN  And how like you this shepherd's life, Master
    Touchstone?

TOUCHSTONE  Truly, shepherd, in respect of itself, it is
    a good life; but in respect that it is a shepherd's life,
    it is naught. In respect that it is solitary, I like             15
    it very well; but in respect that it is private, it is a
    very vild life. Now in respect it is in the fields, it
    pleaseth me well; but in respect it is not in the court,
    it is tedious. As it is a spare life (look you) it fits my
    humor well; but as there is no more plenty in it,          20
    it goes much against my stomach. Hast any philosophy
    in thee, shepherd?

CORIN  No more but that I know the more one
    sickens the worse at ease he is; and that he that
    wants money, means, and content is without three        25
    good friends; that the property of rain is to wet and
    fire to burn; that good pasture makes fat sheep; and
    that a great cause of the night is lack of the sun; that
    he that hath learn'd no wit by nature, nor art, may
    complain of good breeding, or comes of a very dull       30
    kindred.

TOUCHSTONE  Such a one is a natural philosopher.
    Wast ever in court, shepherd?

**2. thrice-crowned queen:** i.e. the divinity who ruled on earth as Diana, in
the heavens as Cynthia the moon-goddess, and in the underworld as Hecate
or Proserpina.  **4. Thy huntress'.** It was a commonplace to represent Diana's
maiden votaries as her companions in the hunt, of which she was patron.
**6. character:** inscribe. Orlando is making literal Duke Senior's metaphor of
"tongues in trees" (2.1.16); cf. also line 127 below.  **8. virtue:** excellence.
**10. unexpressive:** inexpressible; perhaps also lacking expression.★  **13. in . . .
itself:** considered in and for itself.  **14. in respect that:** with regard to the fact
that, in so far as.  **15. naught:** bad.  **16. private:** lonely.  **17. vild:** vile, wretched.
**20. humor:** fancy.  **21. stomach:** inclination (with play on the sense "appetite").
**29. wit:** knowledge. **art:** study.  **30. complain:** lament the lack.  **32. natural:**
born (with play on the sense "fool").

CORIN  No, truly.

TOUCHSTONE  Then thou art damn'd.  35

CORIN  Nay, I hope.

TOUCHSTONE  Truly, thou art damn'd, like an ill-roasted
  egg, all on one side.

CORIN  For not being at court? Your reason.

TOUCHSTONE  Why, if thou never wast at court, thou  40
  never saw'st good manners; if thou never saw'st
  good manners, then thy manners must be wicked,
  and wickedness is sin, and sin is damnation. Thou
  art in a parlous state, shepherd.

CORIN  Not a whit, Touchstone. Those that are  45
  good manners at the court are as ridiculous in the
  country as the behavior of the country is most
  mockable at the court. You told me you salute
  not at the court but you kiss your hands; that
  courtesy would be uncleanly if courtiers were shepherds.  50

TOUCHSTONE  Instance, briefly; come, instance.

CORIN  Why, we are still handling our ewes, and
  their fells you know are greasy.

TOUCHSTONE  Why, do not your courtier's hands sweat?  55
  And is not the grease of a mutton as wholesome as
  the sweat of a man? Shallow, shallow. A better
  instance, I say; come.

CORIN  Besides, our hands are hard.

TOUCHSTONE  Your lips will feel them the sooner.  60
  Shallow again. A more sounder instance, come.

CORIN  And they are often tarr'd over with the
  surgery of our sheep; and would you have us kiss
  tar? The courtier's hands are perfum'd with civet.

TOUCHSTONE  Most shallow man! thou worm's-meat,  65
  in respect of a good piece of flesh indeed! Learn
  of the wise, and perpend: civet is of a baser birth
  than tar, the very uncleanly flux of a cat. Mend
  the instance, shepherd.

---

**37–38. damn'd . . . side:** ruined, like an egg roasted in the ashes that when opened proves to be done on one side but still raw on the other.  **41. manners:** (1) deportment; (2) morals.  **44. parlous:** perilous.  **49. but you kiss:** without kissing.  **52. Instance:** proof. **briefly:** quickly.  **53. still:** always.  **54. fells:** skins.  **61. more sounder.** Double comparatives were common in Elizabethan usage.  **62. tarr'd over.** Tar was applied to the sores and cuts of sheep.  **64. civet:** perfume derived from the civet cat.  **66. in respect of:** in comparison with.  **67. perpend:** consider.  **68. flux:** secretion. **Mend:** improve.

CORIN You have too courtly a wit for me, I'll rest.                    70
TOUCHSTONE Wilt thou rest damn'd? God help thee,
  shallow man! God make incision in thee, thou art raw.
CORIN Sir, I am a true laborer: I earn that I eat,
  get that I wear, owe no man hate, envy no man's
  happiness, glad of other men's good, content with my      75
  harm, and the greatest of my pride is to see my ewes
  graze and my lambs suck.
TOUCHSTONE That is another simple sin in you, to bring
  the ewes and the rams together, and to offer to get
  your living by the copulation of cattle; to be bawd to a   80
  bell-wether, and to betray a she-lamb of a twelve-
  month to a crooked-pated old cuckoldly ram, out of
  all reasonable match. If thou beest not damn'd
  for this, the devil himself will have no shepherds;
  I cannot see else how thou shouldst scape.                 85
CORIN Here comes young Master Ganymed, my
  new mistress's brother.

          *Enter* ROSALIND *[with a paper, reading].*

ROSALIND "From the east to western Inde,
          No jewel is like Rosalind.
          Her worth, being mounted on the wind,              90
          Through all the world bears Rosalind.
          All the pictures fairest lin'd
          Are but black to Rosalind.
          Let no face be kept in mind
          But the fair of Rosalind."                         95
TOUCHSTONE I'll rhyme you so eight years together,
  dinners and suppers and sleeping-hours excepted.

70. **rest:** stop, argue no further. Touchstone then quibbles on the sense "remain, continue." **72. make incision:** i.e. to let out his folly, as a surgeon let out "bad" blood. **raw:** untutored, simple; with a play on the sense "sore" (hence requiring surgery). **73. that:** what. **75–76. content . . . harm:** patient in my own misfortune. **78. simple:** (1) foolish; (2) unadulterated, out-and-out. **79. offer:** undertake. **82. cuckoldly:** i.e. horned, as cuckolds supposedly were (?) or like one who cuckolds, i.e. lecherous (?). **out of:** beyond the limits of, contrary to. **83. match:** (1) correspondence, likeness; (2) mating. **84. the devil . . . shepherds:** it will be because the devil refuses to have shepherds in hell. **85. scape:** escape. **88. Inde:** Indies. **92. fairest.** There is play on two sense of *fair,* "beautiful" and "blonde." Lines 92–93 say that all other beautiful women are ugly, all other blondes dark-complexioned, in comparison with (*to*) Rosalind. Blonde beauty was the Elizabethan ideal. See Rosalind's disparagement of Phebe's looks in 3.5.46–47. **lin'd:** drawn. **96. together:** without intermission.

It is the right butter-women's rank to market.

ROSALIND Out, fool!

TOUCHSTONE For a taste:                                                      100

    If a hart do lack a hind,

    Let him seek out Rosalind.

    If the cat will after kind,

    So be sure will Rosalind.

    Wint'red garments must be lin'd,                            105

    So must slender Rosalind.

    They that reap must sheaf and bind,

    Then to cart with Rosalind.

    Sweetest nut hath sourest rind,

    Such a nut is Rosalind.                                      110

    He that sweetest rose will find,

    Must find love's prick and Rosalind.

This is the very false gallop of verses; why do you

infect yourself with them?

ROSALIND Peace, you dull fool, I found them on a tree.          115

TOUCHSTONE Truly, the tree yields bad fruit.

ROSALIND I'll graff it with you, and then I shall graff

it with a medlar. Then it will be the earliest

fruit i' th' country; for you'll be rotten ere you be

half ripe, and that's the right virtue of the medlar.          120

TOUCHSTONE You have said; but whether wisely or no,

let the forest judge.

*Enter* CELIA *with a writing.*

ROSALIND Peace,

Here comes my sister reading, stand aside.

CELIA *[Reads.]*

    "Why should this [a] desert be?                             125

    For it is unpeopled? No!

---

**98. the right ... market:** i.e. precisely like dairy-women riding along one behind another at the same pace on their way to market. **100. taste:** sample. **101. hart ... hind:** (1) male deer ... female deer; (2) man ... woman. (The verses are a series of double entendres.) **103. will after kind:** will behave in accordance with its nature (proverbial). **105. Wint'red:** readied for winter use. **108. to cart.** The harvest was transported on farm-carts, but Touchstone is alluding here to the practice of exposing disreputable women to public derision by driving them about the town in carts. **113. very false gallop:** true canter (suggesting effortlessly regular movement, hence a mechanical and monotonous effect). **117. graff:** graft. What follows is a triple pun: "with *yew,* and *afterward* with a *medlar*"; "with *you,* and *in that case* with a *meddler.*" The medlar is an apple-like fruit that is not ready to eat until it is on the verge of decay. **120. right virtue:** characteristic quality. **126. For:** because.

Tongues I'll hang on every tree,
    That shall civil sayings show:
Some, how brief the life of man
    Runs his erring pilgrimage,         130
That the stretching of a span
    Buckles in his sum of age;
Some, of violated vows
    'Twixt the souls of friend and friend;
But upon the fairest boughs,         135
    Or at every sentence end,
Will I 'Rosalinda' write,
    Teaching all that read to know
The quintessence of every sprite
    Heaven would in little show.         140
Therefore heaven Nature charg'd
    That one body should be fill'd
With all graces wide-enlarg'd.
    Nature presently distill'd
Helen's cheek, but not [her] heart,         145
    Cleopatra's majesty,
Atalanta's better part,
    Sad Lucretia's modesty.
Thus Rosalind of many parts
    By heavenly synod was devis'd,         150
Of many faces, eyes, and hearts,
    To have the touches dearest priz'd.
Heaven would that she these gifts should have,
And I to live and die her slave."

ROSALIND  O most gentle Jupiter, what tedious homily    155
  of love have you wearied your parishioners withal,
  and never cried, "Have patience, good people!"

---

**130. his erring:** its wandering.   **131. span:** distance from the tip of the thumb to the tip of the little finger of a spread hand.   **132. Buckles in:** encompasses. **139. quintessence:** ultimate essence; highest perfection. **sprite:** spirit.   **140. in little:** in small space; probably with reference to man as microcosm or miniature universe.   **143. wide-enlarg'd:** extended to the fullest (?) or hitherto dispersed at large, i.e. gathered from everywhere (?).   **144. presently:** at once.   **145. Helen's cheek:** Helen of Troy's beauty. **her heart:** i.e. her falseness in love.   **147. Atalanta's better part:** i.e. her fleetness of foot (see lines 276–77 below), as contrasted with her greed. Hippomenes defeated her in a race, and thus won her as his bride, by dropping in her way three golden apples which she paused thrice to pick up.   **148. modesty:** scrupulous chastity. The story of Lucretia's rape and suicide is told by Shakespeare in *The Rape of Lucrece*.   **152. touches:** features, traits.   **153. would:** desired.   **155. Jupiter.** Many editors read *pulpiter* (first suggested by Spedding).   **156. withal:** with.

CELIA  How now? back, friends! Shepherd, go off a
    little. Go with him, sirrah.
TOUCHSTONE  Come, shepherd, let us make an honorable          160
    retreat, though not with bag and baggage, yet with
    scrip and scrippage.                    *Exit [with Corin].*
CELIA  Didst thou hear these verses?
ROSALIND  O yes, I heard them all, and more too,
    for some of them had in them more feet than the           165
    verses would bear.
CELIA  That's no matter; the feet might bear the
    verses.
ROSALIND  Ay, but the feet were lame, and could not
    bear themselves without the verse, and therefore stood    170
    lamely in the verse.
CELIA  But didst thou hear without wondering how
    thy name should be hang'd and carv'd upon these trees?
ROSALIND  I was seven of the nine days out of the wonder
    before you came; for look here what I found on a palm     175
    tree. I was never so berhym'd since Pythagoras'
    time, that I was an Irish rat, which I can hardly
    remember.
CELIA  Trow you who hath done this?
ROSALIND  Is it a man?                                        180
CELIA  And a chain, that you once wore, about his
    neck. Change you color?
ROSALIND  I prithee who?
CELIA  O Lord, Lord, it is a hard matter for friends
    to meet; but mountains may be remov'd with earthquakes,   185
    and so encounter.
ROSALIND  Nay, but who is it?
CELIA  Is it possible?
ROSALIND  Nay, I prithee now, with most petitionary
    vehemence, tell me who it is.                             190
CELIA  O wonderful, wonderful, and most wonderful

---

**159. sirrah:** form of address to inferiors.   **161. not . . . baggage:** i.e. not with
as much equipment as a retreating army would carry.   **162. scrip and scrip-
page:** a pouch and its contents.   **166. bear:** permit (with following pun on the
sense "carry").   **170. without:** (1) without the help of; (2) outside.   **173. should
be:** came to be.   **176–77. Pythagoras' time.** An allusion to the Pythago-
rean doctrine of transmigration of souls.   **177. that:** when. **Irish rat.** Alluding to an old belief that Irish enchanters could rhyme rats and other animals to
death.   **179. Trow you:** have you any idea.   **181. And a chain:** i.e. yes, it is a man,
and one with a chain.   **185. remov'd with:** moved by.   **189–190. petitionary
vehemence:** urgent entreaty.

wonderful! and yet again wonderful, and after that,
out of all hooping!

ROSALIND  Good my complexion, dost thou think,
though I am caparison'd like a man, I have a doublet      195
and hose in my disposition? One inch of delay more is
a South-sea of discovery. I prithee tell me who is
it quickly, and speak apace. I would thou couldst
stammer, that thou mightst pour this conceal'd man
out of thy mouth, as wine comes out of a narrow-         200
mouth'd bottle, either too much at once, or none at all.
I prithee take the cork out of thy mouth that I may
drink thy tidings.

CELIA  So you may put a man in your belly.

ROSALIND  Is he of God's making? What manner of          205
man? Is his head worth a hat? or his chin worth a
beard?

CELIA  Nay, he hath but a little beard.

ROSALIND  Why, God will send more, if the man will
be thankful. Let me stay the growth of his beard, if      210
thou delay me not the knowledge of his chin.

CELIA  It is young Orlando, that tripp'd up the
wrastler's heels, and your heart, both in an instant.

ROSALIND  Nay, but the devil take mocking. Speak sad
brow and true maid.                                       215

CELIA  I' faith, coz, 'tis he.

ROSALIND  Orlando?

CELIA  Orlando.

ROSALIND  Alas the day, what shall I do with my doublet
and hose? What did he when thou saw'st him?              220
What said he? How look'd he? Wherein went he?
What makes he here? Did he ask for me? Where
remains he? How parted he with thee? And when
shalt thou see him again? Answer me in one word.

CELIA  You must borrow me Gargantua's mouth              225
first; 'tis a word too great for any mouth of this

---

**193. out of:** beyond. **hooping:** whooping, i.e. power to utter.  **194. Good my
complexion:** have mercy on my temperament, i.e. on my woman's impatient
curiosity.  **195. caparison'd:** decked out (ordinarily used of a horse's ornamental
trappings).  **196–97. is . . . discovery:** will seem as long as the time needed to
explore the South Seas.  **205. of God's making:** i.e. not of the tailor's making
(the usual antithesis).  **210. stay:** await.  **214–15. sad . . . maid:** seriously and truly.
**221. Wherein went he:** how was he dressed.  **222. makes he:** is he doing.
**225. Gargantua's mouth.** Rabelais' giant swallowed five pilgrims in a salad.

age's size. To say ay and no to these particulars is
more than to answer in a catechism.

ROSALIND  But doth he know that I am in this forest
and in man's apparel? Looks he as freshly as he did          230
the day he wrastled?

CELIA  It is as easy to count atomies as to resolve the
propositions of a lover. But take a taste of my finding
him, and relish it with good observance. I found him
under a tree, like a dropp'd acorn.                          235

ROSALIND  It may well be call'd Jove's tree, when it
drops [such] fruit.

CELIA  Give me audience, good madam.

ROSALIND  Proceed.

CELIA  There lay he, stretch'd along, like a wounded          240
knight.

ROSALIND  Though it be pity to see such a sight, it well
becomes the ground.

CELIA  Cry "holla" to [thy] tongue, I prithee; it curvets unseasonably.
He was furnish'd like a hunter.                              245

ROSALIND  O ominous! he comes to kill my heart.

CELIA  I would sing my song without a burthen;
thou bring'st me out of tune.

ROSALIND  Do you not know I am a woman? when
I think, I must speak. Sweet, say on.                        250

*Enter* ORLANDO *and* JAQUES.

CELIA  You bring me out. Soft, comes he not here?

ROSALIND  'Tis he. Slink by, and note him.

JAQUES  I thank you for your company, but, good
faith, I had as lief have been myself alone.

ORLANDO  And so had I; but yet for fashion sake I          255
thank you too for your society.

JAQUES  God buy you, let's meet as little as we can.

ORLANDO  I do desire we may be better strangers.

---

**228. catechism:** catechizing.  **230. freshly:** fresh, youthfully vigorous.
**232. atomies:** atoms, minute specks.  **233. propositions:** questions.  **234. relish it:**
enhance its flavor. **good observance:** close attention.  **236. Jove's tree:** i.e. the oak,
the king of trees, as the eagle, also connected with Jove, is the king of birds.  **238. audience:** hearing, attention.  **240. along:** full length.  **244. holla:** stop.  **244–45. curvets
unseasonably:** frisks about at the wrong time.  **245. furnish'd:** dressed,
equipped.  **246. heart.** With pun on *hart* (and so spelled in F1).  **247. burthen:**
burden, ground-bass, repeated undersong.  **248. bring'st:** puttest.  **251. bring me
out:** put me off, confuse me.  **257. God buy you:** God be with you; goodbye.

JAQUES  I pray you mar no more trees with writing
   love-songs in their barks.                          260

ORLANDO  I pray you mar no moe of my verses with
   reading them ill-favoredly.

JAQUES  Rosalind is your love's name?

ORLANDO  Yes, just.

JAQUES  I do not like her name.                       265

ORLANDO  There was no thought of pleasing you when
   she was christen'd.

JAQUES  What stature is she of?

ORLANDO  Just as high as my heart.

JAQUES  You are full of pretty answers; have you not     270
   been acquainted with goldsmiths' wives, and conn'd
   them out of rings?

ORLANDO  Not so; but I answer you right painted
   cloth, from whence you have studied your
   questions.                                 275

JAQUES  You have a nimble wit; I think 'twas made
   of Atalanta's heels. Will you sit down with me?
   and we two will rail against our mistress the world,
   and all our misery.

ORLANDO  I will chide no breather in the world but myself,   280
   against whom I know most faults.

JAQUES  The worst fault you have is to be in love.

ORLANDO  'Tis a fault I will not change for your best
   virtue. I am weary of you.

JAQUES  By my troth, I was seeking for a fool when I   285
   found you.

ORLANDO  He is drown'd in the brook; look but in,
   and you shall see him.

JAQUES  There I shall see mine own figure.

ORLANDO  Which I take to be either a fool or a cipher.   290

JAQUES  I'll tarry no longer with you. Farewell, good
   Signior Love.

ORLANDO  I am glad of your departure. Adieu, good
   Monsieur Melancholy.               *[Exit Jaques.]*

ROSALIND  *[Aside to Celia.]* I will speak to him like a   295

---

**261. moe:** more.   **262. ill-favoredly:** in an unattractive way, badly.   **264. just:**
just so, exactly.   **271–72. conn'd . . . rings:** i.e. memorized the mottoes or "po-
sies' (i.e. poesies) engraved on rings.   **273. right:** true, genuine.   **273–74. painted
cloth.** The cheapest type of wall-hanging, customarily decorated with scenes
and mottoes, and thus another source of clichés.   **280. breather:** living person.
**290. cipher:** zero (punning on a second sense of *figure*), nonentity.

saucy lackey, and under that habit play the knave
with him.—Do you hear, forester?

ORLANDO Very well. What would you?

ROSALIND I pray you, what is't a' clock?

ORLANDO You should ask me what time o' day; there's                    300
no clock in the forest.

ROSALIND Then there is no true lover in the forest,
else sighing every minute and groaning every hour
would detect the lazy foot of Time as well as a
clock.                                                                 305

ORLANDO And why not the swift foot of Time? Had
not that been as proper?

ROSALIND By no means, sir. Time travels in divers
paces with divers persons. I'll tell you who Time
ambles withal, who Time trots withal, who Time                        310
gallops withal, and who he stands still withal.

ORLANDO I prithee, who doth he trot withal?

ROSALIND Marry, he trots hard with a young maid
between the contract of her marriage and the day
it is solemniz'd. If the interim be but a se'nnight,                  315
Time's pace is so hard that it seems the length of
seven year.

ORLANDO Who ambles Time withal?

ROSALIND With a priest that lacks Latin, and a rich
man that hath not the gout; for the one sleeps easily                 320
because he cannot study, and the other lives merrily because
he feels no pain; the one lacking the
burthen of lean and wasteful learning, the other
knowing no burthen of heavy tedious penury. These
Time ambles withal.                                                   325

ORLANDO Who doth he gallop withal?

ROSALIND With a thief to the gallows; for though he
go as softly as foot can fall, he thinks himself too
soon there.

ORLANDO Who stays it still withal?                                    330

ROSALIND With lawyers in the vacation; for they sleep
between term and term, and then they perceive not
how Time moves.

ORLANDO Where dwell you, pretty youth?

**296. habit:** guise.   **299. a' clock:** by (of) the clock.   **304. detect:** reveal.
**310. withal:** with.   **313. hard:** with an uneasy pace (the discomfort of the pace
making the ride seem long).   **315. se'nnight:** week.   **323. wasteful:** consuming.
**328. go as softly:** walk as slowly.   **332. term:** session.

ROSALIND With this shepherdess, my sister; here in                                                335
the skirts of the forest, like fringe upon a
petticoat.

ORLANDO Are you native of this place?

ROSALIND As the cony that you see dwell where she is
kindled.                                                                                          340

ORLANDO Your accent is something finer than you
could purchase in so remov'd a dwelling.

ROSALIND I have been told so of many; but indeed an
old religious uncle of mine taught me to speak, who
was in his youth an inland man, one that knew                                                     345
courtship too well, for there he fell in love. I have
heard him read many lectures against it, and I
thank God I am not a woman, to be touch'd with
so many giddy offenses as he hath generally tax'd
their whole sex withal.                                                                           350

ORLANDO Can you remember any of the principal
evils that he laid to the charge of women?

ROSALIND There were none principal, they were all
like one another as halfpence are, every one fault
seeming monstrous till his fellow-fault came to                                                   355
match it.

ORLANDO I prithee recount some of them.

ROSALIND No; I will not cast away my physic but
on those that are sick. There is a man haunts the
forest, that abuses our young plants with carving                                                 360
"Rosalind" on their barks; hangs odes upon hawthorns,
and elegies on brambles; all, forsooth,
[deifying] the name of Rosalind. If I could meet that
fancy-monger, I would give him some good counsel,
for he seems to have the quotidian of love upon                                                   365
him.

ORLANDO I am he that is so love-shak'd, I pray you
tell me your remedy.

ROSALIND There is none of my uncle's marks upon you.
He taught me how to know a man in love; in which                                                  370
cage of rushes I am sure you [are] not prisoner.

---

**339. cony:** rabbit.   **340. kindled:** born.   **342. purchase:** acquire.   **remov'd:**
remote.   **344. religious:** belonging to a religious order.   **346. courtship:** (1) the
ways of court life; (2) wooing.   **348. touch'd:** tainted.   **349. generally:** universally.
**358. physic:** knowledge of medicine.   **364. fancy-monger:** dealer in love.
**365. quotidian:** an ague with daily attacks of chills and fever.   **371. cage of rushes:**
i.e. insubstantial prison, easy to escape from.

ORLANDO  What were his marks?

ROSALIND  A lean cheek, which you have not; a blue
eye and sunken, which you have not; an unquestionable
spirit, which you have not; a beard neglected,                              375
which you have not (but I pardon you for that,
for simply your having in beard is a younger brother's revenue);
then your hose should be ungarter'd,
your bonnet unbanded, your sleeve unbutton'd,
your shoe untied, and every thing about you                                 380
demonstrating a careless desolation. But you are
no such man; you are rather point-device in your
accoutrements, as loving yourself, than seeming the
lover of any other.

ORLANDO  Fair youth, I would I could make thee believe                      385
I love.

ROSALIND  Me believe it? You may as soon make her
that you love believe it, which I warrant she is
apter to do than to confess she does. That is one
of the points in the which women still give the lie                        390
to their consciences. But in good sooth, are
you he that hangs the verses on the trees, wherein
Rosalind is so admir'd?

ORLANDO  I swear to thee, youth, by the white hand of
Rosalind, I am that he, that unfortunate he.                               395

ROSALIND  But are you so much in love as your rhymes
speak?

ORLANDO  Neither rhyme nor reason can express how
much.

ROSALIND  Love is merely a madness, and I tell you,                        400
deserves as well a dark house and a whip as madmen
do; and the reason why they are not so punish'd and
cur'd is, that the lunacy is so ordinary that the
whippers are in love too. Yet I profess curing it
by counsel.                                                                405

ORLANDO  Did you ever cure any so?

---

**373. blue:** i.e. with dark circles caused by weeping and lack of sleep.
**374–75. unquestionable:** disinclined to converse.    **377. simply:** frankly. **your having in:** what you own in the way of.    **379. bonnet unbanded:** hat without a
band around the crown, a fashion described by Stubbes in *The Anatomy of Abuses* as
"unseemly (I will not say how assy)."    **381. careless:** i.e. heedless of appearance.
**382. point-device:** very correct.    **383. accoutrements:** accoutrements.
**389. apter:** readier.    **390. still:** regularly.    **391. consciences:** inmost thoughts,
"hearts." **sooth:** truth.    **400. merely a:** an utter.    **401. dark . . . whip.** The common
treatment for the insane.    **404. profess:** claim to have skill in.

ROSALIND Yes, one, and in this manner. He was to
  imagine me his love, his mistress; and I set him
  every day to woo me. At which time would I, being
  but a moonish youth, grieve, be effeminate,                    410
  changeable, longing and liking, proud, fantastical,
  apish, shallow, inconstant, full of tears, full of smiles;
  for every passion something, and for no passion
  truly any thing, as boys and women are for the
  most part cattle of this color; would now like                 415
  him, now loathe him; then entertain him, then forswear
  him; now weep for him, then spit at him; that I
  drave my suitor from his mad humor of love to a
  living humor of madness, which was, to forswear
  the full stream of the world, and to live in a nook            420
  merely monastic. And thus I cur'd him, and this
  way will I take upon me to wash your liver as clean
  as a sound sheep's heart, that there shall not be one
  spot of love in't.

ORLANDO I would not be cur'd, youth.                              425

ROSALIND I would cure you, if you would but call me
  Rosalind, and come every day to my cote and woo me.

ORLANDO Now, by the faith of my love, I will. Tell
  me where it is.

ROSALIND Go with me to it, and I'll show it you; and             430
  by the way, you shall tell me where in the forest you
  live. Will you go?

ORLANDO With all my heart, good youth.

ROSALIND Nay, you must call me Rosalind. Come,
  sister, will you go?                            *Exeunt.* 435

## SCENE 3

*Enter* CLOWN [TOUCHSTONE], AUDREY; *and* JAQUES *[behind].*

TOUCHSTONE Come apace, good Audrey; I will fetch
  up your goats, Audrey. And how, Audrey? am I

---

**410. moonish:** given to changing moods. **be effeminate:** act like a woman.
**411. fantastical:** fanciful, capricious. **412. apish:** affected. **416. entertain.**
welcome, admit. **418. drave:** drove. **humor:** whim. **419. living humor:** actual state. **421. merely monastic:** exactly like a hermit. **422. liver.** The supposed seat of the passions. **423. sound sheep's heart.** Perhaps suggesting that
Orlando, by being freed of love, will be reduced to one of the stupidest of animals.
**425. would not:** do not wish to be. Rosalind then picks up *would* in the ordinary
sense. 3.3. Location: The forest.

the man yet? Doth my simple feature content
you?

AUDREY Your features, Lord warrant us! what                5
features?

TOUCHSTONE I am here with thee and thy goats as the
most capricious poet, honest Ovid, was among the
Goths.

JAQUES *[Aside.]* O knowledge ill-inhabited, worse        10
than Jove in a thatch'd house!

TOUCHSTONE When a man's verses cannot be understood,
nor a man's good wit seconded with the forward
child, understanding, it strikes a man more
dead than a great reckoning in a little room. Truly,      15
I would the gods had made thee poetical.

AUDREY I do not know what "poetical" is. Is it
honest in deed and word? Is it a true thing?

TOUCHSTONE No, truly; for the truest poetry is the
most feigning, and lovers are given to poetry;           20
and what they swear in poetry may be said as lovers
they do feign.

AUDREY Do you wish then that the gods had made
me poetical?

TOUCHSTONE I do, truly; for thou swear'st to me           25
thou art honest. Now if thou wert a poet, I might
have some hope thou didst feign.

AUDREY Would you not have me honest?

TOUCHSTONE No, truly, unless thou wert hard-favor'd;
for honesty coupled to beauty is to have honey a         30
sauce to sugar.

JAQUES *[Aside.]* A material fool!

AUDREY Well, I am not fair, and therefore I pray
the gods make me honest.

TOUCHSTONE Truly, and to cast away honesty upon           35
a foul slut were to put good meat into an unclean
dish.

**3. feature:** form and appearance. **5. warrant:** protect. **5–6. what features?** To Audrey
the noun is simply unintelligible. **8. capricious:** ingenious, full of witty conceits;
with play on Latin *caper,* "he-goat," which further suggests the sense "goatish, lascivious." **9. Goths.** Pronounced *goats.* **10. ill-inhabited:** meanly lodged. **11. Jove . . .
house.** Jupiter and Mercury, disguised, stayed as guests in the lowly cottage of Baucis
and Philemon. **13–14. forward:** precocious. **15. great . . . room:** exorbitant bill
for food in a small, mean tavern. Some find here an allusion to Christopher Marlowe's death at the hands of Ingram Frizer in 1593 in a quarrel over a tavern bill.
**18. honest:** honorable, true. **20. feigning:** based on imagination. **26. honest:** chaste.
**29. hard-favor'd:** ugly. **32. material:** full of "matter" or good sense. **36. foul:** ugly.

AUDREY  I am not a slut, though I thank the gods
    I am foul.

TOUCHSTONE  Well, prais'd be the gods for thy foulness!    40
    sluttishness may come hereafter. But be it
    as it may be, I will marry thee; and to that end
    I have been with Sir Oliver Martext, the vicar of
    the next village, who hath promis'd to meet me in
    this place of the forest and to couple us.    45

JAQUES  *[Aside.]* I would fain see this meeting.

AUDREY  Well, the gods give us joy!

TOUCHSTONE  Amen. A man may, if he were of a fearful
    heart, stagger in this attempt; for here we have
    no temple but the wood, no assembly but horn-    50
    beasts. But what though? Courage! As horns
    are odious, they are necessary. It is said, "Many
    a man knows no end of his goods." Right! many
    a man has good horns, and knows no end of them.
    Well, that is the dowry of his wife, 'tis none of    55
    his own getting. Horns? even so. Poor men
    alone? No, no, the noblest deer hath them as huge
    as the rascal. Is the single man therefore bless'd?
    No, as a wall'd town is more worthier than a village,
    so is the forehead of a married man more honorable    60
    than the bare brow of a bachelor; and by how
    much defense is better than no skill, by so much is a
    horn more precious than to want.

*Enter* SIR OLIVER MARTEXT.

Here comes Sir Oliver. Sir Oliver Martext, you
are well met. Will you dispatch us here under    65
this tree, or shall we go with you to your chapel?

SIR OLIVER MARTEXT  Is there none here to give the woman?

TOUCHSTONE  I will not take her on gift of any man.

SIR OLIVER MARTEXT  Truly, she must be given, or the marriage
    is not lawful.    70

---

43. **Sir:** courtesy title for a priest; "Mar-"echoes Martin Marprelate, the pseud-
onym on pamphlets critical of the English church.★  49. **stagger:** hesitate, waver.
50–51. **horn-beasts.** With allusion to the horns of the cuckolded husband.
51. **what though:** what of that. **As:** though.  52. **necessary:** inevitable.  53. **knows
. . . goods:** thinks his well inexhaustible.  54. **knows . . . them:** isn't aware of their
points coming into view on his forehead.  55. **dowry:** i.e. what his wife brings him.
56. **getting.** With play on "begetting," with reference to his wife's children.
58. **rascal:** young, lean deer, hence inferior.  62. **defense:** skill in self-defense.
63. **want:** i.e. lack one  65. **dispatch:** i.e. marry.

JAQUES *[Discovering himself.]* Proceed, proceed. I'll
    give her.
TOUCHSTONE  Good even, good Master What-ye-call't;
    how do you, sir? You are very well met. God
    'ild you for your last company. I am very glad to        75
    see you. Even a toy in hand here, sir. Nay, pray
    be cover'd.
JAQUES  Will you be married, motley?
TOUCHSTONE  As the ox hath his bow, sir, the horse his
    curb, and the falcon her bells, so man hath his        80
    desires; and as pigeons bill, so wedlock would be
    nibbling.
JAQUES  And will you (being a man of your breeding)
    be married under a bush like a beggar? Get you
    to church, and have a good priest that can tell        85
    you what marriage is. This fellow will but join
    you together as they join wainscot; then one of you
    will prove a shrunk panel, and like green timber
    warp, warp.
TOUCHSTONE  *[Aside.]* I am not in the mind but I were        90
    better to be married of him than of another, for
    he is not like to marry me well; and not being well
    married, it will be a good excuse for me hereafter
    to leave my wife.
JAQUES  Go thou with me, and let me counsel thee.        95
[TOUCHSTONE]  Come, sweet Audrey,
    We must be married, or we must live in bawdry.
    Farewell, good Master Oliver: not
            "O sweet Oliver,
            O brave Oliver,        100
      Leave me not behind thee;"
but
           "Wind away,
           Be gone, I say,

---

**71.** s.d. **Discovering:** revealing.   **75. 'ild:** yield, i.e. reward. **your last company.**
Referring to their earlier meeting (II.vii.12 ff.).   **76. Even . . . hand:** first a trifling
matter is being undertaken.   **77. be cover'd:** put on your hat. Touchstone speaks as
if to a social inferior who has respectfully bared his head.   **79. bow:** yoke.   **85–86.
tell . . . is:** instruct you in the responsibilities of marriage (as the ignorant Sir Oliver cannot).   **87. wainscot.** oak used in panelling.★   **90–91. not . . . better:** not
sure but that it would be better for me.   **97. married:** i.e. properly in church. **in
bawdry:** i.e. in sin.   **99–101. O . . . thee.** From a ballad of the 1580's, now lost; but
lines 103–5 may be Touchstone's improvisation.   **103. Wind:** wander, go.

I will not to wedding with thee." 105

*[Exeunt Jaques, Touchstone, and Audrey.]*

SIR OLIVER MARTEXT 'Tis no matter; ne'er a fantastical knave
of them all shall flout me out of my calling. *Exit.*


## SCENE 4

*Enter* ROSALIND *and* CELIA.

ROSALIND Never talk to me, I will weep.

CELIA Do, I prithee, but yet have the grace to
consider that tears do not become a man.

ROSALIND But have I not cause to weep?

CELIA As good cause as one would desire, therefore 5
weep.

ROSALIND His very hair is of the dissembling color.

CELIA Something browner than Judas's. Marry,
his kisses are Judas's own children.

ROSALIND I' faith, his hair is of a good color. 10

CELIA An excellent color. Your chestnut was ever
the only color.

ROSALIND And his kissing is as full of sanctity as the
touch of holy bread.

CELIA He hath bought a pair of cast lips of Diana. 15
A nun of winter's sisterhood kisses not more religiously,
the very ice of chastity is in them.

ROSALIND But why did he swear he would come this
morning, and comes not?

CELIA Nay certainly there is no truth in him. 20

ROSALIND Do you think so?

CELIA Yes, I think he is not a pick-purse nor a
horse-stealer, but for his verity in love, I do think
him as concave as a cover'd goblet or a worm-eaten
nut. 25

ROSALIND Not true in love?

---

**106. fantastical:** full of ridiculous notions.  **3.4.** Location: The forest.  **7. of . . .
color:** i.e. red—like Judas Iscariot's, according to tradition.  **8. Something:** somewhat.  **9. Judas's own children:** i.e. traitorous, like the kiss with which Judas
betrayed Jesus.  **11. Your.** The indefinite use; a colloquialism.  **14. holy bread:**
ordinary leavened bread which was blessed after the Eucharist and given to non-
communicants.  **15. cast:** cast-off; also possible play on "castus" (Latin "pure"). I.e.
one whom he kissed might think that his lips had once belonged to Diana, the
goddess of chastity.★  **16. of winter's sisterhood:** i.e. devoted to cold and barren
chastity.  **23. verity:** truthfulness.  **24. concave:** hollow. **cover'd goblet.** A goblet
would have its cover on only when not in use, hence empty.

CELIA  Yes, when he is in—but I think he is not
   in.

ROSALIND  You have heard him swear downright he was.

CELIA  "Was" is not "is." Besides, the oath of [a]         30
   lover is no stronger than the word of a tapster;
   they are both the confirmer of false reckonings.
   He attends here in the forest on the Duke your
   father.

ROSALIND  I met the Duke yesterday, and had much      35
   question with him. He ask'd me of what parentage
   I was. I told him of as good as he, so he laugh'd
   and let me go. But what talk we of fathers, when
   there is such a man as Orlando?

CELIA  O, that's a brave man! he writes brave      40
   verses, speaks brave words, swears brave oaths, and
   breaks them bravely, quite traverse, athwart
   the heart of his lover, as a puisne tilter, that spurs
   his horse but on one side, breaks his staff like a
   noble goose. But all's brave that youth mounts and    45
   folly guides. Who comes here?

*Enter* CORIN.

CORIN  Mistress and master, you have oft inquired
   After the shepherd that complain'd of love,
   Who you saw sitting by me on the turf,
   Praising the proud disdainful shepherdess      50
   That was his mistress.

CELIA                Well; and what of him?

CORIN  If you will see a pageant truly play'd
   Between the pale complexion of true love
   And the red glow of scorn and proud disdain,
   Go hence a little, and I shall conduct you,      55
   If you will mark it.

ROSALIND          O, come, let us remove,
   The sight of lovers feedeth those in love.
   Bring us to this sight, and you shall say
   I'll prove a busy actor in their play.          *Exeunt.*

---

**36. question:** conversation.   **38. what:** why.   **40. brave:** excellent, splendid (but used with irony and some suggestion of the related word *bravado* [= boasting without intention of action]).   **42. traverse:** awry.   **43. puisne:** inexperienced (literally, younger).   **44. staff:** spear.   **45. noble goose:** young, foolish courtier.   **52. pageant:** drama, scene.   **53. pale.** Every sigh was thought to draw a drop of blood from the heart.   **56. will mark:** desire to witness.

## SCENE 5

*Enter* SILVIUS *and* PHEBE.

SILVIUS  Sweet Phebe, do not scorn me, do not, Phebe;
  Say that you love me not, but say not so
  In bitterness. The common executioner,
  Whose heart th' accustom'd sight of death makes hard,
  Falls not the axe upon the humbled neck      5
  But first begs pardon. Will you sterner be
  Than he that dies and lives by bloody drops?

*Enter, [behind,]* ROSALIND, CELIA, *and* CORIN.

PHEBE  I would not be thy executioner;
  I fly thee for I would not injure thee.
  Thou tell'st me there is murder in mine eye:      10
  'Tis pretty, sure, and very probable,
  That eyes, that are the frail'st and softest things,
  Who shut their coward gates on atomies,
  Should be called tyrants, butchers, murtherers!
  Now I do frown on thee with all my heart,      15
  And if mine eyes can wound, now let them kill thee.
  Now counterfeit to swound; why, now fall down,
  Or if thou canst not, O, for shame, for shame,
  Lie not, to say mine eyes are murtherers!
  Now show the wound mine eye hath made in thee;      20
  Scratch thee but with a pin, and there remains
  Some scar of it; lean upon a rush,
  The cicatrice and capable impressure
  Thy palm some moment keeps; but now mine eyes,
  Which I have darted at thee, hurt thee not,      25
  Nor I am sure there is no force in eyes
  That can do hurt.
SILVIUS          O dear Phebe,
  If ever (as that ever may be near)
  You meet in some fresh cheek the power of fancy,
  Then shall you know the wounds invisible      30
  That love's keen arrows make.

---

3.5. Location: The forest.  **5. Falls:** lets fall.  **6. But first begs:** without first asking.  **7. dies and lives:** spends his whole life and thus earns his whole living.  **9. for:** because.  **11. pretty:** clever (ironic). **sure:** surely.  **17. counterfeit to swound:** pretend to swoon.  **23. cicatrice:** i.e. mark. **capable impressure:** perceptible impression.  **29. fresh:** young and beautiful. **fancy:** love.

PHEBE                          But till that time
    Come not thou near me; and when that time comes,
    Afflict me with thy mocks, pity me not,
    As till that time I shall not pity thee.
ROSALIND *[Advancing.]* And why, I pray you? Who
    might be your mother,                                    35
    That you insult, exult, and all at once,
    Over the wretched? What though you have no beauty—
    As, by my faith, I see no more in you
    Than without candle may go dark to bed—
    Must you be therefore proud and pitiless?                40
    Why, what means this? why do you look on me?
    I see no more in you than in the ordinary
    Of nature's sale-work. 'Od's my little life,
    I think she means to tangle my eyes too!
    No, faith, proud mistress, hope not after it.            45
    'Tis not your inky brows, your black silk hair,
    Your bugle eyeballs, nor your cheek of cream
    That can entame my spirits to your worship.
    You foolish shepherd, wherefore do you follow her,
    Like foggy south, puffing with wind and rain?            50
    You are a thousand times a properer man
    Than she a woman. 'Tis such fools as you
    That makes the world full of ill-favor'd children.
    'Tis not her glass, but you that flatters her,
    And out of you she sees herself more proper              55
    Than any of her lineaments can show her.
    But, mistress, know yourself, down on your knees,
    And thank heaven, fasting, for a good man's love;
    For I must tell you friendly in your ear,
    Sell when you can, you are not for all markets.          60
    Cry the man mercy, love him, take his offer;
    Foul is most foul, being foul to be a scoffer.
    So take her to thee, shepherd. Fare you well.

---

**33. mocks:** ridicule.   **36. all at once:** i.e. in the same breath.   **38–39. no . . . bed:** i.e. not enough beauty to lighten the dark.   **43. sale-work:** run-of-the-mill products. **'Od's:** God save.   **44. tangle:** ensnare.   **47. bugle eyeballs:** eyes like shiny black beads. **cream:** yellow.   **48. entame:** subdue. **your worship:** worship of you.   **50. south:** south wind (which in England brings fog and rain). **wind and rain:** i.e. sighs and tears.   **51. properer:** handsomer.   **54. glass:** mirror.   **55. out of you:** i.e. with you as her mirror.   **59. friendly:** as a friend. **61. Cry . . .mercy:** beg the man's pardon.   **62. Foul . . . scoffer:** i.e. an ugly woman is seen at her worst when, ugly though she is, she scoffs at proffered love.

PHEBE Sweet youth, I pray you chide a year together,
   I had rather hear you chide than this man woo.    65
ROSALIND He's fall'n in love with your foulness—and
   she'll fall in love with my anger. If it be so, as
   fast as she answers thee with frowning looks, I'll
   sauce her with bitter words.—Why look you so
   upon me?    70
PHEBE For no ill will I bear you.
ROSALIND I pray you do not fall in love with me,
   For I am falser than vows made in wine.
   Besides, I like you not. If you will know my house,
   'Tis at the tuft of olives here hard by.    75
   Will you go, sister? Shepherd, ply her hard.
   Come, sister. Shepherdess, look on him better,
   And be not proud; though all the world could see,
   None could be so abus'd in sight as he.
   Come, to our flock.    *Exit [with Celia and Corin].*   80
PHEBE Dead shepherd, now I find thy saw of might,
   "Who ever lov'd that lov'd not at first sight?"
SILVIUS Sweet Phebe—
PHEBE              Hah! what say'st thou, Silvius?
SILVIUS Sweet Phebe, pity me.
PHEBE Why, I am sorry for thee, gentle Silvius.    85
SILVIUS Where ever sorrow is, relief would be.
   If you do sorrow at my grief in love,
   By giving love, your sorrow and my grief
   Were both extermin'd.
PHEBE Thou hast my love; is not that neighborly?    90
SILVIUS I would have you.
PHEBE              Why, that were covetousness.
   Silvius, the time was that I hated thee;
   And yet it is not that I bear thee love,

---

**64. together:** without intermission.   **69. sauce:** rebuke sharply.   **75. tuft . . . by:**
bunch of olive trees nearby.★   **78. could see:** should be able to look (on you).
**79. abus'd in sight:** deceived by his eyes.   **81. Dead shepherd:** i.e. Marlowe (died
1593); line 82 is quoted from his *Hero and Leander* (I.176), published in 1598. **find . . .
might:** perceive the force of your saying.   **86. Where . . . be:** i.e. wherever sorrow
is felt, a desire to give relief should follow.   **89. Were both extermin'd:** would
both be banished.   **90. is . . . neighborly:** i.e. doesn't that follow from the fact that
I am your neighbor (and hence, with reference to Christ's second commandment,
am bound as a good Christian to love you).   **91. covetousness.** Referring to the
Mosaic tenth commandment, "Thou shalt not covet . . . anything that is thy neighbor's." Phebe thus makes it appear that she is following the Biblical injunctions,
while Silvius is breaking them.   **93. yet . . . that:** the time has not yet come when.

But since that thou canst talk of love so well,
Thy company, which erst was irksome to me,                        95
I will endure; and I'll employ thee too.
But do not look for further recompense
Than thine own gladness that thou art employ'd.

SILVIUS  So holy and so perfect is my love,
And I in such a poverty of grace,                                 100
That I shall think it a most plenteous crop
To glean the broken ears after the man
That the main harvest reaps. Loose now and then
A scatt'red smile, and that I'll live upon.

PHEBE  Know'st thou the youth that spoke to me yerwhile?           105

SILVIUS  Not very well, but I have met him oft,
And he hath bought the cottage and the bounds
That the old carlot once was master of.

PHEBE  Think not I love him, though I ask for him;
'Tis but a peevish boy—yet he talks well—                         110
But what care I for words? Yet words do well
When he that speaks them pleases those that hear.
It is a pretty youth—not very pretty—
But sure he's proud—and yet his pride becomes him.
He'll make a proper man. The best thing in him                    115
Is his complexion; and faster than his tongue
Did make offense, his eye did heal it up.
He is not very tall—yet for his years he's tall;
His leg is but so so—and yet 'tis well;
There was a pretty redness in his lip,                            120
A little riper and more lusty red
Than that mix'd in his cheek; 'twas just the difference
Betwixt the constant red and mingled damask.
There be some women, Silvius, had they mark'd him
In parcels as I did, would have gone near                         125
To fall in love with him; but for my part
I love him not, nor hate him not; and yet
Have more cause to hate him than to love him,
For what had he to do to chide at me?

---

**95. erst:** once, before.  **100. poverty of grace:** dearth of favor.  **103–104. Loose . . .
scatt'red:** let fly . . . random (a figure from archery).  **105. yerwhile:** erewhile, just
now.  **107. bounds:** pasturage.  **108. carlot:** peasant.  **123. constant:** uniform.
**mingled damask:** mixture of red and white.  **125. In parcels:** part by part, in
detail.  **125–26. gone . . . fall:** come close to falling.  **129. what . . . do:** what
business had he.

He said mine eyes were black and my hair black,                    130
And, now I am rememb'red, scorn'd at me.
I marvel why I answer'd not again.
But that's all one; omittance is no quittance.
I'll write to him a very taunting letter,
And thou shalt bear it; wilt thou, Silvius?                        135
SILVIUS  Phebe, with all my heart.
PHEBE                      I'll write it straight;
The matter's in my head and in my heart.
I will be bitter with him and passing short.
Go with me, Silvius.                                   *Exeunt.*

---

**131. am rememb'red:** recall.   **133. omittance . . . quittance:** failure to assert a claim does not imply renunciation of the claim (legal proverb); i.e. I am still entitled to reply.   **138. passing short:** exceedingly curt.

# Act 4

SCENE I

*Enter* ROSALIND *and* CELIA *and* JAQUES.

JAQUES  I prithee, pretty youth, let me [be] better
acquainted with thee.

ROSALIND  They say you are a melancholy fellow.

JAQUES  I am so; I do love it better than laughing.

ROSALIND  Those that are in extremity of either are      5
abominable fellows, and betray themselves to every
modern censure worse than drunkards.

JAQUES  Why, 'tis good to be sad and say nothing.

ROSALIND  Why then 'tis good to be a post.

JAQUES  I have neither the scholar's melancholy,      10
which is emulation; nor the musician's, which is
fantastical; nor the courtier's, which is proud; nor
the soldier's, which is ambitious; nor the lawyer's,
which is politic; nor the lady's, which is nice; nor
the lover's, which is all these: but it is a melancholy      15
of mine own, compounded of many simples,
extracted from many objects, and indeed the sundry
contemplation of my travels, in which [my]
often rumination wraps me in a most humorous
sadness.      20

ROSALIND  A traveller! By my faith, you have great
reason to be sad. I fear you have sold your own
lands to see other men's; then to have seen much,
and to have nothing, is to have rich eyes and poor
hands.      25

JAQUES  Yes, I have gain'd my experience.

---

4.1. Location: The forest.  **5. are . . . of:** go to extremes in.  **7. modern censure:** ordinary judgment.  **8. sad:** sober-minded. Rosalind then quibbles on the sense "heavy."  **11. emulation:** envy.  **12. fantastical:** highly fanciful.  **14. politic:** shrewd, calculated. **nice:** delicate, fastidious.  **16. simples:** ingredients.  **17. objects:** sights, observations.  **17–18. sundry contemplation of:** contemplation of various details during (?) or various ways of thinking about (?).  **18–19. in . . . rumination:** in which (melancholy) my frequent meditation.  **19. humorous:** moody.

136

*Enter* ORLANDO.

ROSALIND  And your experience makes you sad. I had
    rather have a fool to make me merry than experience
    to make me sad—and to travel for it too!
ORLANDO  Good day and happiness, dear Rosalind!         30
JAQUES  Nay then God buy you, and you talk in
    blank verse.
ROSALIND  Farewell, Monsieur Traveller: look you
    lisp and wear strange suits; disable all the benefits of
    your own country; be out of love with your        35
    nativity, and almost chide God for making you
    that countenance you are; or I will scarce think
    you have swam in a gundello. Why,         [*Exit Jaques.*]
    how now, Orlando, where have you been all this
    while? You a lover! And you serve me such another    40
    trick, never come in my sight more.
ORLANDO  My fair Rosalind, I come within an hour of
    my promise.
ROSALIND  Break an hour's promise in love! He that
    will divide a minute into a thousand parts, and    45
    break but a part of the thousand part of a minute
    in the affairs of love, it may be said of him that
    Cupid hath clapp'd him o' th' shoulder, but I'll
    warrant him heart-whole.
ORLANDO  Pardon me, dear Rosalind.         50
ROSALIND  Nay, and you be so tardy, come no more in
    my sight. I had as lief be woo'd of a snail.
ORLANDO  Of a snail?
ROSALIND  Ay, of a snail; for though he comes slowly,
    he carries his house on his head; a better jointure    55
    I think than you make a woman. Besides,
    he brings his destiny with him.
ORLANDO  What's that?
ROSALIND  Why, horns! which such as you are fain to
    be beholding to your wives for. But he comes    60

---

**29. travel.** With pun on *travail,* "labor."   **31. God buy you:** goodbye. **and:** if.
**34. lisp:** speak affectedly. **disable:** disparage.   **36. nativity:** birth, i.e. nationality
**38. swam . . . gundello:** ridden in a gondola, i.e. seen Venice (a very popular resort
of foreign travellers).   **46. thousand:** thousandth.   **48. clapp'd . . . shoulder:** i.e.
struck him in the back (with his arrow). Cf. *clapp'd i' th' clout* (hit the bull's-eye),
*2 Henry IV,* 3.2.46.   **49. heart-whole:** not wounded in the heart.   **55–56. jointure:**
marriage settlement.   **59. horns:** i.e. cuckold's horns. **fain:** obliged.   **60. beholding:** beholden, indebted.

arm'd in his fortune, and prevents the slander of
his wife.

ORLANDO Virtue is no horn-maker; and my Rosalind
is virtuous.

ROSALIND And I am your Rosalind.                                    65

CELIA It pleases him to call you so; but he hath a
Rosalind of a better leer than you.

ROSALIND Come, woo me, woo me; for now I am in a
holiday humor, and like enough to consent. What
would you say to me now, and I were your very very       70
Rosalind?

ORLANDO I would kiss before I spoke.

ROSALIND Nay, you were better speak first, and when
you were gravell'd for lack of matter, you might
take occasion to kiss. Very good orators when            75
they are out, they will spit, and for lovers lacking
(God warn us!) matter, the cleanliest shift is to kiss.

ORLANDO How if the kiss be denied?

ROSALIND Then she puts you to entreaty, and there
begins new matter.                                       80

ORLANDO Who could be out, being before his belov'd
mistress?

ROSALIND Marry, that should you if I were your mistress,
or I should think my honesty ranker than
my wit.                                                  85

ORLANDO What, of my suit?

ROSALIND Not out of your apparel, and yet out of your
SUIT. Am not I your Rosalind?

ORLANDO I take some joy to say you are, because I
would be talking of her.                                 90

ROSALIND Well, in her person, I say I will not have
you.

ORLANDO Then in mine own person, I die.

ROSALIND No, faith, die by attorney. The poor world
is almost six thousand years old, and in all this        95
time there was not any man died in his own

---

**61. arm'd ... fortune:** already equipped for his future. **prevents:** forestalls. **slander:** ill repute. **67. of ... leer:** better-looking. **74. gravell'd:** stuck, at a loss. **76. out:** confused; excluded.★ **77. warn:** warrant, protect. **cleanliest shift:** cleverest device (with a play on *cleanliest* on kissing versus spitting). **84. honesty:** chastity. **ranker:** more corrupt. **86. suit:** play on double meaning 1)clothing 2)plea.★ **94. attorney:** proxy. **94–95. The poor ... old.** This was the view of some Biblical commentators.

person, *videlicet,* in a love-cause. Troilus had his
brains dash'd out with a Grecian club, yet he did
what he could to die before, and he is one of the
patterns of love. Leander, he would have liv'd                                    100
many a fair year though Hero had turn'd nun, if it
had not been for a hot midsummer night; for, good
youth, he went but forth to wash him in the Hellespont,
and being taken with the cramp was drown'd; and
the foolish chroniclers of that age found it was—                                105
Hero of Sestos. But these are all lies: men have died
from time to time, and worms have eaten them,
but not for love.
ORLANDO  I would not have my right Rosalind of this
    mind, for I protest her frown might kill me.                             110
ROSALIND  By this hand, it will not kill a fly. But
    come, now I will be your Rosalind in a more coming-on
    disposition; and ask me what you will, I will
    grant it.
ORLANDO  Then love me, Rosalind.                                                 115
ROSALIND  Yes, faith, will I, Fridays and Saturdays and
    all.
ORLANDO  And wilt thou have me?
ROSALIND  Ay, and twenty such.
ORLANDO  What sayest thou?                                                       120
ROSALIND  Are you not good?
ORLANDO  I hope so.
ROSALIND  Why then, can one desire too much of a
    good thing? Come, sister, you shall be the priest,
    and marry us. Give me your hand, Orlando. What                          125
    do you say, sister?
ORLANDO  Pray thee marry us.
CELIA  I cannot say the words.
ROSALIND  You must begin, "Will you, Orlando"—
CELIA  Go to! Will you, Orlando, have to wife this                               130
    Rosalind?
ORLANDO  I will.
ROSALIND  Ay, but when?

---

**97. videlicet:** namely. **Troilus:** the lover of Cressida, who proved faithless to
him. **98. brains . . . club.** Troilus died of a wound inflicted by Achilles' spear.
Rosalind makes his end, and Leander's, as unromantic as possible. **98–99. did . . .
before:** i.e. vainly did his utmost to die earlier of frustrated love. **100. patterns:**
models. **105. found:** gave the verdict (the customary term for the handing down
of a verdict by a coroner's jury). **109. right:** real.

ORLANDO  Why, now, as fast as she can marry us.

ROSALIND  Then you must say, "I take thee, Rosalind,                    135
for wife."

ORLANDO  I take thee, Rosalind, for wife.

ROSALIND  I might ask you for your commission, but
I do take thee, Orlando, for my husband. There's
a girl goes before the priest, and certainly a woman's                 140
thought runs before her actions.

ORLANDO  So do all thoughts, they are wing'd.

ROSALIND  Now tell me how long you would have her
after you have possess'd her.

ORLANDO  For ever and a day.                                           145

ROSALIND  Say "a day," without the "ever." No, no,
Orlando, men are April when they woo, December
when they wed; maids are May when they are maids,
but the sky changes when they are wives. I will
be more jealous of thee than a Barbary cock-                           150
pigeon over his hen, more clamorous than a parrot
against rain, more new-fangled than an ape, more
giddy in my desires than a monkey. I will weep for
nothing, like Diana in the fountain, and I will do that
when you are dispos'd to be merry. I will laugh                        155
like a hyen, and that when thou art inclin'd to sleep.

ORLANDO  But will my Rosalind do so?

ROSALIND  By my life, she will do as I do.

ORLANDO  O, but she is wise.

ROSALIND  Or else she could not have the wit to do                     160
this; the wiser, the waywarder. Make the doors
upon a woman's wit, and it will out at the casement;
shut that, and 'twill out at the key-hole; stop that,
'twill fly with the smoke out at the chimney.

ORLANDO  A man that had a wife with such a wit, he                     165
might say, "Wit, whither wilt?"

---

**138. for your commission:** i.e. by what authority you presume to take her.★
**140. goes before:** anticipates.  **150–51. Barbary cock-pigeon:** a kind of pigeon
originally from the Barbary coast of Africa; but the term *Barbary* was also more
widely applied to Eastern non-Christians, particularly Moslems, and is suggestive
here of the vigilance of Eastern husbands in secluding their wives from other
men.  **152. against:** before.  **new-fangled:** delighted by novelty.  **153. giddy:**
variable.  **154. Diana . . . fountain.** There may be some specific reference here;
but the figure of Diana was probably common in garden fountains.  **156. hyen:**
hyena.  **161. Make:** make fast, bar.  **166. Wit, whither wilt.** See note to 1.2.56.

ROSALIND Nay, you might keep that check for it, till
you met your wive's wit going to your neighbor's
bed.

ORLANDO And what wit could wit have to excuse that? 170

ROSALIND Marry, to say she came to seek you there.
You shall never take her without her answer,
unless you take her without her tongue. O, that
woman that cannot make her fault her husband's
occasion, let her never nurse her child herself, for 175
she will breed it like a fool!

ORLANDO For these two hours, Rosalind, I will leave
thee.

ROSALIND Alas, dear love, I cannot lack thee two hours!

ORLANDO I must attend the Duke at dinner. By two 180
a' clock I will be with thee again.

ROSALIND Ay, go your ways, go your ways; I knew
what you would prove; my friends told me as
much, and I thought no less. That flattering tongue
of yours won me. 'Tis but one cast away, and so 185
come death! Two a' clock is your hour?

ORLANDO Ay, sweet Rosalind.

ROSALIND By my troth, and in good earnest, and so
God mend me, and by all pretty oaths that are not
dangerous, if you break one jot of your promise, or 190
come one minute behind your hour, I will think
you the most pathetical break-promise, and the
most hollow lover, and the most unworthy of her
you call Rosalind, that may be chosen out of the
gross band of the unfaithful; therefore beware my 195
censure, and keep your promise.

ORLANDO With no less religion than if thou wert indeed
my Rosalind; so adieu.

ROSALIND Well, Time is the old justice that examines
all such offenders, and let Time try. Adieu. 200

*Exit [Orlando].*

CELIA You have simply misus'd our sex in your love-
prate. We must have your doublet and hose

---

**168. wive's:** wife's. **174–75. her husband's occasion:** a chance to put her husband in the wrong. **179. lack:** do without. **189. pretty:** pleasant-sounding,
inoffensive. **192. pathetical:** pitiable, miserable. **195. gross:** entire. **197. religion:** faithfulness. **200. try:** determine. **201. simply:** stupidly (?) or utterly (?).
**misus'd:** abused, slandered.

pluck'd over your head, and show the world what
the bird hath done to her own nest.

ROSALIND O coz, coz, coz, my pretty little coz, that     205
thou didst know how many fathom deep I am
in love! But it cannot be sounded; my affection
hath an unknown bottom, like the bay of Portugal.

CELIA Or rather, bottomless—that as fast as you
pour affection in, [it] runs out.     210

ROSALIND No, that same wicked bastard of Venus
that was begot of thought, conceiv'd of spleen, and
born of madness, that blind rascally boy that abuses
every one's eyes because his own are out, let him be
judge how deep I am in love. I'll tell thee, Aliena,     215
I cannot be out of the sight of Orlando. I'll go find
a shadow, and sigh till he come.

CELIA And I'll sleep.     *Exeunt.*


### SCENE 2

*Enter* JAQUES *and* LORDS [*as*] *foresters.*

JAQUES Which is he that kill'd the deer?

[1.] LORD Sir, it was I.

JAQUES Let's present him to the Duke like a Roman
conqueror, and it would do well to set the deer's horns
upon his head, for a branch of victory. Have you     5
no song, forester, for this purpose?

[2.] LORD Yes, sir.

JAQUES Sing it. 'Tis no matter how it be in tune,
so it make noise enough.     *Music.*

SONG

[2. LORD] What shall he have that kill'd the deer?     10
    His leather skin and horns to wear.
        Then sing him home.
      *The rest shall bear this burthen.*

---

**202–4. We . . . nest:** i.e. we must expose you as a member of the sex that you have defamed. There is an allusion to the proverb "It is a foul bird that fouls its own nest." **211. bastard of Venus:** Cupid. **212. thought:** melancholy. **spleen:** caprice, waywardness. **213. abuses:** deludes. **214. his . . . out:** he himself is blind. **217. shadow:** shady place. 4.2. Location: The forest. This short scene is introduced to indicate the passing of the specified two hours between Scenes 1 and 3. **8. how . . . tune:** whether you sing it on key (?) or whether the tune be good or bad (?). **12. s.d. bear this burthen:** i.e. sing the words "Then sing him home" as a ground-bass or undersong throughout (?). On the stage direction see the Textual Notes. **13. Take . . . scorn:** do not disdain.

Take thou no scorn to wear the horn,
It was a crest ere thou wast born;
Thy father's father wore it,                                          15
And thy father bore it.
The horn, the horn, the lusty horn
Is not a thing to laugh to scorn.                    *Exeunt.*


## SCENE 3

*Enter* ROSALIND *and* CELIA.

ROSALIND  How say you now? Is it not past two a'
  clock? And here much Orlando!
CELIA  I warrant you, with pure love and troubled
  brain, he hath ta'en his bow and arrows and is gone
  forth—to sleep. Look who comes here.                             5

*Enter* SILVIUS.

SILVIUS  My errand is to you, fair youth,
  My gentle Phebe did bid me give you this.

                                               [*Gives a letter.*]

  I know not the contents, but as I guess
  By the stern brow and waspish action
  Which she did use as she was writing of it,                      10
  It bears an angry tenure. Pardon me,
  I am but as a guiltless messenger.
ROSALIND  Patience herself would startle at this letter,
  And play the swaggerer: bear this, bear all!
  She says I am not fair, that I lack manners;                     15
  She calls me proud, and that she could not love me
  Were man as rare as phoenix. 'Od's my will,
  Her love is not the hare that I do hunt;
  Why writes she so to me? Well, shepherd, well,
  This is a letter of your own device.                             20
SILVIUS  No, I protest, I know not the contents,
  Phebe did write it.
ROSALIND                   Come, come, you are a fool,
  And turn'd into the extremity of love.
  I saw her hand, she has a leathern hand,

---

**14. crest:** (1) heraldic device; (2) something growing on the head. **4.3.** Location: The forest. **11. tenure:** tenor. **17. phoenix.** Supposedly unique bird.★  **23. turn'd:** brought.

A freestone-colored hand. I verily did think 25
That her old gloves were on, but 'twas her hands;
She has a huswive's hand—but that's no matter.
I say she never did invent this letter,
This is a man's invention and his hand.
SILVIUS Sure it is hers. 30
ROSALIND Why, 'tis a boisterous and a cruel style,
A style for challengers. Why, she defies me,
Like Turk to Christian. Women's gentle brain
Could not drop forth such giant-rude invention,
Such Ethiop words, blacker in their effect 35
Than in their countenance. Will you hear the letter?
SILVIUS So please you, for I never heard it yet;
Yet heard too much of Phebe's cruelty.
ROSALIND She Phebes me. Mark how the tyrant writes.
(*Read.*) "Art thou god to shepherd turn'd, 40
That a maiden's heart hath burn'd?"
Can a woman rail thus?
SILVIUS Call you this railing?
ROSALIND (*Read.*)
"Why, thy godhead laid apart,
Warr'st thou with a woman's heart?" 45
Did you ever hear such railing?
"Whiles the eye of man did woo me,
That could do no vengeance to me."
Meaning me a beast.
"If the scorn of your bright eyne 50
Have power to raise such love in mine,
Alack, in me what strange effect
Would they work in mild aspect?
Whiles you chid me, I did love;
How then might your prayers move? 55
He that brings this love to thee
Little knows this love in me;
And by him seal up thy mind,
Whether that thy youth and kind
Will the faithful offer take 60

---

**25. freestone-colored:** brownish-yellow. **35. Ethiop:** black. **36. countenance:** physical appearance. **39. Phebes me:** behaves like Phebe towards me, i.e. addresses me in cruel words. **44. laid apart:** put aside (for human shape). **48. vengeance:** harm. **50. eyne:** eyes (archaic even in Elizabethan English; used here for the sake of rhyme). **53. aspect:** looks. **58. seal . . . mind:** i.e. send your decision in a letter. **59. youth and kind:** youthful nature.

   Of me, and all that I can make,
   Or else by him my love deny,
   And then I'll study how to die."
SILVIUS Call you this chiding?
CELIA Alas, poor shepherd!          65
ROSALIND Do you pity him? No, he deserves no pity.
 Wilt thou love such a woman? What, to make thee
 an instrument, and play false strains upon thee? not
 to be endur'd! Well, go your way to her (for I see
 love hath made thee a tame snake) and say this to her:  70
 that if she love me, I charge her to love thee; if she
 will not, I will never have her unless thou entreat for
 her. If you be a true lover, hence, and not a word;
 for here comes more company.     *Exit Silvius*

*Enter* OLIVER.

OLIVER Good morrow, fair ones. Pray you (if you know) 75
 Where in the purlieus of this forest stands
 A sheep-cote fenc'd about with olive-trees?
CELIA West of this place, down in the neighbor bottom,
 The rank of osiers by the murmuring stream
 Left on your right hand brings you to the place.   80
 But at this hour the house doth keep itself,
 There's none within.
OLIVER If that an eye may profit by a tongue,
 Then should I know you by description—
 Such garments and such years. "The boy is fair,   85
 Of female favor, and bestows himself
 Like a ripe sister; the woman low,
 And browner than her brother." Are not you
 The owner of the house I did inquire for?
CELIA It is no boast, being ask'd, to say we are.   90
OLIVER Orlando doth commend him to you both,
 And to that youth he calls his Rosalind
 He sends this bloody napkin. Are you he?
ROSALIND I am. What must we understand by this?
OLIVER Some of my shame, if you will know of me   95
 What man I am, and how, and why, and where
 This handkercher was stain'd.

---

**68. instrument:** (1) tool; (2) musical instrument. **76. purlieus:** land bordering a
forest, subject to special regulations.* **78. neighbor bottom:** neighboring
dell. **79. rank of osiers:** row of willows. **86. female favor:** feminine features. **be-**
**stows:** conducts. **87. ripe:** mature, i.e. elder. **low:** short. **93. napkin:** handkerchief.

CELIA                    I pray you tell it.
OLIVER  When last the young Orlando parted from you
    He left a promise to return again
    Within an hour, and pacing through the forest,                    100
    Chewing the food of sweet and bitter fancy,
    Lo what befell! He threw his eye aside,
    And mark what object did present itself
    Under an old oak, whose boughs were moss'd with age
    And high top bald with dry antiquity:                             105
    A wretched ragged man, o'ergrown with hair,
    Lay sleeping on his back; about his neck
    A green and gilded snake had wreath'd itself,
    Who with her head nimble in threats approach'd
    The opening of his mouth; but suddenly                            110
    Seeing Orlando, it unlink'd itself,
    And with indented glides did slip away
    Into a bush, under which bush's shade
    A lioness, with udders all drawn dry,
    Lay couching, head on ground, with cat-like watch                 115
    When that the sleeping man should stir; for 'tis
    The royal disposition of that beast
    To prey on nothing that doth seem as dead.
    This seen, Orlando did approach the man,
    And found it was his brother, his elder brother.                  120
CELIA  O, I have heard him speak of that same brother,
    And he did render him the most unnatural
    That liv'd amongst men.
OLIVER                    And well he might so do,
    For well I know he was unnatural.
ROSALIND  But to Orlando: did he leave him there,                    125
    Food to the suck'd and hungry lioness?
OLIVER  Twice did he turn his back, and purpos'd so;
    But kindness, nobler ever than revenge,
    And nature, stronger than his just occasion,
    Made him give battle to the lioness,                              130
    Who quickly fell before him, in which hurtling
    From miserable slumber I awaked.

---

103. **what object:** what a sight.   11. **unlink'd:** uncoiled.   112. **indented:** undulating.   114. **udders . . . dry.** Hence hungry.   122. **render him:** depict him as. **unnatural:** devoid of natural feeling. Cf. *nature* (= natural affection) in line 129. 125. **to:** with regard to.   128. **kindness:** feeling proper to his (human) kind. 129. **just occasion:** chance to get even.   131. **hurtling:** commotion.

CELIA  Are you his brother?
ROSALIND                        Was't you he rescu'd?
CELIA  Was't you that did so oft contrive to kill him?
OLIVER  'Twas I; but 'tis not I. I do not shame                    135
    To tell you what I was, since my conversion
    So sweetly tastes, being the thing I am.
ROSALIND  But for the bloody napkin?
OLIVER                                By and by.
    When from the first to last betwixt us two
    Tears our recountments had most kindly bath'd,          140
    As how I came into that desert place—
    [In] brief, he led me to the gentle Duke,
    Who gave me fresh array and entertainment,
    Committing me unto my brother's love,
    Who led me instantly unto his cave,                     145
    There stripp'd himself, and here upon his arm
    The lioness had torn some flesh away,
    Which all this while had bled; and now he fainted,
    And cried in fainting upon Rosalind.
    Brief, I recover'd him, bound up his wound,             150
    And after some small space, being strong at heart,
    He sent me hither, stranger as I am,
    To tell this story, that you might excuse
    His broken promise, and to give this napkin,
    Dy'd in [his] blood, unto the shepherd youth           155
    That he in sport doth call his Rosalind.
                             [*Rosalind faints.*]
CELIA  Why, how now, Ganymed, sweet Ganymed?
OLIVER  Many will swoon when they do look on blood.
CELIA  There is more in it. Cousin Ganymed!
OLIVER  Look, he recovers.                                         160
ROSALIND  I would I were at home.
CELIA                        We'll lead you thither.
    I pray you, will you take him by the arm?
OLIVER  Be of good cheer, youth. You a man?
    You lack a man's heart.
ROSALIND  I do so, I confess it. Ah, sirrah, a body              165
    would think this was well counterfeited! I pray

---

134. **contrive:** plan, devise ways.   138. **for:** i.e. what about.   140. **recountments:**
stories told to each other.   150. **Brief:** in brief. **recover'd:** revived.   159. **Cousin.**
In her excitement Celia forgets that Rosalind is supposed to be her brother.
165. **I do so.** She lacks a man's heart in two senses not suspected by Oliver.

you tell your brother how well I counterfeited.
Heigh-ho!

OLIVER This was not counterfeit, there is too great
testimony in your complexion that it was a passion       170
of earnest.

ROSALIND Counterfeit, I assure you.

OLIVER Well then, take a good heart and counterfeit
to be a man.

ROSALIND So I do; but i' faith, I should have been a       175
woman by right.

CELIA Come, you look paler and paler. Pray you
draw homewards. Good sir, go with us.

OLIVER That will I, for I must bear answer back
How you excuse my brother, Rosalind.       180

ROSALIND I shall devise something; but I pray you
commend my counterfeiting to him. Will you go?

                                            *Exeunt.*

---

**170–71. passion of earnest:** genuine seizure.

# Act 5

### SCENE I

*Enter Clown* [TOUCHSTONE] *and* AUDREY.

TOUCHSTONE  We shall find a time, Audrey, patience,
    gentle Audrey.
AUDREY  Faith, the priest was good enough, for all
    the old gentleman's saying.
TOUCHSTONE  A most wicked Sir Oliver, Audrey, a most          5
    vile Martext. But, Audrey, there is a youth here
    in the forest lays claim to you.
AUDREY  Ay, I know who 'tis; he hath no interest
    in me in the world. Here comes the man you mean.

*Enter* WILLIAM.

TOUCHSTONE  It is meat and drink to me to see a clown.        10
    By my troth, we that have good wits have much to
    answer for; we shall be flouting; we cannot hold.
WILLIAM  Good ev'n, Audrey.
AUDREY  God ye good ev'n, William.
WILLIAM  And good ev'n to you, sir.                           15
TOUCHSTONE  Good ev'n, gentle friend. Cover thy head,
    cover thy head; nay, prithee be cover'd. How old
    are you, friend?
WILLIAM  Five and twenty, sir.
TOUCHSTONE  A ripe age. Is thy name William?                 20
WILLIAM  William, sir.
TOUCH.  A fair name. Wast born i' the forest
    here?
WILLIAM  Ay, sir, I thank God.
TOUCHSTONE  "Thank God"—a good answer. Art rich?            25

---

5.1. Location: The forest.  **8–9. interest in:** claim to.  **10. clown:** country yokel.
**12. shall:** must. **flouting:** making sport. **hold:** hold back, refrain.  **14. God ye:**
God give you.  **16. Cover thy head:** William has respectfully removed his hat.

WILLIAM  Faith, sir, so, so.

TOUCHSTONE  "So, so" is good, very good, very excellent
good; and yet it is not, it is but so, so. Art thou wise?

WILLIAM  Ay, sir, I have a pretty wit.

TOUCHSTONE  Why, thou say'st well. I do now remember          30
a saying, "The fool doth think he is wise,
but the wise man knows himself to be a fool." The
heathen philosopher, when he had a desire to eat a
grape, would open his lips when he put it into
his mouth, meaning thereby that grapes were made          35
to eat and lips to open. You do love this maid?

WILLIAM  I do, [sir].

TOUCHSTONE  Give me your hand. Art thou learned?

WILLIAM  No, sir.

TOUCHSTONE  Then learn this of me: to have, is to have.          40
For it is a figure in rhetoric that drink, being pour'd out
of a cup into a glass, by filling the one doth empty the
other. For all your writers do consent that *ipse* is he:
now, you are not *ipse,* for I am he.

WILLIAM  Which he, sir?          45

TOUCHSTONE  He, sir, that must marry this woman.
Therefore, you clown, abandon—which is in the
vulgar leave—the society—which in the boorish is
company—of this female—which in the common
is woman; which together is, abandon the society of          50
this female, or, clown, thou perishest; or to thy better
understanding, diest; or (to wit) I kill thee, make thee
away, translate thy life into death, thy liberty into
bondage. I will deal in poison with thee, or in bastinado,
or in steel; I will bandy with thee in faction; I          55
will o'errun thee with [policy]; I will kill thee a
hundred and fifty ways: therefore tremble and depart.

AUDREY  Do, good William.

WILLIAM  God rest you merry, sir.          *Exit.*

---

**27. good, very good.** Touchstone is punning on another meaning of *so, so:* "just so;
very good." **33–35. heathen . . . mouth.** Capell suggests that this notion occurs
to Touchstone because William is standing with his mouth open, gaping at him in
bewilderment. The inference is that Audrey is no grape for William's swallowing.
**43. your writers:** authorities (the indefinite *your,* as in 3.4.12). **ipse:** he himself. **52. to wit:** namely. **53. translate:** change. **54–55. bastinado:** beating with
a stick. **55. bandy:** vie, contend. **faction:** factious spirit. **56. o'errun:** over-
whelm. **policy:** craftiness. **59. God . . . merry.** A common form of greeting or
leavetaking.

*Enter* CORIN.

CORIN  Our master and mistress seeks you. Come          60
  away, away!
TOUCHSTONE  Trip, Audrey, trip, Audrey! I attend, I
  attend.                                              *Exeunt.*


SCENE 2

*Enter* ORLANDO *and* OLIVER.

ORLANDO  Is't possible that on so little acquaintance
  you should like her? that but seeing, you should
  love her? and loving, woo? and wooing, she should
  grant? and will you persever to enjoy her?
OLIVER  Neither call the giddiness of it in question,          5
  the poverty of her, the small acquaintance, my sudden
  wooing, nor [her] sudden consenting; but say with me,
  I love Aliena; say with her that she loves me; consent
  with both that we may enjoy each other. It shall be
  to your good; for my father's house and all the          10
  revenue that was old Sir Rowland's will I estate upon
  you, and here live and die a shepherd.

*Enter* ROSALIND.

ORLANDO  You have my consent. Let your wedding
  be to-morrow; thither will I invite the Duke and
  all's contented followers. Go you and prepare Aliena;          15
  for look you, here comes my Rosalind.
ROSALIND  God save you, brother.
OLIVER  And you, fair sister.                                   [*Exit.*]
ROSALIND  O my dear Orlando, how it grieves me to
  see thee wear thy heart in a scarf!                           20
ORLANDO  It is my arm.
ROSALIND  I thought thy heart had been wounded with
  the claws of a lion.
ORLANDO  Wounded it is, but with the eyes of a lady.

5.2. Location: The forest.  **4. persever:** persevere.  **5. giddiness:** dizzying
speed.  **6. sudden:** swift.  **11. estate:** bestow as an estate.  **15. all's:** all his. **contented:** ready, willing.  **17. brother:** (prospective) brother-in-law.  **18. sister.**
Oliver is presumably entering into the supposed Ganymed's pretense of being
Rosalind.  **20. heart . . . scarf.** Rosalind pretends to assume that any bandage (*scarf*)
worn by Orlando must cover the part that he has long proclaimed wounded—his
heart—and further that he has been wearing it on his sleeve.

ROSALIND  Did your brother tell you how I counterfeited                25
    to sound when he show'd me your
    handkercher?
ORLANDO  Ay, and greater wonders than that.
ROSALIND  O, I know where you are. Nay, 'tis true.
    There was never any thing so sudden but the fight of           30
    two rams, and Caesar's thrasonical brag of "I came,
    saw, and [overcame]." For your brother and my
    sister no sooner met but they look'd; no sooner look'd
    but they lov'd; no sooner lov'd but they sigh'd; no
    sooner sigh'd but they ask'd one another the                  35
    reason; no sooner knew the reason but they sought the
    remedy: and in these degrees have they made a pair
    of stairs to marriage, which they will climb incontinent,
    or else be incontinent before marriage. They
    are in the very wrath of love, and they will together.        40
    Clubs cannot part them.
ORLANDO  They shall be married to-morrow; and I
    will bid the Duke to the nuptial. But O, how bitter
    a thing it is to look into happiness through another
    man's eyes! By so much the more shall I to-morrow be           45
    at the height of heart-heaviness, by how much I shall
    think my brother happy in having what he wishes for.
ROSALIND  Why then to-morrow I cannot serve your
    turn for Rosalind?
ORLANDO  I can live no longer by thinking.                             50
ROSALIND  I will weary you then no longer with idle
    talking. Know of me then (for now I speak to some
    purpose) that I know you are a gentleman of good
    conceit. I speak not this that you should bear a
    good opinion of my knowledge, insomuch I say I know            55
    you are; neither do I labor for a greater esteem than
    may in some little measure draw a belief from you, to
    do yourself good, and not to grace me. Believe then, if
    you please, that I can do strange things. I have,
    since I was three year old, convers'd with a magician,         60

---

**26. sound:** swoon.  **29. where you are:** what you mean.  **31. thrasonical:** vaunting.
Thraso is a braggart soldier in Terence's *Eunuchus*.  **37. degrees.** With a pun on
the meaning "steps." **pair:** flight.  **38–39. incontinent:** immediately (with following pun on the sense "unchaste").  **40. wrath:** rage, passionate ardor.  **41. Clubs.**
Regularly used for breaking up street fights.  **43. bid:** invite.  **52–53. to some
purpose:** with serious intent.  **54. conceit:** understanding.  **55. insomuch:** inasmuch as.  **58. grace:** do honor to.  **60. convers'd:** associated.

most profound in his art, and yet not damnable. If
you do love Rosalind so near the heart as your gesture
cries it out, when your brother marries Aliena, shall
you marry her. I know into what straits of fortune
she is driven, and it is not impossible to me, if it                    65
appear not inconvenient to you, to set her before your
eyes to-morrow, human as she is, and without any
danger.

ORLANDO  Speak'st thou in sober meanings?

ROSALIND  By my life I do, which I tender dearly,                       70
though I say I am a magician. Therefore put you
in your best array, bid your friends; for if you will
be married to-morrow, you shall; and to Rosalind,
if you will.

*Enter* SILVIUS *and* PHEBE.

Look, here comes a lover of mine and a lover of                         75
hers.

PHEBE  Youth, you have done me much ungentleness,
To show the letter that I writ to you.

ROSALIND  I care not if I have. It is my study
To seem despiteful and ungentle to you.                                 80
You are there followed by a faithful shepherd—
Look upon him, love him; he worships you.

PHEBE  Good shepherd, tell this youth what 'tis to
love.

SILVIUS  It is to be all made of sighs and tears,
And so am I for Phebe.                                                   85

PHEBE  And I for Ganymed.

ORLANDO  And I for Rosalind.

ROSALIND  And I for no woman.

SILVIUS  It is to be all made of faith and service,
And so am I for Phebe.                                                   90

PHEBE  And I for Ganymed.

ORLANDO  And I for Rosalind.

ROSALIND  And I for no woman.

---

**61. not damnable:** i.e. not a practicer of black magic, which involved trafficking
with evil spirits and invited damnation.  **62. gesture:** bearing.  **63. cries it out:**
plainly reveals.  **66. inconvenient:** unfitting.  **67–68. human . . . danger:** i.e. in her
own person, not a spirit in her shape who might endanger Orlando's soul (cf. the
apparition of Helen in Marlowe's *Doctor Faustus*).  **69. sober:** serious.  **70. tender
dearly:** value highly.  **71. though . . . magician:** i.e. though I endanger my life by
saying openly that I practice magic (some forms of which were punishable by death).
**77. ungentleness:** discourtesy.  **79. study:** diligent endeavor.  **80. despiteful:** cruel.

SILVIUS  It is to be all made of fantasy,
 All made of passion, and all made of wishes,                         95
 All adoration, duty, and observance,
 All humbleness, all patience, and impatience,
 All purity, all trial, all observance;
 And so am I for Phebe.
PHEBE  And so am I for Ganymed.                                       100
ORLANDO  And so am I for Rosalind.
ROSALIND  And so am I for no woman.
PHEBE  If this be so, why blame you me to love you?
SILVIUS  If this be so, why blame you me to love you?
ORLANDO  If this be so, why blame you me to love you?                105
ROSALIND  Why do you speak too, "Why blame you
 me to love you?"
ORLANDO  To her that is not here, nor doth not hear.
ROSALIND  Pray you no more of this, 'tis like the howling
 of Irish wolves against the moon. [*To Silvius.*] I              110
 will help you if I can. [*To Phebe.*] I would love
 you if I could.—To-morrow meet me all together.
 [*To Phebe.*] I will marry you, if ever I marry woman,
 and I'll be married to-morrow. [*To Orlando.*] I will
 satisfy you, if ever I satisfied man, and you shall be           115
 married to-morrow. [*To Silvius.*] I will content
 you, if what pleases you contents you, and you
 shall be married to-morrow. [*To Orlando.*] As you
 love Rosalind, meet. [*To Silvius.*] As you love Phebe,
 meet. And as I love no woman, I'll meet. So fare                 120
 you well; I have left you commands.
SILVIUS  I'll not fail, if I live.
PHEBE  Nor I.
ORLANDO  Nor I.                                                    *Exeunt.*


## SCENE 3

*Enter Clown* [TOUCHSTONE] *and* AUDREY.

TOUCHSTONE  To-morrow is the joyful day, Audrey,
 tomorrow will we be married.

**96. observance:** devoted service.   **98. trial:** being tested, proving one's constancy.
**observance.** Some editors, taking this repetition as an error, emend to *obedi-
ence.*   **106–7. Why . . . to.** Emended by some editors to *Who . . . to,* to accord with
Orlando's reply.   **109–10. howling . . . moon:** proverbs often refer to howling
wolves; Shakespeare's culture stereotyped the Irish, with whom they were at war
when *As You Like It* was written, as bestial.★   5.3. Location: The forest.

AUDREY  I do desire it with all my heart; and I hope
　　it is no dishonest desire to desire to be a woman
　　of the world. Here come two of the banish'd Duke's　　　5
　　pages.

*Enter two* PAGES.

1. PAGE  Well met, honest gentleman.
TOUCHSTONE  By my troth, well met. Come, sit, sit,
　　and a song.
2. PAGE  We are for you, sit i' th' middle.　　　　　　　10
1. PAGE  Shall we clap into't roundly, without
　　hawking or spitting or saying we are hoarse, which
　　are the only prologues to a bad voice?
2. PAGE  I' faith, i' faith, and both in a tune, like
　　two gipsies on a horse.　　　　　　　　　　　　　15

SONG

It was a lover and his lass,
　　With a hey, and a ho, and a hey nonino,
That o'er the green corn-field did pass,
　　In spring time, the only pretty [ring] time,
When birds do sing, hey ding a ding, ding,　　　　　20
Sweet lovers love the spring.

Between the acres of the rye,
　　With a hey, and a ho, and a hey nonino,
These pretty country folks would lie,
　　In spring time, etc.　　　　　　　　　　　　　25

This carol they began that hour,
　　With a hey, and a ho, and a hey nonino,
How that a life was but a flower,
　　In spring time, etc.

And therefore take the present time,　　　　　　　30
　　With a hey, and a ho, and a hey nonino,
For love is crowned with the prime,
　　In spring time, etc.

**4. dishonest:** immodest.　**4–5. woman . . . world:** married woman.　**10. We . . .
you:** i.e. that suits us.　**11. clap into't roundly:** strike into it briskly.　**13. only:** i.e.
only proper, i.e. customary.　**14. in a tune:** (1) in unison; (2) keeping in time. Both
here and in the next line *a* = one.　**18. corn-field:** wheatfield.　**19. ring time:**
season for weddings.　**22. Between . . . rye:** i.e. on the unploughed strips separating the planted fields.　**30. take:** seize for enjoyment.　**32. prime:** springtime.

TOUCHSTONE  Truly, young gentlemen, though there
    was no great matter in the ditty, yet the note was     35
    very untuneable.
1. PAGE  You are deceiv'd, sir, we kept time, we
    lost not our time.
TOUCHSTONE  By my troth, yes; I count it but time lost
    to hear such a foolish song. God buy you, and God     40
    mend your voices! Come, Audrey.            *Exeunt.*

### SCENE 4

*Enter* DUKE SENIOR, AMIENS, JAQUES,
ORLANDO, OLIVER, CELIA.

DUKE SENIOR  Dost thou believe, Orlando, that the boy
    Can do all this that he hath promised?
ORLANDO  I sometimes do believe, and sometimes do not,
    As those that fear they hope, and know they fear.

*Enter* ROSALIND, SILVIUS, *and* PHEBE.

ROSALIND  Patience once more, whiles our compact is urg'd:     5
    You say, if I bring in your Rosalind,
    You will bestow her on Orlando here?
DUKE SENIOR  That would I, had I kingdoms to give
    with her.
ROSALIND  And you say you will have her, when I
    bring her.
ORLANDO  That would I, were I of all kingdoms king.     10
ROSALIND  You say you'll marry me, if I be willing?
PHEBE  That will I, should I die the hour after.
ROSALIND  But if you do refuse to marry me,
    You'll give yourself to this most faithful shepherd?
PHEBE  So is the bargain.     15
ROSALIND  You say that you'll have Phebe, if she will?
SILVIUS  Though to have her and death were both one thing.
ROSALIND  I have promis'd to make all this matter even:
    Keep you your word, O Duke, to give your daughter;
    You, yours, Orlando, to receive his daughter;     20
    Keep you your word, Phebe, that you'll marry me,
    Or else, refusing me, to wed this shepherd;

---

**35. ditty:** words. **note:** music. **36. untuneable:** untuneful. **39. yes:** i.e. yes, you did lose (waste) your time. 5.4. Location: The forest. **4. fear they hope:** fear they are merely hoping (without prospect of fulfillment). **5. urg'd:** put forward. **8. had I:** even if I had. **18. even:** smooth, unobstructed by difficulty.

Keep your word, Silvius, that you'll marry her
If she refuse me; and from hence I go
To make these doubts all even.                                          25

*Exeunt Rosalind and Celia.*

DUKE SENIOR  I do remember in this shepherd boy
   Some lively touches of my daughter's favor.
ORLANDO  My lord, the first time that I ever saw him
   Methought he was a brother to your daughter.
   But, my good lord, this boy is forest-born,                          30
   And hath been tutor'd in the rudiments
   Of many desperate studies by his uncle,
   Whom he reports to be a great magician,
   Obscured in the circle of this forest.

*Enter Clown* [TOUCHSTONE] *and* AUDREY.

JAQUES  There is sure another flood toward, and                        35
   these couples are coming to the ark. Here comes a
   pair of very strange beasts, which in all tongues are
   call'd fools.
TOUCHSTONE  Salutation and greeting to you all!
JAQUES  Good my lord, bid him welcome. This is                         40
   the motley-minded gentleman that I have so often
   met in the forest. He hath been a courtier, he swears.
TOUCHSTONE  If any man doubt that, let him put me to my
   purgation. I have trod a measure, I have flatt'red a
   lady, I have been politic with my friend, smooth with                45
   mine enemy, I have undone three tailors, I have had
   four quarrels, and like to have fought one.
JAQUES  And how was that ta'en up?
TOUCHSTONE  Faith, we met, and found the quarrel was
   upon the seventh cause.                                              50
JAQUES  How seventh cause? Good my lord, like
   this fellow.
DUKE SENIOR  I like him very well.
TOUCHSTONE  God 'ild you, sir, I desire you of the like.
   I press in here, sir, amongst the rest of the country                55

---

**26. do remember:** am reminded (of).   **27. lively:** lifelike. **touches:** aspects, details.
**favor:** appearance.   **32. desperate:** dangerous.   **34. Obscured:** hidden; with a
possible allusion in *Obscured in the circle* to the magic circle within which a magician was supposed safe during his dealing with spirits.   **35. toward:** on the way.
**43–44. put . . . purgation:** challenge me to clear myself (of the charge of lying).
**44. measure:** a slow, stately dance.   **46. undone:** bankrupted (by running up huge
bills and failing to pay).   **47. like . . . fought:** almost had to fight.   **48. ta'en up:**
settled.   **54. desire . . . like:** wish you the same.

copulatives, to swear and to forswear, according as
marriage binds and blood breaks. A poor virgin, sir, an
ill-favor'd thing, sir, but mine own; a poor humor of
mine, sir, to take that that no man else will. Rich
honesty dwells like a miser, sir, in a poor house, as                    60
your pearl in your foul oyster.

DUKE SENIOR  By my faith, he is very swift and
sent0entious.

TOUCHSTONE  According to the fool's bolt, sir, and such
dulcet diseases.                                                         65

JAQUES  But for the seventh cause—how did you find
the quarrel on the seventh cause?

TOUCHSTONE  Upon a lie seven times remov'd (bear your
body more seeming, Audrey), as thus, sir. I did dislike
the cut of a certain courtier's beard. He sent                          70
me word, if I said his beard was not cut well, he was in
the mind it was: this is call'd the Retort Courteous.
If I sent him word again, it was not well cut, he
would send me word he cut it to please himself: this
is call'd the Quip Modest. If again, it was not well                    75
cut, he disabled my judgment: this is call'd the
Reply Churlish. If again, it was not well cut, he
would answer I spake not true: this is call'd the
Reproof Valiant. If again, it was not well cut, he
would say I lie: this is call'd the Countercheck                        80
Quarrelsome; and so to Lie Circumstantial and the Lie
Direct.

JAQUES  And how oft did you say his beard was not
well cut?

TOUCHSTONE  I durst go no further than the Lie Circumstantial,          85
nor he durst not give me the Lie Direct;
and so we measur'd swords and parted.

JAQUES  Can you nominate in order now the degrees
of the lie?

---

**56. copulatives:** people about to marry.  **57. blood:** passion.  **58. humor:**
whim.  **60. honesty:** chastity.  **62–63. swift and sententious:** ready-witted
and pithy.  **64. fool's bolt.** Alluding to the proverb "A fool's bolt [arrow] is
soon shot."  **65. dulcet diseases:** pleasing discomfort. A jester's shafts of wit are
entertaining but can strike painfully home.  **69. more seeming:** in a more
seemly fashion.  **69–70. dislike:** find fault with.  **75. Modest:** moderate.
**76. disabled:** belittled, declared incompetent.  **80. Countercheck:** counter-
rebuff, contradiction.  **81. Circumstantial:** indirect.  **87. measur'd swords:** i.e.
prepared for duelling.  **88. nominate:** name over.

TOUCHSTONE  O sir, we quarrel in print, by the book—                90
    as you have books for good manners. I will name you
    the degrees. The first, the Retort Courteous; the
    second, the Quip Modest; the third, the Reply
    Churlish; the fourth, the Reproof Valiant; the
    fift, the Countercheck Quarrelsome; the sixt, the                95
    Lie with Circumstance; the seventh, the Lie Direct.
    All these you may avoid but the Lie Direct; and you
    may avoid that too, with an If. I knew when seven
    justices could not take up a quarrel, but when the
    parties were met themselves, one of them thought but                100
    of an If, as, "If you said so, then I said so"; and they
    shook hands and swore brothers. Your If is the only
    peacemaker; much virtue in If.
JAQUES  Is not this a rare fellow, my lord? He's as
    good at any thing, and yet a fool.                105
DUKE SENIOR  He uses his folly like a stalking-horse,
    and under the presentation of that he shoots his wit.

          *Enter* HYMEN, ROSALIND, *and* CELIA.                *Still music.*

HYMEN  Then is there mirth in heaven,
    When earthly things made even
        Atone together.                110
    Good Duke, receive thy daughter,
    Hymen from heaven brought her,
        Yea, brought her hither,
    That thou mightst join [her] hand with his
    Whose heart within his bosom is.                115
ROSALIND  [*To Duke Senior.*] To you I give myself, for I
    am yours.
[*To Orlando.*] To you I give myself, for I am yours.
DUKE SENIOR  If there be truth in sight, you are my daughter.
ORLANDO  If there be truth in sight, you are my Rosalind.

---

**90. by the book:** according to established rules. There were, in fact, such books, hardly less fantastic than Touchstone's "lie seven times remov'd." One which may be glanced at here is Vincent Saviolo's *Practice of the Rapier and Dagger* (1594–5), the second part of which treats of "Honor and Honorable Quarrels," with a section headed "Of the manner and diversity of Lies."  **99. take up:** settle.  **102. swore brothers:** i.e. became sworn brothers, pledged to the mutual loyalty proper to actual brothers.  **106. stalking-horse:** any deceptive cover used by a game-stalker to get within shooting distance of his quarry.  **107. under . . . that:** i.e. using his assumed folly as a protective disguise.  **107.** s.d. **Hymen:** god of marriage. **Still:** soft.  **108. mirth:** joy.  **110. Atone:** are at one, accord.  **114. [her].** This common editorial emendation replaces "his" in the Folio. ★

PHEBE  If sight and shape be true,                                        120
    Why then my love adieu!
ROSALIND  I'll have no father, if you be not he;
    I'll have no husband, if you be not he;
    Nor ne'er wed woman, if you be not she.
HYMEN   Peace ho! I bar confusion,                                       125
        'Tis I must make conclusion
            Of these most strange events.
        Here's eight that must take hands
        To join in Hymen's bands,
            If truth holds true contents.                                130
    [To Orlando and Rosalind.]
        You and you no cross shall part;
    [To Oliver and Celia.]
        You and you are heart in heart;
    [To Phebe.]
        You to his love must accord,
        Or have a woman to your lord;
    [To Touchstone and Audrey.]
        You and you are sure together,                                   135
        As the winter to foul weather.—
    Whiles a wedlock-hymn we sing,
    Feed yourselves with questioning;
    That reason wonder may diminish
    How thus we met, and these things finish.                            140

SONG

    Wedding is great Juno's crown,
        O blessed bond of board and bed!
    'Tis Hymen peoples every town,
        High wedlock then be honored.
    Honor, high honor, and renown                                        145
    To Hymen, god of every town!

DUKE SENIOR  O my dear niece, welcome thou art to me,
    Even daughter, welcome, in no less degree.
PHEBE  I will not eat my word, now thou art mine,
    Thy faith my fancy to thee doth combine.                             150

130. If . . . contents: i.e. if truth is true.  131. cross: disagreement.  133. accord:
assent.  134. to: for.  135. sure together: securely joined.  138. Feed: satisfy.
139. reason: rational explanation.  141. Juno's. Juno was the goddess of marriage.  144. High: solemn.  148. Even . . . degree: i.e. you are no whit less welcome to me than a daughter.  150. combine: unite.

*Enter Second Brother* [JAQUES DE BOYS].

JAQUES DE BOYS  Let me have audience for a word or two.
  I am the second son of old Sir Rowland,
  That bring these tidings to this fair assembly.
  Duke Frederick, hearing how that every day
  Men of great worth resorted to this forest,                          155
  Address'd a mighty power, which were on foot
  In his own conduct, purposely to take
  His brother here, and put him to the sword;
  And to the skirts of this wild wood he came;
  Where, meeting with an old religious man,                            160
  After some question with him, was converted
  Both from his enterprise and from the world,
  His crown bequeathing to his banish'd brother,
  And all their lands restor'd to [them] again
  That were with him exil'd. This to be true,                          165
  I do engage my life.
DUKE SENIOR                Welcome, young man;
  Thou offer'st fairly to thy brothers' wedding:
  To one his lands withheld, and to the other
  A land itself at large, a potent dukedom.
  First, in this forest let us do those ends                           170
  That here were well begun and well begot;
  And after, every of this happy number,
  That have endur'd shrewd days and nights with us,
  Shall share the good of our returned fortune,
  According to the measure of their states.                            175
  Mean time, forget this new-fall'n dignity,
  And fall into our rustic revelry.
  Play, music, and you brides and bridegrooms all,
  With measure heap'd in joy, to th' measures fall.
JAQUES  Sir, by your patience.—If I heard you rightly,                 180
  The Duke hath put on a religious life,
  And thrown into neglect the pompous court?
JAQUES DE BOYS  He hath.

---

**156. Address'd:** made ready, levied. **power:** army. **157. In . . . conduct:** under his personal command. **161. question:** conversation. **166. engage:** pledge. **167. Thou offer'st fairly:** you bring handsome gifts. **169. A land . . . large:** a whole country in itself. The restoration of the dukedom to Rosalind's father means that her husband will be the next duke. **170. do those ends:** bring to a conclusion those purposes. **171. begot:** conceived. **172. every:** every one. **173. shrewd:** sorely difficult. **175. states:** rank. **176. new-fall'n:** newly acquired. **178. music:** musicians. **180. patience:** indulgence, permission. **182. pompous:** ceremonious.

JAQUES  To him will I. Out of these convertites
    There is much matter to be heard and learn'd.  185
[*To Duke Senior.*] You to your former honor I bequeath,
    Your patience and your virtue well deserves it;
[*To Orlando.*] You to a love, that your true faith doth merit;
[*To Oliver.*] You to your land, and love, and great
    allies;
[*To Silvius.*] You to a long and well-deserved bed;  190
[*To Touchstone.*] And you to wrangling, for thy loving
    voyage
    Is but for two months victuall'd.—So to your pleasures,
    I am for other than for dancing measures.
DUKE SENIOR  Stay, Jaques, stay.
JAQUES  To see no pastime I. What you would have  195
    I'll stay to know at your abandon'd cave.  *Exit.*
DUKE SENIOR  Proceed, proceed. We'll begin these rites,
    As we do trust they'll end, in true delights.
    [*A dance.*]  *Exeunt [all but Rosalind].*

# [EPILOGUE]

ROSALIND  It is not the fashion to see the lady the
    epilogue; but it is no more unhandsome than to
    see the lord the prologue. If it be true that good
    wine needs no bush, 'tis true that a good play needs
    no epilogue. Yet to good wine they do use good  5
    bushes; and good plays prove the better by the help
    of good epilogues. What a case am I in then, that
    am neither a good epilogue, nor cannot insinuate
    with you in the behalf of a good play! I am not
    furnish'd like a beggar, therefore to beg will not  10
    become me. My way is to conjure you, and I'll
    begin with the women. I charge you, O women,
    for the love you bear to men, to like as much of
    this play as please you; and I charge you, O men,
    for the love you bear to women (as I perceive  15
    by your simp'ring, none of you hates them), that
    between you and the women the play may please.
    If I were a woman I would kiss as many of you as

---

**184. convertites:** converts.  **Epi. 2. unhandsome:** unfitting.  **3–4. good . . . bush.**
Proverbial. The ivy bush was formerly the vintner's sign.  **7. case:** predicament.
**8. insinuate:** ingratiate myself.  **10. furnish'd:** dressed, equipped.  **11. conjure:**
earnestly charge.

had beards that pleas'd me, complexions that lik'd
me, and breaths that I defied not; and I am 20
sure, as many as have good beards, or good faces, or
sweet breaths, will for my kind offer, when I make
curtsy, bid me farewell. *Exit.*

## NOTE ON THE TEXT

The First Folio (1623) is our only authority for *As You Like It;* all later texts
are derived from that source. Critics are agreed that (1) the printer's copy
for *As You Like It,* F1, was not a Shakespearean holograph; and (2) the F1
text is clean and essentially sound, showing no signs of significant revision
(*pace* Wilson). But here agreement ends. Knowles argues that the F1 copy
was either a prompt-book (so Greg), a transcript from the prompt-book
(so Latham), or a transcript of the "foul papers," partially annotated by
the book-keeper as copy for the official prompt-book; Wells/Taylor are
similarly uncertain, suggesting that "the copy was either the prompt-book
or a literary transcript, either from the prompt-book itself or the foul
papers." A theatrical provenience is supported by the act and scene divi-
sions in the F1 text and probably by the imperative stage directions at
1.2.212, 215; 2.5.37; 4.2.12; 5.4.107.

For further information, see: J. D. Wilson, ed., New Shakespeare *As
You Like It* (Cambridge, 1926; rev. 1947); W. W. Greg, *The Shakespeare
First Folio* (Oxford, 1955); Agnes Latham, ed., New Arden *As You Like It*
(London, 1975); Richard Knowles, ed., New Variorum *As You Like It*
(New York, 1977); Stanley Wells, Gary Taylor, et al., *William Shakespeare: A
Textual Companion* (Oxford, 1987); Alan Brissenden, ed., New Oxford *As
You Like It* (Oxford, 1993).

**18. If . . . woman.** Women's parts were played by boys. **19. lik'd:** pleased. **20.
defied:** disliked. **23. bid me farewell:** i.e. by applauding.

## TEXTUAL NOTES

**Dramatis personae:** *subs. as first given
by Rowe; an earlier list, which describes
Duke Senior as Ferdinand Old duke of
Burgundy, appears in the Douai MS*
**Act-scene division:** *from F1*

### I.1

**Location:** *Rowe, Pope*
52 **What,**] *Theobald;* What *F1*
52 s.d. **Strikes him.**] *White*
54 s.d. **Collaring him.**] *Johnson*
93 s.d. **Exit Dennis.**] *Johnson*
109 **she**] *F3;* hee *F1*

151, 167 **device**] *F3;* deuise *F1*
156 **anatomize**] *F3;* anathomize *F1*
163 s.p. **Oli.**] *F2*

### I.2

**Location:** *Capell (after Rowe)*
4 **I**] *Rowe*
31 **huswife**] *Capell;* housewife *F1*
53 **and**] *Malone*
57 s.p. **Touch.**] *Malone;* Clow. *F1*
  (*throughout*)
81 **mean'st**] *Rowe;* means't *F1*
83 s.p. **Cel.**] *Theobald;* Ros. *F1*

84 s.d. **Exeunt**] *Rowe (subs.);* Ex. *F1*
87 **wise men**] *F3;* Wisemen *F1*
91 **Le**] *F2;* the *F1*
91 **Beau**] *Steevens;* Beu *F1 (throughout, except in s.d. following l. 91)*
97 **Bon jour**] *Rowe (subs.);* Boon-iour *F1*
149 s.p. **Duke F.**] *Malone;* Duke. *F1 (throughout)*
149-56 **Come . . . wrastling.**] *as prose, Pope; as verse, F1*
208 **You . . . after;**] *Cambridge, following Theobald, suggests reading* And you . . . after, *(i.e.* If you . . . after,) *on the supposition that the compositor took* And *to be part of the speech-prefix* Orland.; *though not necessary, the emendation makes for easier sense*
215 s.d. **Charles is thrown.**] *Rowe*
230 s.d. **with . . . Beau**] *Capell (subs.)*
242 **deserv'd.**] *Pope (subs.);* deseru'd, *F1*
243 **love**] *Singer;* loue; *F1;* love, *F2*
244 **all**] all in *F2*
245 s.d. **Giving . . . neck.**] *Theobald*
251 **quintain**] *Theobald;* quintine *F1*
256 s.d. **with Celia**] *Rowe (subs.)*
272 **smaller**] *Malone;* taller *F1*
286 s.d. **Exit Le Beau.**] *Capell*
289 **Rosalind**] *Rowe;* Rosaline *F1 (through II.v; Compositor D's spelling)*

### 1.3

**Location:** *Theobald (subs.)*
1-2 **Why . . . word?**] *as prose, Rowe; as verse, F1*
12 **working-day**] *hyphen, Rowe*
42 **uncle?**] *Capell;* Vncle. *F1*
52 **traitors:**] *Theobald (subs.);* Traitors, *F1*
57 **likelihood**] *F2;* likelihoods *F1*
78 **her**] *F2;* per *F1*
82 **lips:**] *Pope;* lips *F1;* lips, *F2*
83 **doom**] *Rowe;* doombe *F1*
89 s.d. **with Lords**] *Malone (subs.);* &c. *F1*
126 **be**] *F2;* by *F1*
131 **travel**] *F3;* trauaile *F1*
133 **woo**] *F2* (wooe); woe *F1 (sporadically throughout)*
137 **we in**] *F2;* in we *F1*

### 2.1

**Location:** *Theobald (after Rowe)*
6 **fang**] *Johnson;* phange *F1*
18 **I . . . it.**] *Upton suggested giving these words to Duke Senior and has been followed by many eds.*
18 **it. Happy**] *Rowe (subs.);* it, happy *F1*

31 **antique**] *Pope;* anticke *F1*
45 **similes**] *Steevens;* similies *F1*
49 **much**] *F2;* must *F1*
50 **friends**] *Rowe;* friend *F1*
59 **the**] *F2*

### 2.2

**Location:** *Rowe (subs.)*

### 2.3

**Location:** *Capell (after Rowe)*
o.s.d. **meeting**] *Capell*
10 **some**] *F2;* seeme *F1*
16 s.p. **Orl.**] *F2; continued to Adam, F1*
29 s.p. **Orl.**] *F2;* Ad. *F1*
35 **can.**] *F3* (can:); can, *F1*
39 **sav'd**] *Rowe;* saued *F1*
46 **servant.**] *Theobald (subs.);* seruant, *F1*
71 **seventeen**] *Rowe;* seauentie *F1*

### 2.4

**Location:** *Theobald (after Rowe)*
1 **weary**] *Theobald;* merry *F1*
19 **so,**] *Rowe;* so *F1*
33 **heartily!**] *Dyce (after F4);* hartily, *F1*
38 **Wearing**] Wearying *F2 (adopted by some eds.)*
44 **shepherd!**] *F2;* Shepheard *F1*
44 **thy**] *Rowe;* they *F1;* their *F2*
44 **wound**] *F2;* would *F1*
48 **a-night**] *hyphen, Collier*
69 **you**] *F2;* your *F1*
74 **travel**] *F3;* trauaile *F1*
81 **reaks**] *ed.;* wreakes *F1*
83 **Besides,**] *Rowe;* Besides *F1*

### 2.5

**Location:** *Capell (after Rowe)*
1 s.p. **Ami.**] *Capell*
12-4, 17-9, 34-7, 46-7] *as prose, Pope; as irregular verse, F1*
26 **compliment**] *Pope;* complement *F1*
44-5 **No . . . weather.**] *from ll. 7-8 above;* &c. *F1*
49 s.p. **Jaq.**] *F2;* Amy. *F1*

### 2.6

**Location:** *Capell (after Rowe)*
1-18] *as prose, Pope; as irregular verse, F1*
14,18 **cheerly**] *F4;* cheerely *F1*

### 2.7

**Location:** *Capell (after Rowe)*
o.s.d. **A . . . out.**] *Rowe*

o.s.d. **Amiens**] *Capell*
o.s.d. **Lords**] *Rowe;* Lord *F1*
38 **brain**] *F2;* braiue *F1*
48 **Withal**] *F2,* Wiithall *F1*
55 **Not to**] *Theobald*
56 **wise man's**] *Rowe;* Wise-mans *F1*
56 **anatomiz'd**] *F3;* anathomiz'd *F1*
64 **sin**] *F2;* fin *F1*
75 **city-woman**] *hyphen, Pope*
83 **then! . . . what then?**] *Wilson*
   *(after Theobald);* then, how then,
   what then, *F1*
87 **any man. But**] *F2;* any. man But *F1*
   *(Furness claims that some copies of F1*
   *have been corrected, but Hinman records*
   *no corrected state)*
87 **comes**] *F2;* come *F1*
87 s.d. **with . . . drawn**] *Douai MS,*
   *Theobald*
100-1 **and . . . die.**] *as prose, Capell;*
   *as verse, F1*
135 s.d. **Exit.** *Rowe*
167-8 **Welcome . . . feed.**] *as verse,*
   *Pope; as prose, F1*
174 s.p. **Ami.**] *Johnson*
182 **Then**] *Rowe;* The *F1*
198 **master**] *F2;* masters *F1*

### 3.1

**Location:** *Rowe (subs.)*

### 3.2

**Location:** *Rowe*
o.s.d. **with a paper**] *Capell*
27 **good**] *F2;* pood *F1*
32-3 **Such . . . shepherd?**] *as prose, Pope;*
   *as verse, F1*
87 s.d. **with . . . reading**] *Capell*
89 **Rosalind**] *Kittredge points out that F1*
   *here, and through l. 112, spells the name as*
   Rosalinde *to emphasize the pronunciation*
92 **lin'd**] *Pope;* Linde *F1*
97 **sleeping-hours**] *hyphen, Dyce*
125 s.d. **Reads.**] *Dyce*
125 **a desert be?**] *Rowe;* Desert bee, *F1*
128 **show**] *F4;* shoe *F1*
135 **boughs**] *Rowe;* bowes *F1*
143 **wide-enlarg'd.**] *Rowe (subs.; hyphen,*
   *Dyce);* wide enlarg'd, *F1*
145 **her**] *Douai MS, Rowe;* his *F1*
148 **Lucretia's**] *F4;* Lucrecia's *F1*
158 **now?**] *Theobald;* now *F1;* now! *F2*
158 **back,**] *Dyce;* backe *F1*
162 s.d. **with Corin**] *Rowe (subs.)*
196 **hose**] a hose *F2*

227 **size.**] *F3 (subs.);* size, *F1*
237 **such**] *Capell;* forth *F1;* forth such *F2*
244 **thy**] *Rowe;* the *F1*
246 **heart**] *Rowe;* Hart *F2*
294 s.d. **Exit Jaques.**] *Douai MS, Rowe*
295 s.d. **Aside to Celia.**] *Capell*
347 **lectures**] *F3;* Lectors *F1;* Lecturs *F2*
363 **deifying**] *F2;* defying *F1*
371 **are**] *F2;* art *F1*
382 **point-device**] *hyphen, Theobald*

### 3.3

**Location:** *Capell (after Rowe)*
o.s.d. **behind**] *Collier*
2 **Audrey?**] *Capell;* Audrey *F1*
7 **goats**] *Munro;* Goats, *F1*
10, 32, 46 s.dd. **Aside.**] *Johnson*
14-5 **God 'ild**] *Theobald (after F2 godild);*
   goddild *F1*
56-7 **Horns? . . . alone?**] *Theobald (subs.,*
   *after Rowe);* hornes, euen so poore
   men alone: *F1*
67 s.p. **Sir Oli.**] *Rowe;* Ol. *F1 (throughout)*
71 s.d. **Discovering himself.**] *Johnson*
90 s.d. **Aside.**] *Capell*
90 **mind**] *Capell;* minde, *F1*
96 s.p. **Touch.**] *F2 (Clo.);* Ol. *F1*
99-105 **O . . . thee.**] *subs. as verse,*
   *Warburton conj.; as prose, F1*
105 s.d. **Exeunt . . . Audrey.**] *Capell*
107 s.d. **Exit.**] *Capell;* Exeunt. *F1*

### 3.4

**Location:** *Capell (after Rowe)*
5-14 **As . . . bread.**] *as prose, Pope; as*
   *irregular verse, F1*
30 **a**] *F2*

### 3.5

**Location:** *Rowe (implied)*
1 **Phebe;**] *Rowe;* Phebe *F1;* Phebe, *F3*
7 s.d. **behind**] *Collier (after Capell)*
9 **thee**] *ed.;* thee, *F1*
10 **eye:**] *F4 (subs.);* eye, *F1*
11 **pretty,**] *Theobald;* pretty *F1*
17 **why,**] *Theobald;* why *F1*
20 **thee;**] *thee, F1*
22 **lean**] *Leane but F2*
35 s.d. **Advancing.**] *Capell*
37 **have**] *F2;* hau *F1*
37 **beauty—**] *Pope (subs.);* Beauty *F1*
66-70 **He's . . . me?**] *as prose, Pope; as*
   *irregular verse, F1*
80 s.d. **with . . . Corin**] *Hanmer (subs.)*
80 **love,**] *F4;* loue *F1*

108 **carlot**] *Steevens;* Carlot *F1*
  (*in italics, as a proper name*)
128 **Have**] I haue *F2*
134 **taunting**] *F4;* tanting *F1*

## 4.1

**Location:** *Rowe*
1 **be**] *F2*
6 **abominable**] *F3;* abhominable *F1*
18 **my**] *F2;* by *F1*
19 **rumination**] *Rowe (the comma is very
  faint in F4);* rumination, *F1*
29 **travel**] *F3;* trauaile *F1*
38 s.d. **Exit Jaques.**] *Dyce;* Exit.
  *F2 (after l. 32)*
49 **heart-whole**] *F4;* heart hole *F1*
55 **jointure**] *F2;* ioyncture *F1*
69 **holiday**] *Capell;* holy-day *F1*
97 **love-cause**] *hyphen, Theobald*
105 **chroniclers**] *F2;* Chronoclers *F1*
105 **was—**] *Theobald (subs.);* was *F1*
106 **Sestos**] *F2;* Cestos *F1*
138 **I . . . commission,**] *as prose, Pope;
  as verse, F1*
200 s.d. **Orlando**] *Rowe*
210 **it**] *F2;* in *F1*

## 4.2

**Location:** *Capell (after Rowe)*
o.s.d. **as**] *Malone*
2 s.p. **1. Lord.**] *Malone (after Capell);*
  Lord. *F1*
7 s.p. **2. Lord.**] *Malone (after Capell);*
  Lord. *F1*
10 s.p. **2. Lord.**] *C. J. Hill (in Riverside
  Six Plays)*
12 s.d. **The . . . burthen.**] *as s.d.,
  Theobald; as concluding part of l. 12, F1*

## 4.3

**Location:** *Capell (after Rowe)*
1–5 **How . . . here.**] *as prose, Pope;
  as verse, F1*
5 **forth—to**] *Capell;* forth/To *F1*
5 s.d. **Enter Silvius.**] *placed as in Pope;
  after brain, l. 4, F1*
7 **did**] *om. F2*
7 s.d. **Gives a letter.**] *Johnson (subs.)*
34 **giant-rude**] *hyphen, Capell*
44 **apart**] *F2;* a part *F1*
73 **lover,**] *F4;* louer *F1*
78 **bottom,**] *Rowe;* bottom *F1*
87 **the**] But the *F1*
105 **top**] *F2;* top, *F1*
142 **In**] *F2;* I *F1*

155 **his**] *F2;* this *F1*
156 s.d. **Rosalind faints.**] *Pope*
165 **I . . . it.**] *as prose, Pope; as verse, F1*
170 **a**] *om. F2*

## 5.1

**Location:** *Rowe*
10 **clown.**] *F4 (subs.);* Clowne, *F1*
22 **Wast**] *Pope;* Was't *F1*
32 **wise man**] *F4;* wiseman *F1*
37 **sir**] *F2;* sit *F1*
56 **policy**] *F2;* police *F1*
58 **Do,**] *F4;* Do *F1*
59 **merry,**] *F4;* merry *F1*

## 5.2

**Location:** *Capell (after Rowe)*
7 **her**] *Douai MS, Rowe*
13–6 **You . . . Rosalind.**] *as prose, Pope;
  as verse, F1*
18 s.d. **Exit.**] *Capell*
32 **overcame**] *F2;* ouercome *F1*
46 **heart-heaviness**] *hyphen, Rowe*
56 **are**] *F2;* arc *F1*
67 **human**] *Rowe;* humane *F1*
110 s.d. **To Silvius.**] *Douai MS, Capell*
111 s.d. **To Phebe.**] *Douai MS, Johnson*
112 **all together**] *F4;* altogether *F1*
113 s.d. **To Phebe.**] *Pope*
114 s.d. **To Orlando.**] *Pope*
116 s.d. **To Silvius.**] *Pope*
118 s.d. **To Orlando.**] *Johnson*
119 s.d. **To Silvius.**] *Douai MS, Johnson*

## 5.3

**Location:** *Capell (after Rowe)*
16 **It was**] 'Twas *Morley (in First Booke of
  Ayres, 1600)*
17 **hey, and**] haye with *Morley, Adv. MS
  5.2.14, fol. 18 (in National Library,
  Edinburgh)*
18 **corn-field**] corne fields *Morley*
19 **In**] *Knight (after Adv. MS), Morley;*
  In the *F1*
19 **ring**] *Steevens conj. and Morley, Adv. MS;*
  rang *F1*
20 **a ding, ding**] ading ading *Morley, Adv.
  MS*
23, 27, 31 **hey, and**] hay, with *Morley*
24 **folks**] fooles *Morely, Adv. MS*
24 **would**] did *Adv. MS*
30–3 **And . . . etc.**] *Johnson's arrangement
  (as in Morley and Adv. MS); in F1 these
  lines follow l. 21*

30 **And . . . time**] Then prettie louers
   take the time *Morley, Adv. MS*
36 **untuneable.**] *F2;* vntunable *F1*

## 5.4

**Location:** *Capell (after Rowe)*
25 s.d. **Exeunt**] *Hanmer;* Exit *F1*
34 s.d. **Enter . . . Audrey.**] *placed as in*
   *Rowe; after l. 33, F1*
81 **to**] *F2* (to the); ro *F1*
114 **her**] *F3;* his *F1*
116 s.d. **To Duke Senior.**] *Douai*
   *MS, Rowe*
117 s.d. **To Orlando.**] *Douai MS, Rowe*
121 **adieu!**] *Theobald;* adieu *F1;* adiev. *F2*
130 s.d. **To . . . Rosalind.**] *Johnson*
131 s.d. **To . . . Celia.**] *Johnson*
132 s.d. **To Phebe.**] *Johnson*
134 s.d. **To . . . Audrey.**] *Johnson*
148 **daughter,**] *F4;* daughter *F1*
150 s.d. **Jaques de Boys**] *Rowe*

151, 183 s.pp. **Jaq. de B.**] *Rowe;*
   2. Bro. *F1*
164 **them**] *Douai MS, Rowe;* him *F1*
171 **were**] *F2;* vvete *F1*
186 s.d. **To Duke Senior.**] *Rowe*
186 **bequeath,**] *Rowe;* bequeath *F1;*
   bequeath; *F2*
188 s.d. **To Orlando.**] *Rowe*
189 s.d. **To Oliver.**] *Rowe*
190 s.d. **To Silvius.**] *Rowe*
191 s.d. **To Touchstone.**] *Rowe*
197 **rites**] *Rowe;* rights *F1*
198 **trust they'll end,**] *Pope;* trust,
   they'l end *F1*
198 s.d. **A dance.**] *Capell*
198 s.d. **Exeunt.**] *Craig;* Exit *F1*
198 s.d. **all but Rosalind**] *ed.*

## Epilogue

**Epilogue**] *so titled by Theobald*
23 s.d. **Exit.**] Exit. / FINIS. *F1*

# From *ROSALYNDE. EUPHUES GOLDEN LEGACIE*

### Thomas Lodge

### ROSALYND

There dwelled adjoyning to the citie of *Bourdeaux* a Knight of most honorable parentage, whom Fortune had graced with manie favours, and Nature honored with sundrie exquisite qualities, so beautified with the excellence of both, as it was a question whether Fortune or Nature were more prodigall in deciphering the riches of their bounties. Wise hée was, as holding in his head a supreme conceipt of policie, reaching with *Nestor*[1] into the depth of all civill government; and to make his wisedome more gracious, he had that *salem ingenii*[2] and pleasant eloquence that was so highlie commended in *Ulisses*:[3] his valour was no lesse than his wit, nor the stroake of his Launce no lesse forcible, than the sweetnesse of his tongue was perswasive: for he was for his courage chosen the principall of all the Knights of *Malta.*

This hardie Knight thus enricht with Vertue and Honour, surnamed Sir *John* of *Bourdeaux,* having passed the prime of his youth in sundrie battailes against the *Turkes,* at last (as the date of time hath his course) grew aged: his haires were silver hued, and the map of age was figured on his forehead: Honour sat in the furrowes of his face, and many yeres were pourtraied in his wrinckled liniaments, that all men might perceive his glasse was runne, and that Nature of necessity chalenged her due. Sir *John* (that with the Phenix[4] knewe the tearme of his life was now expyred, and could with the Swanne discover his end by her songs) having three sonnes by his wife *Lynida,* the verie pride of all his forepassed yeres, thought now (seeing death by constraint would

---

**1. Nestor:** Greek leader during the Trojan war  **2. salem ingenii:** wit  **3. Ulisses:** famous hero in Homer's *Odyssey*  **4. Phenix:** a mythological bird that rose again from its own ashes

compell him to leave them) to bestowe upon them such a Legacie as might bewray his love, and increase their ensuing amitie. Calling therefore these yong Gentlemen before him in the presence of all his fellowe Knights of *Malta,* he resolved to leave them a memoriall of his fatherlie care, in setting downe a methode of their brotherlie dueties. Having therefore death in his lookes to moove them to pitie, and teares in his eyes to paint out the depth of his passions, taking his eldest sonne by the hand, hee began thus.

### Sir John of Bourdeaux Legacie He Gave To His Sonnes

Oh my Sonnes, you see that Fate hath set a period of my yeares, and Destinies have determined the finall ende of my daies: the Palme tree waxeth away ward, for he stoopeth in his height, and my plumes are full of sicke feathers touched with age. I must to my grave that dischargeth all cares, and leave you to the world that encreaseth many sorowes: my silver haires conteineth great experience, and in the number of my yeares are pend downe the subtilties of Fortune. Therefore as I leave you some fading pelfe to counter-checke povertie, so I will bequeath you infallible precepts that shall leade you unto vertue. First therefore unto thée *Saladyne* the eldest, and therefore the chiefest piller of my house, wherein should be ingraven as well the excellence of thy fathers qualities, as the essentiall forme of his proportion, to thée I give fouretéene ploughlands, with all my Mannor houses and richest plate. Next unto *Fernandyne* I bequeath twelve ploughlands. But unto *Rosader* the yongest I give my Horse, My Armour and my Launce, with sixteene ploughlands: for if the inward thoughts be discovered by outward shadowes, *Rosader* will excéed you all in bountie and honour. Thus (my Sonnes) have I parted in your portions the substance of my wealth, wherein if you bee as prodigall to spend, as I have béen carefull to get, your friends will grieve to see you more wastfull than I was bountifull, and your foes smile that my fall did begin in your excesse. Let mine honour be the glasse of your actions, and the fame of my vertues the Loadstarre[5] to direct the course of your pilgrimage.

[*After John of Bordeaux's death, his eldest son, Saladyne, experiences intense resentment that his brother Rosader inherited more than he did. Saladyne connives with a wrestler to bring about Rosader's death.*]

At last a lustie *Francklin*[6] of the Countrie came with two tall men that were his Sonnes of good lyniaments and comely personage: the eldest of these dooing his obeysance to the King entered the lyst,

---

**5. Loadstarre:** guiding principle   **6. Francklin:** a type of landowner

and presented himselfe to the *Norman*,[7] who straight coapt[8] with him, and as a man that would triumph in the glorie of his strength, roused himselfe with such furie, that not onely hee gave him the fall, but killed him with the weight of his corpulent personage: which the younger brother seeing, lept presently into the place, and thirstie after the revenge, assayled the *Norman* with such valour, that at the first incounter hee brought him to his knées: which repulst so the *Norman*, that recovering himselfe, feare of disgrace doubling his strength, hee stept so stearnely to the young *Francklin*, that taking him up in his armes he threw him against the ground so violently, that he broake his neck, and so ended his dayes with his brother. At this unlookt for massacre, the people murmured, and were all in a déepe passion of pittie; but the *Francklin*, Father unto these, never changed his countenance; but as a man of a couragious resolution, tooke up the bodies of his Sonnes without any shew of outward discontent.

All this while stoode *Rosader* and sawe this tragedie: who noting the undoubted vertue of the *Francklins* minde, alighted off from his horse, and presentlie sat downe on the grasse, and commaunded his boy to pull off his bootes, making him readie to trie the strength of this Champion; being furnished as he would, hee clapt the *Francklin* on the shoulder and saide thus. Bolde yeoman whose sonnes have ended the tearme of their yeares with honour, for that I sée thou scornest fortune with patience, and thwartest the injurie of fate with content, in brooking the death of thy Sonnes: stand a while and either sée mee make a third in their tragedie, or else revenge their fall with an honourable triumph. The *Francklin* séeing so goodlie a Gentleman to give him such courteous comfort, gave him hartie thankes, with promise to pray for his happie successe.

With that *Rosader* vailed bonnet[9] to the King, and lightlie lept within the lists, where noting more the companie than the combatant, hee cast his eye upon the troupe of Ladies that glistered there like the starres of heaven, but at last Love, willing to make him as amorous as he was valiant, presented him with the sight of *Rosalynd*, whose admirable beautie so inveagled the eye of *Rosader*, that forgetting himselfe, he stoode and fed his lookes on the favour of *Rosalynds* face, which she perceiving, blusht: which was such a doubling of her beauteous excellence, that the bashfull red of *Aurora* of her sight of unacquainted *Phaeton*[10] was not halfe so glorious:

---

**7. the Norman:** the wrestler whom Rosader challenges   **8. coapt:** joined   **9. vailed bonnet:** lifted his hat, a sign of respect   **10. Aurora...Phaeton:** Aurora was goddess of dawn; Phaeton died when he drove a chariot too close to the sun

The *Norman* séeing this young Gentleman fettered in the lookes of the Ladies, drave him out of his *memento*[11] with a shake by the shoulder; *Rosader* looking back with an angrie frowne, as if he had been awakened from some pleasant dreame, discovered to all by the furie of his countenance that he was a man of some high thoughts: but when they all noted his youth, and the swéetenesse of his visage, with a generall applause of favours, they grieved that so goodly a young man should venture in so base an action: but séeing it were to his dishonour to hinder him from his enterprise, they wisht him to be graced with the palme[12] of victorie.

After *Rosader* was thus called out of his *memento* by the *Norman*, hee roughlie clapt to him[13] with so fierce an incounter, that they both fell to the ground, and with the violence of the fall were forced to breathe: in which space the *Norman* called to minde by all tokens, that this was hee whom *Saladyne* had appoynted him to kil; which conjecture made him stretch everie limb, & trie everie sinew, that working his death he might recover the golde, which so bountifully was promised him. On the contrarie part, *Rosader* while he breathed was not idle, but still cast his eye uppon *Rosalynd*, who to incourage him with a favour, lent him such an amorous looke, as might have made the most coward desperate: which glance of *Rosalynd* so fiered the passionate desires of *Rosader*, that turning to the *Norman* hee ran upon him and braved him with a strong encounter; the *Norman* received him as valiantly, that there was a sore combat, hard to judge on whose side fortune would be prodigall.

At last *Rosader* calling to minde the beautie of his new Mistresse, the fame of his Fathers honours, and the disgrace that should fall to his house by his misfortune, roused himselfe and threw the *Norman* against the ground, falling upon his Chest with so willing a waight, that the *Norman* yeelded nature her due, and *Rosader* the victorie. The death of this Champion; as it highlie contented the *Francklin*, as a man satisfied with revenge, so it drew the King and all the Péeres into a great admiration, that so young yeares and so beautifull a personage, should containe such martiall excellence: but when they knew him to be the yongest Sonne of Sir *John* of *Bourdeaux,* the King rose from his seate and imbraced him, and the Péeres intreated him with al favourable courtesie, commending both his valour and his vertues, wishing him to goe forward in such haughtie déedes that he might attaine to the glorie of his Fathers honourable fortunes.

As the King and Lordes graced him with embracing, so the Ladies favored him with their lookes, especially *Rosalynd*, whom the beautie and valour of *Rosader* had alreadie touched: but she accounted love a toye, and fancie a momentarie passion, that as it was taken in with a gaze, might bee shaken off with a winck; and therefore feared not to dallie in the flame, and to make *Rosader* knowe she affected him tooke from hir neck a Jewell, and sent it by a Page to the young Gentleman. The Prize that *Venus* gave to *Paris*[14] was not halfe so pleasing to the *Trojan*, as this Jemme was to *Rosader*: for if fortune had sworne to make him sole Monark of the world, he would rather have refused such dignitie, than have lost the Jewell sent him by *Rosalynd*. To retourne her with the like he was unfurnished, and yet that hee might more than in his lookes discover his affection, he stept into a tent, and taking pen and paper writ this fancie.

> *Two Sunnes at once from one faire heaven there shinde,*
> *Ten branches from two boughes tipt all with roses,*
> *Pure lockes more golden than is golde refinde,*
> *Two pearled rowes that Natures pride incloses:*
>
> *Two mounts faire marble white, downe-soft and daintie,*
> *A snow-dyed orbe; where love increast by pleasure*
> *Full wofull makes my heart, and bodie faintie:*
> *Hir faire (my woe) exceedes all thought and measure.*
>
> *In lines confusde my lucklesse harme appeereth;*
> *Whom sorrow clowdes, whom pleasant smiling cleereth.*

This sonnet he sent to *Rosalynd*, which when she read, she blusht, but with a sweete content in that she perceaved love had alotted her so amorous a servant. Rosalynd meditates on her attraction to Rosader. He has further conflict with his brother Saladyne, and the trusty servant Adam Spencer effects an apparent reconciliation.

[*Rosalynd sings a love song.*]

Scarce had *Rosalynde* ended her Madrigale, before *Torismond* came in with his daughter *Alinda*, and manie of the Péeres of *France,* who were enamoured of her beautie: which *Torismond* perceiving, fearing least her perfection might be the beginning of his prejudice, and the hope of his fruite ende in the beginning of her blossomes, hee thought to banish her from the Court: for quoth he to himselfe, her face is so full of favour, that it pleades pitie in the eye of everie man; her beautie is so heavenly and devine, that she will proove to me as *Helen* did to *Priam*:[15] some one of the Péeres will ayme at her love, ende[16] the

---

**14. Venus…Paris:** Venus, goddess of love, rewarded Paris for selecting her as the most beautiful goddess  **15. Helen…Priam:** the beauty of Helen sparked the Trojan war, thus destroying Priam's kingdom  **16. end:** bring about

marriage, and then in his wifes right attempt the kingdome. To prevent therefore had I wist[17] in all these actions, she tarries not about the Court, but shall (as an exile) either wander to her father, or els séeke other fortunes.

In this humour, with a stearne countenance full of wrath, hee breathed out this censure unto her before the Péeres, that charged her that that night shee were not séene about the Court: For (quoth he) I have heard of thy aspiring speaches, and intended treasons. This doome was strange unto *Rosalynde*, and presently covered with the shield of her innocence, shee boldly brake out in reverend tearmes to have cleared her selfe: but *Torismond* would admit of no reason, nor durst his Lordes plead for *Rosalynde*, although her beautie had made some of them passionate, séeing the figure of wrath portraied in his brow. Standing thus all mute, and *Rosalynde* amazed, *Alinda* who loved her more than her selfe, with griefe in her heart, & teares in her eyes, falling downe on her knées, began to intreate her father thus....

*Torismond* (at this speach of *Alinda*) covered his face with such a frowne, as Tyrannie seemed to sit triumphant in his forehead, and checkt her up with such taunts, as made the Lords (that onlie were hearers) to tremble. Proude girle (quoth he) hath my lookes made thee so light of tung, or my favours incouraged thee to be so forward, that thou darest presume to preach after thy father? Hath not my yeares more experience than thy youth, and the winter of mine age deeper insight into civill policie, than the prime of thy florishing daies? The olde Lion avoides the toyles where the yong one leapes into the net: the care of age is provident and foresees much: suspition is a vertue, where a man holds his enemie in his bosome. Thou fonde[18] girle measurest all by present affection, & as thy heart loves thy thoughts censure: but if thou knewest that in liking *Rosalynd* thou hatchest up a bird to pecke out thine owne eyes, thou wouldst intreate as much for her absence, as now thou delightest in her presence. But why do I alleadge policie to thee? sit you downe huswife and fall to your needle: if idlenesse make you so wanton, or libertie so malipert,[19] I can quicklie tie you to a sharper taske: and you (maide) this night be packing either into *Arden* to your father, or whether best it shall content your humour, but in the Court you shall not abide.

This rigorous replie of *Torismond* nothing amazed *Alinda*, for still she prosecuted her plea in the defence of *Rosalynd*, wishing her father (if his censure might not be reverst) that he would appoint her partner

**17. had I wist:** as I should have known    **18. fonde:** foolish; loving    **19. malipert:** presumptuous

of her exile; which if he refused to doo, either she would (by some secrete meanes) steale out and followe her, or els end her daies with some desperate kinde of death.

When *Torismond* heard his daughter so resolute, his heart was so hardned against her, that he set downe a definitive and peremptorie sentence that they should both be banished: which presentlie was done. The Tyrant rather choosing to hazard the losse of his only child, than any waies to put in question the state of his kingdome: so suspicious and fearefull is the conscience of an usurper. Well, although his Lords perswaded him to retaine his owne daughter, yet his resolution might not bee reverst, but both of them must away from the court without either more companie or delay.

[*The friends run away to the woods. There they encounter shepherds who write and sing love poems, which are not parodically flawed like their analogues in Shakespeare. Meanwhile Saladyne chains up Rosader and pretends to guests that he is insane. Having been released with the help of Adam, Rosader kills many of his brother's visitors, who had been taunting him, and takes over the house. When the sheriff to whom Saladyne has appealed for help and his assistants arrive, Rosader and Adam fight with them, then flee to the forest. There they encounter and are fed by Rosalynd's father Gerismond, the lawful French king, who was exiled by Torismond much as Duke Senior was banished by Duke Frederick. Saladyne is first imprisoned, then banished by Torismond, who wants his lands. Ganimede and Aliena, both disguised, encounter Rosader in the forest, where he talks of his love for Rosalynd. All three then enjoy a meal together.*]

As soone as they had taken their repast, *Rosader* giving them thanks for his good cheere, would have been gone: but *Ganimede,* that was loath to let him pass out of her presence, began thus; Nay Forrester quoth he, if thy busines be not the greater, seeing thou saist thou art so deeply in love, let me see how thou canst wooe: I will represent *Rosalynde,* and thou shalt bee as thou art *Rosader;* see in some amorous Eglogue, how if *Rosalynde* were present, how thou couldst court her: and while we sing of Love, *Aliena* shall tune her pipe, and playe us melodie. Content, quoth *Rosader.* And *Aliena,* shee to shew her willingnesse, drewe foorth a recorder, and began to winde it. Then the loving Forrester began thus.

[*Rosalynd and Rosader sing a song together.*]

When thus they had finished their courting Eglogue[20] in such a familiar clause,[21] *Ganimede* as Augure of some good fortunes to light upon their affections, beganne to be thus pleasant; How now Forrester, have I not fitted your turn? have I not plaide the woman

**20. Eglogue:** a type of pastoral song  **21. clause:** conclusion

handsomely, and shewed my selfe as coy in graunts, as courteous in desires, and béen as full of suspition, as men of flatterie? And yet to salve all, jumpt I not all up with the sweete union of love? Did not *Rosalynde* content her *Rosader?* The Forrester at this smiling, shooke his head, and folding his armes made this merrie replie.

Truth, gentle Swaine, *Rosader* hath his *Rosalynde:* but as *Ixion*[22] had *Juno,* who thinking to possesse a goddesse, onely imbraced a clowde: in these imaginarie fruitions of fancie I resemble the birds that fed themselves with *Zeuxis* painted grapes;[23] but they grewe so leane with pecking at shaddowes, that they were glad with *Aesops*[24] Cocke to scrape for a barley cornell: so fareth it with me, who to féede my selfe with the hope of my Mistres favours, sooth my self in thy sutes, and onely in conceipt reape a wished for content: but if my food be no better than such amorous dreames, *Venus* at the yeares end shall finde mee but a leane lover. Yet doo I take these follies for high fortunes, and hope these fained affections doo devine some unfained ende of ensuing fancies.

And thereupon (quoth *Aliena*) Ile play the priest; from this day forth *Ganimede* shall call thée husband, and thou shalt call *Ganimede* wife, and so wéele have a marriage. Content (quoth *Rosader*) and laught. Content (quoth *Ganimede*) and changed as redde as a rose: and so with a smile and a blush, they made up this jesting match, that after proovde to a marriage in earnest; *Rosader* full little thinking he had wooed and wonne his *Rosalynde*. But all was well, hope is a swéete string to harpe on: and therefore let the Forrester a while shape himselfe to his shaddow, and tarrie Fortunes leasure, till she may make a Metamorphosis fit for his purpose.

I digresse, and therefore to *Aliena*: who said, the wedding was not worth a pinne, unles there were some cheere, nor that bargaine well made that was not striken up with a cuppe of wine: and therefore she wild *Ganimede* to set out such cates as they had, and to drawe out her bottle, charging the Forrester as hee had imagined his loves, so to conceipt these cates[25] to be a most sumptuous banquet, and to take a Mazer[26] of wine and to drinke to his *Rosalynde*: which *Rosader* did; and so they passed awaye the day in manie pleasant devices.

[*Rosader, having debated at some length whether or not to save Saladyne's life, does rescue him from a lion, sustaining a wound. Not knowing that his savior is his brother, Saladyne confesses to this apparent stranger that he has mistreated Rosader; Rosader reveals his identity and forgives his errant sibling for the earlier injuries. Saladyne and Aliena fall in love, and the shepherdess*

---

**22. Ixion:** attacked Juno, queen of the gods   **23. Zeuxis:** a famous painter of life-like works   **24. Aesops Cocke:** in a fable attributed to Aesop, the cock, finding a jewel, observes that it would prefer barley   **25. cates:** provisions   **26. Mazer:** cup

*Phebe, disdaining the shepherd Montanus, falls in love with Ganimede. Gerismond, hearing of Montanus's frustrated love for Phebe, tries to find out more about it.*]

Upon this discourse, the King was desirous to see *Phoebe*: who being brought before *Gerismond* by *Rosader*, shadowed the beautie of her face with such a vermilion teinture, that the Kings eyes began to dazle at the puritie of her excellence. After *Gerismond* had fed his lookes awhile upon her faire, he questioned with her, why she rewarded *Montanus* love with so little regard, seeing his desertes were manie, and his passions extreame. *Phoebe* to make replie to the Kings demaund, answered thus: Love (sir) is charie in his lawes, and whatsoever he sets downe for justice (bee it never so unjust) the sentence cannot be reverst: womens fancies lend favours not ever by desert, but as they are inforst by their desires: for fancy is tied to the wings of Fate, and what the Starres Decree, stands for an infallible doome. I know *Montanus* is wise, & womens eares are greatly delighted with wit, as hardlie escaping the charme of a pleasant tongue, as *Ulisses* the melodie of the *Syrens*.[27] *Montanus* is beautifull, and womens eyes are snared in the excellence of objectes, as desirous to feede their lookes with a faire face, as the Bee to sucke on a sweete flower. *Montanus* is wealthie, and an ounce of give mee perswades a woman more than a pound of heare mee. *Danae* was won with a golden shower, when she could not be gotten with all the intreates of *Jupiter*.[28] I tell you sir, the string of a womans heart reacheth to the pulse of her hand, and let a man rub that with golde, and tis hard but she will proove his hearts golde. *Montanus* is yong, a great clause in fancies court: *Montanus* is vertuous, the richest argument that Love yeelds: and yet knowing all these perfections I praise them, and wonder at them, loving the qualities, but not affecting the person, because the Destenies have set downe a contrarie censure. Yet *Venus* to adde revenge, hath given me wine of the same grape, a sippe of the same sawce, and firing me with the like passion, hath crost me with as ill a penaunce: for I am in love with a Shepheards swaine, as coy to me as I am cruell to *Montanus*, as peremptorie in disdaine as I was perverse in desire, and that is (quoth she) *Alienaes* Page, yong *Ganimede*.

*Gerismond* desirous to prosecute the ende of these passions, called in *Ganimede*: who knowing the case, came in graced with such a blush, as beautefied the Christall of his face with a ruddie brightnesse. The King noting well the phisnomie of *Ganimede*, began by his favours to call to minde the face of his *Rosalynde*, and with that fetcht a deep

---

**27. Ulisses...Syrens:** the hero Ulysses protected himself from the sirens' seductive melodies by being tied to a mast   **28. Danae...Jupiter:** Jupiter came to Danae in the form of a shower of gold

sigh. *Rosader*, that was passing familiar with *Gerismond*, demaunded of him why he sigheth so sore? Because *Rosader* (quoth he) the favour of *Ganimede* puts me in minde of *Rosalynde*. At this word, *Rosader* sight so deepely as though his heart would have burst. And whats the matter (quoth *Gerismond*) that you quite mee with such a sigh? Pardon mee sir (quoth *Rosader*) because I love none but *Rosalynd*. And uppon that condition (quoth *Gerismond*) that *Rosalynde* were heere, I woulde this day make up a marriage betwixt her and thee. At this *Aliena* turnde her head and smilde upon *Ganimede*, and she could scarce keep countenaunce. Yet shee salved[29] all with secrecie, and *Gerismond* to drive away such dumpes, questioned with *Ganimede*, what the reason was hee regarded not *Phoebes* love, seeing she was as faire as the wanton that brought *Troy* to ruine.

Ganimede mildly answered, If I shoulde affect the faire *Phoebe*, I shuld offer poore *Montanus* great wrong to win that from him in a moment, that he hath laboured for so manie mont[h]s. Yet have I promised to the beautifull shepheardesse, to wed my selfe never to woman except unto her: but with this promise, that if I can by reason suppres *Phoebes* love towards me, she shal like of none but of *Montanus*.

To that, quoth *Phoebe*, I stand, for my love is so far beyond reason, as it will admit no perswasion of reason. For justice, quoth hee, I appeale to *Gerismond*: and to his censure wil I stand, quoth *Phoebe*. And in your victorie, quoth *Montanus*, stands the hazard[30] of my fortunes: for if *Ganimede* go away with conquest, *Montanus* is in conceipt Loves Monarch, if *Phoebe* win, then am I in effect most miserable. We will see this controversie quoth *Gerismond*, & then we will to Church: therefore *Ganimede* let us heare your argument.

Nay, pardon my absence a while (quoth she) and you shall see one in store. In went *Ganimede* and drest her selfe in womans attire, having on a gowne of greene, with kirtle of rich sandall,[31] so quaint, that she seemed *Diana*[32] triumphing in the Forrest: upon her head she wore a chaplet of Roses, which gave her such a grace, that she looked like *Flora*[33] pearkt in the pride of all her flowers. Thus attired came *Rosalynde* in, and presented herselfe at her fathers feete, with her eyes full of teares, craving his blessing, and discoursing unto him all her fortunes, how she was banished by *Torismond*, and how ever since she lived in that Countrey disguised.

Gerismond seeing his daughter, rose from his seate and fell upon her necke, uttering the passions of his joy in watrie plaints driven into such an extasie of content, that he could not utter one word. At this

---

**29. salve:** smooth over   **30. hazard:** chance   **31. kirtle of rich sandal:** skirt of rich silk   **32. Diana:** goddess associated with the hunt   **33. Flora:** goddess of flowers

sight, if *Rosader* was both amazed & joyfull, I referre my selfe to the judgement of such as have experience in love, seeing his *Rosalynde* before his face whom so long and deeplie he had affected. At last *Gerismond* recovered his spirites, and in most fatherlie tearmes entertained his daughter *Rosalynde*, after many questions demaunding of her what had past betweene her and *Rosader*. So much sir (quoth she) as there wants nothing but your Grace to make up the marriage. Why then (quoth *Gerismond*) *Rosader* take her, she is thine, and let this day sollemnise both thy brothers and thy nuptialls.

*Rosader* beyond measure content, humblie thanked the King and imbraced his *Rosalynd*, who turning towards *Phoebe*, demaunded if she had shewen sufficient reason to suppresse the force of her loves. Yea, quoth *Phoebe*, and so great a perswasive, that, please it you Madame and *Aliena* to give us leave, *Montanus* and I will make this day the third couple in marriage. She had no sooner spake this word, but *Montanus*, threw away his garland of willow, his bottle, where was painted dispaire, and cast his sonnets in the fire, shewing himselfe as frolicke as *Paris* when he hanseled[34] his love with *Helena*. At this *Gerismond* and the rest smiled, and concluded that *Montanus* and *Phoebe* should keepe their wedding with the two brethren.

*Aliena* seeing *Saladyne* stand in a dumpe,[35] to wake him from his dreame began thus. Why how now my *Saladyne*, all a mort,[36] what! melancholy, man, at the day of marriage? perchaunce thou art sorowfull to thinke on thy brothers high fortunes, and thine owne base desires to choose so meane a shepheardize. Cheere up thy heart man, for this day thou shalt bee married to the daughter of a King: for know *Saladyne*, I am not *Aliena*, but *Alinda* the daughter of thy mortall enemie *Torismond*.

At this all the companie was amazed, especiallie *Gerismond*, who rising up tooke *Alinda* in his armes, and sayd to *Rosalynde*: Is this that faire *Alinda* famous for so many vertues, that forsooke her fathers Court to live with thee exilde in the Countrey? The same, quoth *Rosalynd*. Then, quoth *Gerismond*, turning to *Saladyne*, jollie Forrester be frolick, for thy fortunes are great, and thy desires excellent; thou hast got a Princesse as famous for her perfection as exceeding in proportion. And she hath with her beautie wonne (quoth *Saladyne*) an humble servant as full of faith as she of amiable favour. While every one was amazed with these Comicall eventes, *Coridon* came skipping in and told them that the Priest was at Church and tarried for their comming. With that *Gerismond* led the way, and the rest followed, where to the admiration of all the countrey swaines in *Arden* their mariages were solemnely solemnised.

34. **hanseled:** first enjoyed   35. **dumpe:** reverie   36. **a mort:** as though dead

As soone as the Priest had finished, home they went with *Alinda*, where *Coridon* had made al things in readinesse. Dinner was provided, and the tables beeing spread, and the Brides set downe by *Gerismond*, *Rosader*, *Saladyne* and *Montanus* that day were servitors: homely cheere they had such as their countrey could affoord: but to mend their fare they had mickle[37] good chat, and many discourses of their loves and fortunes. About mid dinner, to make them merie *Coridon* came in with an olde crowder,[38] and plaide them a fit of mirth, to which he sung this pleasant song. . . .

*Coridon* having thus made them merrie: as they were in the midst of all their jollitie, word was brought in to *Saladyne* and *Rosader*, that a brother of theirs, one *Fernandyne* was arrived, and desired to speake with them. *Gerismond* over hearing this newes, demaunded who it was? It is sir (quoth *Rosader*) our middle brother, that lyves a Scholler in *Paris*: but what fortune hath driven him to séek us out I know not. With that *Saladyne* went and met his brother, whom he welcommed with all curtesie, and *Rosader* gave him no lesse friendly entertainment: brought hee was by his two brothers into the parlour where they al sate at dinner. *Fernandyne* as one that knewe as manie manners as he could points of sophistrie,[39] & was aswell brought up as well lettered, saluted them all.

But when hee espied *Gerismond*, knéeling on his knée he did him what reverence belonged to his estate: and with that burst foorth into these speaches. Although (right mightie Prince) this day of my brothers mariage be a day of mirth, yet time craves another course: and therefore from daintie cates rise to sharpe weapons. And you the sonnes of Sir *John* of *Bourdeaux*, leave off your amors & fall to armes, change your loves into lances, and now this day shewe your selves as valiant, as hethertoo you have been passionate. For know *Gerismond*, that hard by at the edge of this forrest the twelve Peeres of *France* are up in Armes to recover thy right; and *Torismond* troupt with a crue of desperate runnagates is ready to bid them battaile. The Armies are readie to joyne: therfore shew thy selfe in the field to encourage thy subjects; and you *Saladyne* & *Rosader* mount you, and shewe your selves as hardie souldiers as you have been heartie lovers: so shall you for the benefite of your Countrey, discover the *Idea* of your fathers vertues to bee stamped in your thoughts, and prove children worthie of so honourable a parent.

At this alarum given by *Fernandyne*, *Gerismond* leapt from the boord, and *Saladyne* and *Rosader* betook themselves to their weapons. Nay quoth *Gerismond*, goe with me I have horse and armour for us all,

**37. mickle:** much   **38. crowder:** fiddler   **39. sophistrie:** a form of argumentation

and then being well mounted, let us shew that we carrie revenge and honour at our fawchions points. Thus they leave the Brides full of sorrow, especially *Alinda*, who desired *Gerismond* to be good to her father: he not returning a word because his hast was great, hied him home to his Lodge, where he delivered *Saladyne* and *Rosader* horse and armour, and himselfe armed royally led the way: not having ridden two leagues before they discovered where in a Valley both the battailes were joyned.

*Gerismond* séeing the wing wherein the Peeres fought, thrust in there, and cried *Saint Denis, Gerismond* laying on such loade uppon his enemies, that hee shewed how highly he did estimate of a Crowne. When the Peeres perceived that their lawfull King was there, they grewe more eager: and *Saladyne* and *Rosader* so behaved themselves, that none durst stand in their way, nor abide the furie of their weapons. To be short, the Peeres were conquerours, *Torismond*s armie put to flight, & himselfe slaine in battaile. The Peeres then gathered themselves together, and saluting their king, conducted him royallie into *Paris*, where he was received with great joy of all the citizens. As soone as all was quiet and he had received againe the Crowne, hee sent for *Alinda* and *Rosalynde* to the Court, *Alinda* being verie passionate for the death of her father: yet brooking it with the more patience, in that she was contented with the welfare of her *Saladyne*.

Well, as soone as they were come to *Paris*, *Gerismond* made a royall Feast for the Peeres and Lords of his Lande, which continued thirtie dayes, in which time summoning a Parliament, by the consent of his Nobles he created *Rosader* heire apparant to the kingdom: he restored *Saladyne* to all his fathers lande, and gave him the Dukedome of *Nameurs*, he made *Fernandyne* principall Secretarie to himselfe: and that Fortune might everie way seerne frolicke, he made *Montanus* Lord over all the Forrest of *Arden*: *Adam Spencer* Captaine of the Kings Gard, and *Coridon* Master of *Alindas* Flocks.

Heere Gentlemen may you see in *Euphues Golden Legacie*, that such as neglect their fathers precepts, incurre much prejudice; that division in Nature as it is a blemish in nurture, so tis a breach of good fortunes; that vertue is not measured by birth but by action; that yonger brethren though inferiour in yeares, yet may be superiour to honours; that concord is the sweetest conclusion, and amitie betwixt brothers more forceable than fortune. . . .

These selections are from Shakespeare's principal source, Thomas Lodge's prose romance entitled *Rosalynde. Euphues golden legacie* (1590).

# From *A Treatise and Discourse of the Lawes of the Forrest*

### John Manwood

John Manwood's *Treatise and Discourse of the Lawes of the Forrest* is the most important tract on its subject published during Shakespeare's lifetime. It includes lengthy discussions of the history of English forests and the laws and policies regulating them.

### Chapter 1

A FORREST IS a certen Territorie of wooddy grounds & fruitfull pastures, priviledged for wild beasts and foules of, . . . . Forrest, Chase, and Warren,[1] to rest and abide in, in the safe protection of the King, for his princely delight and pleasure, which Territorie of ground, so priviledged, is meered[2] and bounded with un-removeable, markes, meeres, and boundaries, either knowen by matter of record, or els by prescription: And also replenished with wilde beasts of venerie or Chase,[3] and with great coverts[4] of vert,[5] for the succour of the said wild beastes, to have there abode in: For the preservation and continuance of which said place, together with the vert and Venison,[6] there are certen particuler Lawes, Priviledges and Officers, belonging to the same, meete for that purpose, that are onely proper unto a Forrest, and not to any other place. . . .

For the better understanding whereof, it is to be noted, a Forrest is a *certen Territorie* of ground, this word (*Territorie*) is most properly a circuit of ground, contayning a libertie[7] within itselfe, wherein divers men have land within it, and yet the same Territorie it selfe doth lie open and not inclosed, although perhaps there may be divers inclosures within it, for this worde *Territorie*, as I take it, is derived from the Latin word *Territorium*, which is a Territorie, or all the fields & countrey

---

**1. Forrest, Chase, and Warren:** the chase, park, and warren were subdivisions of the forest, associated with different regulations and animals.   **2. meered:** bounded   **3. venerie or Chase:** venery and chase were both terms for hunting, although Manwood emphasizes some differences in their procedures   **4. coverts:** a covering, often used in relation to sheltering wild animals   **5. vert:** vegetation in a wooded area   **6. Venison:** the flesh of any animal killed in hunting   **7. libertie:** an area under the control of a person or corporate body; sometimes used for an area of a city on its margins

lying within the bounds and libertie of a Citie, which doth extend farre without the walles of the Citie round about, by certen meeres & boundaries, without any other inclosure belonging to the same: And, because a Forrest doth likewise lie open and not inclosed, having onely but meeres and boundaries to know the Ring and uttermost Skirtes of the Forrest by, therefore this word *Territorie*, is used as a meete word for that purpose.

(pp. 1-3)

## Chapter 18

. . . . Hitherto it hath been declared, how and in what manner, men may Hunt, that have any aucthoritie thereunto, and of such as have any lawfull colour[8] or shaddowe[9] to justifie their Hunting in the Forrest. Now it shall not be amisse, here in this place to speake some thing, of such as have no Color or Shadowe at all, to justifie their Hunting by, and yet neverthelesse do Hunt in the Forrest, and kill and destroy her Majesties wild beastes there, or at the leastwise in their Hunting, if they do not kill anie beast of the Forrest, yet they doo vehementlie disquiet the wilde beastes there, to the breach of their firme peace, which, all the Kinges and Princes of this Realme, have always graunted, mayntained, and allowed, and that the Lawes of the Forrest doo yet allow them, and, these are generally called Trespassers or Malefactors in Hunting in the Kings Forrestes. And if any Forrester or Keeper shall finde or take any such person or persons with the manner, then he shall arrest their bodies, and carrie them to prison, from whence they shall not be delivered, without a speciall warrant from the King, or from his Justice. . . .

(p. 113)

## Chapter 20

Purlieu, or *Pourallee,* is a certain Territorie of ground adjoining unto the Forest, meered and bounded wyth unmoveable markes, meeres, and boundaries, knowen by matter of Record onely: which Territorie of ground was also once Forest, and afterwards disafforrested againe by the perambulations made for the severing of the new Forrestes from the old. . . .

And although that such new afforestations were disafforrested againe by the Perambulations, as aforesaid, and so thereby the same became *Pourallee,* (or *Pour Lieu* as some men abusively do call it,) yet the same is not so absolutely disafforrested thereby for every man, but

---

8. **colour:** reason, excuse   9. **shaddowe:** a trace of something

that in some sort the same doth remain Forrest still to some men, and yet disafforrested and freed insome [sic] sort for some men. . . .

Although that the *Pourallee* be Forest still to those, that have neither woods nor lands of freehold therin, yet those, that have woodes and lands of freehold within the *Pourallees* to the yerely value of fortie shillings by the yere, may keepe Greyhounds by the Statute of 13.R.2.cap. 13. And when that they do find the wild beastes of the Forrest within their woods & lands in the *Pourallee,* they may chase the same wild beastes with their Greyhounds towards the Forrest: for, the owners of such woods and lands in the *Pourallees* have property in those wild beasts, so long as they are in their owne woods and lands. . . .But if the wild beasts will returne home againe to the kings Forrest to challenge[10] the benefit of their sanctuarie of peace therein, they must have their free passage thereunto, without any forestalling or foresetting[11] of them, in their returne and course between the *Forrest* and the *Pouralle,* either with dogges, gunne, cros bow, longbow, dead hey,[12] quick hey, or any manner of engin or let[13] whatsoever: for, all such manner of forestalling or foresetting of the wild beastes betweene the *Forrest* and the *Pourallee,* is absolutely forbidden by the Assises[14] of *Woodstock,* made by king *Henry the second,* upon paine of one yeres imprisonment, and the offenders therein to be fined also at the kings pleasure, and so the *Pourralle* in some sort is free for some men, as aforesaid, to hunt there. . . .

But those, that have woods and lands within the *Pourallees,* they are without the regard[15] of the Forrest, and therefore they are absolutely free from the bondage of the Forrest, in respect of selling of their woods, and converting of their meadowes and pastures into arable land and tillage, and otherwise to improve the same at their owne pleasure to their best advauntage and profit, but yet, the woods and lands in the *Pouralles,* although they be without the Regard of the Forrest, are not absolutely freed of the bondage of the Forrest, in respect of the wild beasts, to have their haunt and being therein, at such times, as they shall chance to wander out of the Forrest, so that the woods and lands in the *Pourallees* were once absolutely *Forrest,* and now they are but conditionally in some sort *Forrest.*

(pp. 127-153)

This excerpt is taken from the 1598 edition.

10. **challenge:** claim   11. **foresetting:** entrapping (variant spelling of "forsetting")   12. **hey:** the hay or hey was a type of net for trapping wild animals   13. **let:** hindrance   14. **Assises:** court sessions   15. **without the regard:** without reference to

# ORDERING CONSERVATION OF GAME
## IN HONOR OF CRAFTON

*[Westminster, 2 May 1554, 2 Mary I]*

FORASMUCH AS our old and ancient forests of Whittlewood and Sawcy within our honor of Grafton sithen the death of our most dear father of famous memory, King Henry VIII, have been greatly abused, not only by the great and wasteful falling of woods and excessive making of coppices[1] within the same (whereby our forest too much instraighted, our game are enforced from thence to fly for lack of hold[2] and covert[3] into divers our other woods and grounds of greater thick[4] adjoining to the same for their relief and safeguard, which woods and grounds now being forest doth minister occasion of daily hunting to their destruction) but also by the evil entry and extreme dealing of such light[5] persons of the meaner sort, whose calling nor reason thereto serveth, which continually practice with hounds, greyhounds, crossbows, handguns, shewels,[6] and other unlawful engines, as well by night as by day, do kill, disquiet, and utterly destroy the same, and that most unreasonable and at times not convenient, without respect of their bounden duty and allegiance towards us and contrary to good laws and statutes[1] heretofore in that behalf ordained, whose naughty[7] doings declare that they have rather sought the utter ruin and destruction of our game for the commodity of the flesh, although out of season, and to abuse all gentlemen bordering the same in preventing their sports and hunting than otherwise; without remedy whereof our game at length must needs be brought unto such decay that, neither it shall be able to accomplish our pleasure at any time hereafter having access unto these parts, neither yet replenish the purlieus[8] about the same, as well to satisfy the expectation and pastime of those our gentlemen abordering the same, which in hunting thereof we shall have no cause to mislike their doings at all:

---

**1. coppice:** a small wooded area   **2. hold:** shelter   **3. covert:** a covering, often used in relation to protecting wild animals   **4. thick:** most crowded section (of a wood etc.)   **5. light:** immoral   **6. shewels:** objects hung up to prevent a deer from moving in a particular direction   **7. naughty:** blameworthy   **8. purlieu:** area near forest subject to some but not all of its regulations

We let you wit therefore, our full mind and pleasure is, as well for the replenishing and restoring our game there decayed as also for the preservation of other our pleasures and realties within our said honor, that from henceforth no manner of person or persons, of what estate, degree, or condition soever he or they be, which hunt without license of us or of our officers there for the time being in any of these our woods or grounds hereafter ensuing and adjoining to our forests of Whittlewood, and being within our honor of Grafton, that is to say, Haybourne Fields, Hollowbrook, Catwellhole, the Briars, Blackpits, Aldrington Woods, Plompton Park, Woodel, and the Bullet, and also those woods and grounds adjoining to the forest of Sawcy hereafter ensuing, that is to say, Ashewood, Rowley, and Sawcy Green, either with hounds, greyhounds, crossbows, longbows, handguns, shewels, or any other unlawful engines:

And that all and every such person or persons which shall hereafter offend in any of the premises, we in consideration thereof do fully authorize and appoint by virtue of this our proclamation that the high steward of our said honor, the master of our game, and his or their deputy or deputies, keepers of grounds near unto where any such unlawful acts shall be committed or done, to take from such offenders and breakers of this proclamation their hounds, greyhounds, and guns, crossbows, and his or their engines, and the same incontinent[9] to convey to us or to the lords of our said Privy Council, with a bill of the names of such offenders as a declaration of their act or acts in that behalf committed, so that there may be such punishment as shall seem by us and our said council meet to be ministered unto them in that behalf; and also that he our steward of our said honor for the time being shall not suffer any light person within the liberties of our said honor to take any partridge, pheasant, or quail, or to keep any hounds or greyhounds, or use any crossbow or handgun, otherwise than he or they may do by our laws in that behalf provided.

And further we assuredly trust, and our good opinion is such, that all gentlemen having liberty of purlieu near or adjoining to any our said forests will so use and hunt the same in such convenient times and hours without killing unseasonable deer, which might rather be a destruction of our game than otherwise either pleasure or commodity to themselves, so as we shall have no just occasion to think ourself to be ungently treated or to have any cause to mislike their doings therein.

From Paul L. Hughes and James F. Larkin's collection of proclamations issued by the later Tudor monarchs.

**9. incontinent:** immediately

# ROBIN HOOD AND MAID MARIAN

*Anon.*

The "folk" or "traditional" ballad is a kind of narrative poem that often focuses on a single event. "Robin Hood and Maid Marian," a relatively late addition to the extensive tradition of Robin Hood ballads, probably goes back to the sixteenth or seventeenth century and hence may or may not have preceded *As You Like It.*

A BONNY FINE-MAID of noble degree,
  *With a hey down, down, a down, down,*
  Maid Marian call'd by name,
Did live in the North, of excellent worth,
  For shee was a gallant dame.

For favour and face, and beauty most rare,           5
  Queen Hellen shee did excell:
For Marian then was prais'd of all men
  That did in the country dwell.

'Twas neither Rosamond nor Jane Shore,[1]
  Whose beauty was clear and bright,            10
That could surpass this country lass,
  Beloved of lord and knight.

The earl of Huntington, nobly born,
  That came of noble blood,
To Marian went, with a good intent,           15
  By the name of Robin Hood.

With kisses sweet their red lips did meet,
  For she and the earl did agree;
In every place, they kindly embrace,
  With love and sweet unity.                   20

But fortune bearing these lovers a spight,

---

**1. Rosamond nor Jane Shore:** mistresses of Henry II and Edward IV respectively

That soon they were forc'd to part,
To the merry green-wood then went Robin Hood,
   With a sad and sorrowfull heart.

And Marian, poor soul, was troubled is mind, 25
   For the absence of her friend;
With finger in eye, shee often did cry,
   And his person did much comend

Perplexed and vexed, and troubled in mind,
   She drest herself like a page, 30
And ranged the wood, to find Robin Hood,
   The bravest of men in that age.

With quiver and bow, sword, buckler, and all,
   Thus armed was Marian most bold,
Still wandering about, to find Robin out, 35
   Whose person was better then gold.

But Robin Hood, hee himself had disguis'd,
   And Marian was strangly attir'd,
That they prov'd foes, and so fell to blowes,
   Whose vallour bold Robin admir'd. 40

They drew out their swords, and to cutting they went,
   At least an hour or more,
That the blood ran apace from bold Robins face,
   And Marian was wounded sore,

"O hold thy hand, hold thy hand," said Robin Hood, 45
   "And thou shalt be one of my string,
To range in the wood with bold Robin Hood,
   To hear the sweet nightingall sing."

When Marian did hear the voice of her love,
   Her self shee did quickly discover,
And with kisses sweet she did him greet, 50
   Like to a most loyall lover.

When bold Robin Hood his Marian did see,
   Good lord, what clipping[2] was there!
With kind embraces, and jobbing of faces,[3] 55
   Providing of gallant cheer.

---

**2. clipping:** kissing   **3. jobbing:** thrusting (for kissing)

For Little John took his bow in his hand,
   And wandred in the wood,
To kill the deer, and make good chear
   For Marian and Robin Hood.                   60

A stately banquet they had full soon,
   All in a shaded bower,
Where venison sweet they had to eat,
   And were merry that present hour.

Great flaggons of wine were set on the board,     65
   And merrily they drunk round
Their boules of sack, to strengthen the back,
   Whilst their knees did touch the ground.

First Robin Hood began a health
   To Marian his onely dear;                   70
And his yeomen all, both comly and tall,
   Did quickly bring up the rear.

For in a brave vein they tost off the bouls,
   Whilst thus they did remain;
And every cup, as they drunk up,              75
   They filled with speed again.

At last they ended their merryment,
   And went to walk in the wood,
Where Little John and maid Marian
   Attended on bold Robin Hood.               80

In sollid content together they liv'd,
   With all their yeomen gay;
They liv'd by their hands, without any lands,
   And so they did many a day.

But now to conclude, an end I will make,     85
   In time as I think it good;
For the people that dwell in the north can tell
   Of Marian and bold Robin Hood.

From Francis James Child, ed., *English and Scottish Ballads.* Vol 5. Boston: Little, Brown and Company, 1860.

# IN MEMORY OF DAVID KALSTONE
## WHO DIED OF AIDS

*Anthony Hecht*

Lime-and-mint mayonnaise and salsa verde
Accompanied poached fish that Helen made
For you and J.M. when you came to see us
Just at the salmon season. Now a shade,

A faint blurred absence who before had been
Funny, intelligent, kindness itself,
You leave behind, beside the shock of death,
Three of the finest books upon my shelf.

"Men die from time to time," said Rosalind,
"But not," she said, "for love." A lot she knew!
From the green world of Africa the plague
Wiped out the Forest of Arden, the whole crew

Of innocents, of which, poor generous ghost,
You were among the liveliest. Your friend
Scattered upon the calm Venetian tides
Your sifted ashes so they might descend

Even to the bottom of the monstrous world
Or lap at marble steps and pass below
The little bridges, whirl and eddy through
A liquified Palazzo Barbaro.

That mirrored splendor briefly entertains
Your passing as the whole edifice trembles
Within the waters of the Grand Canal,
And writhes and twists, wrinkles and reassembles.

# Day-Lilies at Night

*Stephen Burt*

Sent to bed without supper
and half-undressed, they fear

success. They are Celia
nearing the end of *As You Like It*;

each one a planetarium
about to close for good, a buckling dome
in which stars rise, bleached stains.

*(I'll put myself in poor and mean attire*
*and with a kind of umber smirch my face—)*

Tongue-tied at dawn, we stay up till
the constellations part; my petals curl

into a coat I shiver in, brown lace—
The sun rides at us through thin
trees, so strong

I fall for him, for Oliver. I have
been made into something unable to live on my own.

# From *Notes on The Plays*

*Samuel Johnson*

O F THIS play the fable is wild and pleasing. I know not how the ladies will approve the facility with which both *Rosalind* and *Celia* give away their hearts. To *Celia* much may be forgiven for the heroism of her friendship. The character of *Jaques* is natural and well preserved. The comick dialogue is very sprightly, with less mixture of low buffoonery than in some other plays; and the graver part is elegant and harmonious. By hastening to the end of his work *Shakespeare* suppressed the dialogue between the usurper and the hermit, and lost an opportunity of exhibiting a moral lesson in which he might have found matter worthy of his highest powers.

# From *Characters of Shakespear's Plays*

*William Hazlitt*

## AS YOU LIKE IT

Shakespear has here converted the forest of Arden into another Arcadia, where they "fleet the time carelessly as they did in the golden world." It is the most ideal of any of this author's plays. It is a pastoral drama, in which the interest arises more out of the sentiments and characters than out of the actions or situations. It is not what is done, but what is said, that claims our attention. Nursed in solitude, "under the shade of melancholy boughs," the imagination grows soft and delicate, and the wit runs riot in idleness, like a spoiled child, that is never sent to school. Caprice and fancy reign and revel here, and stern necessity is banished to the court. The mild, sentiments of humanity are strengthened with thought and leisure; the echo of the cares and noise of the world strikes upon the ear of those "who have felt them knowingly," softened by time and distance. "They hear the tumult, and are still." The very air of the place seems to breathe a spirit of philosophical poetry: to stir the thoughts, to touch the heart with pity, as the drowsy forest rustles to the sighing gale. Never was there such beautiful moralising, equally free from pedantry or petulance:

> "And this our life, exempt from public haunt,
> Finds tongues in trees, books in the running brooks,
> Sermons in stones, and good in everything."

Jaques is the only purely contemplative character in Shakespear. He thinks, and does nothing. His whole occupation is to amuse his mind, and he is totally regardless of his body and his fortunes. He is the prince of philosophical idlers; his only passion is thought; he sets no value upon anything but as it serves as food for reflection. He can "suck melancholy out of a song, as a weasel sucks eggs;" the motley fool, "who morals on he time," is the greatest prize he meets with in the forest. He resents Orlando's passion for Rosalind as some disparagement of his own passion for abstract truth; and leaves the Duke, as soon as he is restored to his sovereignty, to seek his brother out who has quitted it, and turned hermit.

"Out of these convertites
There is much matter to be heard and learn'd."

Within the sequestered and romantic glades of the, forest of Arden, they find leisure to be good and wise or to play the fool and fall in love. Rosalind's character is made up of sportive gaiety and natural tenderness: her tongue runs the faster to conceal the pressure at her heart. She talks herself out of breath, only to get deeper in love. The coquetry with which she plays with her lover in the double character which she has to support is managed with the nicest address. How full of voluble, laughing grace is all her conversation with Orlando:

"In heedless mazes running
With wanton haste and giddy cunning."

How full of real fondness and pretended cruelty is her answer to him when he promises to love her "For ever and a day!"

．　　　．　　　．

The silent and retired character of Celia is a necessary relief to the provoking loquacity of Rosalind, nor can anything be better conceived or more beautifully described than the mutual affection between the two cousins:

"We still have slept together,
Rose at an instant, learn'd, play'd, eat together.
And wheresoe'er we went, like Juno's swans,
Still we went coupled and inseparable."

The unrequited love of Silvius for Phebe shows the perversity of this passion in the commonest scenes of life, and the rubs and stops which nature throws in its way, where fortune has placed none. Touchstone is not in love, but he will have a mistress as a subject for the exercise of his grotesque humour, and to show his contempt for the passion, by his indifference about the person. He is a rare fellow. He is a mixture of the ancient cynic philosopher with the modern buffoon, and turns folly into wit, and wit into folly, just as the fit takes him. His courtship of Audrey not only throws a degree of ridicule on the state of wedlock itself, but he is equally an enemy to the prejudices of opinion in other respects. The lofty tone of enthusiasm, which the Duke and his companions in exile spread over the stillness and solitude of a country life, receives a pleasant shock from Touchstone's sceptical determination of the question:

"*Corin.* And how like you this shepherd's life, Master Touch-stone?

*Clown.* Truly, shepherd, in respect of itself, it is a good life; but in respect that it is a shepherd's life, it is naught. In respect that it is solitary, I like it very well; but in respect that it is private, it is a very vile life. Now in respect it is in the fields, it pleaseth me well; but in respect it is not in the court, it is tedious. As it is a spare life, look you, it fits my humour; but as there is no more plenty in it, it goes much against my stomach."

&bull;   &bull;   &bull;

There is hardly any of Shakespear's plays that contains a greater number of passages that have been quoted in books of extracts, or a greater number of phrases that have become in a manner proverbial. If we were to give all the striking passages, we should give half the play. We will only recall a few of the most delightful to the reader's recollection. Such are the meeting between Orlando and Adam, the exquisite appeal of Orlando to the humanity of the Duke and his company to supply him with food for the old man, and their answer, the Duke's description of a country life, and the account of Jaques moralising on the wounded deer, his meeting with Touchstone in the forest, his apology for his own melancholy and his satirical vein, and the well-known speech on the stages of human life, the old song of "Blow, blow, thou winter's wind," Rosalind's description of the marks of a lover and of the progress of time with different persons, the picture of the snake wreathed round Oliver's neck while the lioness watches her sleeping prey, and Touchstone's lecture to the shepherd, his defence of cuckolds, and panegyric on the virtues of "an If."—All of these are familiar to the reader: there is one passage of equal delicacy and beauty which may have escaped him, and with it we shall close our account of 'As You Like It.' It is Phebe's description of Ganimed, at the end of the third act.

"Think not I love him, tho' I ask for him;
'Tis but a peevish boy, yet he talks well;—
But what care I for words I yet words do well,
When he that speaks them pleases those that hear:
It is a pretty youth—not very pretty—
But sure he's proud, and yet his pride becomes him;
He'll make a proper man; the best thing in him
Is his complexion; and faster than his tongue
Did make offence, his eye did heal it up:
He is not very tall, yet for his years he's tall;
His leg is but so so, and yet 'tis well;
There was a pretty redness in his lip,
A little riper and more lusty red
Than that mixed in his cheek; 'twas just the difference
Betwixt the constant red and mingled damask.

There be some women, Silvius, had they mark'd him
In parcels as I did, would have gone near
To fall in love with him: but for my part
I love him not, nor hate him not; and yet
I have more cause to hate him than to love him;
For what had he to do to chide at me?"

# From SHAKESPERE: A CRITICAL STUDY OF HIS MIND AND ART

*Edward Dowden*

UPON THE whole, *As You Like It* is the sweetest and happiest of all Shakspere's comedies. No one suffers; no one lives an eager intense life; there is no tragic interest in it as there is in *The Merchant of Venice*, as there is in *Much Ado about Nothing*. It is mirthful, but the mirth is sprightly, graceful, exquisite; there is none of the rollicking fun of a Sir Toby here; the songs are not "coziers' catches" shouted in the night-time, "without any mitigation or remorse of voice," but the solos and duets of pages in the wild-wood, or the noisier chorus of foresters. The wit of Touchstone is not mere clownage, nor has it any indirect serious significances; it is a dainty kind of absurdity worthy to hold comparison with the melancholy of Jaques. And Orlando, in the beauty and strength of early manhood, and Rosalind—

> "A gallant curtle-axe upon her thigh,
> A boar-spear in her hand,"

and the bright, tender, loyal womanhood within—are figures which quicken and restore our spirits, as music does which is neither noisy nor superficial, and yet which knows little of the deep passion and sorrow of the world.

Shakspere, when he wrote this idyllic play, was himself in his Forest of Arden. He had ended one great ambition—the historical plays—and not yet commenced his tragedies. It was a resting-place. He sends his imagination into the woods to find repose. Instead of the courts and camps of England and the embattled plains of France, here was this woodland scene, where the palmtree, the lioness, and the serpent are to be found; possessed of a flora and fauna that flourish in spite of physical geographers. There is an open-air feeling throughout the play. The dialogue, as has been observed, catches freedom and freshness from the atmosphere. "Never is the scene within-doors, except when something discordant is introduced to heighten, as it were, the harmony."[*]

---

[*] C. A. Brown, "Shakespere's Autobiographical Poems," p. 283.

After the trumpet-tones of *Henry V* comes the sweet pastoral strain, so bright, so tender. Must it not be all in keeping? Shakspere was not trying to control his melancholy. When he needed to do that, Shakspere confronted his melancholy very passionately, and looked it full in the face. Here he needed refreshment, a sunlight tempered by forest-boughs, a breeze upon his forehead, a stream murmuring in his ears.

# From OXFORD LECTURES ON POETRY
## A. C. Bradley

I F WE were obliged to answer the question which of Shakespeare's plays contains, not indeed the fullest picture of his mind, but the truest expression of his nature and habitual temper, unaffected by special causes of exhilaration or gloom, I should be disposed to choose *As You Like It*. It wants, to go no further, the addition of a touch of Sir Toby or Falstaff, and the ejection of its miraculous conversions of ill-disposed characters. But the misbehaviour of Fortune, and the hardness and ingratitude of men, form the basis of its plot, and are a frequent topic of complaint. And, on the other hand, he who is reading it has a smooth brow and smiling lips, and a heart that murmurs,

> Happy is your grace,
> That can translate the stubbornness of fortune
> Into so quiet and so sweet a style.

And it is full not only of sweetness, but of romance, fun, humour of various kinds, delight in the oddities of human nature, love of modesty and fidelity and high spirit and patience, dislike of scandal and censure, contemplative curiosity, the feeling that in the end we are all merely players, together with a touch of the feeling that

> Then is there mirth in heaven
> When earthly things made even
> Atone together.

And, finally, it breathes the serene holiday mood of escape from the toil, competition, and corruption of city and court into the sun and shadow and peace of the country, where one can be idle and dream and meditate and sing, and pursue or watch the deer as the fancy takes one, and make love or smile at lovers according to one's age.[1]

---

1. It may be added that *As You Like It*, though idyllic, is not so falsely idyllic as some critics would make it. It is based, we may roughly say, on a contrast between court and country; but those who inhale virtue from the woodland are courtiers who bring virtue with them, and the country has its churlish masters and unkind or uncouth maidens.

## BRINGING CHEEK BY JOWL'S
## *AS YOU LIKE IT* OUT OF THE CLOSET:
## THE POLITICS OF GAY THEATER

*James C. Bulman*

ALL-MALE CASTING of Shakespeare's plays, once regarded as a quaint anachronism and rarely practiced outside British public schools, has become commonplace during the past decade and found wide acceptance among audiences in Britain and North America.[1] The reasons for this sea change are not hard to fathom. For more than twenty years feminist and gay rights movements have raised public awareness of gender issues, and while such movements have met resistance, they nevertheless have brought homosexuality out of the closet and prompted even conservative segments of society to consider the extent to which gender may be a cultural construct, and sexual desire dependent on forces other than biological difference. In the academy, queer theorists have been instrumental in promoting such questions by arguing that gender is always performative, never fixed. According to Judith Butler and her disciples, there is no such thing as an essential or interior gender identity; rather, gender can be discerned only by external codes of conduct and by citational behavior (Butler 1990, 1993; Traub 1992a). This post-modern impulse to de-essentialize gender, to regard it as a social performance played to an audience who tacitly set the rules of representation, provides a compelling lens through which to view early modern plays; for in them—and especially in Shakespeare's comedies—gender is often interrogated as a form of role-play, and the historical practice of boys performing women's roles would have challenged the comfortable certainties of how one comes to know a person's sex. Unsurprisingly, then, some contemporary directors have responded to this performative "queering" of gender identity by staging Shakespeare's plays with all-male casts, recuperating an Elizabethan practice to explore the ways in which gender is *now* perceived to be radically contingent, easily elided, always in a state of play.

Bulman, James C. "Bringing Cheek by Jowl's As You Like It out of the Closet: The Politics of Gay Theater." Shakespeare Bulletin 22:3 (Fall 2004): 31–46. Reprinted with permission of The Johns Hopkins University Press.

Cheek by Jowl's audacious 1991 *As You Like It* deserves to be revisited in light of queer theory, because it was the first all-male production of Shakespeare to gain international popularity—revived in 1994, it again toured internationally—and to introduce the convention of the all-male cast to audiences primed by recent social movements to view as "queer" the sexual politics of cross-dressing. Not only did the original staging occur just as Butler's ideas were becoming known but, like most revolutionary theater productions, it gave voice to culturally contested ideas even as they were being theorized by the academy, leading Alisa Solomon, for one, to comment on how "a sexist old stage practice" could unleash an erotic dynamics with the power to deconstruct gender itself (Solomon 1997: 27).[2] Indeed, by exploring vexed notions of gender formation and sexual desire, Cheek by Jowl's *As You Like It* served as a touchstone for all-male productions during the following decade.

One might surmise that the academy's obsessive theorizing about sex and gender would have fueled controversy over how all-male productions of Shakespeare since 1991 have deconstructed gender and kept contested ideas about cross-dressing and homosexuality in play. But with few exceptions, most notably Solomon, this has not been the case. Instead, critics have turned their gaze on the Elizabethan stage, using feminism and queer theory to debate the extent to which casting boys in women's roles had the power to destabilize gender identity and denaturalize sexual desire. In other words, they have applied contemporary thinking about gender and sexuality not to performances they have seen, but to historical performances they have only *imagined*, hoping that speculation about original all-male casting might help them to recover the Elizabethan cultural moment. In the view of some, the Elizabethan stage was "a site where there was considerable fluidity and multiplicity in the channeling of sexual energies" (Howard 1994: 111), and cross-dressing boy actors became both a source and a reflection of cultural anxieties about gender identity and homoeroticism. These boys, it is argued—like the women and pages they played, marginalized figures without power or social position—were invariably subjugated to the controlling desires of men. Stephen Orgel's "Nobody's Perfect, or Why Did the English Stage Take Boys for Women?" (1989) remains the most influential expression of this point of view. Positing that homosexuality was the dominant form of eroticism for Elizabethans, Orgel argues that the feminized bodies of cross-dressing boys stirred vivid imaginings and sexual longings among men in the audience; for in Elizabethan England's misogynist culture, boys, serving as female analogues or substitutes, were apparently less threatening than women as objects of male sexual desire.[3]

Such speculation draws strength from the diatribes of puritan moralists who inveighed against the sins of theatrical representation and warned that the display of adult male actors embracing cross-dressed boys on stage could provoke men in the audience to sodomitical thoughts and acts (Howard 1988, 1994; Garber 1992; Traub 1992a; Levine 1994; Senelick 2000).

The danger of such arguments, according to David Cressy, "lies in projecting present preoccupations onto the past, and in bringing our opinions to the evidence rather than deriving them from it" (2000: 114). Indeed, other critics have countered that acceptance of male actors as women was such a long-standing stage convention, dating back to the Greeks, that it would have passed unnoticed. Elizabethan spectators, they argue, didn't "take" boy actors as eroticized bodies at all, but understood that during the two hours' traffic on the stage, they were to read as female the character as played: the boy actor "himself" became invisible, immersed in the role he assumed, his sex occluded by spectators' tacit complicity in the fiction. Bruce Smith, for example, insists that despite the puritan moralists' objections, "all the unpolemical witnesses we have from the seventeenth century ... register no erotic interest whatsoever in the characters they saw onstage, much less a specifically homoerotic interest in the boy actors;" and further, "the all-male composition" of the company would have made the boys' gender unexceptional and inconspicuous (1992: 129–30). Anthony Dawson writes that "the audience by convention simply ignored the gender of the actor, reading him as her" (1996: 32); John Astington concurs that Elizabethans "didn't think twice" about boys performing female roles (2000: 109); and Juliet Dusinberre asserts that "[t]he actual biological male body of the boy is erased by the performative energy of the theatrical experience" (1996: 57). These critics dismiss the application of Butler's ideas to historical performance as a distortion of the available evidence. In effect, they accuse those who view cross-dressing boy actors through the lens of queer theory of foisting their own cultural anxieties onto the Elizabethans. As Carol Rutter concludes, "cross-dressing was an unremarkable stage convention, no more sensational, anxious or trangressive when practised by the Chamberlain's Men in 1601 than by Cheek by Jowl in 1991" (2001:xiv).

Implicitly, such thinking assumes that audiences in 1991 not only regarded cross-dressed adult male actors in the same way that Elizabethan audiences would have perceived boy actors, as "an unremarkable stage convention," but willingly surrendered to the play's heterosexual fictions, ignoring the male bodies beneath the skirts. This curious cultural elision needs to be examined in light of the recent surge in all-male performances, for in Cressy's terms, one would expect queer theory and arguments about the fluidity of gender identity to be more pertinent to present-day than to Elizabethan performances. Yet critics have been strangely reluctant to apply queer theory to contemporary all-male productions; and even those few who have used Butler to explore the deconstruction of gender in same-sex productions at London's new Globe Theatre have been guided more by a historicizing impulse—by artistic director Mark Rylance's claim to use original practices as a recuperative act—than by an attempt to view the productions in light of current debates over gender, cross-dressing and homosexuality.[4]

This reluctance was certainly evident in critical responses to Cheek by Jowl's *As You Like It*, whose all-male cast was widely praised for the effectiveness with which it rendered invisible, or at least irrelevant, the sex of those actors who played women. "Donnellan's production reveals that *As You Like It* is not about sexuality hetero-, homo-, bi-, or trans- but about love," exulted John Peter (*The Sunday Times* 8 December 1991). Michael Billington agreed that while the production "brings out the polymorphous perversity of Shakespearean comedy ... Donnellan's real emphasis is on the transforming potency of love" (*The Times* 14 October 1991). Of the 1994 revival, the reviewer for *Shakespeare Bulletin* wrote approvingly, "Soon, one forgot transvestism and gender-bending entirely." Even the reviewer for *Shakespeare Survey*, who was perceptive enough to note that the cross-dressed actors "enabled a subtle consideration [of] the play's homosexuality," asserted that "the tremendous erotic charge between Rosalind and Orlando had nothing glibly homoerotic about it" and that finally, "[t]he problem of love and desire was defined as lying beyond gender."[5] More surprisingly, the reviewer for a special issue of *Theatre Journal* devoted to queer theory, even as she acknowledged "the virtues of gender play" in the production, concluded that "same-sex casting ... makes explicit the point that gender is ultimately unimportant in human relationships." Such accounts are tantamount to avoidance behavior: they betray a discomfort with the production's sexual politics and a refusal to grapple with the homophobic social attitudes and government policies which, I shall argue, formed the context through which the production should be viewed. It is time to bring Cheek by Jowl's *As You Like It* out of the closet.

Deeply influenced by Brecht's conviction that theater should alienate its audience by making strange what has been comfortably familiar, director Declan Donnellan made spectators immediately aware of gender at play. Onto a bare stage strode fourteen men wearing white shirts and black pants, clearly marked as actors in modern dress. As they faced the audience, the actor who would play Jaques spoke the opening lines of his Seven Ages of Man speech transposed from Act 2 scene 7: "All the world's a stage,/And all the *men*"—on men, those actors who would play male roles moved stage right—"and *women*"—on women, the actors playing Rosalind and Celia broke from the group to move stage left—"[are] merely players" (139–40).[6] Asking spectators to take two of these male actors, in clothing indistinguishable from the others, as women at once signaled the performative nature of both the play they were about to watch and of the gender identities within it. In Brechtian fashion, the performers were insisting that spectators maintain a double consciousness of both the character and of the actor playing the role.[7] And while Peter Holland argued that "the production allowed character to exist dissociated from performer" so that "sexuality was placed within the control of character, not actor," as if the gender of the actor were inconsequential (1997: 91), Benedict Nightingale countered that the production never lets us "forget the gender behind the gender" (*The Times* 5 December 1991), and Dominic Cavendish, in an article titled "What kind of man do you take me for?," concurred that "however good the performances, you never forget you are watching men" (*Independent* 5 January 1995).

This double consciousness was crucial to the early scenes in which Rosalind is banished by the Duke and Celia vows to join her in exile. Usually of little dramatic impact and paced to move speedily to the Forest of Arden, these scenes were informed by a sexual tension unparalleled in modern productions. The mature male actors playing Celia (attired in a red silk dress) and Rosalind (in blue) could clearly be seen beneath their female garments; and though they made some effort to lighten their voices, their intention was to gesture towards femaleness, not to efface the maleness of their own bodies, a doubleness that lent a particular erotic frisson to their playing. During their initial conversation (1.2), Rosalind lay on the stage while Celia hovered over her, fondling and kissing her playfully; then Rosalind knelt next to Celia and brushed her hair. Their intimacy read as girlish: the adult actors were playing "young." But when reinforced by observations such as Le Beau's that their "loves/Are dearer than the natural bonds of sisters'" (260–61), the potential for an erotic attraction between them became palpable, and it was fully realized after Rosalind fell in love with Orlando at the wrestling match. As she lay with her head on Celia's lap praising Orlando (1.3), Celia became jealous and eventually slapped Rosalind on the back in frustration. Intimations of an erotic relationship between them grew more pointed when Celia defended Rosalind to her father; she grabbed Rosalind's hand defiantly on "We still have slept together" (1.3.71); and when she taunted her father further with "I cannot live out of her company" (85), the

Duke hurled his daughter to the floor. The clear implication was that the Duke suspected Celia of being infatuated with Rosalind—perhaps of having a sexual relationship with her—and, not understanding the depth of their attachment, viewed Rosalind as an unhealthy sexual predator.[8] Later, as Rosalind prepared to leave the court, Celia burst into tears and begged to be taken along, pawing Rosalind's body and holding her face between her hands as she sobbed, "Shall we be sundered? Shall we part, sweet girl?" (97). What ordinarily is played as a comic scene here became emotionally compelling. But what was the audience watching? Two women (for they clearly were too old to be called girls) involved in a lesbian relationship?[9] Or two male actors whose playing of homoerotic attraction informed, but was not fully submerged in, the relationship of the two women? In Donnellan's staging, spectators were constantly made aware that their perception of gender was contingent and determined by performance.[10] Such awareness helped them to maintain a distance from the fiction sufficient to allow them to perceive in the characters an elision of heterosexual and homosexual identities, and thereby to understand how cross-dressing could subvert a heteronormative reading of the text.

This elision of identities became more pronounced when Rosalind disguised herself as Ganymede and swore to cure Orlando of his love for Rosalind. In these scenes, spectators observed two men playing at love—the actor cast as Orlando (Patrick Toomey in 1991; Scott Handy in 1994), and Adrian Lester as Ganymede, a 6'2" actor who, in the viewer's eye, was not in disguise at all. In one dimension, Lester's Ganymede performed credibly as Rosalind trying valiantly to act like a boy in the presence of the man to whom she longs to expose "true" identity, angry that he does not recognize her, frustrated by his lack of demonstrative feeling for her, yet sensible that she can trick him into making love to her by pretending to be his Rosalind as part of the "cure." In another dimension, however, Lester as Ganymede was blatantly male, playing a love scene with another male actor with a sexual intensity that might become Rosalind, but was charged with homoerotic potential. In the famous wooing scene, Ganymede's passion for Orlando came through repeatedly. When, finding it increasingly hard to maintain the game, Ganymede confessed that he was "like enough to consent" (4.1.63) to be wooed by Orlando, all feigning ceased: the scene was played unabashedly as two men pledging their love to one another. When Ganymede asked Celia to marry them, a disapproving Celia refused even to look at them—a reminder of her earlier jealousy; and when Orlando threatened to depart, Ganymede threw a tantrum and tore up his love poems so convincingly that Orlando applauded as a performance what Ganymede had played it in earnest. For spectators like Solomon, steeped in new theories of gender formation and sexual desire, this scene embodied the "transgressive reinscription" of gender and erotic codes which Jonathan Dollimore (1991) thinks characterized Elizabethan performances. It also helped to advance the subversive sexual politics of Donellan's production.

These sexual politics were revealed in the program, which quoted at length from John Boswell's book *Christianity, Social Tolerance and Homosexuality*: "Like that of the modern West," Boswell writes, "the gay subculture of the High Middle Ages appears to have had its own slang, which gradually became diffused among the general population. The equivalent of 'gay,' for example, was 'Ganymede.' The similarity of this word to 'gay' in its cultural setting is striking. In an age addicted to classical literature, the invocation of Greek mythology to describe homosexual relationships not only tacitly removed the stigma conveyed by the biblical 'sodomita,' the only word in common use before or after this period, but also evoked connotations of mythological sanctions, cultural superiority, and personal refinement which considerably diminished negative associations in regard to homosexuality. Although 'Ganymede' was also used derisively, it was basically devoid of moral context and could be used by gay people themselves without misgivings" (1980: 253).

This program note reads like pseudo-historical wishful thinking; for the idea of a homosexual identity as such was unknown in the Renaissance (in Boswell's text, the High Middle Ages); only sodomy as a sexual practice was condemned; and certainly the term Ganymede did not sanitize sodomites any more than the word "gay," among conservative circles today, erases the moral revulsion with which homophobia is tinged.[11] But Boswell's remarks reveal a will to invest Elizabethan culture with present day attitudes towards identity politics, and, even if anachronistically, they address how issues of gender formation have entered the discourse of educated Western audiences. Any attempt to read homoerotics into *As You Like It* reveals the contemporary significance we attach to cross-dressing. Arguing that "Ganymede" signifies gayness as an identity, Boswell's history was invoked by Check by Jowl to validate Donellan's decision to use the gender elisions of *As You Like It* to foreground a contemporary political agenda.

Nowhere was that agenda revealed more clearly than in his decision to have Jaques played as a Noel Cowardesque queen.[12] Where Lester's Ganymede was virile, devoid of camp, and invested in the maleness of his ostensibly cross-dressed body, the Jaques of Joe Dixon (1991; Michael Gardiner in 1994) was a flamboyant dandy, dressed in a white morning suit and cashmere overcoat, heavily made up, a beauty spot on his cheek. Next to his effete gayness, the sexual ambiguities of the principals seemed more "natural." He was a character whose status as an outsider could be stereotypically explained by his homosexuality—his failure to find a mate in the Forest of Arden. Forever trying to pick up young men, he first attempted to hook the hunky Silvius by offering him a cigarette; but his supercilious come-on, "I prithee, pretty youth, let me be better acquainted with thee" (4.1.1–2)—a line directed to Rosalind in Shakespeare's text, but here appropriated for the conclusion of the preceding scene—was apparently misunderstood by Silvius, who happily accepted the cigarette and ran off. The bumpkin clearly had not picked up on the courtier's covert invitation for sex.

Jaques' next target was the more knowing Ganymede. When Ganymede inquired why Jaques was so melancholy, the older man broke down and wept in his lap. But Ganymede-as-Rosalind was not about to accept Jaques' attentions, even if Ganymede-as-pretty-youth (or male actor) might have. When Ganymede stood to bid him farewell, however, striking a masculine pose and extending his hand, Jaques would not let go of it. In self-defense, Ganymede reverted to playing "Rosalind" and disabused him by putting Jaques' hand on her "breast" as she told him emphatically to "chide God for making you that countenance you are" (4,1.33)—in this context, the line sounded like homophobic chastisement. Jaques recoiled: he had been mistaken about Ganymede's sex; Ganymede was a female cross-dresser. The audience laughed at his confusion. But Ganymede-as-Rosalind put her fingers to her lips, swearing him to secrecy. A pact of homosexual kinship thus made Jaques complicit in maintaining Rosalind's disguise. But what disguise? In what was Jaques complicit? Although, in the fiction of the play, he had discovered that Ganymede was female—she had a breast and therefore was not a youth at all—the audience knew there *was* no breast.[13] The actor of Rosalind was feigning femaleness, and while spectators on one level might have imagined the breast to be there and thus been willing to buy into the fiction, on another, they knew that Jaques had felt Adrian Lester's chest and found only a pectoral muscle. This confusion, in the doubleness of vision encouraged by the feigning, heightened the sense of homoerotics at play.

In the ensuing scene, the production's political agenda grew more overt and topical: Jaques became the victim of a vicious gay-bashing. With the hunt for deer over, Jaques now was the hunted—surrounded by hunters, who in this production's gay aesthetic were burly men, shirtless and sweaty. When he asked sardonically, "Which is he that killed the deer?" (4.2.1), they manhandled him; and when they burst into song about "the lusty horn" (18)—goading him with its obvious phallic references—they pushed him around the stage with derisive brutality. If the machismo of the staging was redolent of gay culture, the bashing of the "fem" smacked of conservative cultural backlash. Yet these uncomfortable moments had a specific topicality—at least in 1991. In an article tellingly titled "The Worst of Times," Colin Richardson writes: "The violent homophobia inspired by the advent of AIDS in the early 80s, inflamed by the tabloids and indulged by Thatcherism, had fostered in gay Britain a siege mentality. . . . In 1988 Section 28, the first anti-gay legislation in a hundred years, became law. The re-criminalisation of male homosexuality was high on the Tory wishlist . . . arrests of gay men for 'gross indecency' doubled . . . [and] violence against gay people was spiraling out of control. In September 1989 a gay barrister . . . was murdered in his west London home. He was stabbed more than 40 times. . . . Three months later, in another part of London, a gay hotelier . . . was stabbed to death at home. The following month [a] gay hotel porter . . . was found unconscious on a roadside in Acton [and] died soon after from severe head injuries." The list of atrocities grows more ominous, because apparently sanctioned by the government: "In 1990 police [were] staking out the [public] toilets, arresting gay men in unprecedented numbers," and in one infamous case, on 29 April 1990, a man was lured into a toilet, savagely beaten by a gang of a half dozen men, and died of internal bleeding. "The reaction of the gay community was angry and terrified;" and out of their protests came the activist group OutRage which "campaigned for the police to stop arresting gay men and start protecting them." More extraordinarily, in September of 1990 "gay [police] officers met anxiously in private to set up the Lesbian and Gay Police Association (Lagpa)" (*The Guardian* 14 August 2002). This inflammatory chain of events provides a crucial context for understanding why, in the deer hunting scene, Cheek by Jowl's agenda turned activist, going beyond merely dramatizing elisions of gender and same-sex desire to warn explicitly of the violence against homosexuals to which Thatcherism had given rise.

The final scene of pairings brought the political agenda full circle, but more gently. Ganymede had promised Orlando, "I will satisfy you if ever I satisfy man" (5.2.109), and the audience had been encouraged to hear his promise as a wryly gay threat. Would Orlando, at Rosalind's unveiling, see anything more than the "boy" whom he had been taught to think of as Rosalind until he complained that he could no longer live by thinking? When Rosalind appeared in a wedding dress—"To you I give myself, for I am yours" (5.4.112)—she went to take his hand, but he refused it. Shocked, he moved away from her; and she, dismayed, threw down her bouquet and wept in her father's arms. What did spectators see here? Through the lens of the play's fiction, an Orlando who was disturbed at having been tricked by a woman wiser than he, confused that the boy he had rejected as a poor substitute for Rosalind was in fact female? Or, through lens of the production's sexual politics, a man confronting the fact that the object of his desire had all along been a male, here simply cross-dressed in woman's attire—a man disturbed to discover "the scope and contradictions of his sexuality" (Nightingale, *The Times* 5 December 1991)?[14] In this production, both were possibilities; each assumed the audience's active and unflagging awareness of the male actor beneath Rosalind's skirt. When at last Orlando came 'round and embraced her, asking incredulously, "You *are* my Rosalind?" (118)—the text's declarative, "If there be truth in sight, you are my Rosalind," delivered here as a tentative question—they indulged in a passionate kiss. Spectators of course saw two male actors kissing, but even in suspending their disbelief would perceive, with Orlando, that this Rosalind was, or could be, a man. The moment was richly nuanced: it satisfied the heteronormative fiction of the play yet admitted of homosexual self-realization—the queering of Orlando and, in so far as spectators had been taught by the production to see sexuality as fluid and gender as contingent, the queering of the audience as well.

The indeterminacy of sexual identity was playfully preserved in the Epilogue spoken by Adrian Lester, who removed the bandana that he had worn as Rosalind and, in his own person, toyed with the audience when he said, "If I were a woman, I would kiss as many of you as had beards that pleased me" (16–18), teasing them with the possibility of homoerotic contact. The statement's conditionality reinforced the conflation of gender and performance in which spectators had been complicit and reminded them that the heterosexual couplings they had just seen sanctioned might be as deceptive as the disguise by which Lester-as-Rosalind-as-Ganymede had presumed, ultimately, to fool no one. Lester's speaking the lines in his own voice, as male actor, challenged audiences to consider that when Rosalind had donned the attire of Ganymede, "she was perhaps not adding a layer of disguise so much as stripping one away, revealing the homoerotic foundations of the play's marital structure" (DiGangi 1996: 286).[15]

Cheek by Jowl's production has become a landmark in performance studies because it so brilliantly destabilized gender assumptions which had characterized productions of Shakespeare since the Restoration. Actresses playing cross-dressing women's roles create a different sexual dynamic; such casting does not encourage so playful an awareness of gender difference among spectators, and the homoerotic potentials of performance are buffered by safe assurances that the real attraction Orlando feels, albeit unconscious, is to the woman's body beneath Ganymede's male disguise. Yet to effect such a change in the audience's way of looking, Cheek by Jowl's *As You Like It* was suffused with a gay aesthetic that politicized the production in a manner consistent with queer advocacy in late '80s and early '90s Britain. The erotic play between Ganymede and Orlando was the most prominent way in which the staging foregrounded same-sex relations; but the lesbian force of Celia's jealousy of Rosalind, the flaunting of macho versus fern culture, and hunky foresters with bare chests taunting a queenly Jaques carrying a cigarette lighter, made explicit an identity politics that a production which played the cross-dressing "straight" would have left unexplored. Intriguingly, even with such explicit references to gay culture, some critics insisted on seeing the production's cross-dressing as uninflected by a political agenda, "an unremarkable stage convention," not at all transgressive or reflective of contemporary cultural anxieties over gender identity and sexual desire. In 1991, I would argue, when AIDS was still regarded as God's revenge on homosexuals and homophobic violence was commonplace, it would have been impossible for a production as daring as this *not* to ground itself in gay political discourse.

## NOTES

1. Clifford Williams's 1967 all-male *As You Like It* (National Theatre at the Old Vic) is a notable exception. An isolated experiment, it occurred when audiences were not yet ready seriously to entertain questions of gender construction and when representations of homosexuality were still banned from the British stage. Although the Lord Chamberlain had eased some restrictions on the *discussion* of homosexuality in the theatre in 1958, his power of censorship ceased only with passage of the Theatres Act in 1968. For a history of the censorship of homosexuality on stage, see deJongh 1992.

2. Suggesting that Cheek by Jowl's *As You Like It* might reveal how transvestism worked on the Elizabethan stage, Solomon quotes Susan Zimmerman about the play's power to unleash "an erotic dynamics that deconstructs gender itself, leaving conventional categories of sexuality blurred, confused—or absent" (Zimmerman 1992: 8). I am indebted to Solmon's use of Butler's theory of performativity to queer the Cheek by Jowl production, but I differ from her in regarding the production as more overtly political, its insistent queerness impelled by the pressing social contexts—and homophobic policies—of Thatcherite Britain.

3. Several years earlier than Orgel, Lisa Jardine (1983: 9–36) had argued that cross-dressing boys were especially exciting to male spectators: "'Playing the women's part'—male effeminacy—is an act for a male audience's appreciation" (31). Orgel and Jardine differ, however, on the extent to which male transvestism was a symptom of a pervasive

cultural misogyny: for Orgel, the homoeroticism of the Elizabethan stage was not *inevitably* misogynist. See also Orgel's essay on "The performance of desire" in *Impersonations* (1996: 10–30).

4. One such essay is John R. Ford's perceptive analysis of gender performativity and the all-male cast as a manifestation of an original practice in the Globe's *Twelfth Night* (2002; revived in 2003). I take issue with Rylance's claim to use original practices as a recuperative strategy and argue instead that it serves as a tactical ruse for getting audiences to think about sex and gender transgressively in my essay "Queering the Audience: All-Male Casts in Recent Shakespeare Productions," in *A Companion to Shakespeare and Performance*, ed. Barbara Hodgdon and William B. Worthen (Oxford: Blackwell, forthcoming).

5. See Margaret Loftus Ranald, *Shakespeare Bulletin* 12.4 (Fall 1994) 10; Peter Holland, *Shakespeare Survey* 45 (1992) 128; and Katie Laris, *Theatre Journal* 47 (May 1995) 300; and compare Ben Brantley's assertion in his review for *The New York Times* that "[t]he fact that men are portraying women here is less a statement about sexual role playing than about playing roles in its broadest and most resonant sense" (6 October 1994). Holland's analysis of the production's depiction of gender was unchanged in his collection *English Shakespeares* (91–94) which appeared in 1997, the same year as Solomon's more Butlerian account of the effect of all-male casting. This inclination to de-emphasize the production's sexual role play in the interest of universalizing its performativity—and a sentimental insistence on subsuming gender in the transcendent power love—was perhaps the most common critical response to the all-male casting.

6. All references are to the Oxford *As You Like It* (1993).

7. Shapiro (1994) argues that such double consciousness operated in the Elizabethan theatre, wherein audience awareness of the sex of the boy actor was activated in specific situations, particularly those involving cross-gender disguise. While Shapiro's theory has been qualified with regard to early modern stage practices (e.g., Dawson 1996), it is readily applicable to performances with cross-dressed male casts today.

8. Benedict Nightingale, alone among critics for the London dailies in 1991, acknowledged the production's "strong homoerotic feel," particularly in the early scenes with Rosalind and Celia. The suggestion of sexual play between "the two men-women" makes us wonder, he writes, whether Duke Frederick "hasn't more than one reason for ridding his court of Rosalind" (*The Times* 5 December 1991).

9. In her study of lesbian desire in early modern England, Traub (1992b) argues that because the plot of *As You Like It* moves towards a heterosexual union, "an implicit power asymmetry" distinguishes the woman who clings to homoerotic desire, Celia, from the woman who abandons it, Rosalind (158).

10. Donnellan had to break down his actors' essentialized views of gendered behavior as well. Dominic Cavendish interviewed Simon Coates, who played Celia in the revival, about this very topic (*Independent* 30 January 1994); "In rehearsal, Coates started repressing traits he considered too testosterone-based. 'The second I became in any way aggressive on stage, I thought, "Oh my God, I'm being masculine." But Declan said "You've really got to go for the aggression."'"

11. The most influential studies of the representation of homosexuality in the early modern period are Bray 1982, Smith 1991, Goldberg 1994, DiGangi 1997, and Masten 1997. These writers help to clarify cultural differences between how homosexuality is viewed today, as a form of sexual identity, and how it was viewed in Shakespeare's time, when identifying oneself by sexual preference was unheard of and the only term for same-sex relations was sodomy. The myth of Ganymede as a vehicle for expressing same-sex desire in the period has been the subject of books by Saslow 1986 and Barkan 1991, and shorter studies by Smith (1991:199–223) and DiGangi (1996: 281–85).

12. The discrepant ways in which critics commented on the playing of Jaques reveal the degree to which they were willing or unwilling to engage with the production's radical sexual politics. John Peter, for example, praised "a fine, saturnine Jaques from Joe Dixon, a self-absorbed, melancholy, slightly precious dandy," skirting around the issue of his sexuality (*The Sunday Times* 8 December 1991), and Jeremy Kingston complained that Jaques' "propositioning man after man, even at the wedding, feels wrong" (*The Times* 21 January 1995). Benedict Nightingale, however, pegged him more receptively as "a would-be sugar-daddy to both Ganymede and Patrick Toomey's pale, intent Orlando. Homo, bi, and trisexuality is all about" (*The Times* 5 December 1991).

13. Stallybrass (1992; rpt. in Jones and Stallybrass 2000) writes revealingly about the "fetishistic staging of the boy actor" on the Elizabethan stage and particularly about how an early modern audience would have responded to allusions to the female breast, presumably an essential figure of gender, when that breast had to be imagined on the body of the cross-dressed boy actor. Mazer (2004) discusses a similar moment of breast awareness later in the Cheek by Jowl production when Rosalind, after fainting, lets Oliver in on her secret by placing his hand inside her shirt and pressing it against her "breast."

14. Holland's unambiguous interpretation of this moment, typical of that of many critics, is consistent with his view of the actor's gender being irrelevant to the character: "When Rosalind lifted her bridal veil and offered herself to Orlando . . . Orlando turned on his heel and stormed to the back of the stage, shocked at the trick and shamed at his failure to have recognized her" (1992: 130). I deviate from Holland in regarding this as only one way in which the

audience could have understood the moment. Katie Laris's take on the same moment is more reflective of a queer reading of the production. In her view, Donnellan used the play to impart a "message" of "tolerance" of sexual difference and of gender as a *choice*; the vehicle for that message was Rosalind; and Orlando's "eventual acceptance of her for what she chooses to be is painfully poignant and serves as the final test of the lessons he's been taught" (*Theatre Journal* 47 [May 1995] 301–02).

15. Solomon (1997: 24–26) reads the whole Epilogue as a playful projection of the actor's sexual ambiguity onto the audience. The reference to beards, which presumably would apply only to male spectators, may in fact have been understood as a bawdy reference to female pubic hair; and therefore the actor could be implying that if he were a woman, he would willingly have sex with other women. DiGangi reads the Epilogue as more exclusively, if no less playfully, male in its homoeroticism. The audience's tendency—tinged with homophobia—to identify a character's sexual ambiguity with the actor who plays him/her is a phenomenon that affected Cheek by Jowl. As reported by Dominic Cavendish, while the sexuality of the actors themselves was never an issue for the company, "Coates and Lester are widely (and wrongly) assumed to be gay by audiences. 'The men never look you in the eye if they come back-stage,' says Coates" (*Independent* 30 January 1994).

## WORKS CITED

Astington, John H. "Playhouses, Players, and Playgoers in Shakespeare's Time." *The Cambridge Companion to Shakespeare*. Ed. Margareta de Grazia and Stanley Wells. Cambridge: Cambridge UP, 2001.

Barkan, Leonard. *Transuming Passion: Ganymede and the Erotics of Humanism*. Stanford: Stanford UP, 1991.

Boswell, John. *Christianity, Social Tolerance, and Homosexuality: Gay People in Western Europe from the Beginning of the Christian Era to the Fourteenth Century*. Chicago: U of Chicago P, 1980.

Bray, Alan. *Homosexuality in Renaissance England*. London: Gay Men's P, 1982.

Butler, Judith. *Gender Trouble: Feminism and the Subversion of Identity*. New York: Routledge, 1990.

—. *Bodies That Matter: On the Discursive Limits of* "Sex." New York: Routledge, 1993.

Cressy, David. *Travesties and Transgressions in Tudor and Stuart England*. Oxford: Oxford UP, 2000.

Dawson, Anthony. "Performance and Participation: Desdemona, Foucault, and the Actor's Body." *Shakespeare, Theory, and Performance*. Ed. James C. Bulman. London: Routledge, 1996.

de Jongh, Nicholas. *Not in Front of the Audience: Homosexuality On Stage.* London: Routledge, 1992.

DiGangi, Mario. "Queering the Shakespearean Family." *Shakespeare Quarterly* 47 (1996): 269–90.

——. *The Homoerotics of Early Modern Drama.* Cambridge: Cambridge UP, 1997.

Dollimore, Jonathan. *Sexual Dissidence: Augustine to Wilde, Freud to Foucault,* Oxford: Clarendon P, 1991.

Dusinberre, Juliet. "Squeaking Cleopatras: Gender and Performance in *Antony and Cleopatra.*" *Shakespeare, Theory, and Performance.* Ed. James C. Bulman. London: Routledge, 1996.

Ford, John R. "Estimable Wonders and Hard Constructions: Recognizing *Twelfth Night* at the Globe." *Shakespeare Bulletin* 21.3 (2003): 47–60.

Garber, Marjorie. *Vested Interests: Cross-Dressing and Cultural Anxiety.* New York: Routledge, 1992.

Goldberg, Jonathan. *Sodometrics: Renaissance Texts, Modern Sexualities.* Stanford: Stanford UP, 1992.

Holland, Peter. *English Shakespeares: Shakespeare on the English Stage in the 1990s.* Cambridge: Cambridge UP, 1997.

Howard, Jean E. "Cross-Dressing, the Theater, and Gender Struggle in Early Modern England," *Shakespeare Quarterly* 39.4 (1988) 418–40.

——. *The Stage and Social Struggle in Early Modern England.* London: Routledge, 1994.

Jardine, Lisa. *Still Harping on Daughters: Women and Drama in the Age of Shakespeare.* Totowa: Barnes and Noble, 1983.

Jones, Ann Rosalind and Peter Stallybrass. *Renaissance Clothing and the Materials of Memory.* Cambridge: Cambridge UP, 2000.

Levine, Laura. *Men in Women's Clothing: Anti-Theatricality and Effeminization, 1579–1642.* Cambridge: Cambridge UP, 1994.

Masten, Jeffrey. *Textual Intercourse: Collaboration, Authorship, and Sexualities in Renaissance Drama.* Cambridge: Cambridge UP, 1997.

Mazer, Cary M. "Rosalind's Breast." Unpublished paper written for a seminar on cross-dressing in contemporary performances of Shakespeare. New Orleans: meeting of the Shakespeare Association of America, 2004.

Orgel, Stephen. "Nobody's Perfect, or Why Did the English Stage Take boys for Women?" *Displacing Homophobia: Gay Male Perspectives in Literature and Culture.* Ed. Ronald R. Butters, John M. Clum, and Michael Moon. Durham: Duke UP, 1989,

——. *Impersonations: The Performance of Gender in Shakespeare's England.* Cambridge: Cambridge UP, 1996.

Rutter, Carol. *Enter the Body: Women and Representation on Shakespeare's Stage.* London: Routledge, 2001.

Saslow, James M. *Ganymede in the Renaissance: Homosexuality in Art and Society.* New Haven: Yale UP, 1986.

Senelick, Laurence. *The Changing Room: Sex, Drag and Theatre*. London: Routledge, 2000.

Shakespeare, William. *As You Like It*. Ed. Alan Brissenden. Oxford: Clarendon P, 1993.

Shapiro, Michael. *Gender in Play on the Shakespearean Stage: Boy Heroines and Female Pages*. Ann Arbor: U of Michigan P, 1994.

Smith, Bruce R. *Homosexual Desire in Shakespeare's England: A Cultural Poetics*. Chicago: U of Chicago P, 1991.

—. "Making a Difference: Male/Male 'Desire' in Tragedy, Comedy, and Tragic-Comedy." *Erotic Politics: Desire on the Renaissance Stage*. Ed. Susan Zimmerman. London: Routledge, 1992.

Solomon, Alisa. *Re-Dressing the Canon: Essays on Theater and Gender*. London: Routledge, 1997.

Stallybrass, Peter. "Transvestism and the 'Body Beneath': Speculating on the Boy Actor." *Erotic Politics: Desire on the Renaissance Stage*. Ed. Susan Zimmerman. London: Routledge, 1992.

Traub, Valerie. *Desire and Anxiety: Circulations of Sexuality in Shakespearean Drama*. London: Routledge, 1992a.

—. "The (In)significance of 'Lesbian' Desire on Early Modern England." *Erotic Politics: Desire on the Renaissance Stage*. Ed. Susan Zimmerman. London: Routledge, 1992b.

Zimmerman, Susan, ed. *Erotic Politics: Desire on the Renaissance Stage*. London: Routledge, 1992.

# THEATRICAL PRACTICE AND THE
# IDEOLOGIES OF STATUS IN *AS YOU LIKE IT*

*Mary Thomas Crane*

I N *As You Like It*, even more directly than in *The Comedy of Errors*, Shakespeare explores the relationships between theater, language, and ideology in the formation of early modern subjectivity. In *As You Like It* Shakespeare seems to be interested in words that are directly implicated in the mediation of ideological structures, in Marxist terms, in the "reproduction of the conditions of production," specifically the shift from feudal to capitalist ideologies of social mobility and status hierarchy.[1] In this play, as in *The Comedy of Errors*, the material practices of theatrical production are an integral part of the lexical web on which Shakespeare's attention seems focused. Here Shakespeare seems fascinated by the changing connotations of the words *villain* and *clown*, especially as they are inflected by the possibilities for upward or downward mobility within a theatrical company. Although most critics have seen this play as clearly working to reproduce the currently dominant ideologies of limited mobility and social hierarchy, I find that its relation to those ideologies is actually uneven and at times problematic.

Cognitive theory might seem initially to support this current critical orthodoxy since it suggests that the concept of hierarchy and a sense that it is better to be up than down are based in early image schemas and are therefore powerful discursive formations in most cultures because of their grounding in fundamental mental structures.[2] Certainly this play seems especially focused on forms of social hierarchy in a range of cultural settings. However, Shakespeare's interest in the ways words can work to shore up hierarchical discursive structures seems to be shaped significantly by feelings of anger, sympathy, and regret. In this play the issue of authorial agency is directly addressed, but this too is both ambivalently presented and marked by mixed feelings. Cognitive theory has begun to suggest how affect or emotion shapes the very nature of human thought and conceptualization.

Crane, Mary Thomas. "Theatrical Practice and the Ideologies of Status in *As You Like It*." Shakespeare's Brain: Reading with Cognitive Theory. Princeton University Press. 2001. 67–82; 92–93. Used by permission.

*As You Like It* provides an especially useful example of the ways in which the power of language to shape the subject (in a process like Althusserian interpellation) is itself shaped and complicated not just by cognitive structures and motivations but also by feeling.

Hamlet's famous complaint, probably performed in the year after *As You Like It*, about William Kemp's style of clowning ends with a significant phrase that glances back at and sums up the issues of agency and social mobility that are of central concern in the earlier play. Having urged the players to "let those that play your clowns speak no more than is set down for them, for there be of them that will themselves laugh to set on some quantity of barren spectators to laugh too, though in the mean time some necessary question of the play be then to be consider'd," he concludes: "That's villainous, and shows a most pitiful ambition in the fool that uses it" (3.2.38–44). We should be cautious in taking Hamlet's words here to be Shakespeare's, but the collocation of *clown, villainous,* and *ambition* returns us to the preoccupations of *As You Like It*, where the words *villain* and *clown* are used both to justify and to apologize for Shakespeare's own attempt to gain control over the text by banishing Kemp from the Globe stage. The meditations on *villain* and *clown* in *As You Like It* must thus be read in the context of the social implications of Kemp's jig performances and the ambitions of the Chamberlain's Men around 1600.

In 1612 the general sessions of the peace for Middlesex added yet another document to ongoing attempts at regulation of the theater, this time ordering suppression of the jigs that usually followed performances of plays:

> Whereas Complaynte have [*sic*] beene made at this last Generall Sessions, that by reason of certayne lewde Jigges songes and daunces vsed and accustomed at the play-house called the Fortune in Gouldinglane, divers cutt-purses and other lewd and ill disposed persons in great multitudes doe resorte thither at th'end of euerye playe, many tymes causinge tumultes and outrages wherebye His Majesties peace is often broke and much mischiefe like to ensue thereby, Itt was hereuppon expresslye commaunded and ordered by the Justices of the said benche, That all Actors of euerye playhouse in this cittye and liberties thereof and in the County of Middlesex that they and euerie of them utterlye abolishe all Jigges Rymes and Daunces after their playes.[3]

C. R. Baskervil speculated that the infamous jig "Garlic," probably performed by the clown named Shank, was the immediate catalyst for this order.[4] But the scattered references to jig performances that survive suggest that most of them were boisterous and obscene and that large crowds of vagrant and criminal persons who could not afford (or were not interested in affording) the minimal price of groundling admission to the featured play gathered outside the theater and somehow gained admission to the postperformance jig.[5] These jigs evidently involved plots centered on cuckoldry or rustic wooing, bawdy songs, and exuberant (and sometimes obscene) dances; there was a fashion around 1612 for dances performed by a man in a baboon costume, and *The Two Noble Kinsmen* describes "the beast-eating clown, and next the Fool/ The Bavian [baboon], with long tail and eke long tool, / *cum multis aliis* that make a dance" (3.5.131–33).[6] The jig probably also included exchanges with the audience, who in any event by all accounts participated in the performance through shouts, loud laughter, and applause.[7]

Evidence suggests that by 1612 jigs (and the clowns who performed them) were held in contempt by some audiences because of their obscenity, rowdiness, and, to use Baskervil's term, "low art." Hamlet, of course, denigrates Polonius's taste in theater when he says that "he's for a jig or a tale of bawdry, or he sleeps" (2.2.500). Similarly, a contemporary satirist describes the audiences for the jigs of the celebrated clown William Kemp as decidedly lower class: "Whores, Bedles, bawdes, and Sergeants filthily/Chaunt Kemps Iigge."[8] Nevertheless, jigs remained enormously popular, especially in the theaters of the northern suburbs, from the opening of the first theaters until at least 1612.

During William Kemp's tenure as lead clown of the Chamberlain's Men from 1594 until around 1599, Shakespeare's plays, like most other plays performed in the period, would have been followed by such a jig, in this case one written and performed by Kemp himself. David Wiles, in his excellent study of Kemp's career, persuasively argues that these jigs had a complex relationship to their preceding plays, tending toward an anarchic "deconstruction" of the values of the main play.[9] In addition, a role appropriate for Kemp's popular persona of rustic clown had to be included in each play; once onstage, Kemp was notoriously liable to improvise. Shakespeare was, of course, probably thinking of Kemp when he had Hamlet voice the complaint about improvisation cited above. The presence of the clown and the jig, then, assured that plays would be subject to interruption and qualification by unruly voices that were not under the control of the author of the play. And there is evidence that Shakespeare, far from accepting this collaborative structure, took steps to regain a measure of authorial control over his texts by replacing Kemp with a clown who would speak his lines as written.

Concern over the unruliness of the audience (and the performing clown), as well as a desire to appeal to a more exclusive audience may have led the Chamberlain's Men to decide to abolish or curtail performances of jigs when they moved south to Bankside and the new

Globe Theatre in 1599, well before the court order suppressing them. What we know for sure is that Kemp, a shareholder in the company and perhaps its most popular actor, suddenly sold his share and left the company at that time. *As You Like It*, probably first performed in 1599, introduces Kemp's replacement, Robert Armin, as the fool, Touchstone. Kemp subsequently made some (unsuccessful) attempts at raising money through spectacular solo performances, for example, an attempt to dance from London to Norwich, and ultimately appeared with Worcester's men, a company located in the northern suburbs, where jigs remained popular until their suppression.[10] But he never again regained the prosperity and standing that he had achieved with the Chamberlain's Men. A number of scholars speculate that Kemp left the company because of a decision to curtail the role of the jig.[11] Certainly the Lord Chamberlain's company had by this time begun to set its sights on a slightly different audience, and as Wiles has argued, "the jig did nothing to raise the status of the company, and increased the risk of crowd trouble."[12] With the purchase and renovation of the Blackfriars Theatre in 1596 (although the company could not perform there until 1608), and with a move south to Bankside in 1599, the Chamberlain's Men dissociated themselves from the existing public theaters in the north and created a repertory that could ultimately be performed at both the public Globe and the private Blackfriars. The move to the Globe, then, marked a point of upward mobility for the Chamberlain's Men and one of downward mobility for the excluded Kemp and his jigs.

David Wiles and Richard Helgerson have noted the important implications of these jigs for our understanding of authorship in the period.[13] With the exception of Wiles and Helgerson, however, arguments over subversion and containment and over Shakespeare's role in the cultural work of reproducing differences in social class have for the most part proceeded based on assumptions about the nature of Shakespeare's authorship alone rather than an uneasy collaboration with Kemp or, for that matter, the rest of the company.[14] Those who argue that the dominant (hierarchical) ideologies of early modern culture essentially construct and contain both author and play correlate cultural work in the interests of the ruling hierarchies with lack of authorial agency.[15] On the other hand, those who want to see Shakespeare's plays as furthering the interests of lower- or working-class persons correlate that alignment with a high degree of authorial independence, individuality, and agency.[16]

Helgerson, on the other hand, allies authorial agency with support of class hierarchy. He argues that the Shakespearean history plays written around the same time as *As You Like It* "purge" the common, the festive, and other lingering signs of the collaborative popular "player's theater" from his plays. In comedy, however, Shakespeare treated the potential conflicts between high and low, elite and popular, rulers and ruled, in a different and less clearly purgative way. A cognitive reading may also offer a more flexible way to think about the competing interests represented in the play than does Helgerson's New Historicism. While a historicist or materialist reading such as Helgerson's can note the presence of competing ideologies in a text—for example, his admission that Shakespeare's history plays do offer some "exposure" of the "brutal and duplicitous strategies by which power maintained itself," as well as some limited "festive power of inversion"—such readings seem to feel obligated to identify a text with some dominant ideological position.[17] A cognitive reading, with its broader sense of agency and its assumption that all meaning is polysemic, allows greater weight for multiplicity and the coexistence of competing interests. It also acknowledges a factor that is of particular importance in this play, namely, the central role of feelings—of regret, anger, envy—in inflecting the ideological forces present in the play.

An examination of the representation of relations between different social classes in *As You Like It* thus reveals that the connection between ideology and agency is neither simple nor uniform. The performance of Shakespeare's *As You Like It* marked a pivotal moment in the status negotiations of the Chamberlain's Men; it was perhaps the first play performed at their new Globe Theatre, and in what seems to have been an attempt to appeal to a "better" audience it was the first play to be performed with the new, more refined clown Robert Armin (and probably without an attendant jig). More importantly, the play links the exclusion of the rustic clown and jig from the Globe to the social mechanisms that helped to justify the exclusion of lower-class persons from the limited upward mobility then becoming possible in the culture as a whole. These mechanisms included the semantic shift of what previously had been status terms (e.g., *villain, churl,* and *clown*) to almost exclusively ethical connotations, a linguistic change that was deeply implicated in the reformulation of attitudes toward social class that accompanied the decline of the feudal system. The play uses these terms, however, in ways that reveal the implication of language in the reproduction of the ideologies of class, just as it uses the figure of the clown and several jig motifs to reveal the problematic ambitions of the play itself.

The "divers cutt-purses and other lewd and ill disposed persons in great multitudes" who provided the jig with its unruly audience were most probably members of the group of persons identified as "vagrants" or "vagabonds," whose numbers were increasing significantly as a result of far-reaching changes in social and economic organization in this period.[18] Many of these vagrants were descended from the feudal "villein" class, the serfs or "churls" who were "unfree" workers bound to till their lords' fields and subject to burdensome manorial fees and royal taxes. By the end of the sixteenth century, villenage was in practice obsolete in England, having been replaced in most cases by copyhold tenures, which left workers free to move from place to place and protected, in some instances, by royal courts. The end of villenage, so long sought by English peasants, actually left many of them in an even less desirable condition, as vagrants lacking land and work. While feudal custom bound peasants to the land, landowners in the early modern period realized that the enclosure of tenantless land for sheep farming could bring greater profits. Thus, many villeins formerly attached to the land became vagrants, whose new prominence was reflected in the Elizabethan period by increased legislation attempting to control them.[19]

As semanticists have noted, and as the play makes clear, language itself played a role in mediating the changing attitudes toward class and social mobility in this period. Of particular interest in *As You Like It* is a set of terms that were in the process of shifting from essentially neutrally designating status to indicating something about a subject's personal character. In contrast to the prototype shifts that were a center of interest in *The Comedy of Errors*, the kind of semantic change that Shakespeare seems to have emphasized in *As You Like It* has been widely noted. C. S. Lewis. described it as the "moralisation of status-words," whereby "words which originally referred to a person's rank—to legal, social, or economic status and the qualifications of birth which have often been attached to these—have a tendency to become words which assign a type of character and behaviour. Those implying superior status can become terms of praise; those implying inferior status, terms of disapproval. *Chivalrous, courteous, frank, generous, gentle, liberal,* and *noble* are examples of the first; *ignoble, villain,* and *vulgar,* of the second."[20] The second type of shift, from inferior status to moral disapproval, was categorized by the semanticist Gustaf Stern as "depreciative specialization," a category that also includes words such as *huswife* and *gossip*, which depreciate on the basis of gender rather than class.[21]

Of central concern in *As You Like It* are the terms *villain, churl,* and *clown*. By the time Shakespeare wrote that play *villein* had become *villain* and had lost most of its legal imputation of status, having come to mean instead "an unprincipled or depraved scoundrel" *(OED)*. Lewis attributed such shifts to essentially benign and apolitical causes: to "optimism" that social superiors were also superior in ethical behavior and to a desire to encourage the socially ambitious to act in ethically acceptable ways (22–23). But more recent work on the ideologies of class in the medieval and early modern periods reveals the extent to which this semantic shift can be implicated in the strategies of changing social orders to constitute and reproduce themselves.[22] Lee Patterson has traced the medieval ideological formation insisting that "serfdom is a permanent condition of moral inferiority inherent in the peasant's very being rather than a social status capable of being both assumed and (at least in theory) left behind."[23] This concept of inferiority was based on the idea that peasants were descended from Cain or from Noah's son Ham and thus were especially tainted by sin.[24] The revolutionary slogan "When Adam dalf and Eve span/Who was thanne a gentil man," perennially cited by English peasants, especially during the revolts of 1381, 1450, 1536, and 1549, can thus be seen as an attempt to counter the dominant ideology of status by establishing a common ancestry for all people.[25] Of course, such assertions of equality prompted attempts to oppose this revolutionary doctrine with reassertions of orthodoxy: "A bonde man or a churle wyll say, 'All we be cummyn of Adam.' So Lucifer with his cumpany may say, 'All we be cummyn of heuyn.'" In fact, because of his sin "did Cayn become a chorle and all his ofsprung after hym."[26] Such statements reveal the extent to which the correlation of inferior moral and social status was a highly charged ideological maneuver.

Increased possibilities for social mobility in the early modern period necessarily changed how ideologies of status were articulated. In order to accommodate upward mobility, the idea that people are born with qualities suitable to their permanent station in life shifts slightly to suggest that each person's status will ultimately suit his qualities. Richard Halpern, among others, has identified the role of such a "discourse of capacities" in this period, which associated upward mobility with such personal qualities as "intelligence, talent, creativity . . . industry, parsimony, and persistence." Halpern argues that this discourse took on new significance in the sixteenth century, when it was used "to explain *downward* mobility and to cope ideologically with the swelling tides of the new poor," created in part by the deterritorialization and displacement that followed the end of villenage and widespread enclosures.[27] The upwardly mobile Edmund Spenser illustrates a typically mixed ideological formation, when he describes the witch's son in book 3 of the *Faerie Queene* as a "chorle" and "villain" on the basis of low status (he and his mother live in "a little cottage, built of stickes and reedes/In homely, wize" [3.7.6]), natural moral baseness (he feels "no love, but brutish lust" for Florimel [3.7.15]), and inferior capacity (he would not "ply him selfe to any honest trade/ . . . Such laesinesse both lewd and poor attonce him made" [3.7.12]).

The word *clown*, though related in some ways to words such as *villain* and *churl,* has a semantic history that differs in significant ways. *Clown* was not an official status term during the feudal period and in fact seems not to have occurred at all until the sixteenth century.[28] When it did begin to appear, it had simultaneous status and ethical connotations, meaning both "countryman, rustic, or peasant," and "an ignorant, rude, uncouth, ill-bred man" (*OED*). Wiles argues, persuasively I think, that "the concept of a 'clown' emerged within a neo-chivalric discourse centered on the notion of 'gentility.' The word 'gentle' has ambiguously genetic and ethical connotations, and to be a 'clown' is the obverse of being 'gentle.'"[29] As *villain* came to be applicable, in its ethical sense, to upper-class subjects, the term *clown* was needed to convey the special connections between rusticity, low status, and lack of "gentle" qualities.[30] Also unlike *villain* and *churl* in this period (although something similar happened to *villain* in the nineteenth century), *clown* appreciated rather than depreciated as it became a technical theatrical term for a particular (and very popular) kind of actor. In its theatrical sense the term initially retained connotations of low status, but at almost precisely the moment when this play was performed, it began to lose those associations and began to denote simply a comic actor without reference to status. Although in Kemp's persona rudeness and rusticity were inextricably linked to his role as clown, Armin, who appears first in *As You Like It*, preferred to represent a learned "fool" who had courtly and even gentle status.[31]

In general, critics of *As You Like It* have argued that the play represents upper-class concerns. Louis Montrose, for example, has argued that the romance plot and the pastoral genre of this play function to align it with the concerns about status and mobility that were current in the late sixteenth century for its essentially upper-class audience.[32] Montrose sees both the play and the pastoral mode in general as addressing issues of status at the upper end of the social scale and shows how *As You Like It* specifically works through anxieties about social class raised for younger sons by the practice of primogeniture. Similarly, Richard Wilson has traced the assimilation into the play of motifs of popular revolt current during the enclosure riots of the 1590s, arguing that the play finally works to "depoliticize Carnival" and neutralize "the rites of collective action," again associating the play with conservative and upper-class interests.[33]

But it is also possible to see in the play signs of sympathy with lower-class interests, though in an essentially contestatory relationship to the cultural work of the play as a whole.[34] On a verbal level, the insistent and ideologically charged uses of such shifting status terms as *villain* and *clown* insinuate into the play questions about the implications of upward (and downward) mobility for precisely those "poorest laborers and indigent" who were largely absent from the main play (although evidently sometimes present for the jig). Although these questions are for the most part not explicitly raised in the play, they are persistently suggested from its margins and are sufficiently present to ruffle the surface of the romance plot. The play repeatedly hints at the counterideologies of the peasant or vagrant class but usually diffuses these potentially disruptive ideas either by shifting the class referent to gradations of status within the "gentle" classes or by means of a distancing and neutralizing layer of classical allusion.[35] Nevertheless, because the play calls attention to the linguistic strategies at work in the culture to manage the threat of disruptive mobility from below, its representation of lower-class concerns is, finally, incompletely contained.

The negotiation of issues related to social mobility in *As You Like It* is complicated by theatrical practice in ways that remind us of the extent to which text and performance cannot be separated. The evidence of theater history suggests that in using a more refined clown designed to appeal to a more exclusive audience the play itself enacts the very mobility it examines and, at times, enables. Just as it uses words like *villain* and *churl* to allude to the concerns of those for whom upward mobility was largely impossible, the play also gestures toward the missing "clown" Will Kemp and his jig; the play is in part about the replacement of the clownish (but popular) Kemp with the more refined "fool," Robert Armin.[36] Just as the play includes partially managed bits of peasant ideology, it also incorporate some incompletely assimilated elements of the jig within itself. Like the "villains" to which the play alludes, Kemp is absent from the text, but his absence is treated in such a way as to raise a hint of discomfort about the implications of upward mobility for those left out and for those who benefit. In its emphasis on shifting terms and the changing conditions of theatrical production, *As You Like It* seems to question the self-justifications of hierarchy that it seems concerned, in other ways, to uphold.

The relationship between these potentially subversive moments and the agency of Shakespeare as author is, however, more complex than we might expect. On the one hand, the assimilation of elements of the jig into the play itself and exclusion of the extemporizing Kemp increased authorial agency since the author could now count on controlling the words spoken by the actors during the play and end the play as he liked, without facing the possibility of a disruptive coda. At the same time, however, this act of exclusion and assimilation transformed what had been an unruly lower-class voice into a "gentled" critique over which a single author now had more control.

In this sense, increased authorial agency is not, as some have argued, to be inevitably associated with a more subversive text. On the other hand, wordplay focused on the ideologies of hierarchy and limited mobility as manifested in language seems to mark an attempt to evade interpellation with irony, to play on the language of the dominant classes in such a way as to render transparent the linguistic strategies at work to reproduce the conditions of their dominance. Whether an author can, in fact, attain a measure of control over the ideo logical workings of language is not only questioned by many critics today but significantly questioned in the play itself. What we do seem to see in the play is an increase in authorial control and agency coupled with various kinds of upward mobility—for the author himself, for the theatrical company, and, indirectly, for the audience. Along with its ambition, however, the play seems to manifest an awareness of and a sense of regre about what it must exclude to achieve its ambition, including the incipien rejection of the theater's festive roots and established tradition of collaborative work.

The emotional shadings inextricably attached through individual experience to words such as *villain* and *clown* complicate their ideological functions. Althusser has described ideology as a condition of "obviousness" that, "like all obviousnesses, including those that make a word 'name a thing,' or 'have a meaning' (therefore including the obviousness of the 'transparency' of language), the 'obviousness' that you and I are subjects—and that that does not cause any problems—is an ideological effect, the elementary ideological effect."[37] Individuals are interpellated as subjects when family structures inculcate in them "the rituals of ideological recognition, which guarantee for us that we are indeed concrete, individual, distinguishable and (naturally) irreplaceable subjects" (173).

This Althusserian theory of interpellation was, of course, influenced by Lacanian subject formation and is thus open to similar critique from a cognitive perspective, namely, that we perceive ourselves to be "concrete, individual, distinguishable" because of our physiologically based spatial and sensory experiences of selfhood as well as because our culture "hails" us as such. Daniel Stern's work on the development of selfhood in infants stresses the centrality of affect to all early learning, including the formation of this "core sense of self": "Affective and cognitive processes cannot be readily separated. In a simple learning task, activation builds up and falls off. Learning itself is motivated and affect-laden."[38] Antonio Damasio stresses the necessary involvement of feeling in the most rational decision-making processes, and Gerald Edelman similarly argues that feeling and "value" play a central role in the cumulative history of an individual "self": "Meaning takes shape in terms of concepts that depend on categorizations based on value. It grows with the history of remembered body sensations and mental images. The mixture of events is individual and, in large measure unpredictable. When, in society, linguistic and semantic capabilities arise and sentences involving metaphor are linked to thought, the capability to create new models of the world grows at an explosive rate. But one must remember that, because of its linkage to value and to the concept of self, this system of meaning is almost never free of affect; it is charged with emotions."[39] The Althusserian "transparency of language," then, must be complicated by a cognitive sense of the lexical field that defines the meaning of even the simplest word, as well as by the necessary inflection of that field by feelings that will be different (and not always consistent) for each individual.

It is in the context of Orlando's concerns about the relationship between social status, natural capacity, financial means, and education that the play introduces its concern with the ideological uses of status terms. Throughout the play, Orlando seems confused by his culture's contradictory ideologies of status and social mobility. On the one hand, he feels that he has been relegated to "peasant" (1.1.68) status by his brother's failure to educate him and provide him with the means to live as a gentleman, complaining that his brother "keeps me rustically here at home" and "mines my gentility with my [lack of] education" (1.1.7, 20). Here Orlando seems to distrust his native capacities and to assume that gentle status depends upon suitable education and financial resources. His desire to "go buy my fortunes," however, plays on the contemporary shift in the meaning of the word *fortune*, from an original sense of "chance" to a new meaning, emerging in the late sixteenth century, "amount of wealth."[40] As such, it works as a part of the "discourse of capacities" so important in justifying the limitation of upward mobility to the already privileged.

It is no surprise, then, that Orlando also insists that he possesses gentlemanly capacities conferred by birth: "the spirit of my father, which I think is within me, begins to mutiny against this servitude" (1.1.22–24). He subsequently suggests that his "gentleman-like qualities" have been merely hidden from him rather than undermined, by his lack of education. Thus, Orlando's seemingly egalitarian belief in the importance of education for the achievement of true gentility is based on a more conservative sense that someone born to the gentle class possesses both an innate superiority and an innate right to development through education.[41]

In *As You Like It* the status and ethical senses of *villain* are separated and recombined in ways that seem motivated by powerful feelings and that call attention to its role in the mediation and limitation of social mobility. It is always used to indicate a person of gentle status, and it is almost always used by one brother to describe another in an emotionally charged situation; as a result, questions are raised about the connections between birth, social class, and ethical worth. It is Oliver who prods Orlando toward a bolder claim to a natural capacity for gentle status when he first calls him a "villain" (1.1.55). Oliver uses the term angrily, in its ethical sense (Orlando has just threatened him with violence), but he also intends to taunt Orlando with his own perception that a lack of education has lowered his social status. Orlando responds indignantly, as if this were the case. He clearly perceives an accusation of "villainy" to be an insult with particular force in his case, asserting indignantly that "I am no villain; I am the youngest son of Sir Rowland de Boys. He was my father, and he is thrice a villain that says such a father begot villains" (1.1.56–59). Caught up in their intense and emotional rivalry, these brothers fail to see the irony that their exchange makes clear to an audience. Since the two are brothers, according to an ideology of inherited capacity and status, if one is a villain, the other must also be a villain. Just as clearly, however, if Orlando has been relegated to "villain" or "peasant" status by lack of education and means, Oliver reveals himself to be the true "villain" in the ethical sense.

The troubled brothers in the play continue to repeat emotionally laden accusations of "villainy" in ways that reinforce its ethical sense and stress the ironies of its connection with status. The irony works to reveal the ways in which language is complicitous in the self-serving attitudes of the supposedly "gentle." Oliver, for example, twice describes Orlando as "villainous" (1.1.144, 154) to Charles the wrestler but in soliloquy admits that his brother is in fact by nature just the opposite: "gentle, never school'd and yet learned, full of noble device" (1.1.166–67). Here Oliver admits the confluence in Orlando of both status and ethical "gentility" and "nobility" while revealing that "my own people" recognize his own lack of those capacities: "I am altogether mispris'd." In similarly ironic uses, Duke Frederick, who has dispossessed his own older brother, believes that "some villains of my court" (2.2.2) must have helped Rosalind and Celia escape, and he terms Oliver "more villain" (3.1.15) because he admits that he hates Orlando.

These uses of moralized status terms initially seem to function as a part of the negotiation of upper-class issues in that they uphold both meritocratic and nativist views of status. By implying that some supposedly gentle persons behave as villains, the play opens the possibility of the converse: that some persons of lower status might possess the capacities for advancement. On the other hand, by insisting on the correlation of status and capacity in Orlando's case, the play obscures the question of how far down the social scale such gentle qualities might extend. The word *villain* thus participates in the play's negotiation of limited mobility by smoothing over contradictions in the system and allowing education and money to erode the status system, but only to a limited extent.

On the other hand, repetition of words such as *villain* in emotionally charged familial disputes emphasizes the purposeful use of such words to shore up one's own position at the expense of another. This insistence on their semantic shift and resulting double meanings calls our attention to their implication in the ideologies that both protected hierarchy and promoted limited individual ambition (at the upper end of the social scale) within it. The very presence of the word conjures up the plight of former feudal "villeins," many of whom were now vagrants and criminals, and what this ideology means for them. The control of just such "Roges Vacabonds or Sturdy Beggars" was the object of repeated statutes during this period, typically ordering, for example, that "all and everye persone and persones beynge whole and mightye in Body and able to labour, havinge not Land or Maister, nor using any lawfull Marchaundize Crafte," shall be considered vagabonds and "grevouslye whipped, and burnte through the gristle of the right Eare with a hot Yron of the compasse of an Ynche about."[42] It was also against such people that the "discourse of capacities" worked, justifying their downward mobility as resulting from a lack of the natural capacities that enabled others to rise. Whether such persons attended the public theaters has been debated, but clearly they lacked the financial means to make up a significant portion of the paying audience for the main play.[43] There is evidence that they attended jigs, but the decision of the Chamberlain's Men to curtail the jig suggests an attempt to discourage such an audience. Despite this, or perhaps because of it, *As You Like It* continually hints at the situation of real "base" persons and a revolutionary ideology of class leveling.

As in many plays by Shakespeare, the upper-class characters of the main plot coexist with various characters lacking gentle status; this play includes the old servant Adam, the shepherds Corin, Silvius, and Phebe, the goatherd Audrey, and the "clown" William. In each case pressing issues of status and material conditions of life are suggested but for the most part undeveloped. Old Adam, the faithful servant, for example, represents a person who clearly possesses the prized capacities of the upwardly mobile merchant class: thrift, persistence, prudence, and temperance. He has a nest egg saved "by thrifty hire" during his years of service, he has provided for his old age, and he has avoided strong drink. Nevertheless, he realizes that his fate, once "service should in my old limbs lie lame," will be to become a masterless man, describing the ultimate fate of the geriatric servant in the period as "unregarded age in corners thrown" (2.3.38–51). Despite these capacities, he feels no compulsion to use his means "to mutiny against this servitude" (as Orlando does); instead, recognizing Orlando's natural status as his "master," he not only gives him all of his money but promises to do him "the service of a younger man" (2.3.54). Orlando recognizes Adam's attitude as that of a prior age, before the possibility of upward mobility:

> O good old man, how well in thee appears
> The constant service of the antique world,
> When service sweat for duty, not for meed!
> Thou art not for the fashion of these times,
> Where none will sweat but for promotion.
>
> (2.3.56–60)[44]

Orlando and Adam both attempt to rename Adam's lack of interest in promotion as a virtue: "loyalty." But since the rest of the play depicts Orlando's own striving for (and attainment of) a higher place in the world, it makes sense that after Orlando demonstrates a reciprocal loyalty to Adam (by refusing to abandon him to starve), Adam disappears from the play. His combination of capacity and inability to get ahead disrupts the ideology that would correlate low social and ethical status.

The biblical Adam was, of course, a central figure in the competing accounts of the role of inheritance in determining social class.[45] Louis Montrose and Lee Patterson have both noted the contradiction between the aristocratic belief that base persons were descended from Cain and a peasant belief in the common ancestry of all persons: "When Adam dalf and Eve span, who was then the gentle man."[46] Adam's presence in this play as a worthy person who seems to be relegated to servitude by birth and without regard for his capacities alludes to the revolutionary slogan. *As You Like It* conjures up the orthodox myth of class ancestry (Cain and Abel) as a parallel to the destructive intraclass rivalries between the gentry and the nobility; it brings in Adam to show a worthy but slighted servant.

The questions raised by Adam are given emphasis by the oblique presence of a spinning Eve (who, in a strategy typical of the play, is transformed into a classical spinster). When Celia and Rosalind discuss their own differences in status, they seem similarly concerned with the relationship between "Nature" (native gifts and inherited status) and "Fortune" (formerly "chance" but now "money") (1.2.42, 41). Rosalind and Celia both seem disturbed that Rosalind, who is the daughter of the rightful Duke, has been displaced by Celia, who has less inherited right to that status. As in the case of Oliver and Orlando, Rosalind's birth claim to higher status is also correlated with superior capacities: even Celia's father admits that "thou wilt show more bright and seem more virtuous/When she is gone" (1.3.81–82). Rosalind implies that Celia's upward mobility is the result of superior (but undeserved) financial means, punning on the new financial meanings of words like *estate* and *fortune*: "I will forget the condition of my estate to rejoice in yours"; "Fortune reigns in the gifts of the world, not in the lineaments of Nature" (1.2.15, 42). Celia brings in the spinster, here named "Fortune" rather than "Eve," although her take on social status seems similar: "Let us sit and mock the good huswife Fortune from her wheel, that her gifts may henceforth be bestow'd equally" (1.2.31–33). Celia calls not for a return to their former situation, with Rosalind as superior and she inferior, but rather for a more equitable distribution of fortune. It is Rosalind who insists that "Nature" is superior to "Fortune" even though her fortune is temporarily in decline. Of course, the implication of social leveling in Celia's invocation of Fortune is, literally, "gentle," since it only calls for a slight redistribution of resources among the nobility. But her spinning "Fortune," taken in tandem with Adam, similarly gestures toward more radical implications of a truly equitable bestowal of fortune in the monetary sense.

The play makes another covert gesture toward a counterideology of the peasant class when it mentions the myth of Robin Hood.[47] Rodney Hilton has argued that the popular Robin Hood ballads of the Middle Ages must be seen in the context of peasant insistence that the products of nature itself, particularly wood and game, should belong to all men, not only to the nobility.[48] The unlawful gathering of "the lord's wood," which was necessary for warmth and shelter, is frequently recorded in manorial court records, and royal proclamations into the sixteenth century abjure "you our loving subjects, from henceforth to abstain and forbear to murder, kill, or destroy, chase or hunt, any of our said deer."[49] Hilton suggests that the Robin Hood ballads represent at least in part a "Utopian vision of free communities of hunters eating their fill of forbidden food."[50] In "A Gest of Robin Hode" (ca. 1492–1534), for example, Robin addresses the king himself, who is disguised as an abbot:

> We be yemen of this foreste
> Under the grene-wode tre;
> We lyve by our kynges dere,
> Other shyft haue not we.[51]

The disguised king is impressed by Robin's "courteysy" and the "wonder semely syght" of his followers kneeling before him; he shares a meal

with them—"Anone before our kynge was set/The fatte venyson"—
and ultimately pardons them, and he invites Robin to come to his court
(lines 385–417). This ballad clearly represents a fantasy involving gentle
qualities ("courteysy") among men of low status that are recognized by
the king himself, as well as an assertion of a right to eat the king's deer.[52]

When it appears in *As You Like It*, however, the ideological content of the Robin Hood myth is blunted—"made gentle"—in several
ways.[53] In the first place, as Richard Wilson notes, it is an exiled Duke
and "many young gentlemen" who "live like the old Robin Hood
of England" and "fleet the time carelessly, as they did in the golden
world" (1.1.116–20).[54] In this case, the Duke is probably killing deer
that would be rightfully his if his position had not been wrongfully
usurped. The insistence on the outlaws' leisured existence ("fleet the
time carelessly") signals that these exiles retain that mark of nobility
even in the forest. Their hunting bears a resemblance closer to the
sanctioned hunt as aristocratic pastime than to the poacher's illicit
hunt.[55] Thus, when the "civility" of the Duke's banquet is emphasized by Orlando's rude interruption, the class logic of the meal in the
Robin Hood ballad is reversed: here it is the nobleman who represents
courtesy in the forest and a person of (slightly) lower status who
recognizes it. At the same time, the reference to "the golden world"
distances class issues by transposing them onto a classical landscape.

The Duke's account of his misgivings about hunting in the forest
of Arden curiously inflects these class issues, introducing relations
between nobility and the merchant class and downward mobility
among merchants. He claims to be distressed ("it irks me") that

> the poor dappled fools,
> Being native burghers of this desert city,
> Should in their own confines with forked heads
> Have their round haunches gor'd.
>
> (2.1.21–25)

An attendant lord cites Jacques's opinion that "you do more usurp/
Than doth your brother that hath banish'd you" (2.1.27–28) when
he wrongfully kills the animals "in their assign'd and native dwelling
place" (2.1.63). The lord further quotes Jacques's description of the
deer who abandon their wounded comrade: "sweep on, you fat
and greasy citizens,/'Tis just the fashion. Wherefore do you look/
Upon that poor and broken bankrupt there" (55–57). Here the lord's
right to game is questioned, but it is rather oddly seen not as the
right of peasants (who live close to nature) but as that of a bourgeois
economy of the animals themselves. On the one hand, these animals
are described as free "burghers" and "citizens," who nevertheless

disregard the downward mobility of a fellow citizen who is "bankrupt." On the other hand, they have an "assign'd and native dwelling place"—assigned, like that of peasants tied to their lord's land. Until the sixteenth century the word *native* meant "one born in thralldom," and *nativus* was the Latin word used in manorial court records for "villein."[56] Whatever their putative class affiliation, these deer rather fancifully reflect the effects of usurpation and downward mobility both within a class and between classes.

The human inhabitants of the forest of Arden are depicted as having a similarly ambivalent status. Here again the play hints at the problems of "base" persons in the period and in some cases deflects direct treatment of such problems. Corin, Silvius, and Phebe are all identified as "shepherds," yet they seem to bridge several important social gaps: Corin is a wage laborer, while Silvius is a potential purchaser of the flock and seems relatively leisured; Corin is a "natural philosopher" who eschews courtly ways, while Silvius and Phebe seem versed (or rather saturated) in courtly love conventions. In this sense, these "shepherds" seem a part of what Montrose has identified as the role of the pastoral in the "mediation of status distinctions."[57] Their classicized names and participation in such literary conventions as Petrarchan love discourse, formal debate, and the "beatus ille" topos suggest that questions about their social status may be irrelevant.

And yet, at other points the text clearly foregrounds issues of status and the material realities of these characters' existence. Corin, for example, calls attention to the plight of the shepherd as wage laborer at the mercy of an absentee master:

> But I am shepherd to another man,
> And do not shear the fleeces that I graze.
> My master is of churlish disposition,
> And little reaks to find the way to heaven
> By doing deeds of hospitality.
> Besides, his cote, his flocks, and bounds of feed
> Are now on sale, and at our sheep-cote now
> By reason of his absence there is nothing
> That you will feed on.
>
> (2.4.78–86)

Significantly, Corin uses a depreciated status term—*churlish*—in its ethical sense to describe his "master."[58] His description of this particular gentleman shepherd works against the pastoral negotiation of status difference by pointing up the sharp *difference* between the shepherd who owns the sheep and the real shepherd who does the work. Corin's use of *churlish* to describe his master is a more pointed critique of depreciation than Oliver's use of *villain* to describe his brother since Corin is (most probably) a "churl" in status who suffers because of churlish treatment by his (ostensibly) "gentle" master. Corin suggests that his master fails in the duties of a truly "gentle" manorial proprietor since he does not take care of his workers and does not practice hospitality. In this he resembles the newly rich courtiers of the period, who neglected traditional country practices in order to spend time at court and who often were forced to sell lands to finance conspicuous expenditures in London.

Even Corin's critique is partially deflected by the romance plot, however, when Celia and Rosalind purchase the sheep farm and proceed to demonstrate truly "gentle" shepherd behavior. They will "mend" Corin's "wages" (2.4.94), and they plan to spend their time, at least for the time being, in the country and not at court. Of course, like all the gentle people in the forest, they plan a leisured existence ("I like this place, / And willingly could waste my time in it" [2.4.94–95]; as in the case of Orlando and Adam, Corin recognizes their superior gentility and offers to serve them faithfully ("I will your faithful feeder be" [2.4.99]). Once again the play raises the possibility of "villainous" or "churlish" behavior on the part of those of high status, only to suggest that this is an exception rather than the rule. Once again it raises the issue of a worthy servant mistreated by a less worthy master, only to suggest that the servant simply needs a better, more "gentle" master.

Below the classicized shepherds are the truly menial rustics Audrey and William. Montrose has argued that the pastoral, because wealthy sheep owners could describe themselves as shepherds and also because of the traditional association of shepherds with a leisured life, was a form easily assimilated to courtly interests. In order for the pastoral to perform the cultural work of the upper classes, however, shepherds had to be rigorously separated from truly lower-class "plowmen," the traditional agricultural workers of the villein class.[59] It was in this context that the word *clown* arose in the sixteenth century to define civilized gentility with reference to its opposites. The roles of Audrey and William, then, must be seen in connection with Touchstone, and with the changes in personnel and policy relating to clowns that the Chamberlain's Men seem to have made when they moved to the Globe, changes that first surface in *As You Like It*.

•   •   •

Beyond the ironies of this play, however, I think a note of regret can be felt—regret over the loss of Kemp and the jigs, over a gain in authorial control at the cost of distance from comedy's festive roots and the theater's collaborative fertility. It is this emotional shading, the subtle inflection of concepts by complex social feelings, that both Antonio Damasio and Leslie Brothers have emphasized as an integral part of human cognition.[60] It is also this affective content that Marxist and New Historicist criticism, with their tendency to focus on ideology and power relations, can sometimes fail to note. Shakespeare's ability both to participate in the mobility made possible by the cultural changes mediated by words such as *villain* and *clown* and, at the same time, to perceive the uses of these words as if from a distance and to regret the work that they do might, in more traditional criticism, be seen as a characteristic of his famous "negative capability." It might be possible here to redefine that capability as involving an unusual awareness of the complexities of thought and feeling that lie behind the lexical and conceptual structures in the brain—an awareness that prevents meaning from seeming transparent or obvious.

That such awareness might complicate interpellation within family structures may be suggested by Shakespeare's representation in the play of hostility located in both older and younger brothers. Although Montrose emphasizes reasons why Shakespeare might represent the plight of younger sons with more sympathy in order to appeal to an audience that probably contained a large proportion of those disinherited by primogeniture, psychoanalytic critics have tended to emphasize Shakespeare's own family position as an oldest son displaced by several younger brothers (and effectively "disinherited" by his father's financial failure).[61] Shakespeare's feelings about the failure of Will Kemp may have been colored by his feelings about another actor who, like Kemp, died in poverty and without a will. Edmund Shakespeare evidently followed his successful older brother to London, where the Parish register of St. Giles Cripplegate records him simply as "player, base born." William Shakespeare, of course, is recorded in the Stratford register as "Will Shakspere, gent." when he died in 1616, nine years after his younger brother, the base-born player. These complex events suggest that for Shakespeare, conceptions of status, mobility, brotherhood, and brothers who accuse each other of villainy were shaped and colored by mixed and contradictory emotions.

*As You Like It* thus takes us to the forest in order to sever, or at least to transform, the connection between drama and rustic festivity; later Shakespeare comedies have urban or country-house settings more appropriate to Armin's "gentle" fool. Finally, the play uses the question whether "nature" or "fortune" plays a greater role in the attainment and maintenance of status simultaneously to obscure and reveal the real issue: that those terms and other status terms were changing in ways that could be beneficial to those who had the power to use them, with full awareness of their double-edged ironies, for their own benefit. Shakespeare was preeminently able to do so, and the play reveals his dexterity, but also his misgivings about that project.

1. On the workings of ideology to reproduce conditions of production see Louis Althusser, "Ideology and Ideological State Apparatuses," in *Lenin and Philosophy and Other Essays*, trans. Ben Brewster (New York: Monthly Review, 1971), 127–88.

2. See George Lakoff, *Women, Fire, and Dangerous Things: What Categories Reveal about the Mind* (Chicago: University of Chicago Press, 1987), 283 ff., for the idea that "hierarchical structure is understood in terms of PART-WHOLE schemas and UP-DOWN schemas."

3. E. K. Chambers, *The Elizabethan Stage*, 4 vols. (Oxford: Clarendon, 1923), 4:340–41.

4. Charles Read Baskervil, *The Elizabethan Jig and Related Song Drama* (Chicago: University of Chicago Press, 1929), 113–19. Contemporary references, cited at length by Baskervil, suggest that the jig centered around an itinerant garlic seller and included a prostitutes' dance.

5. On postperformance admission to jigs, see David Wiles, *Shakespeare's Clown* (Cambridge: Cambridge University Press, 1987), 46–47, who speculates, partly based on the passage cited above, that the "anarchy" attendant upon jig performances was in part caused by "the swelling of the audience by many who could not afford the entry fee for the main play," although "whether they paid, stampeded their way in, or entered freely is still unclear."

6. Baskervil, *Elizabethan Jig*, 55, 117, gives evidence for such baboon dances, including the passage cited above.

7. Wiles, *Shakespeare's Clown*, 14–16, describes the practice of Richard Tarlton, the first famous Elizabethan clown, who would reply to rhymes suggested by the audience.

8. Baskervil, *Elizabethan Jig*, 110–11, cites both quotations and several more. The satirist is Edward Guilpin, in his *Skialetheia*, satire 5.

9. Wiles, *Shakespeare's Clown*, 56.

10. On Kemp's Norwich undertaking, see Max W. Thomas, "*Kemps Nine Daies Wonder*: Dancing Carnival into Market," *PMLA* 107 (1992): 511–23. Thomas argues that Kemp's published account of his journey is part of "a larger cultural transition, which effectively replaced the liminal space offered by the car-nivalesque with the fungible com-modity of Renaissance theatrical representation" (521). I am arguing that Shakespeare in *As You Like It* uses the absence of Kemp to do something very similar.

11. See Peter Thomson, *Shakespeare's Theatre*, 2nd ed. (New York: Routledge, 1992), 12; Wiles, *Shakespeare's Clown*, 47; and Baskervil, *Elizabethan Jig*, 114, which suggests that "after 1600 the policy of private houses probably tended to discredit the jig and to throw it

more definitely into the hands of companies that catered to the populace. The fact that by 1600 Kemp had left the Chamberlain's Men and by 1602 had joined Worcester's may reflect a shift in attitude on the part of his old company." Max Thomas, "*Kemps Nine Daies Wonder,*" similarly attributes Kemp's departure from the company to possible "resentment" over his tendency to improvise, his "derogatory jests and exaggerated gestures" (511).

12. Wiles, *Shakespeare's Clown,* 47.

13. Wiles suggests that the jigs highlight the "communal" nature of authorship in the Elizabethan theater (ibid.). I see the assimilation of the jig into the main play as a more difficult and problematic process, however. Richard Helgerson, *Forms of Nationhood: The Elizabethan Writing of England* (Chicago: University of Chicago Press, 1992), 199, sees the move away from Kemp and jigs as a step toward what he calls an "author's theater."

14. Margreta de Grazia and Peter Stallybrass, "The Materiality of the Shakespearean Text," *Shakespeare Quarterly* 44 (1993): 255–83, suggest some of the ways the problematic status of the text forces us to "reconceptualize the fundamental category of a *work* by Shakespeare" (255). A consideration of material conditions of performance is beyond the scope of their essay, but I believe that the presence of the jig similarly problematizes our conception of the Shakespearean play.

15. I would associate this position with most American New Historicist work done in the 1980s. Certainly Montrose makes such an assumption in both "Of Gentlemen and Shepherds: The Politics of Elizabethan Pastoral Form," *ELH* 50 (1983): 415–59 and " The Place of a Brother' in *As You Like It*: Social Process and Comic Form," *Shakespeare Quarterly* 32 (1988): 28–54. Stephen Greenblatt, *Shakespearean Negotiations* (Berkeley and Los Angeles: University of California Press, 1988), seems to make a similar assumption, despite his focus on a more complex circulation of "social energy" (6). Leonard Tennenhouse, *Power on Display: The Politics of Shakespeare's Genres* (London: Methuen, 1986), is another example. Richard Wilson, "'Like the old Robin Hood': *As You Like It* and the Enclosure Riots," *Shakespeare Quarterly* 43 (1992): 1–19, argues that the play includes elements of popular revolt only to "incorporate the energies of charivari in a reconstituted order" (14).

16. A recent example of this approach is Annabel Patterson, *Shakespeare and the Popular Voice* (Oxford: Blackwell, 1989), who ties some very persuasive evidence of interest in popular political goals to be found in Shakespeare's plays with insistence on a "common-sense" (87) view of agency and authorship, arguing that Shakespeare was engaged in a "conscious analytic project" (65) in his plays.

17. Thus Helgerson sees the history plays as standing for "a particularly anachronistic state formation based at least symbolically on the monarch and an aristocratic governing class" (*Forms of Nationhood*, 244).

18. See A. L. Beier, *Masterless Men: The Vagrancy Problem in England*, 1560–1640 (London: Methuen, 1985).

19. For one account of this familiar story of sheep enclosure, deracination, and increasing vagrancy, see Richard Halpern, *The Poetics of Primitive Accumulation: English Renaissance Culture and the Genealogy of Capital* (Ithaca: Cornell University Press, 1991), 71–73.

20. C. S. Lewis, *Studies in Words*, 2nd ed. (Cambridge: Cambridge University Press, 1967), 21.

21. For "depreciative specialization," see Gustaf Stern, *Meaning and Change of Meaning*, 3rd ed. (Bloomington: Indiana University Press, 1931), 411–14. He includes "specialization" under the class of semantic change called "adequation," whereby a referent is initially named "by a single characteristic which happens to strike us" but "may be of subordinate importance for the real status of the referent in our universe of action and discourse." The "most important" characteristic of the referent subsequently "becomes more closely associated with the name than any other," and "the meaning undergoes adequation to what is now considered by speakers as the main characteristic of the referent, and the basis of naming, now considered relatively unimportant, recedes, and eventually disappears" (380–81). For a list of gendered depreciations, see Joseph M. Williams, *Origins of the English Language: A Social and Linguistic History* (New York: Macmillan, 1975), 196–97. For an extended account of "the semantic legacy of the Middle Ages," including a section on the moralization of status terms, see Geoffrey Hughes, *Words in Time: A Social History of English Vocabulary* (Oxford: Blackwell, 1988), 32–66.

22. Geoffrey Hughes, for example, has suggested that this pattern of change has its roots in the Anglo-Saxon legal system and its "concept of *wergild*, an equation between a person's status and material value, and a strong correlation between status and implied moral quality" (*Words in Time*, 47).

23. Lee Patterson, *Chaucer and the Subject of History* (Madison: University of Wisconsin Press, 1991), 262. Patterson cites Rodney Hilton, *Class Conflict and the Crisis of Feudalism* (London: Hambledon Press, 1985), 138, for this "caste interpretation of peasant status."

24. Patterson, *Chaucer and the Subject of History*, cites, among others, Honorius of Autun, *De imagine mundi*, for peasants' descent from Ham.

25. For this proverb, see Albert B. Friedman, "'When Adam Delved …': Contexts of an Historic Proverb," in *The Learned and the Lewd: Studies in Chaucer ana Medieval Literature*, ed. Larry D. Benson (Cambridge: Harvard University Press, 1974), 213–30.

26. Quotation from *The Boke of Seynt Albans* (St. Albans, 1486) in Patterson, *Chaucer and the Subject of History*, 268.

27. Halpern, *Poetics of Primitive Accumulation*, 88.

28. The etymology of *clown* is obscure. Wiles notes a spurious etymology deriving it from the Latin *colonus* (farmer) (*Shakespeare's Clown*, 61), but the *OED* suspects a derivation from Germanic terms for "clod, clot, lump."

29. Wiles, *Shakespeare's Clown*, 62.

30. Helgerson argues that "most of the status abuse—terms like *villain, clown, churl, hind, peasant, swain*—refers specifically to countrymen. Perhaps the city dwellers who populated the theaters thought themselves exempt. But if so, it was an uncomfortable and unstable exemption, for this conceptual universe allotted no terms, whether favorable or unfavorable, specifically to them" (*Forms of Nationhood*, 206). Comedy seems more directly *about* the new range of uses for such terms, within semantic fields of court, countryside, and pastoral. *As You Like It* in particular is concerned with the ways context can alter the meanings of words.

31. Wiles traces this shift in a chapter called "'The Clown' in Playhouse Terminology" (*Shakespeare's Clown*, 61–72).

32. On the "cultural work" of pastoral in this regard, see Montrose, "Of Gentlemen and Shepherds," and for the negotiations of status and mobility in this play, see idem, "The Place of a Brother."

33. Wilson, "'Like the old Robin Hood,'" 17, 16.

34. Annabel Patterson finds moments of social critique in sympathy with lower-class interests in *A Midsummer Night's Dream, Hamlet, King Lear, Coriolanus,* and *The Tempest,* arguing that earlier plays "could cross social boundaries without obscuring them, and by these crossings imagine the social body whole again." She argues that with *King Lear,* "Shakespeare was forced to admit that the popular voice had grievances that the popular theater could no longer express comedically" (*Shakespeare and the Popular Voice*, 69).

35. Wilson, "'Like the old Robin Hood,'" similarly notes the ways in which the play "[grafts] the old rural games" onto classical mythology in order to "neutralize" their disruptive force (16–17). He does not see the irony and regret about this neutralization that I argue for here.

36. Thomson, *Shakespeare's Theatre*, 66–68, 94–96, discusses the roles of Kemp and Armin in the company and suggests that *As You Like It* alludes to the change. Wiles, *Shakespeare's Clown*, 146, makes a similar argument.

37. Althusser, "Ideology and Ideological State Apparatuses," 171–72.

38. Daniel Stern, *The Interpersonal World of the Infant: A View from Psychoanalysis and Developmental Psychology* (New York: Basic Books, 1985), 42.

39. Gerald Edelman, *Bright Air, Brilliant Fire: On the Matter of the Mind* (New York: Basic Books, 1992), 170.

40. Hughes has noted that this linguistic change involves movement from viewing fortune as "something which controlled one" to "something which can be 'made,' allowing one control over one's life" (*Words in Time*, 69).

41. Madeline Doran, "Yet am I inland bred," *Shakespeare Quarterly* 15 (1964): 105, suggests that Oliver here reflects "the belief, always present in Shakespeare, that in spite of all, birth will tell, that the gently born, with or without nurture, are naturally gentle in behavior." Doran, I think, overestimates the extent to which such a view, usually held by "gentle" characters, can be attributed to Shakespeare himself.

42. Quoted from *An Acte for the punishment of Vacabondes and for Releif of the Poore and Impotent* (14 Eliz., c. 5), of 29 June 1572, as cited in Chambers, *Elizabethan Stage*, 4:269–70.

43. For the argument about the class affiliation and financial means of Shakespeare's audience, see Ann Jennalie Cook, *The Privileged Playgoers of Shakespeare's London, 1576–1642* (Princeton: Princeton University Press, 1981), who argues against an earlier view that the theaters brought together a socially heterogeneous audience; and Andrew Gurr, *Playgoing in Shakespeare's London* (Cambridge: Cambridge University Press, 1987), who argues that different theaters had different audiences.

44. Wilson, " 'Like the old Robin Hood,'" 6–7, suggests that Orlando, with his "combination of rebelliousness and conservatism," represents a "noble robber" or upper-class leader of a peasant revolt. In my view, Orlando, as upper-class "rebel," voices a more conservative view than the play as a whole seems to support.

45. Montrose has suggested the importance of a character named Adam in establishing "resonances" between the brotherly animosities in the play and the story of Cain and Abel in Genesis ("The Place of a Brother," 45–46).

46. Montrose, "Of Gentlemen and Shepherds," 432. Montrose argues that pastoral forms, "by reconstituting the leisured gentleman as the gentle shepherd, obfuscates a fundamental distinction in cultural logic: a contradiction between the secular claims of aristocratic prerogative and the religious claims of common origins" (432). See also Patterson, *Chaucer and the Subject of History*, 262.

47. Wilson, "'Like the old Robin Hood,'" 8–9, notes that "the outlaw ballads of medieval England legitimated peasant protest, but *As You Like It* is one of a cluster of plays written in the late 1590s that exalt the rank of Robin Hood to make him a gentleman or even … an aristocrat" in order to dramatize "the divided loyalty of the propertied." Wilson cites a contemporary document describing the denizens of the woods as "people of very lewd lives and conversa-

tions, leaving their own and other counties and taking the place for a shelter as a cloak to their villainies" (9). *As You Like It*, however, represents the court as the source of "villainy."

48. Rodney Hilton, *Bond Men Made Free* (London: Methuen, 1977), 72.

49. Quoted from a proclamation "Prohibiting Encroachment in Waltham Forest," Westminster, 17 June 1548, 2 Edw. 6, in *Tudor Royal Proclamations*, ed. Paul L. Hughes and James F. Larkin, vol. 1, *The Early Tudors* (1485–1553) (New Haven: Yale University Press, 1964), 430. For the frequency of charges of stealing wood in manorial court records, see John West, *Village Records* (London: Macmillan, 1962), 35.

50. Hilton, *Bond Men Made Free*, 72. Lee Patterson connects this peasant desire for control over nature to a desire to return to the prelapsarian state of equality, "when Adam dalf, and Eve span" (*Chaucer and the Subject of History*, 265).

51. Helen Child Sargent and George Lyman Kittredge, eds., *English and Scottish Popular Ballads* (Boston: Houghton Mifflin, 1904), 274.

52. Anne Barton, "The King Disguised: Shakespeare's *Henry V* and the Comical History," in *The Triple Bond*, ed. Joseph G. Price (University Park: Pennsylvania State University Press, 1975), 97, alludes to this ballad as illustrating the motif of "the King-in-disguise," a "wish-dream of a peasantry harried and perplexed by a new class of officials" that they could have recourse to the king himself. Barton sees a critique of this motif in *Henry V*; however, Annabel Patterson, *Shakespeare and the Popular Voice,* 89–90, argues that Henry's appropriation of the motif is questioned by a lower-class voice.

53. See Helgerson, *Forms of Nationhood*, 231–32, which suggests that Shakespeare's *Henry V* alludes to the dream of "commonality … between the ruler and the ruled" found in the Robin Hood ballads but then "unequivocally denies it."

54. Wilson, "'Like the old Robin Hood.'" 8.

55. On hunting and other leisure activities as manifestations of aristocratic privilege, see Mervyn James, *Society, Politics, and Culture: Studies in Early Modern England* (Cambridge: Cambridge University Press, 1986), 271–78; Frank Whigham, *Ambition and Privilege: The Social Tropes of Elizabethan Courtesy Theory* (Berkeley and Los Angeles: University of California Press, 1984), 88; and Mary Thomas Crane, *Framing Authority: Sayings, Self, and Society in Sixteenth-Century England* (Princeton: Princeton University Press, 1993), 101–2.

56. Orlando Patterson, *Freedom in the Making of Western Culture* (New York: Basic Books, 1991), 344–75, discusses the use of such terms as *nativus* and *villanus* initially to distinguish between slaves and serfs, but as these two categories fused during the medieval period, the words became synonyms.

57. Montrose, "Of Gentlemen and Shepherds," 452.

58. *Ceorl* was the Anglo-Saxon term for "serf"; it was replaced after 1066 by its French equivalent, *villein*. However, the term depreciated in a similar way.

59. Montrose, "Of Gentlemen and Shepherds." 429–33.

60. Antonio Damasio, *Descartes' Error: Emotion, Reason, and the Human Brain* (New York: Avon, 1994); Leslie Brothers, *Friday's Footprint: How Society Shapes the Human Mind* (New York: Oxford University Press, 1997).

61. See esp. C. L. Barber and Richard P. Wheeler, *The Whole Journey: Shakespeare's Power of Development* (Berkeley and Los Angeles: University of California Press, 1986); and Marianne Novy, "The Bonds of Brotherhood" in *Shakespeare's Personality*, ed. Norman N. Holland, Sidney Homan, and Bernard J. Paris (Berkeley and Los Angeles: University of California Press, 1989), 103–15.

# As You Like It
## Who's Who in The Greenwood

### Penelope Gay

PRETTY PASTORAL or exploration of the dark recesses of the psyche?[1] Or damning indictment of a power-hungry urban society? The conventions of pastoral, which Shakespeare drew on so extensively in *As You Like It*, allow for all these interpretive emphases, and more. The play's social framework is clear, but in commentaries it tends to take second place to the fantasy of transformation in the greenwood—self-sufficiency, sudden conversions, and above all, a marvellously fluid sexuality, independent of conventional gender signs and embodied in the image of the free woman in love, Rosalind. Recent critics have stressed the way the powerful fantasy of liberation, particularly sexual liberation, is contained by a reassertion of the patriarchal system, which is always there in the greenwood anyway (in a fantastically benign version) in the exiled Duke's 'court'. Rosalind's last two speeches in the play's narrative are a ritual of voluntary re-entry into the patriarchy:

(*To the Duke*) To you I give myself, for I am yours.
(*To Orlando*) To you I give myself, for I am yours.
… I'll have no father, if you be not he.
I'll have no husband, if you be not he.

(5.4, 114–15, 120–1)

But as Valerie Traub argues, this submission does not take place until after Rosalind has led the play 'into a mode of desire neither heterosexual nor homoerotic, but both heterosexual *and* homoerotic'. Her last line before the teasing epilogue is the provocative reminder to Phoebe: 'Nor e'er wed woman, if you be not she.'

Rosalind's elaborate courtship game with Orlando throws into question not only the regulation and organisation of desire, but also

Gay, Penny. "As You Like It: Who's Who in the Greenwood." *As She Likes: Shakespeare's Unruly Women.* London: Routledge. 1994. 48–52; 54–59; 75–85. Used by permission.

1. This excerpt retains the parenthetical documentation within the text but omits endnotes because of space considerations.

the construction of gender. What *is* the proper behaviour for a young woman in love? 'You have simply misused our sex in your love-prate', says Celia (4.1, 189); yet Celia herself is of just such a 'coming-on disposition' when occasion finally arises in the person of Oliver—and so too is Phoebe, taking 'Ganymede's' outward signs of masculinity as a licence to desire. *As You Like It* effects, through Rosalind's behaviour, the most thorough deconstruction of patriarchy and its gender roles in the Shakespearean canon; yet it is a carnival licence allowed only in the magic space of the greenwood. At the end, all must return to the real world and its social constraints—though we can read Rosalind's epilogue as a liberating reminder of a world of alternative possibilities: is she/he finally boy or girl? By comparison, *Twelfth Night* seems the more troubled and troubling play, since no exit from Illyria is implied for the characters, despite Feste's reminders to the audience of *their* real world.

Stephen Greenblatt comments that Rosalind belongs to 'a social system that marks out singularity, particularly in women, as prodigious, though the disciplining of singularity is most often represented in Shakespearean comedy as romantic choice, an act of free will, an expression of love.' Greenblatt's second clause has been privileged over the first in the critics' response to Rosalind in performance: she is thought of as *society's* ideal young woman, on the verge of marriage— and when an actress presents Rosalind's 'singularity' as disruptive of social norms, there is often considerable unease in the ranks of critics. The play's history at Stratford over the last forty years reflects most strongly our culture's fascination with this figure of the marriageable daughter; inevitably also it responds to a changing view of the nature of social bonds, in the depiction of the two Dukes' courts, and most notably in the figure of Jaques.

## 1952–57

The 1952 production by Glen Byam Shaw has all the hallmarks of post-war glamour that are typical of this period. The lovers were the youthful and attractive Margaret Leighton and Laurence Harvey. The sets and costumes by Motley were elaborately pretty—'the scene is France', the programme tells us—and had the look of tapestries from the court of Louis XIII, though some critics found the foliage 'subtropical'. The greensward extended beyond the proscenium arch, and included a fake rock-pool (33 years later the water would be real, a stream across the front of the stage, and much use would be made of it, from narcissism to ritual cleansing). Tellingly, the commonest critical epithet for Motley's greenwood was 'Neverland'—with Margaret Leighton clearly recognisable as Peter Pan; her boyish looks and figure made this a natural association (she played Ariel in the same season at Stratford). In Arden, she was comfortably dressed in a floppy shirt, breeches, and short jacket, and seemed quite at home in her role as commander of various Lost Boys (and girls). She was not reluctant to sit inelegantly on the ground, and many critics commented on her 'sprightliness', her vitality, her 'tomboyish fun and high spirits'. This quality in the performance was perceived by the critic of the *Western Daily Press* (1 May 1952):

> Livened by the sprightly personality of Margaret Leighton, this 'As You Like It'... bubbled up to an enchanting make-believe of Spring song. Miss Leighton was a gay deceiver of infectious spirit, boyish and girlish together in swift changing moods that rippled like a babbling brook through the still beauty of Motley's Arden.

Others, however, found all this energy somewhat exhausting, even unladylike:

> Perhaps Miss Leighton's interpretation would be even more satisfying if her apparently inexhaustible vitality were subjected to firmer control. Her gestures sometimes gave the impression of restlessness.
>
> (*Birmingham Post*, 1 May 1952)

> Margaret Leighton had taken her pattern of a boy from an attractive but underfed, overexcitable *gamin*, rather than from the sturdy English adolescent, who can be among the most beautiful of living creatures. She was, it is true, hampered by the clothes designed for Ganymede, for, in an effort to get away from the hackneyed (but becoming) doublet and hose, Motley provided her with an adaptation of the costume affected by girl cyclists on long, dusty tours. This scruffy attire could not obliterate the actress' great beauty, but 'heavenly Rosalind' was almost too well disguised.
>
> (Ruth Ellis, *Stratford Herald*, 2 May 1952)

Clearly there were some members of the audience who didn't care for the image of the modern young woman in her freedom-bestowing pedal-pushers. Another aspect of ladylikeness which Leighton flouted came under the heading of 'reserve' or 'poise'. Philip Hope-Wallace thoughtthat she 'ha[d] not the aristocratic sense of comedy of the greatest Rosalinds ... she was obliged to work too hard, in order to save the play, to allow for many of those contrasts of silent happiness which can so well set off the raillery' (*Manchester Guardian,* 30 April 1952). Such vitality and independence might even bring on social disaster:

> If she conceives the part as Shakespeare wrote it, for an Elizabethan boy, her straddle-legged disguise as Ganymede looks right. If she

supposes this Princess of Harden [*sic*] to be of courtly breeding, such inelegant posturing is of old-maid inclination.

(Kenneth Pearson, *Manchester Daily Despatch*, 30 April 1952)

Perhaps the oddest of these observations from those who have seen the writing on the wall and realise, with fear, that the day of the dutiful, charming daughter is passing came from the critic of the *Sunday Times* (4 May 1952):

> Miss Leighton does not have that bubbling gaiety that Dame Edith Evans brought to the part. She is younger, sadder; she is paler, thinner; dressed as a boy, she is too short in the coat, too long and flimsy, frail and wasted in the leg. What an actress Miss Leighton would be, if only she could be persuaded to transfer her reverence for Stanislavski to steak-and-kidney pie!

It's the foreignness, the un-Englishness of this new image of women that is such a threat to conservative critics: the transatlantic girl bicyclist or androgynous French *gamine* look, lacking feminine curves; intellectual, even. The critics were of Margaret Leighton's parents' generation, and they were not reassured (though often, despite themselves, charmed) by what they saw.

Laurence Harvey's Orlando, on the other hand, was perfectly acceptable: adjectives such as handsome, sturdy, virile, manly and romantic were applied to him, and he was particularly congratulated on his wrestling. He was evidently secure about both his status (despite the play's opening scenes) and his sexuality. Did Leighton's Rosalind, however, perhaps find him a little dull? Ivor Brown reported that 'confronted with the double affection of Rosalind, love of Orlando in his simplicity and of her own wit in its complexity, [she] throws the more emphasis on the latter' (*Observer*, 4 May 1952).

Other aspects of the production brought general approval. Though *The Times* did not care to be shown 'Arden in winter', others welcomed the response to the text's suggestions that it was not always summer in an idealised pastoral greenwood (though the play did in fact move from winter through spring to final summer). Similarly an unusually 'chirpy' Celia (Siobhan McKenna), obviously responding to Leighton's spiritedness, brought enthusiastic comments, particularly as 'Miss McKenna controlled her performance with such tact that the competition was never serious' (*Birmingham Post*, 1 May 1952)—*she* remained a lady. Michael Hordern's Jaques was commended for his 'sad, gentle music' (*Western Daily Press*, 1 May 1952) in a generally admired performance of the conventional melancholic.

• • •

# 1961–73

Almost thirty years after Vanessa Redgrave's barefoot, denim-capped Rosalind stepped onto the Stratford stage, critics were still recalling her with wonder and delight. Julian Holland of the *Evening News* (5 July 1961) was one of several reviewers who declared themselves 'madly and desperately in love' with Redgrave, who at 24, tall and slim, had no need of heavy stage makeup to give her beauty. Overwhelmed critics attempted to convey the essence of her charismatic performance: it was 'sunny', 'luminous', 'radiant'. *Punch* managed a slightly more telling analysis:

> she is immensely natural, and her gentle mockery is always near the surface, so that even in the extravagance of adoration she is never mawkish. Of course she is an entirely modern Rosalind. She might be any of our daughters, bowled head over heels, and it is a pleasure to watch her.
>
> (Eric Keown, *Punch*, 12 July 1961)

Redgrave's 'modernity' was a matter of her personal style and presence. Her costume (by Richard Negri, as were the sets) was quite remarkably similar to that of Margaret Leighton nine years earlier— floppy shirt and breeches (called 'jeans' by some confused critics, just as Leighton's were), worn with an air of comfort and gaiety. Where Leighton was berated for sitting inelegantly on the ground, Redgrave's naturalness was expressed in her *lying* on the greensward next to Orlando, chatting animatedly, at times grabbing hold of him quite unself-consciously (plate 7). 'Prone or supine, kneeling or crouching, hugging her knees, or flinging herself backwards before Orlando when in "a more coming-on disposition", she is exquisite,' said Felix Barker, (*Evening News*, 11 January 1962). Some critics thought her 'gawky', but to none of them did this seem a disadvantage; on the contrary,

> Miss Redgrave had the audience in the hollow of her hand. Perhaps it is not playing fair to Shakespeare to turn his Rosalind into a twentieth-century gamin, a fantasticated Bisto kid, a terror of the lower fifth. Miss Redgrave's Rosalind is like all these things. It may be, on the other hand, that 'As You Like It' has had to wait until the 1960s for someone to appreciate that this is what Rosalind is.
>
> (*Birmingham Mail*, 11 January 1962)

'She achieved something rare in acting—she was at once timeless and contemporary': Julian Holland's tribute to Redgrave's quality is typical of the critics' capitulation. No longer are they prescribing ladylike behaviour, describing their own ideal girl: they have been forced to recognise that the part of Rosalind is there to be filled out by an actress who can put into it her own sense of what it is to be a young woman 'fathom deep' in love. But she is also a character thrown on her own resources when exiled by an authoritarian state. It seems entirely appropriate that Redgrave, between the Stratford season and the London revival, became a political activist, for what she was demonstrating on the Stratford stage was literally 'actresses' liberation'.

Michael Elliott's production was a breakthrough on many levels. A minor, but not insignificant, point was that the play had only one interval, rather than the two that were *de rigueur* at the time: going to the theater was no longer quite so dominated by social considerations—rather, the audience members were expected to concentrate on the play for over an hour and a half before resuming their social selves. The first half of the play took place in winter, the second in summer (the evocative lighting, by Richard Pilbrow, was much admired). For the first time, also, a 'movement director', Litz Pisk, was credited in the programme; many reviewers found this idea somewhat risible, but henceforward no production of a Shakespearean comedy would be complete without its dances. For both these developments the publication of C.L. Barber's *Shakespeare's Festive Comedy* in 1959 may have been partly responsible; by the later 1960s, Barber's influence was clearly acknowledged in Peter Hall's and other directors' work on the comedies.

Richard Negri's set was another departure from tradition: a single, stylised, huge tree placed on a steepish rising mound. The only changes were in lighting, props, and backcloth. Reviewers complained, not for the last time, about the lack of a forest, but by eschewing picturesqueness Elliott and Negri obliged the audience to concentrate on the characters' relationships and on the symbolic significance of the pastoral. 'At the opening', one critic pointed out, the director 'underlines the tension and violence which is often ignored as a mere prelude to the pastoral sweetness to come … the early scenes uncover moments of unexpected force' (*Leamington Spa Courier*, 7 July 1961). Similarly, life in the forest was not, for once, an unalloyed 'golden time': 'The lugubrious tone in which "This life is most jolly" is uttered suggests that most of the banished Duke's followers are thoroughly fed up with picnics and the pastoral life, and will welcome their return to court' (*Daily Telegraph*, 6 January 1962). Jaques was played by Max Adrian, whose wry, rueful, stylish performance emphasised the character's role as cynical commentator on pastoral fantasies; no longer could the actor of Jaques get away with being either slightly daffy or a sonorously venerable court philosopher. Most strikingly, the killing of the deer became a crucial symbolic set-piece which acted as a critique of naive pastoralism and affected the characterisation of the court-in-exile:

> By staging the stalking of the prey, its killing amid bestial cries from men momentarily turned to wolves, Mr Elliott gives point to Jaques' wincing—and suggests a reason for his melancholy, the old nightmare of the horns.
>
> (J.W. Lambert, *Sunday Times*, 9 July 1961)

Thus Elliott brought into question the 'naturally superior' attributes of the male on which a patriarchal social order is based.

This questioning of received ideas about masculinity was also evident in the Orlando of Ian Bannen, who had recently played a neurotic, slouching Hamlet. He at first eschewed the role of romantic hero, taking refuge in a self-burlesquing style. 'He is too complex a character to convey simplicity', said T.C. Worsley (*Financial Times*, 5 July 1961); and J.C. Trewin admitted unself-consciously that Bannen 'has not been my idea of Orlando. He is a lank figure with a weary eye, [looking] iike someone from a contemporary novel who has lost his way in the forest' (*Birmingham Post*, 5 July 1961). This modernist consciousness allowed Bannen to explore a possibility in Orlando's character that has been generally ignored—a hint of bisexuality, which, according to Lambert, made him 'respond much more eagerly to the apparent boy than to the dream of the lost girl'. By the time the production moved to London, either Bannen had become more extrovert or the critics had adjusted their spectacles to the contemporary emotional world, for there were no further complaints about miscasting.

The final scene of the play focused on Rosalind, a shining image spotlighted in her white dress, surrounded by flickering torches and the dark night. The irradiating power of the young woman's personality was here most strikingly presented, a challenge to the darkness of the patriarchal system which the young couples are about to re-enter, and to the symbolic winter which inevitably will come again. The adjectives 'sunny', 'radiant', and so forth, describing Redgrave's presence, chimed with Michael Elliott's apparent intention to encourage the audience to receive, however subliminally, a symbolic reading, rather than just another lovely night in the theater.

'Director's theater' was underway, and *The Times*'s reviewer was canny enough to comment on it:

> Mr Elliott sees clearly into the double game that Shakespeare was playing. His production reflects both sides of it. We are made to

feel both how pleasant it may be for courtiers to seek release from themselves in dreaming of Arcady in Arden, and how preposterous is their dream. Human nature in Arden is still human nature.

(*The Times*, 11 January 1962)

This critic went on to commend Patrick Wymark's Touchstone, 'at the centre of the play . . . the natural gross man who blurts out in every crisis just those undesirable facts, even those touching his own af-fairs, which it is the whole object of romance to refine away.' In none of the previous productions had Touchstone had such an accolade (Wymark replaced Colin Blakely from the Stratford production), and his role as counterweight to Jaques—deflating the pastoral from a low-life perspective rather than that of the court—is increasingly emphasised hereafter. Elliott's production thus became the first the-atrically self-conscious reading of the play, recognising the court-country opposition as a metaphor enabling exploration of the human psyche in its social construction.

•       •       •

## 1985–90

Adrian Noble's 1985 production took the perhaps inevitable next step and psychoanalysed the fairytale in a contemporary (modern-dress) reading, set in the country of the modern mind. Here court and country were but flipsides to each other, both metaphors of the prisons/landscapes we construct for ourselves out of our desires and their repressions. Designed by Bob Crowley, the play began in an 'attic' filled with shapes of furniture draped in white material—here Rosalind and Celia had come to escape the oppressive court, but (of course) it pursued them. The move to Arden simply involved the lifting of the covers, with a huge piece of white silk pulled up in the centre of the stage to suggest a tree-trunk, and, eventually, a green silken canopy. 'We wanted something that was genuinely plastic, that would change shape according to what the actors did, according to the moment in the play, because the Forest of Arden in *As You Like It* changes shape, dimension, character, according to the perception of each person.' Over all loomed a huge moon: we were clearly in the realm of the unconscious ('Within the Forest/the Forest within', as the programme directed us). In the Stratford version, much play was made with a large carved looking-glass, through which characters entered and exited, and a clock, which began ticking only when the play was over. In the transfer to London these perhaps over-insistent symbolic props disappeared, and 'key moments of transition [were] reserved for a great luminous port-hole in the back wall, where figures poised for flight or return appear[ed] in silhouette' (Irving Wardle, *The Times*, 18 December 1985).

Instead of the usual educational material on the pastoral, the programme contained poems and prose related to the thematic idea that to enter the 'wood' is to enter a dream or fantasy. It quoted Heinrich Zimmer: 'it is only after ... a journey in a distant region, in a new land that ... the inner voice ... can make itself understood by us.' There were also quotations relating transvestism to the Jungian animus/anima, and the query 'What is love *anyway*?' Juliet Stevenson, the Rosalind, in an interview in *Plays & Players* (May 1985), explained that the play is 'a vital exploration of gender, the male and the female within us all. Rosalind is very released when her masculine aspect is allowed release'. Arden is 'a realm where you can dress up and change your gender, change your way of life'. Bob Crowley's set, she went on to explain, 'is mostly to do with colours, and space, and different moons. These moons get larger and larger as you get into the forest'. Jung's symbolism has probably never had such a thorough outing in the Shakespearean theater. In another example, the deer-hunt became Celia's dream of defloration:

> Adrian Noble had equated the deer with the virginal Celia, who lay asleep beneath the towering, white, lingam-like mountain of silk that dominated the stage for the forest scenes. Her body had been caught by a snaking, blood-stained trail of cloth, pulled across the stage as she slept ... and she would awaken to fall in love with Oliver.
>
> (Barry Russell, *Drama*, 3, 1985)

The critics' response was astonished but on the whole quite enthusiastic; some made complimentary comparisons with the effect of Peter Brook's revolutionary *Midsummer Night's Dream* of 1970. John Barber thought that the design 'had the effect of cleansing the text ... of the greasy fustian of painted scenery and the varnish of old conventions gone stale'—an *As You Like It* for this generation (*Daily Telegraph*, 25 April 1985). Benedict Nightingale's review is typical—resistant but fascinated despite his principles:

> I dislike seeing texts strongly slanted by a director.... I dislike being violently and superfluously reminded of a play's contemporary 'relevance' by performers wearing bowlers, braces, tuxedos, donkey-jackets, as happens here.... And yet there are times at Stratford—for instance, when Juliet Stevenson's marvellously bright, buoyant and sexy Rosalind becomes marvellously grave, melancholy and sombre too—when [Noble] achieves a complexity and, yes, a depth I don't recall seeing in any previous production of the play.
>
> (*Listener*, 25 April 1985)

Michael Billington was not so convinced of the success of the production's dealings with the erotic; for him, it was

> a highly original reading but one that undercuts the play's sheer Mozartian joy. . . . [Noble's] chief conceit is to suggest that the court and the forest are not continents apart but simply opposite sides of the same human coin. . . . I don't mind the absence of real trees. . . . But Arden is also a place of discovery filled with the 'madness' of love and what I find missing in this production is transforming human ecstasy. . . . [Hilton McRae and Juliet Stevenson] embody the Jungian animus and anima (hello Jung lovers wherever you are), each having something of the other's sexual nature . . . . But rarely in their encounters did I feel I was witnessing the marriage of two minds or even two souls.
>
> (*Guardian*, 26 April 1985)

'Better a production with a concept than a bland retread; and Mr Noble's intelligence shines through', he concluded, '[b]ut I would beg him to remember that *As You Like It* is still billed as a comedy.' What Noble may well have intuited, however, is that his working definition of comedy as 'a ceremony or initiation leading towards matrimony' is not necessarily in this age a recipe for joyous laughter or sexual delight. Rather such an 'initiation' might be the opportunity for an examination of power-structures within the community and within the individual psyche (for example, the 'doubling' of the two Dukes' courts indicated two 'aspects of the same person' for each actor).

Juliet Stevenson is an actress ever willing to explore the intellectual issues raised by the character she is playing. She obviously followed Noble's directorial concept with enthusiasm (see her comments in Plays & Players above); but she also found herself going beyond Noble to discover a strong feminist reading of the play. For Stevenson,

> what happens to [Orlando] is classically what happens to women in Shakespeare. His love is tested. Rosalind/Ganymede uproots his idea of the wooing process. Not only is Orlando being wooed, not wooing, but his hopelessly romantic notions of wooing are deconstructed in the process.

Further, Stevenson together with Fiona Shaw, who played Celia, considered that an important aspect of the play is the story of the friendship between the two women:

> Armed with this resolve to jettison stereotype, we began work. . . . To liberate Shakespeare's women from the confines of literary and theatrical tradition requires an analysis of the nature and effects of those social structures which define and contain them—the opening

of this play sees Rosalind and Celia already contained within a structure that is oppressive and patriarchal, namely the court of Duke Frederick, Celia's father. The modern dress decision served to remind us that such structures are by no means 'ancient history', and that the freedom and self-definition that the two girls are seeking remain prevalent needs for many of their contemporaries today. This insistence on the contemporary reality of the women's emotional and psychological experience produced a compelling and admirable performance from Stevenson. Irving Wardle's review describes the effect:

> Rosalind begins as a prisoner of a stifling court and discovers her real powers through playing games.... She begins as a rather plain downcast girl, very much the house guest of Fiona Shaw's sharp-eyed Celia; then she gets into a white suit and begins to discover herself, first in . . . clown routines with Hilton McRae's Orlando, and then entering deeper waters where neither she, her lover, nor the audience can tell truth from masquerade. I have never seen their later dialogue played with equivalent erotic force; nor seen the mock-marriage take on such sacramental qualities.
>
> (*The Times*, 24 April 1985)

What was evidently lost in this reading of Rosalind was the comic vitality with which actresses have traditionally been able to imbue the role. Stevenson was intense and sincere rather than naturally playful (none of the production pictures shows her laughing or smiling, in strong contrast to the photos of virtually all earlier productions—see, for example, plate 9). Nicholas Shrimpton commented on this quality in her performance:

> Juliet Stevenson's Rosalind is touching in her vulnerable moments but desperately unconfident when she is required to be witty, flirtatious or high-spirited. Possibly she is weighed down by the psychological lumber of the interpretation. More probably this gifted actress is . . . simply not a comedienne.
>
> (*Times Educational Supplement*, 10 May 1985)

Nor need Rosalind be, in such a reading of the play as this; and 'Fortunately', Shrimpton continues, 'the production reminds us that the play has not one but two heroines, and supplies a superb Celia to take up the slack.' Fiona Shaw's Celia brought many appreciative comments, most notably Billington's sense that the production's 'one igniting spark of passion ... was when Fiona Shaw's Celia (beautifully played as a slightly woozy Mitfordesque deb who turns to mantras and meditation in the forest) exchange[d] instant glances with Bruce

Alexander's transformed Oliver.' (*Guardian*, 26 April 1985.) The archival videotape confirms this observation: Celia and Oliver's long, hypnotised stares at each other, ignoring Rosalind's faint, and their comically awkward, mutually absorbed exit, brought, a round of applause.

The play's male characters were less complex, except for the directorial concept of doubling the Dukes and their courts (a practice followed by John Caird in the 1989 production). Alan Rickman's Jaques was an arrogant but vulnerable lone intellectual: 'He did not care who married whom, nor who was in power. He had been there and seen it, and cared for it no longer' (Barry Russell, *Drama*, 3, 1985). Hilton McRae's Orlando, according to Michael Ratcliffe, 'is the sole reference to any resolved humanity warming the cerebral chill of the [play's] first half. . . . Into the world of hatchet faces and long over-coats at the start, [he] erupts scruffy, humorous, brave and enormously likeable, if in need of a bath' (*Observer*, 24 April 1985). His wrestling match was a comic epic in the manner of television's rock 'n' roll wrestling, with McRae in a very fetching G-string; at one crucial point he released himself from the grunting Charles by giving him a hearty kiss. 'One might even say', wrote Barry Russell,

> that this Orlando was used as the 'token male'. He took his clothes off, showed us his body, was pretty, long-haired and attractive. He was the romantic dreamer who spent much time in thought, but actually seemed incapable of achieving very much if left to his own devices. Rosalind, by contrast, looked strong and played strong.

So the production achieved its aim of presenting the feminine in the masculine, the masculine in the feminine. But, according to Stevenson, this deconstruction of gender roles presented problems as the play approached its end—a magical, joyous celebration which insists on the characters' return to the patriarchal 'hierarchies of the structured world', which is also the 'real world'. Stevenson and Noble argued about the staging of the ending:

> Having spent three hours challenging notions of gender, we couldn't then end with a final stage picture which was cliched and stereotypical, which threw the whole play away. Adrian did point out to me that, whether I liked it or not, Shakespeare was a monarchist, a reactionary, a bourgeois and a conservative, but I said, 'I think it's irrelevant what Shakespeare was. The fact is the *play* asks the most anarchic questions. It doesn't attempt to resolve them, so why should we?

Eventually, by the time the production came to London, the actors and director had re-worked the ending so that the play continued its challenge to the audience:

the dance culminated in a moment of still suspension, as the characters took in the Arden they were about to leave, and absorbed the *consequences* of the return to the ordered world. They then exited, through a moon-shaped hole in the backdrop, which both told the story more clearly and laid emphasis on the fantastical nature of the whole event. . . . These changes meant that the issues explored were no longer smothered, at the end, by excesses of 'merry-making', and we no longer felt obliged to abandon ourselves on the stage to some imposed inevitability.

Stevenson hoped that 'the audience would go out of the theater talking to each other', that the production's serious re-thinking of this comedy would in some way affect the lives of the spectators:

> I don't expect audiences to go skipping out of *As You Like It* humming the tunes, because the play isn't about that. It isn't about confirming cosy opinions or settled stereotypes. It isn't about a woman in search of romantic love. The search is for knowledge and for faith, and in that search Rosalind is clamorous.

This clarion call from one of the new generation of feminist classical actresses was, astonishingly, ignored in subsequent RSC productions of the play. Nineteen eighty-nine brought John Caird's new production, and a question from a somewhat weary Michael Billington: is *As You Like It* being done too often? (*Guardian*, 15 September 1989). Stewart McGill found the production 'a major disappointment':

> As the theatre world awaits the announcement of a successor to Terry Hands, the focus of the debate must be on what kind of Shakespeare should this company be doing as we move toward the 1990s. . . . Caird, his designer Ultz and composer Ilona Sekacz have destroyed the play in a quest for yet another way of reviving Shakespeare for today's audiences. The RSC production is loud, expensive, spectacular and utterly heartless.
>
> (*Plays & Players*, November 1989)

Caird clearly had a 'concept' for the play: an even more radical questioning of the power of the comic paradigm than Noble's. The problem lay in the communicating of these ideas. A case in point is the opening scene, as striking a directorial imposition as Nunn's operatic masque in 1977. The audience entered the theater to find a 1930s cocktails-and-tango party going on on stage. The effect was overwhelmingly funeral, not to say sinister. These were the bored, idle, and corrupt rich; no-one smiled; the men grimly challenged each other in toreador postures; Duke Frederick's heavies eyed the auditorium; and no-one danced with Rosalind. Yet for the two male critics quoted above, 'The aim, I take it, is to build up a party atmosphere' (McGill); 'Why, if Duke Frederick's court is an incipient tyranny, is everyone having such a good time?' (Billington). Billington incorrectly describes the event as a 'tea-dance'—apparently unaware that people don't wear black and diamonds, and dance with cold formality, at a *tea*-dance. The brutalist mood continued with a wrestling match in which Orlando appeared to be badly injured, spitting blood, and which he finally won by fighting dirty. The Duke's henchmen pulled guns on him when he revealed whose son he was: this 'court' was the home, of a tough, loveless gangster, whose conversion is never remotely likely.

The 'forest' was created by the same henchmen (with a change into brown overcoats; the Dukes too were doubled, by the actor Clifford Rose) simply pulling up the black boards of the floor, to reveal a small patch of wintry ground, which was gradually enlarged, as the forest ethos took over. All this provided a strong moral contrast between court and country—or rather, as Caird was clearly reflecting the ethical concerns of the 1980s, between the City and those who try to escape its circle of power—while at the same time indicating, as Noble did, that the two are inextricably linked. It was, however, the image of Arden which most worried the critics—an alien, vaguely sinister world in the play's first half, all piles of planks and swirling mist, and in the second half, a pool surrounded by surrealistic bullrushes; no trees (again). Its inhabitants, most notably Silvius and Phoebe, behaved very oddly indeed, pursuing their courtships in underwear (eventually, in the 'summertime', the court in exile was also reduced to boxer shorts). The audience was clearly invited to take a patronising view of the absurd behaviour of these pastoral types ineptly aping their betters (by contrast, an admired aspect of Noble's production was that the yokels were treated with respect as people, not caricatures). As Irving Wardle commented, 'they, no less than the courtiers, are giving a performance . . . the forest has no claims to reality' (*The Times*, 15 September 1989)—as opposed to the all-too-grim reality of the court.

The programme was little help: it carried a number of Blake's *Songs of Innocence and Experience* which reflected the production's ambivalence about the relation between the loveless adult world and 'the echoing green', but it was hard to tell what value was placed upon the green world. Perhaps the portrayal of Rosalind as a bored young sophisticate released into her true self, a tomboyish schoolgirl, was meant to present an image of Blakean energy which 'might transform the oppressive social world. Certainly Sophie Thompson's performance offered an excess of manic vitality. But if this was Caird's intention, it was somewhat skewed in performance by Thompson's comic genius. She used the role of Rosalind to create a highly inventive and amusing study of the tomboy schoolgirl in love. For Michael Coveney this was enough:

> a performer of blazing comic personality, powerful voice, dimpled, darting radiance and quixotic charm. . . . Sophie Thompson joins an exalted company of tomorrow's Denches and Smiths in a performance that ripples with invention, bubbles with high spirits and delights at every turn.
>
> (*Financial Times*, 15 September 1989)

Others were less enchanted:

> Sophie Thompson's Rosalind emerges as a simpering St Trinian's schoolgirl, dressed in shorts, gym shoes, straw hat and a satchel. Eschewing any hint of androgynous appeal Miss Thompson runs a gamut from bawling declamation to the doleful quaver, whose nasal stresses are reminiscent of Maggie Smith.
>
> (Nicholas de Jongh, *Guardian*, 13 April 1990)

As one might expect from such a characterisation the production was short on sexual excitement, a lack which disappointed de Jongh:

> there is small hint of sexual pathos, flirtatious mockery or erotic tension in her larkish, gamey performance when set against Jerome Flynn's morose Orlando, a youth whom you almost feel would prefer to be otherwise engaged.

Hugo Williams of the *Sunday Correspondent* (17 September 1989) offered a more generous judgement—which also reminded theatergoers of the ephemerality of the art they support, dependent on performers and performances:

> As usual, the play's success depends on Rosalind, with a little help from Touchstone. It is almost thirty years since Vanessa Redgrave's Rosalind, and yet one goes on comparing succeeding Rosalinds to her lanky principal boy. Sophie Thompson could not be more different: short, knock-kneed, Chaplinesque, it is a knockabout characterisation which takes some getting used to because of its lack of physical allure, but which finally triumphs by radical conviction and wholeness. . . . Though never 'luminous', she is finally loveable.

As, one might add, small children or clowns are loveable. Thompson's Rosalind and Mark Williams's red-nosed Touchstone provided between them many laughs; but it might be argued that this directorial emphasis suggests a curious desperation: does 'comedy' now only mean a brilliantly-performed joke? Has it, at the end of the twentieth century, lost its power to reconcile and renew? Ultz's design for Arden had created a surrealist dream-world—Wonderland, or a return to the Neverland of the 1950s. Now, however, it is a dream-escape from an extremely unpleasant contemporary real world. Perhaps the biggest clue to the production's perspective is given by the poster advertising the show. Rosalind and/or the greenwood are nowhere to be seen; instead, Charles the wrestler throws Orlando, in front of a grim-faced male courtier. The sources of power and energy are not to be found in Rosalind or the greenwood, but in the world of macho games ruled by the men in suits (these games were grimly parodied in the deer-killing, whose primitivism disgusted the cold dandy Jaques). The same pessimism underlay the uncomfortably jokey 'business' surrounding the Epilogue: Orlando stepped forward to speak it, had a fit of stage-fright, and Rosalind came to his rescue—she was not *in herself* an authoritative figure, just a Blakean 'happy child'. One wondered how these children of the greenwood would survive on the outside, lacking even the empowerment of sexual desire.

# "THE PLACE OF A BROTHER" IN *AS YOU LIKE IT*: SOCIAL PROCESS AND COMIC FORM

*Louis Adrian Montrose*

## I

*A**S YOU LIKE IT* creates and resolves conflict by mixing what the characters call Fortune and Nature—the circumstances in which they find themselves, as opposed to the resources of playfulness and boldness, moral virtue and witty deception, with which they master adversity and fulfill their desires.

The romantic action is centered on the meeting, courtship, and successful pairing of Rosalind and Orlando. This action is complicated, as Leo Salingar reminds us, by "a cardinal social assumption . . . (which would have been obvious to . . . Shakespeare's first audiences)—that Rosalind is a princess, while Orlando is no more than a gentleman. But for the misfortune of her father's exile, they might not have met in sympathy as at first; but for the second misfortune of her own exile, as well as his, they could not have met in apparent equality in the Forest".[1] The personal situations of Rosalind and Orlando affect, and are affected by, their relationship to each other. Rosalind's union with Orlando entails the weakening of her ties to her natural father and to a cousin who has been closer to her than a sister; Orlando's union with Rosalind entails the strengthening of his ties to his elder brother and to a lord who becomes his patron. Orlando's atonements with other men—a natural brother, a social father—precede his atonement with Rosalind. They confirm that the disadvantaged young country gentleman is worthy of the princess, by "nature" and by "fortune." The atonement of earthly things celebrated in Hymen's wedding song

Montrose, Louis Adrian. "The Place of a Brother in *As You Like It*": Social Process and Comic Form". Shakespeare Quarterly 32:1 (1981), 28–40, 45–54. © 1981 Folger Shakespeare Library. Reprinted with permission of The Johns Hopkins University Press.

1. Leo Salingar, *Shakespeare and the Traditions of Comedy* (Cambridge: Cambridge Univ. Press, 1974), pp. 297–98. On the *topos,* see John Shaw, "Fortune and Nature in *As You Like It*," *Shakespeare Quarterly,* 6 (1955), 45–50; *A New Variorum Edition of Shakespeare: "As You Like It*," ed. Richard Knowles, with Evelyn Joseph Mattern (New York: MLA, 1977), pp. 533–37.

incorporates man and woman within a process that reunites man with man. This process is my subject.

As the play begins, Orlando and Adam are discussing the terms of a paternal will; the first scene quickly explodes into fraternal resentment and envy, hatred and violence. By the end of the second scene, the impoverished youngest son of Sir Rowland de Boys finds himself victimized by "a tyrant Duke" and "a tyrant brother" (I. iii. 278).[2] The compact early scenes expose hostilities on the manor and in the court that threaten to destroy both the family and the state. Although modern productions have shown that these scenes can be powerful and effective in the theater, modern criticism has repeatedly downplayed their seriousness and significance. They are often treated merely as Shakespeare's mechanism for propelling his characters—and us—into the forest as quickly and efficiently as possible. Thus Harold Jenkins, in his influential essay on the play, writes of "the inconsequential nature of the action" and of "Shakespeare's haste to get ahead"; for him, the plot's interest consists in Shakespeare's ability to get "most of it over in the first act."[3] If we *reverse* Jenkins' perspective, we will do justice to Shakespeare's dramaturgy and make better sense of the play. What happens to Orlando at home is not Shakespeare's contrivance to get him into the forest; what happens to Orlando in the forest is Shakespeare's contrivance to remedy what has happened to him at home. The form of *As You Like It* becomes comic in the process of resolving the conflicts that are generated within it; events unfold and relationships are transformed in accordance with a precise comic teleology.

## II

Jaques sententiously observes that the world is a stage; the men and women, merely players; and one man's time, a sequence of acts in which he plays many parts. Shakespeare's plays reveal many traces of the older drama's intimate connection to the annual agrarian and ecclesiastical cycles. But more pervasive than these are the connections between Shakespearean comic and tragic forms and the human life cycle—the sequence of acts performed in several ages by Jaques' social player. Action in Shakespearean drama usually originates in combinations of a few basic kinds of human conflict: conflict among

---

2. *As You Like It* is quoted from the new Arden edition, ed. Agnes Latham (London: Methuen, 1975); all other plays are quoted are quoted from *The Riverside Shakespeare,* gen. ed. G. Blakemore Evans (Boston: Hughton Mifflin, 1974).   3. Harold Jenkins, "*As You Like It*," *Shakespeare Survey,* 8 (1955), 40–51; quotation from p. 41. There is an exception to this predominant view in Thomas McFarland, *Shakespeare's Pastoral Comedy* (Chapel Hill: Univ. of North Carolina Press, 1972), pp. 98–103.

members of different families, generations, sexes, and social classes. Shakespeare tends to focus dramatic action precisely *between* the social "acts," between the sequential "ages," in the fictional lives of his characters. Many of the plays turn upon points of transition in the life cycle—birth, puberty, marriage, death—where discontinuities arise and where adjustments are necessary to basic interrelationships in the family and in society. Such dramatic actions are analogous to rites of passage. Transition rites symbolically impose markers upon the life cycle and safely conduct people from one stage of life to the next; they give a social shape, order, and sanction to personal existence.[4]

In *As You Like It*, the initial conflict arises from the circumstances of inheritance by primogeniture. The differential relationship between the first born and his younger brothers is profoundly augmented at their father's death: the eldest son assumes a paternal relationship to his siblings; and the potential for sibling conflict increases when the relationship between brother and brother becomes identified with the relationship between father and son. The transition of the father from life to death both fosters and obstructs the transition of his sons from childhood to manhood. In *As You Like It*, the process of comedy accomplishes successful passages between ages in the life cycle and ranks in the social hierarchy. By the end of the play, Orlando has been brought from an impoverished and powerless adolescence to the threshold of manhood and marriage, wealth and title.

A social anthropologist defines inheritance practices as "the way by which property is transmitted between the living and the dead, and especially between generations."

> Inheritance is not only the means by which the reproduction of the social system is carried out . . . it is also the way in which interpersonal relationships are structured. . . .
>
> The linking of patterns of inheritance with patterns of domestic organization is a matter not simply of numbers and formations but of attitudes and emotions. The manner of splitting property is a manner of splitting people; it creates (or in some cases reflects) a particular

---

4. The paradigm for transition rites—the triadic movement from separation through marginality to reincorporation—was formulated in Arnold Van Gennep's classic, *The Rites of Passage* (1909), trans. M. B. Vizedom and G. L. Caffee (Chicago: Univ. of Chicago Press, 1960). Among more recent discussions, see *Essays on the Ritual of Social Relations*, ed. Max Gluckman (Manchester: Manchester Univ. Press, 1962); Victor Turner, *Dramas, Fields, and Metaphors* (Ithaca: Cornell Univ. Press, 1974); and Edmund Leach, *Culture and Communication* (Cambridge: Cambridge Univ. Press, 1976). For further discussion of analogies to transition rites in Shakespearean drama and Elizabethan theatre, see Louis Adrian Montrose, "The Purpose of Playing: Reflections on a Shakespearean Anthropology," *Helios*, NS, 7 (Winter 1980), 51–74.

constellation of ties and cleavages between husband and wife, parents and children, sibling and sibling, as well as between wider kin.[5]

As Goody himself concedes, the politics of the family are most powerfully anatomized, not by historians or social scientists, but by playwrights. Parents and children in Shakespeare's plays are recurrently giving or withholding, receiving or returning, property and love. Material and spiritual motives, self-interest and self-sacrifice, are inextricably intertwined in Shakespearean drama as in life.

Lear's tragedy, for example, begins in his division of his kingdom among his daughters and their husbands. He makes a bequest of his property to his heirs before his death, so "that future strife/May be prevented now" (I. i. 44–45). Gloucester's tragedy begins in the act of adultery that begets an "unpossessing bastard" (II.i.67). Edmund rails against "the plague of custom . . . the curiosity of nations" (I. ii. 3–4); he sees himself as victimized by rules of legitimacy and primogeniture. *As You Like It* begins with Orlando remembering the poor bequest from a dead father and the unnaturalness of an elder brother; he is victimized by what he bitterly refers to as "the courtesy of nations" (I.i.45–46). Rosalind dejectedly remembers "a banished father" (I.ii.4) and the consequent loss of her own preeminent social place. Celia responds to her cousin with naive girlhood loyalty: "You know my father hath no child but I, nor none is like to have; and truly when he dies, thou shalt be his heir; for what he hath taken away from thy father perforce, I will render thee again in affection" (I. ii. 14–19). The comic action of *As You Like It* works to atone elder and younger brothers, father and child, man and woman, lord and subject, master and servant. Within his play, Rosalind's magician-uncle recreates situations that are recurrent sources of ambiguity, anxiety, and conflict in the society of his audience; he explores and exacerbates them, and he resolves them by brilliant acts of theatrical prestidigitation.

The tense situation which begins *As You Like It* was a familiar and controversial fact of Elizabethan social life. Lawrence Stone emphasizes that "the prime factor affecting all families which owned property was . . . primogeniture"; that "the principle and practice of primogeniture . . . went far to determine the behaviour and character of both parents and children, and to govern the relationship between siblings."[6] In the sixteenth and seventeenth centuries, primogeniture was more widely and rigorously practiced in England—by the gentry and lesser landowners, as well as by the aristocracy—than anywhere else in Europe. The consequent hardships,

**5.** Jack Goody, "Introduction," in *Family and Inheritance: Rural Society in Western Europe, 1200–1800,* ed. Jack Goody, Joan Thirsk, and E. P. Thompson (Cambridge: Cambridge Univ. Press, 1976), pp. 1, 3.   **6.** Lawrence Stone, *The Family, Sex and Marriage in England 1500–1800* (New York: Harper & Row, 1977), pp. 87–88.

frequent abuses, and inherent inequities of primogeniture generated a "literature of protest by and for younger sons" that has been characterized as "plentiful," "vehement" in tone, and "unanimous" in its sympathies.[7]

Jaques was not the only satirist to "rail against all the first-born of Egypt" (II. v. 57–58). John Earle included the character of a "younger Brother" in his *Micro-Cosmographie* (1628):

> His father ha's done with him, as *Pharaoh* to the children of Israel, that would have them make brick, and give them no straw, so he taskes him to bee a Gentleman, and leaves him nothing to maintaine it. The pride of his house has undone him, which the elder Knighthood must sustaine, and his beggery that Knighthood. His birth and bringing up will not suffer him to descend to the meanes to get wealth: but hee stands at the mercy of the world, and which is worse of his brother. He is something better then the Servingmen; yet they more saucy with him, then hee bold with the master, who beholds him with a countenance of sterne awe, and checks him oftner then his Liveries. . . . Nature hath furnisht him with a little more wit upon compassion; for it is like to be his best revenew. . . . Hee is commonly discontented, and desperate, and the forme of his exclamation is, that Churle my brother.[8]

As a class, the gentry experienced a relative rise in wealth and status during this period. But the rise was achieved by inheriting eldest sons at the expense of their younger brothers. As Earle and other contemporaries clearly recognized, the gentry's drive to aggrandize and perpetuate their estates led them to a ruthless application of primogeniture; this left them without the means adequately to provide for their other offspring. The psychological and socio-economic consequences of primogeniture for younger sons (and for daughters) seem to have been considerable: downward social mobility and relative impoverishment, inability to marry or late marriage, and fewer children.

In 1600, about the time *As You Like It* was first performed, Thomas Wilson wrote a valuable analysis of England's social structure. His description of gentlemen reveals a very personal involvement:

> Those which wee call Esquires are gentlemen whose ancestors are or have bin Knights, or else they are the heyres and eldest of their houses and of some competent quantity of revenue fitt to be called to office and authority in their Country. . . . These are the elder brothers.

---

**7.** Joan Thirsk, "Younger Sons in the Seventeenth Century," *History* (London), 54 (1969), 358–77; quotation from p. 359. Thirsk cites *As You Like It*, I.i, as part of that literature.   **8.** Ed. Edward Arber (1869; rpt., New York: AMS Press, 1966), pp. 29–30. I have modernized obsolete typographical conventions in quotations from this and other Renaissance texts.

I cannot speak of the number of yonger brothers, albeit I be one of the number myselfe, but for their estate there is no man hath better cause to knowe it, nor less cause to praise it; their state is of all stations for gentlemen most miserable.... [A father] may demise as much as he thinkes good to his younger children, but such a fever hectick hath custome brought in and inured amongst fathers, and such fond desire they have to leave a great shewe of the stock of their house, though the branches be withered, that they will not doe it, but my elder brother forsooth must be my master. He must have all, and all the rest that which the catt left on the malt heape, perhaps some smale annuytye during his life or what please our elder brother's worship to bestowe upon us if wee please him.[9]

The foregoing texts characterize quite precisely the situation of Orlando and his relationship to Oliver at the beginning of *As You Like It*. They suggest that Shakespeare's audience may have responded with some intensity to Orlando's indictment of "the courtesy of nations."

In his constitutional treatise, *De Republica Anglorum* (written ca. 1562; printed 1583), Sir Thomas Smith observes that "whosoever studies the laws of the realm, who studies at the universities, who professes liberal sciences and to be short, who can live idly and without manual labour, and will bear the port, charge and countenance of a gentleman ... shall be taken for a gentleman"[10] The expected social fate of a gentleborn Elizabethan younger son was to lose the ease founded upon landed wealth that was the very hallmark of gentility. Joan Thirsk suggests that, although there were places to be had for those who were industrious and determined to make the best of their misfortune,

the habit of working for a living was not ingrained in younger sons of this class, and no amount of argument could convince them of the justice of treating them so differently from their elder brothers. The contrast was too sharp between the life of an elder son, whose fortune was made for him by his father, and who had nothing to do but maintain, and perhaps augment it, and that of the younger sons who faced a life of hard and continuous effort, starting almost from nothing. Many persistently refused to accept their lot, and hung around at home, idle, bored, and increasingly resentful.[11]

At the beginning of *As You Like It*, Orlando accuses Oliver of enforcing his idleness and denying him the means to preserve the gentility

---

**9.** Thomas Wilson, *The State of England Anno Dom. 1600*, ed. F. J. Fisher, Camden Miscellany, 16 (London: Camden Society, 1936), pp. 1–43; quotation from pp. 23–24. **10.** Rpt. in *Social Change and Revolution in England 1540–1640*, ed. Lawrence Stone (New York: Barnes & Noble, 1965), p. 120. **11.** Thirsk, "Younger Sons," p. 368.

which is his birthright: "My brother Jaques he keeps at school, and report speaks goldenly of his profit; for my part, he keeps me rustically at home, or, to speak more properly, stays me here at home unkept; for call you that keeping for a gentleman of my birth, that differs not from the stalling of an ox? . . . [He] mines my gentility with my education" (I.i. 5–10, 20–21). Orlando is "not taught to make anything" (l. 30); and his natural virtue is marred "with idleness" (ll. 33–34). When Adam urges him to leave the family estate, Orlando imagines his only prospects to be beggary and highway robbery (II. iii. 29–34). He finally agrees to go off with Adam, spending the old laborer's "youthful wages" in order to gain "some settled low content" (II. iii. 67–68).

Shakespeare's opening strategy is to plunge his characters and his audience into the controversy about a structural principle of Elizabethan personal, family, and social life. He is not merely using something topical to get his comedy off to a lively start: the expression and resolution of sibling conflict and its social implications are integral to the play's form and function. The process of comedy works against the seemingly inevitable prospect of social degradation suggested at the play's beginning, and against its literary idealization in conventions of humble pastoral retirement. In the course of *As You Like It*, Orlando's gentility is preserved and his material well-being is enhanced. Shakespeare uses the machinery of pastoral romance to remedy the lack of fit between deserving and having, between Nature and Fortune. Without actually violating the primary Elizabethan social frontier separating the gentle from the base, the play achieves an illusion of social leveling and of unions across class boundaries. Thus, people of every rank in Shakespeare's socially heterogeneous audience might construe the action as they liked it.

Primogeniture is rarely mentioned in modern commentaries on *As You Like It*, despite its obvious prominence in the text and in the action.[12] Shakespeare's treatment of primogeniture may very well have been a vital—perhaps even the dominant—source of engagement for many in his Elizabethan audience. The public theater brought together people from all the status and occupational groups to be found in Shakespeare's London (except, of course, for the poorest laborers and the indigent). Alfred Harbage points out that the two groups "mentioned again and again in contemporary allusions to the theaters" are "the students of the Inns of Court and the apprentices of London.[13] In addition to these youthful groups, significant numbers of soldiers, professionals, merchants, shopkeepers, artisans, and household

12. An exception is John W. Draper, "Orlando, the Younger Brother," *Philological Quarterly*, 13 (1934), 72–77. 13. See Alfred Harbage, *Shakespeare's Audience* (New York: Columbia Univ. Press, 1941), pp. 53–91; quotation from p. 80.

servants were also regular playgoers. The careers most available to the younger sons of gentlemen were in the professions—most notably the law, but also medicine and teaching—as well as in trade, the army, and the church.[14] Thus, Shakespeare's audience must have included a high proportion of gentleborn younger sons—adults, as well as the youths who were students and apprentices. Among these gentleborn younger sons, and among the baseborn youths who were themselves socially subordinate apprentices and servants, it is likely that Orlando's desperate situation was the focus of personal projections and a catalyst of powerful feelings. "During the sixteenth century," Thirsk concludes, "to describe anyone as '*a younger son*' was a short-hand way of summing up a host of grievances. . . . *Younger son* meant an angry young man, bearing more than his share of injustice and resentment, deprived of means by his father and elder brother, often hanging around his elder brother's house as a servant, completely dependent on his grace and favour."[15] Youths, younger sons, and all Elizabethan playgoers who felt that Fortune's benefits had been "mightily misplaced" (II. i. 33–34) could identify with Shakespeare's Orlando.

## III

It is precisely in the details of inheritance that Shakespeare makes one of the most significant departures from his source. Sir John of Bordeaux is on his deathbed at the beginning of Lodge's *Rosalynde*; he divides his land and chattels among his three sons:

> Unto thee *Saladyne* the eldest, and therefore the chiefest piller of my house, wherein should be ingraven as well the excellence of thy fathers qualities, as the essentiall forme of his proportion, to thee I give fourteene ploughlands, with all my Mannor houses and richest plate. Next unto *Fernadyne* I bequeath twelve ploughlands. But unto *Rosader* the youngest I give my Horse, my Armour and my Launce, with sixteene ploughlands: for if inward thoughts be discovered by outward shadowes, *Rosader* will exceed you all in bountie and honour.[16]

The partible inheritance devised by Lodge's Sir John was an idiosyncratic variation on practices widespread in Elizabethan society among

---

**14.** See Thirsk, "Younger Sons," pp. 363, 366–68.   **15.** Thirsk, "Younger Sons," p. 360.   **16.** *New Variorum* ed. of *AYL*, p. 382; future page references will be to this text of *Rosalynde*, which follows the First Quarto (1590). On the relationship of *AYL* to *Rosalynde*, see *Narrative and Dramatic Sources of Shakespeare*, ed. Geoffrey Bullough (London: Routledge & Kegan Paul, 1958), II, 143–57; Marco Mincoff, "What Shakespeare Did to *Rosalynde*," *Shakespeare Jahrbuch*, 96 (1960), 78–89; *New Variorum* ed. of *As You Like It*, pp. 475–83.

those outside the gentry.[17] Saladyne, the eldest born, inherits his father's authority. Rosader receives more land and love—he is his father's joy, although his last and least. Saladyne, who becomes Rosader's guardian, is deeply resentful and decides not to honor their father's will: "What man thy Father is dead, and hee can neither helpe thy fortunes, nor measure thy actions: therefore, burie his words with his carkasse, and bee wise for thy selfe" (p. 391).

Lodge's text, like Thomas Wilson's, reminds us that primogeniture was not a binding law but rather a flexible social custom in which the propertied sought to perpetuate themselves by preserving their estates intact through successive generations. Shakespeare alters the terms of the paternal will in Lodge's story so as to alienate Orlando from the status of a landed gentleman. The effect is to intensify the differences between the eldest son and his siblings, and to identify the sibling conflict with the major division in the Elizabethan social fabric: that between the landed and the unlanded, the gentle and the base. (Within half a century after Shakespeare wrote *As You Like It*, radical pamphleteers were using "elder brother" and "younger brother" as synonyms for the propertied, enfranchised social classes and the unpropertied, unenfranchised social classes.) Primogeniture complicates not only sibling and socio-economic relationships but also relationships between generations: between a father and the eldest son impatient for his inheritance; between a father and the younger sons resentful against the "fever hectic" that custom has inured among fathers.

Shakespeare's plays are thickly populated by subjects, sons, and younger brothers who are ambivalently bound to their lords, genitors, and elder siblings—and by young women moving ambivalently between the lordships of father and husband. If this dramatic proliferation of patriarchs suggests that Shakespeare had a neurotic obsession, then it was one with a social context. To see father-figures everywhere in Shakespeare's plays is not a psychoanalytic anachronism, for Shakespeare's own contemporaries seem to have seen father-figures everywhere. The period from the mid-sixteenth to the mid-seventeenth century in England has been characterized by Lawrence Stone as

---

**17.** See Joan Thirsk, "The European Debate on Customs of Inheritance, 1500–1700," in *Family and Inheritance*, pp. 177–91: "The inheritance customs of classes below the gentry did not give rise to controversy: practices were as varied as the circumstances of families. Primogeniture in the original sense of advancing the eldest son, but nevertheless providing for the others, was common, perhaps the commonest custom among yeoman and below, but it did not exercise a tyranny. Among the nobility primogeniture was most common. . . . In general it did not cause excessive hardship to younger sons because the nobility had the means to provide adequately for all" (p. 186).

"the patriarchal stage in the evolution of the nuclear family."[18] Writing of the early seventeenth-century family as "a political symbol and a social institution," Gordon J. Schochet documents that

> virtually all social relationships—not merely those between fathers and children and magistrates and subjects—were regarded as patriarchal or familial in essence. The family was looked upon as the basis of the entire social order. . . .
>
> So long as a person occupied an inferior status within a household—as a child, servant, apprentice, or even as a wife—and was subordinated to the head, his social identity was altogether vicarious. . . .
>
> Before a man achieved social status—if he ever did—he would have spent a great many years in various positions of patriarchal subordination.[19]

This social context shaped Shakespeare's preoccupation with fathers; and it gave him the scope within which to reshape it into drama, satisfying his own needs and those of his paying audience. His plays explore the difficulty or impossibility of establishing or authenticating a self in a rigorously hierarchical and patriarchal society, a society in which full social identity tends to be limited to propertied adult males who are the heads of households.

Shakespeare's Sir Rowland de Boys is dead before the play begins. But the father endures in the power exerted by his memory and his will upon the men in the play—his sons, Adam, the dukes—and upon their attitudes toward each other. The play's very first words insinuate that Orlando's filial feeling is ambivalent "As I remember, Adam, it was upon this fashion bequeathed me by will but poor a thousand crowns, and, as thou sayst, charged my brother on his blessing to breed me well; and there begins my sadness" (I.i. 1–4). Orlando's diction is curiously indirect; he conspicuously avoids naming his father. Absent from Shakespeare's play is any expression of the special, compensatory paternal affection shown to Lodge's Rosader. There is an implied resentment against an unnamed father, who has left his son a paltry inheritance and committed him to an indefinite and socially degrading

---

**18.** Stone, *Family, Sex and Marriage*, p. 218. *Contra* Stone, there is evidence to suggest that the nuclear family was in fact the pervasive and traditional pattern in English society outside the aristocracy; that the English family at this period was profoundly patriarchal remains, however, undisputed. The assumptions and conclusions of Stone's massive study have not found complete acceptance among his colleagues. See the important review essays on Stone's book by Christopher Hill, in *The Economic History Review*, 2nd. Ser., 31 (1978), 450–63; by Alan Macfarlane, in *History and Theory*, 18 (1979), 103–26; and by Richard T. Vann, in *The Journal of Family History*, 4 (1979), 308–14. **19.** *Patriarchalism in Political Thought* (New York: Basic Books, 1975), pp. 65–66.

dependence upon his own brother. Ironically, Orlando's first explicit acknowledgment of his filial bond is in a declaration of personal *independence*, a repudiation of his bondage to his eldest brother: "The spirit of my father, which I think is within me, begins to mutiny against this servitude" (I. i. 21–23). Orlando's assertions of filial piety are actually self-assertions, directed against his father's eldest son. As Sir Rowland's inheritor, Oliver perpetuates Orlando's subordination within the patriarchal order; he usurps Orlando's selfhood.

In a private family and household, the eldest son succeeds the father as patriarch. In a royal or aristocratic family, the eldest son also succeeds to the father's title and political authority. Thus, when he has been crowned as King Henry V, Hal tells his uneasy siblings, "I'll be your father and your brother too./Let me but bear your love, I'll bear your cares" (*2 Henry IV*, V. ii. 57–58). Like Henry, Oliver is simultaneously a father and a brother to his own natural sibling; he is at once Orlando's master and his peer. Primogeniture conflates the generations in the person of the elder brother and blocks the generational passage of the younger brother. What might be described dispassionately as a contradiction in social categories is incarnated in the play, as in English social life, in family conflicts and identity crises.[20]

Orlando gives bitter expression to his personal experience of this social contradiction: "The courtesy of nations allows you my better in that you are the firstborn, but that same tradition takes not away my blood, were there twenty brothers betwixt us. I have as much of my father in me as you, albeit I confess that your coming before me is nearer his reverence" (I. i. 45–51). Here Orlando asserts that all brothers are equally their father's sons. Oliver might claim a special paternal relationship because he is the first born; but Orlando's own claim actually to incorporate their father renders insubstantial any argument based on age or birth order. Thus, Orlando can indict his brother and repudiate his authority: "You have trained me like a peasant, obscuring and hiding from me all gentlemanlike qualities. The spirit of my father grows strong in me, and I will no longer endure it" (I. i. 68–71). Because the patriarchal family is the basic political unit of a patriarchal society, Orlando's protests suggest that primogeniture involves contradictions in the categories of social status as well as those of kinship. Orlando is subordinated to his sibling as a son to his father; and he

---

**20.** Orlando's predicament may be compared to Hamlet's: for each of these young Elizabethan heroes, the process of becoming himself involves a process of "remembering" the father for whom he is named. But the generational passage of each is blocked by a "usurper" of his spiritual inheritance, who mediates ambiguously between the father and the son: Oliver is a brother-father to Orlando; Claudius, himself the old King's younger brother, is an uncle-father to Hamlet.

is subordinated to a fellow gentleman as a peasant would be subordinated to his lord.

Orlando incorporates not only his father's likeness and name ("Rowland") but also his potent "spirit"—his personal genius, his manliness, and his moral virtue. To Adam, Orlando is "gentle, strong, and valiant" (II.iii.6). He is his father's gracious and virtuous reincarnation: "O you memory of old Sir Rowland!" (II. iii. 3–4). Adam challenges the eldest son's legal claim to be his father's heir by asserting that Oliver is morally undeserving, that he is *spiritually* illegitimate:

> Your brother, no, no brother, yet the son—
> Yet not the son, I will not call him son—
> Of him I was about to call his father.
>
> (II. iii. 19–21)

Orlando's claim to his spiritual inheritance leads immediately to physical coercion: Oliver calls him "boy" and strikes him. Orlando responds to this humiliating form of parental chastisement not with deference but with rebellion: he puts his hands to Oliver's throat. Orlando's assertion of a self which "remembers" their father is a threat to Oliver's patriarchal authority, a threat to his own social identity; "Begin you to grow upon me?" (I.i.85). The brothers' natural bond, in short, is contaminated by their ambiguous social relationship.

Because fraternity is confused with filiation—because the generations have, in effect, been collapsed together—the conflict of elder and younger brothers also projects an oedipal struggle between father and son. In the second scene, the private violence between the brothers is displaced into the public wrestling match. Oliver tells Charles, the Duke's wrestler, "I had as lief thou didst break [Orlando's] neck as his finger" (I. i. 144–45). Sinewy Charles, the "general challenger" (I. ii. 159), has already broken the bodies of "three proper young men" (I.iii) before Orlando comes in to try "the strength of [his] youth" (I.161). In a sensational piece of stage business, Orlando and Charles enact a living emblem of the generational struggle. When Orlando throws Charles, youth is supplanting age, the son is supplanting the father. This contest is preceded by a remarkable exchange:

> CHARLES Come, where is this young gallant that is so desirous to lie
> with his mother earth?
> ORLANDO Ready sir, but his will hath in it a more modest working.
>
> (I. ii. 188–91)

Charles's challenge gives simultaneous expression to a filial threat of incest and a paternal threat of filicide. In this conspicuously motherless play, the social context of reciprocal father-son hostility is a male struggle for identity and power fought between elders and youths, first-born and younger brothers.[21]

Orlando's witty response to Charles suggests that he regards neither his fears nor his threats. Orlando's "will" is merely to come to man's estate and to preserve the status of a gentleman. At the beginning of *As You Like It*, then, Shakespeare sets himself the problem of resolving the consequences of a conflict between Orlando's powerful assertion of identity—his spiritual claim to be a true inheritor—and the social fact that he is a subordinated and disadvantaged younger son. In the forest, Oliver will be spiritually reborn and confirmed in his original inheritance. Orlando will be socially reborn as heir apparent to the reinstated Duke. Orlando will regain a brother by "blood" and a father by "affinity."

# IV

Orlando is not only a younger son but also a youth. And in its language, characterization, and plot, *As You Like It* emphasizes the significance of age categories. Most prominent, of course, is Jaques' disquisition on the seven ages of man. But the play's *dramatis personae* actually fall into the three functional age groups of Elizabethan society: youth, maturity, and old age. Orlando's youth is referred to by himself and by others some two dozen times in the first two scenes: he is young; a boy; a youth; the youngest son; a younger brother; a young fellow; a young gallant; a young man; a young gentleman. Social historians have discredited the notion that adolescence went unexperienced or unacknowledged in early modern England. Lawrence Stone, for example, emphasizes that in Shakespeare's time there was "a strong contemporary consciousness of adolescence (then called 'youth'), as a distinct stage of life between sexual maturity at about fifteen and marriage at about twenty-six."[22] Shakespeare's persistent epithets identify Orlando as a member of the group about which contemporary moralists and guardians of the social order were most obsessively concerned. The Statute of Artificers (1563)

21. Thus, I am not suggesting that the text and action of *As You Like It* displace a core fantasy about mother-son incest. My perspective is socio-anthropological rather than psychoanalytic: allusions to incest amplify the confusion between older and younger generations, kin and non-kin; they exemplify the tension inherent in the power relations between male generations in a patriarchal society. Perhaps one reason for Shakespeare's fascination with kingship as a dramatic subject is that it provides a paradigm for patriarchy and succession. Prince Hal's destiny is to replace his father as King Henry; his father's death is the legal condition for the creation of his own identity. A major aspect of comic form in the *Henry IV* plays is Hal's process of projecting and mastering his patricidal impulse until he comes into his kingdom legitimately. 22. Stone, *Family, Sex and Marriage*, p. 108.

summarizes the official attitude: "Until a man grow unto the age of twenty-four years he . . . is wild, without judgment and not of sufficient experience to govern himself."[23] The youthful members of an Elizabethan household—children, servants, and apprentices—were all supposed to be kept under strict patriarchal control. Stone points out that "it was precisely because its junior members were under close supervision that the state had a very strong interest in encouraging and strengthening the household. . . . It helped to keep in check potentially the most unruly element in any society, the floating mass of young unmarried males."[24] Orlando is physically mature and powerful, but socially infantilized and weak.

That Shakespeare should focus so many of his plays on a sympathetic consideration of the problems of youth is not surprising when we consider that perhaps half the population was under twenty, and that the youthfulness of Shakespeare's society was reflected in the composition of his audience.[25] In his richly documented study, Keith Thomas demonstrates that

> So far as the young were concerned, the sixteenth and seventeenth centuries are conspicuous for a sustained drive to subordinate persons in their teens and early twenties and to delay their equal participation in the adult world. This drive is reflected in the wider dissemination of apprenticeship; in the involvement of many more children in formal education; and in a variety of measures to prolong the period of legal and social infancy.[26]

Elizabethan adolescence seems to have been characterized by a high degree of geographical mobility: youths were sent off to school, to search for work as living-in servants, or to be apprenticed in a regional town or in London. Alan Macfarlane has suggested that, "at the level of family life," this widespread and peculiarly English custom of farming out adolescent children was "a mechanism for separating the generations at a time when there might otherwise have been considerable difficulty." "The changes in patterns of authority as the children approached adulthood would . . . be diminished." He speculates further that, at the collective level, "the whole process was a form of age ritual, a way of demarcating off age-boundaries by movement through space."[27]

---

**23.** Quoted in Keith Thomas, "Age and Authority in Early Modern England," *Proceedings of the British Academy*, 62 (1976), 205–48; quotation from p. 217. **24.** Stone, *Family, Sex and Marriage*, p. 27.   **25.** See Stone, *Family, Sex and Marriage*, p. 72; Thomas, "Age and Authority," p. 212; Harbage, *Shakespeare's Audience*, p. 79. **26.** Thomas, "Age and Authority," p. 214.   **27.** Alan Macfarlane, *The Family Life of Ralph Josselin, A Seventeenth-Century Clergyman: An Essay in Historical Anthropology* (Cambridge: Cambridge Univ. Press, 1970), Appendix B: "Children and servants: the problem of adolescence," pp. 205, 210.

The family was a source of social stability, but most families were short-lived and unstable. Youth was geographically mobile, but most youths were given no opportunity to enjoy their liberty. In schools and in households, the masters of scholars, servants, and apprentices were to be their surrogate fathers. Thomas stresses that, "though many children left home early and child labour was thought indispensable, there was total hostility to the early achievement of economic independence."[28] The material basis of that hostility was alarm about the increasing pressure of population on very limited and unreliable resources. One of its most significant results was delayed marriage: "Combined with strict prohibition on alternative forms of sexual activity, late marriage was the most obvious way in which youth was prolonged. For marriage was the surest test of adult status and on it hinged crucial differences in wages, dress, and economic independence."[29] Most Elizabethan youths and maidens were in their mid or late twenties by the time they entered Hymen's bands.[30] When Touchstone quips that "the forehead of a married man [is] more honourable than the bare brow of a bachelor" (III.iii. 53–55), he is giving a sarcastic twist to a fundamental mark of status. And when, late in his pseudo-mock-courtship of Ganymede, Orlando remarks ruefully that he "can live no longer by thinking" (V.ii.50), he is venting the constrained libido of Elizabethan youth. One of the critical facts about the Elizabethan life cycle—one not noted in Jaques' speech—was that a large and varied group of codes, customs, and institutions regulated "a separation between physiological puberty and social puberty."[31] "Youth," then, was the Elizabethan age category separating the end of childhood from the beginning of adulthood. It was a social threshold whose transitional nature was Manifested in shifts of residence, activity, sexual feeling, and patriarchal authority.

The dialectic between Elizabethan dramatic form and social process is especially conspicuous in the triadic romance pattern of exile and return that underlies *As You Like It*. Here the characters' experience is a fictional analogue of both the theatrical and the social experiences of its audience. "The circle of this forest" (V.iv.34) is equivalent to Shakespeare's Wooden O. When they enter the special space-time of the theater, the playgoers have voluntarily and temporarily withdrawn from "this working-day world" (I.iii. 12) and put on "a holiday humour" (IV.i. 65–66). When they have been wooed to an atonement by the comedy, the Epilogue conducts them back across the threshold

**28.** Thomas, "Age and Authority," p. 216.   **29.** Stone, *Family, Sex and Marriage*, p. 226.   **30.** See Peter Laslett, *The World We Have Lost*, 2nd ed. (New York: Charles Scribner's Sons, 1973), pp. 85–86; Stone, *Family, Sex and Marriage*, pp 46–54; Thomas, "Age and Authority," pp. 225–27.   **31.** Thomas, "Age and Authority," p. 225.

between the world of the theater and the theater of the world. The dramatic form of the characters' experience corresponds, then, not only to the theatrical experience of the play's audience but also to the social process of youth in the world that playwright, players, and playgoers share. In a playworld of romance, Orlando and Rosalind experience separation from childhood, journeying, posing and disguising, altered and confused relationships to parental figures, sexual ambiguity, and tension. The fiction provides projections for the past or ongoing youthful experiences of most of the people in Shakespeare's Elizabethan audience. The forest sojourn conducts Orlando and Rosalind from an initial situation of oppression and frustration to the threshold of interdependent new identities. In one sense, then, the whole process of romantic pastoral comedy—the movement into and out of Arden—is what Macfarlane calls "a form of age ritual, a way of demarcating off age-boundaries by movement through space." The characters' fictive experience is congruent with the ambiguous and therefore dangerous period of the Elizabethan life cycle that is betwixt and between physical puberty and social puberty.

·   ·   ·

# VI

.... Some commentators have seen the outlines of a Christian allegory of redemption in the play. They point to the presence of a character named Adam; the Duke's disquisition on "the penalty of Adam"; the iconography of the serpent, the tree and the *vetus homo*; the heroic virtue of Orlando; the comic rite of atonement.[39]

Perhaps we do better to think of Shakespeare as creating resonances between the situations in his play and the religious archetypes at the foundations of his culture; as invoking what Rosalie Colie, writing of *King Lear*, calls "Biblical echo." What echoes deeply through the scenes I have discussed is the fourth chapter of Genesis, the story of Cain and Abel and what another of Shakespeare's fratricides calls "the primal eldest curse .../ A brother's murther" (*Hamlet*, III. iii. 37–38). Adam's two sons made offerings to the Lord: "and the Lord had respect unto Habel, and to his offering,"

> But unto Kain and to his offring he had no regarde: wherefore Kain was exceding wroth, & his countenance fel downe.

---

**39.** See Richard Knowles, "Myth and Type in *As You Like It*," *ELH* 33 (1966), 1–22; René E. Fortin, "'Tongues in Trees': Symbolic Patterns in *As You Like It*," *Texas Studies in Literature and Language*, 14 (1973), 569–82.

Then the Lord said unto Kain, Why art thou wroth? and why is thy countenence cast downe?

If thou do wel, shalt thou not be accepted? and if thou doest not well, sinne lieth at the dore: also unto thee his desire *shal be subject*, and thou shalt rule over him.

Then Kain spake to Habel his brother. And when they were in the field, Kain rose up against Habel his brother, and slewe him.

Then the Lord said unto Kain, Where is Habel thy brother? Who answered, I canot tel. Am I my brothers keper?

Againe he said, What hast thou done? the voyce of thy brothers blood cryeth unto me from the grounde.

Now therefore thou art cursed from the earth, which hath opened her mouth to receive thy brothers blood from thine hand.[40]

The Geneva Bible glosses the italicized phrase in the seventh verse as a reference to the foundations of primogeniture: "The dignitie of ye first borne is given to Kain over Habel."

The wrath of Cain echoes in Oliver's fratricidal musings at the end of the first scene: "I hope I shall see an end of him; for my soul—yet I know not why—hates nothing more than he. Yet he's gentle, never schooled and yet learned, full of noble device, of all sorts enchantingly beloved, and indeed so much in the heart of the world, and especially of my own people, that I am altogether misprised. But it shall not be so long" (I.i. 162–69). Oliver feels humanly rather than divinely misprized; and it is his tyrannical secular lord to whom he declares that he is not his brother's keeper. Orlando sheds his own blood for his elder brother, which becomes the sign of Oliver's conversion rather than the mark of his fratricidal guilt. Oliver finds acceptance in the old Duke, who commits him to his brother's love. Shakespeare is creating a resonance between his romantic fiction and Biblical history, between the dramatic process of assuaging family conflict in the atonements of comedy and the exegetical process of redeeming the primal fratricide of Genesis in the spiritual fraternity of the Gospel:

For brethren, ye have bene called unto libertie: onely use not *your* libertie as an occasion unto the flesh, but by love serve one another.

For all the Law is fulfilled in one worde, which is this, Thou shalt love thy neighbour as thy self.

If ye byte & devoure one another, take hede lest ye be consumed one of another.

---

**40.** Genesis iv. 4–11, in *The Geneva Bible* (1560), facsimile ed. (Madison: Univ. of Wisconsin Press, 1969). Italics in the original. All further references to the Bible from this source.

Then I say, walke in the Spirit, and ye shal not fulfil the lustes of the flesh.[41]

(Galatians v. 13–16)

The rivalry or conflict between elder and younger brothers is a prominent motif in the fictions of cultures throughout the world. Its typical plot has been described as "the disadvantaged younger sibling or orphan child besting an unjust elder and gaining great fortune through the timely intercession of a benevolent supernatural being."[42] Cultural fictions of the triumphs of younger siblings offer psychological compensation for the social fact of the deprivation of younger siblings. Such fictions are symbolic mediations of discrepancies between the social categories of status and the claims of individual merit, in which the defeat and supplanting of the elder sibling by the younger reconciles ability with status: "The younger outwits, displaces, and becomes the elder; the senior position comes to be associated with superior ability."[43]

The folk-tale scenario of sibling rivalry is clear in the fourteenth-century tale of *Gamelyn*, to which Lodge's Rosader plot and Shakespeare's Orlando plot are indebted.[44] The disinherited Gamelyn and his outlaw cohorts sentence Gamelyn's eldest brother to death by hanging. Their topsy-turvy actions are sanctioned and absorbed by the social order: the King pardons Gamelyn, restores his inheritance, and makes him Chief Justice. In *As You Like It*, Shakespeare's characters emphasize the discrepancy between "the gifts of the world" and "the lineaments of Nature" (I.ii. 40–41), between social place and personal merit. The comedy's task is to "mock the good hussif Fortune from her wheel, that her gifts may henceforth be bestowed equally" (I. ii. 30–32). Shakespeare transcends *Gamelyn* and its folktale paradigm in a wholehearted concern not merely to eliminate social contradictions, but also to redeem and reconcile human beings.[45] Oliver is not defeated, eliminated,

---

**41.** "The flesh lusteth against the Spirit" (Galatians v. 17) is glossed in the Geneva Bible: "That is, the natural man striveth against ye Spirit of regeneration." The spiritually regenerate Oliver marries the aptly named Celia; the socially regenerate Orlando marries a Rosalind brought "from heaven" (V.iv. 111) by Hymen. **42.** Michael Jackson, "Ambivalence and the Last-Born: Birth-order position in convention and myth," *Man,* NS, 13 (1978), 341–61; quotation from p. 350. This anthropological essay, based on comparative ethnography of the Kuranko (Sierra Leone) and Maori (New Zealand), has clarified my thinking about the society of Arden. **43.** Jackson, "Ambivalence and the Last-Born," p. 354. **44.** *New Variorum* ed. of *As You Like It*, pp. 483–87, provides a synopsis of the plot of *Gamelyn* and a digest of opinions about its direct influence on *As You Like It*. **45.** Compare Lodge's address to the reader at the end of *Rosalynde*: "Heere Gentlemen may you see ... that vertue is not measured by birth but by action; that younger brethren though inferiour in yeares, yet may be superiour to honours; that concord is the sweetest conclusion, and amitie betwixt brothers more forceable than fortune" (pp. 474–75).

supplanted; he is converted, reintegrated, confirmed. In the subplot of *King Lear*, the unbrotherly struggle for mastery and possession is resolved by fratricide; the comic resolution of *As You Like It* depends instead upon an expansion of opportunities for mastery and possession.

# VII

In Lodge's *Rosalynde*, the crude heroic theme of *Gamelyn* is already fused with the elegant love theme of Renaissance pastorals. In constructing a romantic comedy of familial and sexual tension resolved in brotherhood and marriage, Shakespeare gives new complexity and cohesiveness to his narrative source. The struggle of elder and younger brothers is not simply duplicated; it is inverted. In the younger generation, the elder brother abuses the younger; in the older generation, the younger abuses the elder. The range of experience and affect is thereby enlarged, and the protest against primogeniture is firmly balanced by its reaffirmation. Myth, Scripture, and Shakespearean drama record "the bond crack'd betwixt son and father" (*King Lear*, I. ii. 113–14). Hostilities between elder and younger brothers and between fathers and sons are homologous: "Yea, and the brother shal deliver the brother to death, and the father the sonne, and the children shal rise against their parents, and shal cause them to dye" (Mark xiii. 14). Because in *As You Like It* the doubling and inversion of fraternal conflict links generations, the relationship of brother and brother can be linked to the relationship of father and son. In the process of atonement, the two families and two generations of men are doubly and symmetrically bound: the younger brother weds the daughter of the elder brother, and the elder brother weds the daughter of the younger brother. They create the figure of *chiasmus*. Whatever vicarious benefit *As You Like It* brings to younger brothers and to youths, it is not achieved by perverting or destroying the bonds between siblings and between generations, but by transforming and renewing them— *through marriage*.

In Arden, Orlando divides his time between courting Rosalind (who is played by Ganymede, who is played by Rosalind) and courting the old Duke who is Rosalind's father. Celia teases Rosalind about the sincerity of Orlando's passion, the truth of his feigning, by reminding her of his divided loyalties: "He attends here in the forest on the Duke your father" (III. iv. 29–30). Rosalind, who clearly resents that she must share Orlando's attentions with her father, responds: "I met the Duke yesterday and had much question with him. He asked me of what parentage I was: I told him of as good as he, so he laughed and let me go. But what talk we of fathers, when there is such a man as Orlando?" (III. iv. 31–35). Celia has already transferred her loyalties from her father to Rosalind; Rosalind is transferring hers from her father and from Celia to Orlando. But she withholds her identity from her lover in order to test and to taunt him. In the forest, while Orlando guilelessly improves his place in the patriarchal order, Rosalind wittily asserts her independence of it. Rosalind avoids her father's recognition and establishes her own household within the forest; Orlando desires the Duke's recognition and gladly serves him in his forest-court.

It is only after he has secured a place within the old Duke's benign all-male community that Orlando begins to play the lover and the poet: "Run, run Orlando, carve on every tree / The fair, the chaste, and unexpressive she" (III. ii. 9–10):

> But upon the fairest boughs,
> Or at every sentence end,
> Will I Rosalinda write,
> Teaching all that read to know
> The quintessence of every sprite
> Heaven would in little show.
> Therefore Heaven Nature charg'd
> That one body should be fill'd
> With all graces wide-enlarg'd.
> Nature presently distill'd
> Helen's cheek, but not her heart,
> Cleopatra's majesty,
> Atalanta's better part,
> Sad Lucretia's modesty.
> Thus Rosalind of many parts
> By heavenly synod was devis'd,
> Of many faces, eyes, and hearts,
> To have the touches dearest priz'd.
> Heaven would that she these gifts should have,
> And I to live and die her slave.
>
> (ll. 132–51)

The Petrarchan lover "writes" his mistress or "carves" her in the image of his own desire, incorporating virtuous feminine stereotypes and scrupulously excluding what is sexually threatening. The lover masters his mistress by inscribing her within his own discourse; he worships a deity of his own making and under his control. When Rosalind-Ganymede confronts this "fancy-monger" (III. ii. 354–55) who "haunts the forest . . . deifying the name of Rosalind" (ll. 350, 353–54), she puts a question to him: "But are you so much in love as your rhymes speak?" (l.386). Rosalind and Touchstone interrogate and undermine self-deceiving amorous rhetoric with bawdy wordplay and relentless insistence upon the power and inconstancy of physical desire. All the love-talk in the play revolves around the issue of mastery in the shifting social relationship between the sexes: in courtship, maidens suspect the faithfulness of their suitors; in wedlock, husbands suspect the faithfulness of their wives. The poems of feigning lovers and the horns of cuckolded husbands are the complementary preoccupations of Arden's country copulatives.

Consider the crucially-placed brief scene (IV. ii) which is barely more than a song inserted between the betrothal scene of Orlando and Rosalind-Ganymede and the scene in which Oliver comes to Rosalind bearing the bloody napkin. In IV. i, Rosalind mocks her tardy lover with talk of an emblematic snail: "He brings his destiny with him. . . . Horns—which such as you fain to be beholding to your wives for" (ll. 54–55, 57–58). Touchstone has already resigned himself to the snail's destiny with his own misogynistic logic: "As horns are odious, they are necessary. It is said, many a man knows no end of his goods. Right. Many a man has good horns and knows no end of them. Well, that is the dowry of his wife, 'tis none of his own getting" (III. iii. 45–49). Now, in IV.ii, Jaques transforms Rosalind's jibes into ironic male self-mockery: "He that killed the deer" is to have the horns set on his head "for a branch of victory" (l. 5). Jaques calls for a song—"'Tis no matter how it be in tune, so it makes noise enough" (ll. 8–9). The rowdy horn song is a kind of *charivari* or "rough music," traditionally the form of ridicule to which cuckolds and others who offended the community's moral standards were subjected.[46] This *charivari*, however, is also a song of consolation and good fellowship, for not only the present "victor" but all his companions "shall bear this burden" (ll. 12–13).

*Take thou no scorn to wear the horn.*
*It was a crest ere thou wast born.*
*Thy father's father wore it,*

46. On *charivari* and cuckoldry, see the masterful 1976 Neale Lecture in English History by Keith Thomas, "The Place of Laughter in Tudor and Stuart England," published in *The Times Literary Supplement*, 21 January 1977, pp. 77–81. Students of Shakespearean comedy would do well to bear in mind Thomas' point that "laughter has a social dimension. Jokes are a pointer to joking situations, areas of structural ambiguity in society itself, and their subject-matter can be a revealing guide to past tensions and anxieties." From this perspective, "Tudor humour about shrewish and insatiable wives or lascivious widows was a means of confronting the anomalies of insubordinate female behaviour which constantly threatened the actual working of what was supposed to be a male-dominated marital system. Hence the ... obsession with cuckoldry" (p. 77).

*And thy father bore it.*
*The horn, the horn, the lusty horn,*
*Is not a thing to laugh to scorn.*

(ll. 14–19)

The play's concern with patriarchal lineage and the hallmarks of gentility is here transformed into an heraldic celebration of the horn—instrument of male potency and male degradation—which marks all men as kinsmen. Thus, although cuckoldry implies the uncertainty of paternity, the song celebrates the paradox that it is precisely the common destiny they share with the snail that binds men together—father to son, brother to brother. Through the metaphor of hunting (with its wordplays on "deer" and "horns") and the medium of song, the threat that the power of insubordinate women poses to the authority of men is transformed into an occasion for affirming and celebrating patriarchy and fraternity.

After the mock-marriage (IV. i) in which they have indeed plighted their troth, Rosalind-Ganymede exuberantly teases Orlando about the shrewishness and promiscuity he can expect from his wife. Naively romantic Orlando abruptly leaves his threatening Rosalind in order "to attend the Duke at dinner" (IV. i. 170). On his way from his cruel mistress to his kind patron, Orlando encounters his own brother. It is hardly insignificant that Shakespeare changes the details of the fraternal recognition scene to include an aspect of sexual differentiation wholly absent from Lodge's romance. He adds the snake which wreathes itself around Oliver's neck; and he makes it into an insidious female, "who with her head, nimble in threats, approach'd/The opening of his mouth" (IV.iii. 109–10). Furthermore, he changes Lodge's lion into a lioness whose nurturing and aggressive aspects are strongly and ambivalently stressed: "a lioness, with udders all drawn dry" (l.114); "the suck'd and hungry lioness" (l.126). Orlando has retreated in the face of Rosalind's verbal aggressiveness. He has wandered through the forest, "chewing the food of sweet and bitter fancy" (l.101), to seek the paternal figure who has nurtured him. Instead, he has found Oliver in a dangerously passive condition, threatened by a double source of oral aggression.

Oliver's fantastic narrative suggests a transformation of the sexual conflict initiated by Rosalind when she teases Orlando in IV. i. Rosalind and the lioness are coyly linked in the exchange between the lovers at their next meeting:

ROSALIND  O my dear Orlando, how it grieves me to see
thee wear thy heart in a scarf!
ORLANDO  It is my arm.
ROSALIND  I thought thy heart had been wounded
with the claws of a lion.

278

ORLANDO Wounded it is, but with the eyes of a lady.

(V.ii. 19–23)

The chain which Rosalind bestows upon Orlando at their first meeting ("Wear this for me" [I.ii. 236]) is the mark by which Celia identifies him in the forest ("And a chain, that you once wore, about his neck" [III. ii. 178]). The "green and gilded snake" (IV. iii. 108) encircling Oliver's neck is a demonic parody of the emblematic stage property worn by his brother throughout the play. The gynephobic response to Rosalind is split into the erotic serpent and the maternal lioness, while Orlando is split into his victimized brother and his heroic self. Orlando's mastery of the lioness ("Who quickly fell before him" [IV. iii. 131]) is, then, a symbolic mastery of Rosalind's challenge to Orlando. But it is also a triumph of fraternal "kindness" (l. 128) over the fratricidal impulse. Relationships between elder and younger brothers and between fathers and sons are purified by what the text suggests is a kind of matricide, a triumph of men over female powers. Thus the killing of the lioness may also symbolize a repudiation of the consanguinity of Orlando and Oliver. If this powerful female—the carnal source of siblings—is destroyed, both fraternity and paternity can be reconceived as male relationships unmediated by woman, relationships of the spirit rather than of the flesh. Orlando's heroic act, distanced and framed in an allegorical narrative, condenses aspects of both the romantic plot and the sibling plot. And these plots are themselves the complementary aspects of a single social and dramatic process.

Before Orlando is formally married to Rosalind at the end of the play, he has reaffirmed his fraternal and filial bonds in communion with other men. Orlando's rescue of Oliver from the she-snake and the lioness frees the brothers' capacity to give and to receive love. Now Oliver can "fall in love" with Celia; and now Orlando "can live no longer by thinking" (V.ii.50) about Rosalind. Oliver asks his younger brother's consent to marry, and resigns to him his birthright: "My father's house and all the revenue that was old Sir Rowland's will I estate upon you, and here live and die a shepherd" (ll.10–12).[47] Orlando agrees with understandable alacrity: "You have my consent. Let your wedding be tomorrow" (ll.13–14). Marriage, the social institution at the heart of comedy, serves to ease or eliminate fraternal strife. And fraternity, in turn, serves as a defense against the threat men feel from women.

47. Of course, Oliver's gallant gesture of social and economic deference to his youngest brother (a spontaneous reversal of the primogeniture rule into the ultimogeniture rule) cannot be made good until there is a profound change in the society from which they have fled. Oliver's lands and revenues are no longer his to give to Orlando; it is because of Orlando that Frederick has confiscated them.

Rosalind-as-Ganymede and Ganymede-as-Rosalind—the woman out of place—exerts an informal organizing and controlling power over affairs in the forest. But this power lapses when she relinquishes her male disguise and formally acknowledges her normal status as daughter and wife: "I'll have no father, if you be not he./I'll have no husband, if you be not he" (V.iv. 121–22). In a ritual gesture of surrender, she assumes the passive role of mediatrix between the Duke and Orlando:

[*To the Duke.*] To you I give myself, for I am yours.
[*To Orlando.*] To you I give myself, for I am yours.

(V.iv. 115–16)

The Duke's paternal bond to Orlando is not established through the natural fertility of a mother but through the supernatural virginity of a daughter: "Good Duke receive thy daughter,/Hymen from heaven brought her" (V.iv. 110–11). The play is quite persistent in creating strategies for subordinating the flesh to the spirit, and female powers to male controls. Hymen's marriage rite gives social sanction to the lovers' mutual desire. But the atonement of man and woman also implies the social subordination of wife to husband. Rosalind's exhilarating mastery of herself and others has been a compensatory "holiday humor," a temporary, inversionary rite of misrule, whose context is a transfer of authority, property, and title from the Duke to his prospective male heir. From the perspective of the present argument, the romantic love plot serves more than its own ends: it is also the means by which other actions are transformed and resolved. In his unions with the Duke and with Rosalind, Orlando's social elevation is confirmed. Such a perspective does not deny the comedy its festive magnanimity; it merely reaffirms that Shakespearean drama

**48.** Several generations of critics—most of them men, and quite infatuated with Rosalind themselves—have stressed the exuberance and ignored the containment. Much the same may be said of some recent feminist critics (see, for example, Juliet Dusinberre, *Shakespeare and the Nature of Women* [London: Macmillan, 1975]), although they approach the character in another spirit. The "feminism" of Shakespearean comedy seems to me more ambivalent in tone and more ironic in form than such critics have wanted to believe. *Contra* Dusinberre, Linda T. Fitz emphasizes that "the English Renaissance institutionalized, where it did not invent, the restrictive marriage-oriented attitude toward women that feminists have been struggling against ever since. ...The insistent demand for the right—nay, obligation—of women to be happpily married arose as much in reaction against women's intractable pursuit of independence as it did in reaction against Catholic ascetic philosophy" ("'What Says the Married Woman?' Marriage Theory and Feminism in the English Renaissance," *Mosaic*, 13, no. 2 [Winter 1980], 1–22; quotations from pp. 11, 18). A provocative Renaissance context for Shakespeare's Rosalind is to be found in the essay, "Women on Top," in Natalie Zemon Davis, *Society and Culture in Early Modern France* (Stanford: Stanford Univ. Press, 1975), pp. 124–51.

registers the form and pressure of Elizabethan experience. If *As You Like It* is a vehicle for Rosalind's exuberance, it is also a structure for her containment.[48]

Jaques de Boys, "the second son of old Sir Rowland" (V.iv. 151), enters suddenly at the end of the play. This Shakespearean whimsy fits logically into the play's comic process. As the narrator of Frederick's strange eventful history, Jaques brings the miraculous news that resolves the conflict between his own brothers as well as the conflict between the brother-dukes. As Rosalind mediates the affinity of father and son, so Jaques—a brother, rather than a mother—mediates the kinship of eldest and youngest brothers; he is, in effect, the incarnate middle term between Oliver and Orlando. The Duke welcomes him:

> Thou offer'st fairly to thy brothers' wedding;
> To one his lands withheld, and to the other
> A land itself at large, a potent dukedom.
>
> (V.iv. 166–68)

Jaques' gift celebrates the wedding of his brothers to their wives and to each other. Solutions to the play's initial conflicts are worked out between brother and brother, father and son—among men. Primogeniture is reaffirmed in public and private domains: the Duke, newly restored to his own authority and possessions, now restores the de Boys patrimony to Oliver. The aspirations and deserts of the youngest brother are rewarded when the Duke acknowledges Orlando as his own heir, the successor to property, power, and title that far exceed Oliver's birthright. The eldest brother regains the authority due him by primogeniture at the same time that the youngest brother is freed from subordination to his sibling and validated in his claim to the perquisites of gentility.

With his patrimony restored and his marriage effected, Oliver legitimately assumes the place of a patriarch and emerges into full social adulthood; he is now worthy to be the son and heir of Sir Rowland de Boys. Orlando, on the other hand, has proved himself worthy to become son and heir to the Duke. Thomas Wilson, another Elizabethan younger brother, made the bitter misfortune of primogeniture the spur to personal achievement: "This I must confess doth us good someways, for it makes us industrious to apply ourselves to letters or to armes, whereby many time we become my master elder brothers' masters, or at least their betters in honour and reputacion."[49] Unlike Thomas Wilson, Shakespeare's Orlando is spectacularly successful, and his success is won more by spontaneous virtue than by

---

49. Wilson, *State of England, 1600*, p. 24.

industry. But like Wilson's, Orlando's accomplishments are those of a gentleman and a courtier. Unlike most Elizabethan younger sons, Orlando is not forced to descend to commerce or to labor to make his way in the world. He succeeds by applying himself to the otiose courtship of his mistress and his prince. Although the perfection of his social identity is deferred during the Duke's lifetime, Orlando's new filial subordination is eminently beneficent. It grants him by affinity what he has been denied by kinship: the social advancement and sexual fulfillment of which youths and younger sons were so frequently deprived. The de Boys brothers atone together when the eldest replaces a father and the youngest recovers a father.

# VIII

Social and dramatic decorum require that, "to work a comedy kindly, grave old men should instruct, young men should show the imperfections of youth."[50] London's city fathers, however, were forever accusing the theaters and the plays of corrupting rather than instructing youth: "We verely think plays and theaters to be the cheif cause . . . of . . . disorder & lewd demeanours which appear of late in young people of all degrees."[51] Shakespeare's play neither preaches to youths nor incites them to riot. In the world of its Elizabethan audience, the form of Orlando's experience may indeed have functioned as a collective compensation, a projection for the wish-fulfillment fantasies of younger brothers, youths, and all who felt themselves deprived by their fathers or their fortunes. But Orlando's mastery of adversity could also provide support and encouragement to the ambitious individuals who identified with his plight. The play may have fostered strength and perseverance as much as it facilitated pacification and escape. For the large number of youths in Shakespeare's audience—firstborn and younger siblings, gentle and base—the performance may have been analogous to a rite of passage, helping to ease their dangerous and prolonged journey from subordination to identity, their difficult transition from the child's part to the adult's.

My subject has been the complex interrelationship of brothers, fathers, and sons in *As You Like It*. But I have suggested that the play's concern with relationships among men is only artificially separable from its concern with relationships between men and women. The androgynous Rosalind—boy actor and princess—addresses Shakespeare's

---

**50.** George Whetstone, Epistle Dedicatory to *Promos and Cassandra* (1578), quoted in Madeleine Doran, *Endeavors of Art* (Madison: Univ. of Wisconsin Press, 1954), p. 220. **51.** From a document (1595) in the "Dramatic Records of the City of London," quoted in Harbage, *Shakespeare's Audience*, p. 104.

heterosexual audience in an epilogue: "My way is to conjure you, and I'll begin with the women. I charge you, O women, for the love you bear to men, to like as much of this play as please you. And I charge you, O men, for the love you bear to women—as I perceive by your simpering none of you hates them—that between you and the women the play may please" (V.iv. 208–14). Through the subtle and flexible strategies of drama—in puns, jokes, games, disguises, songs, poems, fantasies—*As You Like It* expresses, contains, and discharges a measure of the strife between the men and the women. Shakespeare's comedy manipulates the differential social relationships between the sexes, between brothers, between father and son, master and servant, lord and subject. It is by the conjurer's art that Shakespeare manages to reconcile the social imperatives of hierarchy and difference with the festive urges toward leveling and atonement. The intense and ambivalent personal bonds upon which the play is focused—bonds between brothers and between lovers—affect each other reciprocally and become the means of each other's resolution. And as the actions within the play are dialectically related to each other, so the world of Shakespeare's characters is dialectically related to the world of his audience. *As You Like It* is both a theatrical *reflection* of social conflict and a theatrical *source* of social conciliation.

# COUNTRY MATTERS: *AS YOU LIKE IT* AND THE PASTORAL-BASHING IMPULSE

*Linda Woodbridge*

UDIENCES DELIGHT in *As You Like It,* but critics often get twitchy about it, which seems odd. The play after all features cross-dressing, the biggest female speaking role in all of Shakespeare, an intriguingly intimate friendship between two women, an exploited agricultural laborer, and a set speech on animal rights—one would think that this comedy offered satisfactions for gender theorists, feminists, queer theorists, Marxists, and eeocritics alike. What's not to like in *As You Like It?*

The answer, I think, is fairly straightforward: what's not to like is the pastoralism. For a couple of centuries now but especially in recent decades, a wide spectrum of critics has heaped scorn upon the bucolic realm of pastoral, and Shakespeare's most pastoral play has come in for its share of scorn. Shakespeare being who he is, critics are seldom as hard on him as on other writers of pastoral, and some exonerate him entirely by recasting *As You Like It* as itself a sneer at pastoral: Shakespeare is not himself conventional, but uses conventions playfully, self-consciously, mockingly. He writes not pastoral but antipastoral. This move in itself, of course, drives another nail into pastoral's coffin. Excavating the cultural meanings of the critical vendetta against pastoral, and exploring how it plays out in *As You Like It,* may give us not only a fresh perspective on the play, but a route into the enigma of pastoral bashing and what it says about our culture.

## *AS YOU LIKE IT* AND CRITICAL ANTIPASTORALISM

Critics often complain of a lack of action in *As You Like It,* beginning in act 2. It's not so much that they get bored when the wrestling match is over as that they feel uneasy being invited to share in a pastoral life that seems, well, lazy. In this relaxed world, exiled lords entertain each other with songs or gaze thoughtfully into brooks, lovers pin

Woodbridge, Linda. "Country Matters: *As You Like It* and the Pastoral-Bashing Impulse." *Re-Visions of Shakespeare: Essays in Honor of Robert Ornstein.* Ed. Evelyn Gajowski. University of Delaware Press. 2004. 189-214. Used by permission.

poetry to trees, and Jaques and Celia go off to take naps—troubling
evidence of a lack of purposeful action in Arden. Peter Lindenbaum
excoriates pastoral in general for its "life of leisure and freedom from
the cares and responsibilities of the normal world," sternly averring
that responsible Renaissance writers recognized that "in this world of
ours man simply has no time for relaxation or even momentary escape
from the pressing activity of day-to-day living"; Sidney in *Arcadia*
and Shakespeare in *As You Like It* "lodge an objection to the whole
prospect of life in a pastoral setting, to a cast of mind that either seeks
an easy, carefree existence anywhere in our present world or indulges
overmuch in dreams of better times and better places, thereby avoiding full concentration upon the facts of man's present existence."[1] The
shepherd's reprehensible life of ease has offended so many critics that
A. Stuart Daley feels he must explain the habits of sheep to excuse
all the slacking that goes on in an early Arden afternoon: "At midday,
after a long morning of nibbling on the herbage, the animals needed
complete rest, and lay down to ruminate. At noon, a shepherd such as
those in *As You Like It* could expect two or three hours of comparative
freedom. Indeed all English workers had the right to a midday rest,
according to a statute of 1563."[2] The play's adjournment from the
court into a rural world of ease is often belittled as an escapist fantasy.
To avoid being charged with advocating escapism, a responsible author
must "insist upon the need to leave Arcadia," Lindenbaum dictates;[3]
Richard Helgerson insists, "the pastoral world is meant to be left
behind."[4] Critics assume that characters in Arden scramble to get back
to the court: Daley writes, "With the zeal of a reformed sinner, Celia's
fiancé resolves to 'live and die a shepherd'; but his aristocratic calling
obviously forbids the abandonment of his lands and great allies to the
detriment of the commonweal."[5] Critics seem untroubled that *As You
Like It* nowhere articulates this ideal of public service, or that the play
not only leaves open the question of whether Oliver and Celia will stay
in the country, but insists that Duke Frederick and Jaques opt to stay in
Arden—Jaques's decision to stay is given an emphatic position at the very
end of the play. Ignoring all this and focusing on characters who do leave
the pastoral world, Lindenbaum, who is pretty hard on Duke Senior for
using banishment as an excuse for lolling around in the woods, readmits
him to favor when he makes the crucial decision "to leave Arcadia":

> His pastoral dream proves by the end to have been that of a basically
> good man on vacation. His essential moral health is affirmed at the
> play's end by his unhesitating willingness to return to court and
> take up responsible active life in the political world again. This final
> act reflects the whole play's antipastoral argument. The forest is

initially a place of ease, idleness, and escape from normal cares and responsibilities, but that view provides the stimulus for Shakespeare's eventual insistence upon a more active stance.[6]

Albert Cirillo expresses approval that once characters have straightened out their lives, "they can return to the court"; far from pastoral's challenging court values, he sees it the other way around: "the Forest needs the contrast with the court and worldly values to clarify the consciousness of the audience as to the essential illusory quality of the pastoral world."[7]

Renato Poggioli's belief that "the psychological root of the pastoral is a double longing after innocence and happiness, to be recovered not through conversion or regeneration, but merely through a retreat" rings false in *As You Like It*, where Frederick is converted, Oliver regenerated.[8] You'd think the discomfort of Arden, with its wintry wind, would obviate charges of escapism, but critics instead read this as Shakespearean contempt for pastoral. Daley notes that "characters who express an opinion about the Forest of Arden utter mostly dispraise"; taking at face value Touchstone's gripes and Rosalind's "saucy lackey" impertinences, he pronounces "the local women vain and foul and the backwoods dialect lacking in grace and beauty"; the "consistent dispraise of the country" shows that Shakespeare did not intend "a traditional contrast between court and country."[9] But did such dispraise indicate that Shakespeare disdained the country? Traditionally, pastoral figures gain moral authority through asceticism; in pastoral, country harshness obviates charges of hedonism that would undermine pastoral's ability to critique the corruptions of a world of power. Lindenbaum reads dispraise of the country as unhappiness with pastoral, born of frustrated goldenworld expectations, of finding country life "no different from life at court or in the city."[10] Svetlana Makurenkova generalizes about Shakespeare's career, "one may trace throughout the corpus of Shakespeare's work a certain dethroning of idyllic pastoral imagery."[11]

Taking the play's realism for antipastoralism, critics create a no-win situation. Pastorals *do* speak of rural harshness—Meliboeus's dispossession from his farm in Virgil's first eclogue or, in *As You Like It*, Corin's low wages from a churlish absentee master (2.4.75–8) and description of shepherds hands as greasy, work hardened, and "tarr'd over with the surgery of our sheep" (3.2,50–51, 59–60).[12] But such details don't make critics revise their belief that pastoral ignores "real difficulties and hardships" and shuns "realistic description of the actual conditions of country life"; instead, critics consider such realism as "antipastoral sentiment" attributable to frustration at the genre's artificiality and escapism. Cirillo says "every force which would lead to the acceptance of life in Arden as a perfect world is negated by the intrusion of a harsher reality";[13] but the idea of Arden as a perfect world comes only from Cirillo's stereotype that pastorals deal in escapist golden worlds. For such critics, when a pastoral doesn't fit the stereotype, it doesn't negate stereotype but becomes evidence of the author's un happiness with pastoral. This resembles the way that the Renaissance decried as unnatural women who didn't fit its stereotypes, thus preserving the stereotypes intact.

Touchstone finds shepherding "a very vile life" (3.2.16) and many think that his name, implying a test of genuineness, declares him the play's voice of truth. Yet his plans to wriggle out of his marriage discredit him; and anyway, a clown's-eye view of the action is never the whole story in Shakespeare. Against Touchstone's view we have Corin's sensible cultural relativism: "Those that are good manners at the court are as ridiculous in the country as the behavior of the country is most mockable at the court" (3.2.43–46). Touchstone's witty equivocation on "manners" shows how antirural prejudice works: "If thou never wast at court, thou never saw'st good manners; if thou never saw'st good manners; then thy manners must be wicked; and wickedness is sin, and sin is damnation. Thou art in a parlous state, shepherd" (3.2.38–42). The pun has lost its force, since "manners" now means only "etiquette"; in Shakespeare's day it also meant "morals." Considering country etiquette uncouth, courtiers assume that country morals are loose too. Touchstone discovers this untrue of country wench Audrey, who declares (to his disappointment) "I am not a slut" (3.3.35). Orlando too mistakes country manners, expecting violent in hospitality: "I thought that all things had been savage here" (2.7.71). Orlando, says Rawdon Wilson, "fails to understand the nature of Arden"; exiled courtiers need "a period of adjustment to Arden"[14]—a time to revise prejudices about country life?

The play has sometimes been attacked on aesthetic grounds, with complaints that the satiric and the bucolic are awkwardly joined and tonally disjunctive, especially in the person of Jaques, whom critics virulently attack, often on the assumption that a satiric voice doesn't belong in a choir making mellow pastoral music. But satiric voices have always spoken in Arcadia—satire is one thing pastoral is all about. Unwillingness to stomach Jaques echoes criticism of Spenser and Milton for letting sharp attacks on abuses intrude into a pastoral setting. Shakespeare is not alone in being scorned for writing pastoral or praised for allegedly resisting pastoral: the whole pastoral mode has been inimical to our general cultural climate for a good many years now.

## NEW HISTORICISTS VERSUS PASTORAL:
## THE PASSION FOR POWER

It's hard to think of another genre that has been described so patronizingly, attacked so virulently, dismissed so contemptuously over many years. Samuel Johnson called *Lycidas* "a pastoral, easy, vulgar, and therefore disgusting."[15] W. W. Greg said of one of Spenser's eclogues "only a rollicking indifference to its own inanity ... saves it from sheer puerility," and considered eclogues "the type of all that is frigid and artificial in literature," announcing that a "stigma ... attaches to pastoral as, a whole," that even the best pastorals suffer from lack of originality, and that even Lycidas, the best pastoral since Virgil, is so defective that "the form of pastoral instituted by Virgil and handed down without break from the fourteenth century to Milton's own time stand[s] condemned in its most perfect flower."[16] Peter Lindenbaum, disgusted with Sannazaro's representation of Arcadia as "a soothing dwelling place for the troubled human spirit," charges that "the pastoral mode in Sannazaro's hands threatens to become a vehicle for mere indulgence in sentimental feeling."[17] Spenserian retreat from aspiration, Louis Montrose calls "resignation to the poetry of pastoral triviality."[18] Renato Poggioli says pastoral "reduces all human intercourse to an everlasting tête-à-tête."[19] P.V. Krieder thinks the "susceptibilities" of "inexperienced writers" make them "silly victims of an unnatural pastoralism"; he denounces "the tawdry allurements of pastoralism."[20] Feminists too have attacked pastoral: as Lisa Robertson puts it, "Certainly, as a fin de siecle feminist, I cannot in good conscience perform even the simplest political identification with the pastoral genre ... [wherein] the figure of woman appears as eroticized worker—the milkmaid or the shepherdess."[21]

It seems the genre can't put a foot right. If it's political, it is taxed with toadying to repressive regimes; its very attacks on such regimes are inscribed in ideological structures it can't escape. If it speaks of love and spring, it is escapist and trivial. If it treats politics and love, its tone is disjunctive. If its authors are thriving courtiers, they are indicted for hypocrisy in that they praise retired life while living a public life; if they are out of political favor, living in the country, they have a sour grapes attitude. If a pastoral is highly artificial, ignoring agricultural laborers' harsh life, it is suppressing socioeconomic reality; if it includes gritty details of sheep tending, it is called antipastoral, and made an accomplice to its own undoing. Pastoral's very popularity is held against it: the astounding receptivity of readers to legions of Corins, Colins, and Dorindas over centuries—nay, millennia—provokes not praise for the genre's wide appeal and staying power but condemnation for repetitious unoriginality. The charge that pastoral is repetitious is fair in a way, though the sensation of being waterlogged in a sea of oaten piping mainly afflicts those who survey the whole genre; is it fair to adduce against individual pastorals the fact that there are too many pastorals in the world? It would be hard *not* to be repetitious in a mode that has had such a long run as pastoral has—from the ancient Greeks and Romans right through the 1960s. Anyway, the charge is brought selectively against pastoral: other numbingly repetitious genres are tolerated—satire, epigram, sonnet, sermon, or (later) commentaries on football games. The aesthetic complaint about pastoral's repetitiousness seems to mask other causes for distaste. Why the contempt for pastoral? What are the cultural meanings of this vendetta?

The most obvious point of entry into the question is pastoral's relation to a world of power, a feature of the discourse about pastoral since its Greek and Roman beginnings, but most recently of lively interest to new historicists such as Louis Montrose, whose influential essays on Elizabethan pastoral posit its inscription within the ideology of state power. Focusing on court pageants and pastorals produced for Elizabeth on progresses, and extending his critique to all pastorals, Montrose argues that pastoral performs the cultural work of justifying autocratic government, that its authors are state propagandists, encomiasts, sycophants, that Renaissance pastorals mingled "*otium* and *negotium*, holiday and policy"; "Elizabethan pastorals of power combin[ed] intimacy and benignity with authoritarianism."[22] Pastoral professions of power's hollowness, Montrose dismisses as cynical attempts to dissuade lower orders from wanting to share power.

Do propagandistic pageants fairly represent pastoral? It is true that Queen Elizabeth used royal progresses through the countryside to intimate "a beautiful relation between rich and poor," in Empson's sardonic formulation of pastoral's primary mystification. But the pastoral mode can also be dissident and oppositional, attacking specific power abuses.[23] Over centuries, many authors have used pastoral to criticize politics, to attack political and clerical abuses and meddle in current affairs. Virgilian pastoral had implications for current events of its day—civil wars between Brutus and Cassius. Mantuan's pastorals attacked abuses of the Roman church; Naldo Naldi wrote eclogues on the house of Medici; Ariosto wrote an eclogue on the 1506 conspiracy against Alfonso d'Este; Spenser in *The Shepheardes Calender* criticized the proposed French marriage of Queen Elizabeth; Francis Quarles's eclogues dealt with current religious controversies. Pastoral's country cousin, the Georgic, was indeed employed in eighteenthcentury justifications of imperial colonization, but it was also employed to criticize such colonization, as in the ending of "Autumn" in James Thomson's *The Seasons*, 1746.[24] The sixteenth century assumed that pastorals critiqued power: George Puttenham wrote that eclogues "under the veil of homely persons, and in rude speeches insinuate and glance at greater matters, and such as perchance had not been safe to have been disclosed in any other sort."[25]

And pastoral not only attacks specific abuses of power but challenges the power ethic itself. It has a long tradition of discrediting the supposed pleasures of power. The first set of pastoral eclogues in English, by Alexander Barclay, begins with three eclogues on the miseries of court life; the subtitle features "the Miseries of Courtiers and Courts of All Princes in General."[26]

New historicists have also read pastoral as an attempt to curry favor with those in power by justifying that power for them. When pastoral is not read as outright propaganda, as is the case with Queen Elizabeth's pastoral entertainments, it is often read as some courtier's sycophantic bid for career advancement. From Virgil's praise of Caesar onwards, pastoral *has* at times been encomiastic, and no one would deny that the pastoral mode has its sycophantic face. *Iam redit et Virgo, redeunt Saturnia regna;/iam nova progenies caelo demittitur alto* might be a motto for the Elizabethan age: "the Virgin and the rule of Saturn are now returning; a new offspring is now sent from heaven." The words are Virgil's, but just as Christianity took this image from Virgil as a prophecy of the Virgin Mary, so Elizabeth appropriated for herself his image of the Virgin Astraea, and mythmakers heralded her reign as a return of Saturn's golden, pastoral age. This crucial iconography comes from a pastoral, Virgil's fourth eclogue; through it, the Elizabethan explosion of pastoral was implicated in the machinery of state propaganda.

But granted that the Elizabethan propaganda machine did absorb some pastoral writers, the question remains, why pastoral? Why not use trappings of epic or lyric in royal entertainments, rather than shepherds? I think pastoral needed to be co-opted because of its great potential for criticizing governmental abuses, the centralizing policies at the heart of the Tudor project, and the power ethic itself. An autocratic regime that feared criticism needed to disable pastoral. But it was less successful at this than many think. Pastoral has served many purposes that new historicists ignore: why have they gazed so exclusively upon pastoral's more sycophantic face, generalizing to the entire mode from one unsavory posture, seeing "royal pastoral" as contaminating the whole mode?

For example, Montrose and others have read *The Shepheardes Calender* as Spenser's bid for royal favor and career advancement; but much evidence in the poem points in a contrary direction. This pastoral actually criticizes Queen Elizabeth, treading on dangerous ground in its references to Catholic perfidy in the 1572 Huguenot massacre by Charles IX, brother of the duke of Alencon with whom Elizabeth was currently contemplating marriage (*May* eclogue), and the *July* eclogue criticizes the Queen for repressive policies particularly the house arrest of Archbishop Grindal.[27] As Paul Alpers says, "a poet who praised [Grindal's] virtues and lamented his misfortunes was not playing it safe."[28] Montrose astonishingly recognizes July as "a boldly explicit allusion to Elizabeth's reprimand for Grindal's outspokenness that is thoroughly sympathetic to the Archbishop" without modifying his contention that the *Calender* is politically sycophantic; he simply reasserts that the repressive regime curtailed free speech, leaving the reader to wonder why it did not curtail *July*.[29] Further, Montrose shanghais the *February* eclogue into the tradition of sycophancy toward the Tudors by reading the oak/briar fable, I think, upside down: ignoring plain signs identifying the oak with the Catholic Church, the briar with the Tudors, he takes the oak as the Tudor establishment.[30] That so penetrating and logical a writer as Louis Montrose would have risked such strident misinterpretations bespeaks a kind of desperation this poem must be discredited at all costs. *The Shepheardes Calender* appears to me to be a dissident poem, criticizing specific abuses of power and challenging the power ethic itself, condemning those who, prompted by too much "prosperitie," "gape for greedie gouernaunce/And match them selfe with mighty potentates,/Lovers of Lordship" (*May*, 117–24).

Some pastorals, like *The Shepheardes Calender*, challenge the power ethic; others simply evade the world of ambition, offering country contentment as a mute alternative to ambition's frantic frenzies. A move like Montrose's, which relocates the dissident *Shepheardes Calender* within a power-hungry world, makes its protestations against ambition appear merely hypocritical. The whole genre suffers when such major texts are discredited as bids for preferment, inscribed in a court culture of ambitious strivings; this move disables pastoral's challenge to the world of ambition. Why new historicists need to do this is obvious: their whole program is predicated on the assumption that power is what matters in human affairs. As an antipower genre, pastoral is an enemy.

The hypocrisy ascribed to pastoral authors—using an antipower genre to curry favor with the powerful—has rubbed off on the shepherds, undermining their moral authority. This matters to pastoral more than to other modes: pastoral's critique of worldly values depends on the moral authority its speakers gain by refusing participation in the world they indict. As Paul Alpers says, "The literary shepherd's sufficiency to great matters is due to his simplicity and innocence; these confer on him a moral authority."[31] We are seldom interested in the moral authority of a sonnet speaker or the narrator of a prose fiction; but in pastoral it is everything. If a pastoral persona is implicated in the world of power and ambition, the pastoral crumbles.

Even when a pastoral is acknowledged to be oppositional, its dissidence has often been judged politically wrongheaded. Opposition to a centralized court has been seen as atavistic—as powerful central governments emerged all over Europe, the Tudor centralizing project worked to break the baronial power based in the country.

Pastoral satire on the court's emasculated aristocracy is dismissed as nostalgia for "real" feudalism. Even if a pastoral is admittedly political and its political heart is conceded to be in the right place, it may suffer a final dismissal as being ineffective as a means of protest. Some argue that pastoral emasculates itself by indirectness, especially by allegory. Alpers argues that giving moral authority to the powerless renders such authority toothless, since the powerless must speak with impotent indirection. And indirection, for Montrose, spells duplicity: though allegory is "an obfuscation necessary to circumvent governmental hostility to all expressions of dissent or controversy,"[32] he still despises pastoral for such obfuscations.

It's easy to be brave at our historical remove. John Stubbs had his hand cut off for publishing a criticism of the Queen's contemplated French marriage, a criticism that Spenser—in the same year and with the same printer—got away with making in *The Shepheardes Calender*, which was couched in allegory. Montrose judges pastoral "a literary mode specialized to the conditions of a complex, contentious, and authoritarian civilization—a fallen world of duplicity and innuendo. Its enforced deceptiveness epitomizes the very condition it seeks to amend."[33] He concludes that such ignominious "indirection and dissimulation are the rhetorical techniques of poetry and policy."[34] In assuming that only direct frontal assaults really count as dissent, Alpers and Montrose insist on a brash courage I'm not sure we have a right to demand of those living in a repressive society. And dismissing indirection as a literary technique disables not only pastoral but a good deal of literature. Is "A Modest Proposal" less effective dissent than an outraged letter to the authorities? Swift tried straightforward polemical pamphlets; but after the failure of such frontal assaults he took up a more potent weapon, irony.

I have argued that pastoral figures gain moral authority by refusing participation in the world they indict. Removal from the court to the country is paradoxically a condition of making credible critiques of the court. Failure to accept this necessary doubleness, this absent presence in the world of power, helps account for persistent complaints about pastorals' uncouth diction and tonal disunity. Pastoral is damned if it does and damned if it doesn't: couched in artificial court language, it is denounced for evading the material reality of peasant life; couched in rustic diction, it is dismissed as lacking the decorum of serious literature.[35] Dr. Johnson dismissed Spenser's rustic diction as a "studied barbarity"[36] and complained of Milton's using religious allegory in a pastoral: the disjunction of Lycidas's being "now a feeder of sheep, and afterwards an ecclesiastical pastor" is "indecent." It was "improper," Johnson decreed, "to give the title of a pastoral to verses in which the speakers, after the slight mention of their flocks, fall to complaints of errors in the church and corruptions in the government."[37] The unity issue is crucial: readers from Johnson on have faulted pastoral for yoking together by violence bucolic contentment and satire on abuses. Yet the two are intimately linked: it is by eschewing power and comfort that one gains authority to attack the powerful and comfortable. One must depart from power's premises to find the perspective and authority to unmask power's abuses, pretenses, futility. Seeing artistic disunity in pastoral's double tone—contentment in a simple life and criticism of the powerful—destroys the pastoral mode.

The pastoral persona occupies a subject position uniquely suited to challenging the power ethic: a shepherd's critique had moral weight because s/he wasn't implicated in power. But didn't that mean forgoing power? Creating "pastoral counter-worlds," Montrose argues, "is always suspect—potentially dangerous, escapist, or regressive. To make poetry a vehicle of transcendence is tacitly to acknowledge its ethical and political impotence."[38] The dilemma of corrupt implication in power versus irresponsible evasion of power is familiar to those who try to get women into positions of power where they can influence events: they risk reproducing the oppressive, unequal system they oppose. Those who believe that women can oppose the power system only by opting out of it risk lacking the means to change anything. They argue that lack of power is a catastrophe only in a power-obsessed society; the only way to reduce society's obsession with power is for individuals to avoid obsession. But won't the powerful oppress those who eschew power? Others faced with this dilemma, advocates of unilateral disarmament, have argued that someone has to make the first move. However imperfect, cooptable, exploitable the pastoral genre, its merit is that for dismantling oppressive power structures, it offers a position from which to make the first move. It is not a perfect position—it risks political toothlessness—but it is more credible than the position of the powerful. And even if some implicated in power—courtiers or preferment-seekers—choose this subject position, does that necessarily nullify their criticisms or make it less valuable to imagine a less power-obsessed world?

Attacking both royal power and pastoral's critique of royal power creates a damned-if-you-do-and-damned-if-you-don't situation. New historicists cut the ground from under any oppositional stance—one cannot be truly oppositional if one has ever sought social advancement, or values relaxation, or uses irony. As Anne Barton has summed up Stephen Greenblatt's mode of disabling dissent, "what looks to us like subversion in the art of the past is merely something orthodoxy makes strategic use of."[39] Does new historicism really demystify authority, or does it grant authority a mysterious, nearomnipotent power?

Can't criticizing power or articulating an ideal be valuable no matter *who* does it, no matter what their motives or personal lives? It is said that U.S. voters attend not to candidates' policies but to their personalities or private lives, and the same might be said of critics who discredit pastoral if its authors have any link with the world of power. Even Golden Age myths, an extreme manifestation of the pastoral impulse, are not without value—*is* what is irrecoverable in the past (or never existed) necessarily unattainable in the future? Can an ideal, however unrealistic, not at least *correct* reality, creating a synthesis out of the thesis of hierarchical authoritarianism and the antithesis of a classless Golden Age? And if an ideal is worth articulating, how much does it matter who articulates it or how pure his motives?

We are hard on pastoral, but how credible a position for demystifying power do *we* occupy? We are quick to indict the Elizabethan elite, but are we in our tenured positions not ourselves an elite compared to the vast underclasses of our own society? We are nimble at decoding from Elizabethan prefatory epistles the complicity of their authors in a system of court patronage; yet the acknowledgment pages of our scholarly books advertise the elite institutions at which we teach, grants supporting the research, colleagues at prestigious universities who read the manuscript—the appearance of their names is our equivalent of commendatory verses. One can decode such stuff easily enough—authors published by the most prestigious presses, with the most famous friends reading the manuscript, the best fellowships and grants, are those with power in our profession. They are often those who deplore the power and patronage of Elizabeth's time. Does pastoral, that challenger of the life of power and influence, threaten us because it hits too close to home?

## OTHER MOTIVES FOR PASTORAL BASHING

In recent times, literary study has become less preoccupied with power, but other incentives to pastoral bashing remain. Foremost among them is class prejudice. Do we take seriously the passions and

opinions of farm hands? Even Marxist critics accord high seriousness to genres populated by kings and dukes. A variant is city prejudice against the rural. Urban villains get more respectful attention
than kindly rustics. Krieder sniffs at Audrey and William in *As You
Like It*: "These bumpkins are actual shepherds whom, in delusion, the
élite social groups are imitating; the crude life, gross manners, and
dull wits of these uncouth simpletons represent the state of society to
which courtly ladies and gentlemen, in their ignorance, believe they
should like to revert."[40] We don't say aloud that Audrey and William
are only rednecks, but if we aren't too worried about their being taken
advantage of by a courtier, their rustic status—so unlike our own
sophistication—is perhaps not wholly irrelevant.

Second, repugnance for pastoral is the unexamined reaction
of a capitalist, consumer society to a land posited as indifferent to
material goods. Poggioli heaps scorn on pastoral's uncommercial
mentality: "Foremost among the passions that the pastoral opposes
and exposes are those related to the misuse, or merely to the possession, of worldly goods"; it opposes to "an acquisitive society" the
ideal of "contained selfsufficiency," ignoring "industry and trade."[41]
For opposing or ignoring capitalist developments, which indeed were
happening on its bucolic doorstep, pastoral is called reactionary. But
pastoral's unworldliness is often strategic, a mode of critiquing the
crass materialism of a protocapitalist society. Scorn for pastoral's anti-
capitalism emanates most obviously from the political and economic
right; but even opponents of capitalism sometimes judge the countryside an ineffective platform from which to launch salvos against the ills
of an urban society.

But why? Going outside one's own culture can be a precondi-
tion for analyzing its ills. Edward Said argues that Auerbach's exile in
Turkey helped him see European culture with new eyes.[42] And if the
outside place is imaginary, so much the better: the Renaissance iook
an interest in Utopias and the possibility of perfect worlds existing
out in space,[43] and during the sixteenth century, as Sandra Billington
shows, "Misrule entertainments began to draw on the possibilities of
*alterae terrae* for their settings, and the *mundus inversus* changed from
a reductive to an improving concept."[44] Sir Thomas More, in *Utopia*,
went outside Europe *and* reality to reach a standpoint from which to
critique Tudor England's economic and legal ills. Pastoral realms can
operate as such *alterae terrae*. And even when Tudor pastoral left the
world of urban ills behind, there were plenty of economic ills in the
country—enclosures, low agricultural wages, depressions in the textile
industry, rural depopulation. Pastoral does not always ignore these—
the low wages of Corin the shepherd are an issue in *As You Like It*.

A third root of antipastoralism: our workaholic age suffers entrenched resistance to relaxation. In its early days, the Protestant work ethic was still more countercurrent than mainstream: Elizabethans still celebrated some one hundred holidays a year. We moderns have a much worse case of work anxiety than they did. Early modern workers, who put in very long hours, understandably created fantasies of ease. Like the Land of Cockaigne, work-free pastures were a cherished dream, attended with much less guilt than we accord them. Renaissance comedy values sleep; sleeplessness is a plague suffered by *tragic* heroes. Berowne in *Love's Labor's Lost* is aghast at the King's proposed ascetic regimen, which curtails life's most agreeable activities: "O, these are barren tasks, too hard to keep,/Not to see ladies, study, fast, not sleep!" (1.1.47–48). Dogberry speaks for the spirit of comedy in roundly declaring, "I cannot see how sleeping should offend" (*Much Ado* 3.3.40–41). But listen to what modern critics say about ease. Poggioli sneers at ; the convention that "redeems [the shepherd] from the curse of work, Literary shepherds form an ideal kind of leisure class"; "the pastoral imagination exalts the pleasure principle at the expense of the reality principle."[45] Lindenbaum decrees that for Milton, "not even Eden is exempt from strictures against a life of uncomplicated ease and retirement which many in the English Renaissance found suspect."[46] But was it the Renaissance that found ease and retirement suspect, or is it us? Here the Yankee nationality of so many pastoral bashers (Cirillo, Daley, Helgerson, Montrose, Lindenbaum) is suggestive: Americans are infamous for having the longest work week and fewest holidays of any civilized nation on earth.

A grim suspicion of relaxation, inherited from Puritan forebears, disables pastoral for us. But the Renaissance didn't condemn shepherds for luxurious ease. Some pastoral writers saw shepherding as real work; others found it a life of ease but didn't condemn that. Shepherds in *The Shepheardes Calender* work long hours guarding sheep, suffer bitterly from winter while working outside, agonize about whether to take a break to enjoy the holiday sports of May; before they can relax enough to tell a moral fable, they must arrange for a lad to guard their flocks. It looks like work to me; the poem takes it seriously as an important responsibility, both in its literal agrarian sense and its allegorical sense as ministerial or governing duties. That looking after sheep isn't work is probably the attitude of those who have never tried looking after sheep; the same goes at the allegorical level, where shepherds represent bishops or secular administrators. Governing is hard work. Other pastoral writers do represent sheeptending as a relatively easeful, stress free life, and they aren't at all bothered by this. What with our high pressure, highachieving modern sensibility, such an attitude drives us crazy. Many charge that when pastoral shepherds (unlike real peasants) moon around feeling lovelorn or unproductively carping at the clergy, their fantasy world reproduces the idle court from which pastorals emanated—leisured aristocracy, disdainful of manual labor, Poggioli is outraged by this dream of bucolic idleness: "Wishful thinking is the weakest of all moral and religious resorts," he fulminates, and pastoral is but a "retirement to the periphery of life, an attempt to charm away the cares of the world through the sympathetic magic of a rustic disguise."[47] By all means, we must focus squarely on "the cares of the world" at every waking moment!

The issue is not only laziness but also a morally reprehensible evasion of an everyday reality full of trouble. Lindenbaum dubs pastoral a "realm of wish-fulfillment"; he disdains its wishing away of evil, its "miraculous events" such as "the immediate conversion of (Shakespearean) villains as soon as they enter a forest."[48] Pastoral is, in short, escapism.

Well, so what? The Renaissance, I think, wasn't nearly as hard on escapism as we are. If life is harsh and intolerable, why not escape? In Shakespearean comedy Orlando, Camillo, Pericles, and many others find happiness by running away from trouble. Human history is a tale of great escapes, from the biblical exodus to the great refugee migrations of our day, and escaping heroes populate myth and literature—the holy family's flight into Egypt, Aeneas's flight from Troy, the heroes of American literature forever lighting out for the territories. To assume that life is dreadful and then to dictate that we must stay where we are and face up to its full dread fulness at all times, not even yielding to an occasional fantasy of escape, is bleak doctrine indeed. There is something disturbingly humorless, regimented, and censorious about views that approve only of pastorals that manfully resist the escapist urge, decreeing that the shepherd "is morally obligated to leave his pastoral bower."[49]

A fourth impetus to pastoral bashing is our valorization of public over private life. Poggioli denounces pastoral's concern with private life as narcissistic solipsism; Montrose equates private life with "the comforts and safety of mediocrity."[50] Such devaluing of private life has gender implications: the domestic sphere has long been constructed as female and great ideological work has gone into confining women to the home. In this gendered schema, pastoral's opting out of the world of power and public life is effeminizing, emasculating. Pastoral, especially compared with epic or tragedy, has strongly valorized female presence—shepherdesses, milkmaids shepherds in love with lasses. The shepherd's job is a nurturing, one, a kind of ovine babysitting—and we all know how society values child care. Women writers, too, were especially attracted to pastoral: as Josephine Roberts points out, "the seventeenth century witnessed an ... outpouring of pastoral writing by such figures as Aemilia Lanyer, Mary Wroth, Elizabeth Brackley, Jane Cavendish, An Collins, Margaret Cavendish, Katherine Philips, Elizabeth Wilmot, and Aphra Behn."[51]

As the female is often devalued, some read pastoral love lyrics allegorically because they can't believe poets would attend to anything as lowly as love—reading "private" allegorically as "public" seems to make it worthier of their attention. Montrose deems the public life the only important life. That Queen Elizabeth was female obscures what a masculine definition of the important life this is: most Renaissance women had no access to public careers. The *Shepherd's Calender's* concerns, Montrose says, are "erotic desire and social ambition," but erotic desire, inhabiter of a private realm, is really a displacement of ambition, which belongs to the public world. What seems to be love is really politics; private is really public. The assumption is that public life alone merits attention. Montrose extends this widely, finding "an encoding principle that is undoubtedly operative in much of Elizabethan literature: amorous motives displace or subsume forms of desire, frustration, and resentment other than the merely sexual."[52] Elizabethans would leap on a facile reduction of love to "the merely sexual"—Hamlet's "country matters"; but what startles me is not the "sexual" so much as the "merely," which dismisses everything in life but politics and public striving, erasing at a stroke nearly every woman from early modern history. It translates much Renaissance literature too—the loves of Romeo and Juliet, Othello and Desdemona, the Duchess of Malfi and Antonio, become politics in disguise; the merely sexual, the merely private, is not important enough to be a subject of literature.

Helgerson shows how those with a gentleman's education were expected to give up the youthful folly of writing poetry (especially love poetry) in favor of public service, but this expectation was hardly impossible to resist. As Helgerson shows, Spenser during a life of public service never gave up poetry and love. Shakespeare had no gentleman's education, and his characters don't speak of an ideal of public service. Does anyone in Shakespeare counsel that it is anyone's *duty* to seek office? (Volumnia, perhaps; but does *Coriolanus* endorse her views?) Shakespeare presents political power more as a desired good than a public duty; only once in office do rulers discover that it isn't as much fun as in fairy tales. No one needs to urge others toward a duty of power: there are plenty of candidates. If one or two potential or former rulers shirk in a sheep cote or forest, nobody minds.

A fifth cultural obstacle is our preference for action over contemplation, related to the public/private issue because public was linked with action, private with inaction. Lindenbaum ascribes Sidney's alleged "opposition to pastoralism" to the "kind of Humanist training he had received, designed to prepare him for active service to his state and disposing him against any kind of life that might resemble inactivity."[53] Again, anxiety about ease: even though we inhabit the pastorally tinged groves of academe, for us contemplation (unless dignified by a title like basic research) doesn't seem like work. Hallett Smith shows how the Renaissance identified the generic poles of epic and pastoral with the active and contemplative lives;[54] the Renaissance usually (though not always) valued active over contemplative, and here we have outdone them. And again the gender issue—the active life has always been masculine, with women often seen as a drag on purposive activity.

The Renaissance placed literary genres on a spectrum from active to contemplative. The preference for action relegated pastoral to the bottom rung, but it was still a serious genre. Here is Sidney's hierarchy of genres from *The Defense of Poesy*: (1) heroical (i.e., epic); (2) lyric; (3) tragedy; (4) comedy; (5) satire; (6) iambic; (7) elegiac; (8) pastoral.[55] The first three genres belong to the sphere of action (lyrics here are songs praising memorable manly actions) Pastoral, the most reposeful, least action-packed genre, droops at the bottom of the ladder. But while Sidney places pastoral lowest among canonical genres, he defends it stoutly, and it is possible to see pastoral's low position not simply as a value judgment but also as a strategic location from which to make comment on the high.

Bakhtin posits that canonical genres have shadows: noncanonical genres (mimes, satyr plays) are their parodic doubles, with lower-class characters and diction that challenge the values of high literature.[56] We might also see a shadow effect within high literature itself. Genres in the lower half of Sidney's hierarchy are parodic doubles of genres in the upper half, standing apart from and; commenting on the upper tetralogy's world of action, on its strivings after power, fame, glory, wealth, and love. Pastoral, I suggest, is a parodic double of epic. Writers often couple the two: Sidney shows how pastoral paints the epic strivings of Alexander the Great as amounting to no more than a pastoral singing match; Spenser, in the *October* eclogue, writes of a conflict between pastoral and epic. Pastoral looks at the launching of a thousand ships, at the death of Hector, at Cyclops, Sirens, battles, underworld journeys—and asks in its mood of repose what it's all worth. No wonder mighty men who strive and mighty epic poets feel compelled to push pastoral to the bottom of the generic heap.

Seeing pastoral as carnivalized epic—like carnival, it is ruled by lowerclass characters and has the values of *otium* or holiday—sheds light on disagreements over the effectiveness of pastoral's critiques: when some critics see its assaults on the court as potentially effective while others think the court co-opted pastoral for its own uses, what we have is exactly the old "subversion/containment debate" visible in other manifestations of the carnival spirit. The difference is that with pastoral, those arguing for containment have gone almost unopposed by subversionists.

Finally, a Freudian take on our cultural resistance to pastoral might look closely at the long cultural practice wherein male authors wrote pastorals as a first step toward writing epics. In this career trajectory, pastoral occurs at the stage where a boy begins to break away from mother. Nurturing images persist—loving care for sheep beside images of inaccessible, rejecting women (Rosalind, in *The Shepheardes Calender*) or dead women (Dido in the same poem). Poets came of age by writing a pastoral, after which a strong poet might eventually work his way up to that task of manhood, epic. Steven Marx finds signs of coming-of-age rites in pastoral: youth/age conflict, isolation, instruction by elders.[57] If pastoral is partly a dream of childhood, of a world before Mother was lost, then the sternness with which (especially male) critics reject pastoral reflects the way male identity is formed by cutting itself off from Mother and a world of women. Examining responses to pastoral by male and female readers is beyond my scope here; but my impression is that the most vehement pastoral haters have been male. One of the best writers on pastoral, one sympathetic to its aims, is a woman, Annabel Patterson.[58] Montrose finds Spenser's dead Dido (a Queen figure, of course) as a "radical solution" to resentment of Elizabeth's authority: "kill the lady."[59] Boy children, subordinated poets, perhaps even literary critics, experience the matricidal urge to establish male identity by striking out at the Queen, at female Authority, at Mother.

If pastoral, then, speaks to some of our cherished fantasies and needs, it also triggers some of our cultural prejudices. Wildly popular in its own day, Renaissance pastoral has largely been assailed and discredited in later centuries. Nobody listens to this Cassandra among genres. Even in its most oppositional moments, it has been cast as a tool of the establishment. In a protocapitalist age, pastoral attacked the passion for worldly goods. In an urbanizing age, it celebrated country life. In an age of centralized government, it spoke for a decentering, centrifugal force. In an autocratic age, it challenged obsession with power. But this important cultural work has been disallowed.

Is it still possible to resist the tyranny of our own culture and rasp away encrustations of centuries of antipastoralism? Let us have another look at the pastoralism of *As You Like It*.

## SERMONS IN STONES AND GOOD IN EVERY THING

Pastoral's challenge—sometimes overt, sometimes implicit in its withdrawal from the frantic world—is to the assumption that power, public life, hard work, and success are everything. *As You Like It* represents the world of power in Frederick's court as literally repulsive: having banished Duke Senior and his followers, Frederick now banishes Rosalind and sends away Oliver. Through that great tool of patriarchy, male competitive sport, the Duke enacts a public semiotics of power in a scenario of invader-repulsion: the populace is invited to combat Charles the wrestler. The Duke's tyranny betrays paranoia: he banishes Rosalind because her "silence and her patience/Speak to the people, and they pity her," seemingly fearful that "the people" might rise up on behalf of Rosalind and her father (1.3. 79–81). Do those who come to wrestle Charles represent for the Duke the challenge he fears? Does he invite it precisely to demonstrate that he can defeat such challenges? Frederick and Le Beau call Orlando "the challenger," though when asked "have you challenged Charles the wrestler?" Orlando answers "No, he is the general challenger" (1.2.169–78). That the court issues a challenge and then feels it is being challenged betrays a paranoid insecurity that it tries to assuage by violence.

A pivot between the court and Oliver's household, Charles the wrestler flags the sibling competition that is festering in each place. Both paranoid tyrants, Duke Frederick and Oliver, project onto powerless siblings their own murderous impulses. Both keep the brother/competitor at bay by rustication—pushing him into a countryside that prejudice has encoded loathsome. Duke Frederick has pushed his brother Duke Senior into forest banishment, and Oliver has pushed his brother Orlando into a neglected life in a country home. Our initial view of the country is resentful: in the play's opening speech Orlando complains, "my brother keeps me rustically at home, or stays me here at home unkept; for call you that keeping for a gentleman of my birth, that differs not from the stalling of an ox? His horses are bred better. He lets me feed with his hinds" (1.1.3–18). A hind was a farm hand; it is appropriate that the word later occurs in its other meaning, "deer," for this passage superimposes peasant life on animal life. The servant Adam is pushed into the animal kingdom, called "old dog" (1.1.86). Frederick too has pushed his brother/competitor into the countryside where he sleeps outside like an animal. Challengers must not rise; they are pushed out into the country, down among animals. The despised realm is that of peasants and animals, the world of shepherds: pastoral.

Rustication was a Tudor political punishment: noblemen fallen from grace often retreated to a country estate, remaining there under house arrest, an echo of the way pastoral poets were pushed out of the upper canon's polite society into a rustic underworld, for challenging the world of power. But Duke Senior's first speech defends country living and attacks the court, with its artificiality, danger, and competitiveness: "Hath not old custom made this life more sweet/Than that of *painted pomp*? Are not these woods/More free from *peril* than the *envious* court?" (2.1.2–4; emphasis mine). Any fear that his forest society might merely reproduce structures of authority, dominance, and competition of Frederick's court are immediately allayed by Duke Senior's style, a striking departure from Frederick's. By the time we meet Duke Senior in act 2, we are accustomed to Frederick's mode of communication, which like the speech of the early King Lear is performative, his speeches curt and peppered with commands ("Bear him away" (1.2.211); "Dispatch you with your safest haste/And get you from our court" (1.3.39–40); "Open not thy lips" (1.3.80); "You, niece, provide yourself" (1.3.85); "Push him out of doors" (3.1.15). In act 1, the average length of Frederick's speeches is less than three lines, mainly short sentences of staccato monosyllables. His longest flight, a twelve-line speech in act 3, is clogged with curt imperatives: "*Look* to it:/*Find* out thy brother./*Seek* him with candle; *bring* him dead or living/or *turn* thou no more/To seek a living in our territory" (3.1.4–8). Frederick's curt, choppy, commanding language recreates the haste and arbitrariness of his acts—banishing Rosalind, turning Orlando out of favor, dispatching Oliver and seizing his lands. In contrast, Duke Senior's first words are egalitarian: "Now, my co-mates and brothers in exile" (2.1.1). Where Frederick's typical utterances are commands, Duke Senior's are questions: "Hath not old custom made this life more sweet? ... Are not these woods/More free from peril?" (2.1.2–4); "Shall we go and kill us venison?" (2.1.21); "What said Jaques?/Did he not moralize this spectacle?" (2.1.43–44,); "Did you leave him in this contemplation?" (2.1.64); "What would you have?" (2.7.101). Further, Duke Senior listens to the answers. Inquiring rather than commanding, he listens attentively to people, replacing Frederick's banishments and repulsions with hospitable welcomes: "Sit down and feed, and welcome to our table" (2.7.104). Speeches are longer than at court: Duke Senior's first is seventeen lines long, and his courteous questions elicit two unhurried nineteen-line answers. The verse grows relaxed and flowing, its complex sentences and run-on lines a relief after Frederick's tense verbal jabbings. The anthropomorphosed deer, prominent in this first forest scene, is an important reversal: in act 1 humans were pushed down into the animal kingdom, but in Arden, animals rise to the human level.

The exiles, suffering "the icy fang/of the winter's wind" (2.1.6–7), are not luxuriating in sloth; but their life is wholesomely easeful. It is simply not the case that the court is presented as the brisk, responsible world of action, the country as an irresponsible life of ease: the court is paranoid, twitchy, a world of hasty political decisions, its frenetic pace neurotic, born of the knowledge that its power is illegitimate. Its pace is so brisk as to abrogate both justice and courtesy. The relaxed movement, language, and song in the play's pastoral world have the rhythm of a livable environment.

Pastoral, always the wealth-eschewing genre, was well placed to be oppositional to the new capitalism; in the early scenes, set in "a commercial world of exchange and transaction," even good characters speak its language: Orlando's initial lines (1.1.1–27) are strewn with references to types of change and exchange; and some of the same terminology is repeated in Celia's protestation of love to Rosalind … (1.2.17–25). Such words as 'bequeathed,' 'will,' 'profit,' 'hired,' and 'gain' are particularly suggestive."[60] In Arden, such language ebbs.

One of Arden's lessons is how little the world of power matters once it is out of sight. A bracing effect of the time-honored human strategy of running away from trouble—escapism—is that nobody in the new land has heard, of our local tyrant, which shows the world of power striving in a whole new light. Our exiles have arrived where nobody has heard of Duke Frederick's power grab. Corin never speaks of Frederick's usurpation, and the fact that Duke Senior, presumably his former ruler, is living in exile in the immediate neighborhood is something Corin never mentions.

Before his exile, was Duke Senior too a tense, paranoid, competitive ruler? Was it rustication that taught him patience, courtesy, humaneness, relaxation—a conversion as stunning as Frederick's later conversion? We can't know—the play doesn't say what he was like before. If the Duke hasn't changed, if he was always a good, humane man, it might make us uneasy about the vulnerability of patient, courteous, humane, relaxed rulers—but the play doesn't invite us to worry about this, as *The Tempest* does. It doesn't matter what kind of ruler Duke Senior was and will be: the play loses interest in that, and directs our attention elsewhere.

The segregation of *As You Like It*'s twelve pastureland scenes from its four forest scenes makes it possible to drop Duke Senior after act 2 —he reappears only in the last scene. The play moves from the real court to the forest court, to a pastureland with no court. As the play progresses, politics, which comes on strong at first, is entirely replaced by love. Interest is deflected from public to private. Was Shakespeare's pretended interest in the lesser spheres of politics, power, and authority all along a sublimation of his real interest, love and women? To paraphrase

Montrose, political motives here displace or subsume forms of desire, frustration, and resentment other than the merely political.

Strongly approving Rosalind's and Orlando's return to court, Lindenbaum declares, "the pastoral sojourn was not strictly necessary; the love of Rosalind and Orlando was well under way even at the troubled court,"[61] but their return to court isn't strictly necessary either. Theirs is a worldpeopling comedic destiny; one can procreate anywhere. The move from court to country prefigures the shift in the play's center of gravity from politics to love. The exclusionary circle tyranny drew around itself when Frederick forbade Rosalind to come nearer than twenty miles (1.3.41–43) yields to an inclusive circle: Rosalind reigns in "the circle of this forest" (5.4.34). Though many will return to the court, the play doesn't stage the return but ends with *everyone* in Arden, Duke Frederick and all; the court as the play ends is entirely empty. The ending dwells not on resumption of power or return to responsible public sendee but on living happily ever after in a world of love. Country matters.

As Edward Said's Orientalist is outside the Orient, so most pastoral writers have been outside the country, assuming, like Orientalists, that city writers must represent the country, since it cannot represent itself.[62] But where Orientalism projects onto the Orient the West's disowned qualities, creating a worse self against which the West defines itself, pastoral does the opposite. Its rustic is an antienemy, an antiseapegoat: one on whom to project not one's most loathed but one's best qualities, or desired qualities. Like Browning's Setebos, a city writer created in country folk "things worthier than himself," made them "what himself would fain, in a manner, be." Pastoral writers created a standard against which to measure the value of contemporary striving. The potent pastoral dream recurred amid the Industrial Revolution, where it helped spawn Romanticism, and amid the malaise of the industrialized, urban twentieth century—there was a good deal of pastoralism in 1960s counterculture. However we mock and condemn it, pastoralism will likely keep reemerging, disquietingly indicting the way we live by holding out an ideal more attractive than the world we have created.

Country matters. Doesn't it?

## NOTES

1. Peter Lindenbaum, *Changing Landscapes: Anti-Pastoral Sentiment in the English Renaissance* (Athens: University of Georgia Press, 1986), 1, 3, 17.
2. A. Stuart Daley, "Where Are the Woods in *As You Like It?*" *Shakespeare Quarterly* 34 (1983): 176–77.

3. Lindenbaum, *Changing Landscapes*, 96.
4. Richard Helgerson, "The New Poet Presents Himself: Spenser and the Idea of a literary Career," *PMLA* 93 (1978): 906.
5. A. Stuart Daley, "The Dispraise of the Country In *As You Like It*," *Shakespeare Quarterly* 36 (1985): 307.
6. Lindenbaum, *Changing Landscapes*, 110.
7. Albert Cirillo, "*As You Like It*: Pastoralism Gone Awry," *ELH* 38 (1971): 24.
8. Renato Poggioli, *The Oaten Flute: Essays on Pastoral Poetry and the Pastoral Ideal* (Cambridge: Harvard University Press, 1975), 1.
9. Daley, "Dispraise," 306–7, 311–12.
10. Lindenbaum, *Changing Landscapes*, 1.
11. Svetlana Makurenkova, "Intertextual Correspondences: The Pastoral in Marlowe, Raleigh, Shakespeare, and Donne," in *Russian Essays on Shakespeare and His Contemporaries*, ed. Alexandr Parfenov and Joseph G. Price (Newark: University of Delaware Press, 1998), 194.
12. William Shakespeare, *Complete Works*, ed. David Bevington, 4th ed. (Glenview, Ill.: Scott, Foresman, 1992), 292–325. All references to Shakespeare plays are to this edition.
13. Cirillo, "*As You Like It*," 27.
14. Rawdon Wilson, "The Way to Arden: Attitudes Toward Time in *As You Like It*," *Shakespeare Quarterly* 26 (1975): 22, 18.
15. Samuel Johnson, "Milton," in *Lives of the English Poets*, ed. Arthur Waugh (Oxford: Oxford University Press, 1906), 1:116.
16. W. W. Greg, *Pastoral Poetry and Pastoral Drama* (New York: Russell and Russell, 1959), 30, 87, 134, 69, 130, 135.
17. Lindenbaum, *Changing Landscapes*, 12.
18. Louis Montrose, "'The perfecte paterne of a Poete': The Poetics of Courtship in *The Shepheardes Calender*," *Texas Studies in Literature and Language* 21 (1979): 49.
19. Poggioli, *The Oaten Flute*, 21.
20. P. V. Krieder, "Genial Literary Satire in the Forest of Arden," *Shakespeare Association Bulletin* 10 (1935): 21.
21. Lisa Robertson, "How Pastoral: A Manifesto," in *A Poetics of Criticism*, ed. Juliana Spahr, Mark Wallace, Kristin Prevallet, and Pam Rehm (Buffalo, N.Y.: Leave, 1994), 279.
22. Louis Montrose, "'Eliza, Queene of Shepheardes,' and the Pastoral of Power," *English Literary Renaissance* 10 (1980): 169, 180.
23. William Empson, *Some Versions of Pastoral* (London: Chatto and Windus, 1935), 11–12.
24. Karen O'Brien, "Imperial Georgic, 1660–1789," in *The Country and the City Revisited: England and the Politics of Culture, 1550–1850*, ed. Gerald MacLean, Donna Landry, and Joseph P. Ward (Cambridge: Cambridge University Press, 1999), 169.

25. George Puttenham, *The Art of English Poesy*, ed. Gladys Doidge Willcock and Alice Walker (Cambridge: Cambridge University Press, 1936), 38.

26. Alexander Barclay, *Eclogues* (London: P. Treveris, 1530; first published ca. 1523).

27. Edmund Spenser, *The Shepheardes Calender*, in *The Poetical Works of Edmund Spenser*, ed. J. C. Smith and E. De Selincourt (London: Oxford University Press, 1912).

28. Paul Alpers, "Pastoral and the Domain of Lyric in Spenser's *Shepheardes Calender*" in *Representing the English Renaissance*, ed. Stephen Greenblatt (Berkeley and Los Angeles: University of California Press, 1988), 166.

29. Montrose, "'The perfecte paterne of a Poete,'" 48.

30. Louis Montrose, "Interpreting Spenser's *February* Eclogue: Some Contexts and Implications," *Spenser Studies* 2 (1981): 70.

31. Alpers, "Pastoral and the Domain of Lyric," 166.

32. Montrose, " 'The perfecte paterne,' " 47.

33. Louis Montrose, "Of Gentlemen and Shepherds: The Politics of Elizabethan Pastoral Form," *ELH* 50 (1983): 435.

34. Ibid., 439.

35. One refreshing exception is Robert Lane, who argues persuasively that Spenser's casting of *The Shepheardes Calender* in country dialect is a radical sociopolitical move in a milieu wherein theorists such as Puttenham were "establish[ing] the court and its elite as the standard in language use" ("*Shepheards Devises*": Edmund Spenser's Shepheardes Calender *and the Institutions of Elizabethan Society* [Athens: University of Georgia Press], 35).

36. Samuel Johnson, "Principles of Pastoral Poetry," in The *Rambler*, ed. S.C. Roberts (London: Dent, 1953), 84.

37. Johnson, "Milton," 116.

38. Montrose, "'The perfecte paterne,'" 54.

39. Anne Barton, "Perils of Historicism," Review of *Learning to Curse*, by Stephen Greenblatt, *New York Review of Books*, 28 March 1991, 55.

40. Krieder, "Genial Literary Satire," 213.

41. Poggioli, *The Oaten Flute*, 4–5,

42. Edward Said, *The World, the Text, and the Critic* (Cambridge: Harvard University Press, 1983), 5–9.

43. William Empson, "Donne the Space Man," in *William Empson: Essays on Renaissance Culture*, vol. 1, ed. John Haffenden (Cambridge: Cambridge University Press, 1993), 98.

44. Sandra Billington, *Mock Kings in Medieval Society and Renaissance Drama* (Oxford: Clarendon, 1991), 38.

45. Poggioli, *The Oaten Flute*, 6, 14.

46. Lindenbaum, *Changing Landscapes*, 18.

47. Poggioli, *The Oaten Flute*, 2, 11.

48. Lindenbaum, *Changing Landscapes*, 92.

49. Ibid., 5.

50. Montrose, "'The perfecte paterne,'" 49.

51. Josephine Roberts, "Deciphering Women's Pastoral: Coded Language in Wroth's *Love's Victory*," in *Representing Women in Renaissance England*, ed. Claude J. Summers and Ted-Larry Pebworth (Columbia: University of Missouri Press, 1997), 163.

52. Montrose, "Of Gentlemen," 440.

53. Lindenbaum, *Changing Landscapes*, 19.

54. Hallett Smith, *Elizabethan Poetry: A Study in Conventions, Meaning, and Expression* (Cambridge: Harvard University Press, 1952), chap. 1.

55. *The Prose Works of Sir Philip Sidney*, ed. Albert Feuillerat (1912; reprint, Cambridge: Cambridge University Press, 1962), 3:3–46.

56. Mikhail Bakhtin, *The Dialogic Imagination,* ed. Michael Holquist, trans. Caryl Emerson and Michael Holquist (Austin: University of Texas Press, 1981).

57. Steven Marx, *Youth Against Age: Generational Strife in Renaissance Poetry, with Special Reference to Edmund Spenser's "The Shepheardes Calender"* (New York: Peter Lang, 1985), 208 ff.

58. See Annabel Patterson, *Pastoral and Ideology: Virgil to Valéry* (Berkeley and Los Angeles: University of California Press, 1987).

59. Montrose, "'The perfecte paterne,'" 54.

60. Wilson, "The Way to *Arden*," 20.

61. Lindenbaum, *Changing Landscapes*, 127.

62. Edward Said, *Orientalism* (New York: Pantheon, 1978), 8.

# For Further Reading, Viewing, and Listening

In addition to the sources in the Works Cited section of the Critical Introduction and Performance History, readers may find the following useful:

Bardbox. http://bardbox.wordpress.com

Belsey, Catherine. *Why Shakespeare?* New York: Palgrave Macmillan, 2007. Esp. Chapter 2

Berry, Edward I. "Rosalynde and Rosalind." *Shakespeare Quarterly,* 30 (1980), 42–52.

————*Shakespeare and the Hunt: A Cultural and Social Study.* Cambridge, Eng.: Cambridge UP, 2001.

Berry, Wendell. "The Uses of Adversity." *Sewanee Review,* 115 (2007), 211–238.

Dobson, R. B. and J. Taylor. *Rymes of Robyn Hood: An Introduction to the English Outlaw.* Pittsburgh: U of Pittsburgh P, 1976

Doran, Madeleine. "'Yet am I inland bred'," *Shakespeare Quarterly,* 15 (1964), 99–114.

Gardner, Helen, "*As You Like It.*" In *More Talking of Shakespeare,* ed. John Garrett. New York: Theatre Arts Books, 1959.

Halio, Jay L. and Barbara C. Millard. *"As You Like It": An Annotated Bibliography, 1940-1980.* New York: Garland, 1985.

Hayles, Nancy. "Sexual Disguise in *As You Like It* and *Twelfth Night,*" *Shakespeare Survey,* 32 (1979). 63–72.

International Database of Shakespeare on Film, Television, and Radio. http://bufvc.ac.uk/shakespeare

Johnson, Charles. *Love in a Forest.* In *"As You Like It" From 1600 to the Present,* ed. Edward Tomarken

Kott, Jan. *The Gender of Rosalind: Interpretations: Shakespeare, Büchner, Gautier.* Trans. Jadwiga Kosicka and Mark Rosenzweig. Evanston, IL: Northwestern UP, 1992.

Newman, Karen. *Shakespeare's Rhetoric of Comic Character: Dramatic Convention in Classical and Renaissance Comedy.* London: Methuen, 1985.

Panofsky, Erwin. *Studies in Iconology: Humanistic Themes in the Art of the Renaissance.* New York: Oxford UP, 1939. Esp. pp. 212–218 on Ganymede

Rothwell, Kenneth S. *A History of Shakespeare on Screen: A Century of Film and Television.* Cambridge, Eng.: Cambridge UP, 1999.

Saslow, James M. *Ganymede in the Renaissance: Homosexuality in Art and Society.* New Haven: Yale UP, 1986.

Shakespeare Performance in Asia. (SPIA). http://web.mit.edu/shakespeare/asia/

Shapiro, Michael. *Gender in Play on the Shakespearean Stage: Boy Heroines and Female Pages*. Ann Arbor: U of Michigan P, 1994.

Strout, Nathaniel. "*As You Like It, Rosalynde,* and Mutuality," *Studies in English Literature,* 41 (2001), 277-295.

Tomarken, Edward, ed. *"As You Like It" From 1600 to the Present: Critical Essays*. New York: Garland, 1997.

Wheeler, Richard. *Shakespeare's Development and the Problem Comedies: Turn and Counter-Turn*. Berkeley: U of California P, 1981.

Wiles, David. *The Early Plays of Robin Hood*. Cambridge, Eng.: D. S. Brewer, 1981.

White, R. S. "Functions of Poems and Songs in Elizabethan Romance and Romantic Comedy," *English Studies,* 5 (1987), 392-405.